MULTICULTUR

James A. Banks, Series Editor

(continued)

Transforming Multicultural Education Policy
and Practice

Expanding Educational Opportunity

EDITED BY
James A. Banks

Afterword by Margaret Smith Crocco

TEACHERS COLLEGE PRESS

TEACHERS COLLEGE | COLUMBIA UNIVERSITY

NEW YORK AND LONDON

Published by Teachers College Press,® 1234 Amsterdam Avenue, New York, NY 10027

Copyright © 2021 by Teachers College, Columbia University

Library of Congress Cataloging-in-Publication Data

Names: Banks, James A., editor.
Title: Transforming multicultural education policy and practice : expanding
    educational opportunity / Edited by James A. Banks ; Afterword by
    Margaret Smith Crocco.
Description: New York, NY : Teachers College Press, [2021] | Series:
    Multicultural education series | Includes bibliographical references and
    index.
Identifiers: LCCN 2021022352 (print) | LCCN 2021022353 (ebook) | ISBN
    9780807766286 (hardcover) | ISBN 9780807766279 (paperback) | ISBN
    9780807780695 (ebook)
Subjects: LCSH: Multicultural education—United States. | Curriculum
    change—United States. | Educational change—United States. | Education
    and state—United States. | Culturally relevant pedagogy—United States.
Classification: LCC LC1099.3 .T723 2021 (print) | LCC LC1099.3 (ebook) |
    DDC 370.1170973—dc23
LC record available at https://lccn.loc.gov/2021022352
LC ebook record available at https://lccn.loc.gov/2021022353
ISBN 978-0-8077-6627-9 (paper)
ISBN 978-0-8077-6628-6 (hardcover)
ISBN 978-0-8077-8069-5 (ebook)

Printed on acid-free paper
Manufactured in the United States of America

Contents

Acknowledgments

It takes a community to initiate and keep a publication series flourishing for 25 years. The success of the Multicultural Education Series at Teachers College Press results from a team effort. I am immensely grateful to my colleagues at Teachers College Press for the assistance, encouragement, and inspiration they have given me since the Series began. I owe my greatest debt to Brian Ellerbeck, senior acquisitions editor at the Press. Brian invited me to edit the Series and is a stalwart colleague and cherished friend. His contributions to the Series are incisive, diligent, and visionary. I would like to thank the editors at the Press I have worked with over the years—Karl Nyberg, Lori Tate, and John Bylander—for their professionalism, meticulous work, and perceptive editorial eyes. I owe a special thanks to Karl Nyberg for his incisive and discerning work on this commemorative volume. I would also like to thank Jennifer Feldman, director of the Press, for supporting the publication of this commemorative volume.

I am also grateful to the marketing group at Teachers College Press—Emily Freyer, Nancy Power, and Michael McGann—for their creative and innovative ways of marketing the books that are published in the Multicultural Education Series. I would like to thank Kimberly McKaig for helping me to read and correct the proofs for this book.

Cherry A. McGee Banks, my wife and colleague, has supported and enriched my life and work during the more than five decades of our journey. She is also an ardent supporter of the Multicultural Education Series. The Series is one of my most inspiring and professionally rewarding endeavors. I am immensely grateful to the authors who have contributed to it. Without them, the Series would not exist.

—*James A. Banks*

Introduction

The publication of this book commemorates the 25th anniversary of the Multicultural Education Series of books published by Teachers College Press. The Multicultural Education Series developed as a consequence of the compilation and publication of the *Handbook of Research on Multicultural Education* (Banks & Banks, 1995). I was the editor and Cherry A. McGee Banks was the associate editor of the *Handbook* project, which took 3 years from its conceptualization to publication. Macmillan published the first edition of the *Handbook* in 1995; the second edition was published in 2004 by Jossey-Bass (Banks & Banks, 2004). The *Handbook* was highly praised and positively reviewed in a number of influential education journals, including *Teachers College Record* (Semel, 1996), *The Journal of Negro Education* (Ford, 1996), *Urban Education* (Vavrus, 2006), and the *Journal of Education for Students Placed at Risk* (Rivers & Lomotey, 1996).

After the publication of the *Handbook*, Brian Ellerbeck, executive acquisitions editor at Teachers College Press, invited me to edit a series of books on multicultural education that would parallel the series the Press publishes on other topics. I accepted Brian's invitation because I viewed it as an opportunity to extend the work that Cherry and I had initiated with the *Handbook* project. Several of the authors who wrote chapters for the *Handbook* accepted my invitation to write book-length manuscripts for the Multicultural Education Series. I used the dimensions of multicultural education, which are described and illustrated in Chapter 2, to conceptualize the Series. I now use the dimensions to guide the selection of books that I solicit for the Series as well as emerging and significant events and trends related to theory and practice in multicultural education.

THE DEVELOPMENT OF THE MULTICULTURAL EDUCATION SERIES

The first book in the Series, edited by James A. Banks, was published in 1996, *Multicultural Education, Transformative Knowledge, and Action: Historical and Contemporary Perspectives*. This book was the second

1

volume in the Studies in the Historical Foundations of Multicultural Education Series initiated in 1992 by the Center for Multicultural Education at the University of Washington. The major goals of the Studies in the Historical Foundations project were to uncover the roots of multicultural education, to identify the ways in which it is connected to historical antecedents, and to gain insights from the past that can facilitate school reform efforts to expand educational opportunity for all students. Another goal was the mentoring of graduate students. Most of the chapters in the book were first presented as papers in a faculty/student symposia series organized and sponsored by the Center for Multicultural Education at American Educational Research Association (AERA) annual meetings in three consecutive years: 1993, 1994, and 1995. Several professors on campuses beyond the University of Washington presented papers in the AERA symposia that were published in this book, including Gloria Ladson-Billings (1996) at the University of Wisconsin–Madison and Carlos J. Ovando at Indiana University (Ovando & Gourd, 1996).

The third book developed for the Studies in the Historical Foundations of Multicultural Education Series was authored by Cherry A. McGee Banks (2005) and published in the Multicultural Education Series, *Improving Multicultural Education: Lessons from the Intergroup Education Movement.* Chapter 1 is reprinted from this book.

More than 70 books have been published in the Multicultural Education Series, with additional titles in various stages of development and publication. Some of the most eloquent, visionary, and eminent scholars in diversity and multicultural education have published influential and best-selling books in the Series, including Linda Darling-Hammond, Gloria Ladson-Billings, Sonia Nieto, Pedro A. Noguera, Na'ilah Suad Nasir, Daniel G. Solórzano, Guadalupe Valdés, and Geneva Gay.

In addition to publishing well-established scholars, I am pleased that the Multicultural Education Series has been and is a launching venue for younger scholars. Gary Howard was a gifted and visionary school practitioner when I met him in 1976 at a Teacher Corps conference at Florida State University where I gave a keynote address. Gary and I became friends and colleagues. I invited Gary to write a chapter for a book I edited for the National Education Association (Howard, 1981), and an article for a special section of the *Phi Delta Kappan* that I edited (Howard, 1993). Because I was impressed with Gary's lucid and incisive writing, I invited him to develop the book that was published in the Series in 1999, *We Can't Teach What We Don't Know: White Teachers, Multiracial Schools.* This book became a best-seller and is now in its third edition (Howard, 2016). Özlem Sensoy and Robin DiAngelo were my doctoral students at the University of Washington when I invited them to write their influential and popular book in the Series, *Is Everyone Really Equal? An Introduction to Key Concepts in Social Justice Education* (2012), now in its second edition (Sensoy &

DiAngelo, 2017). I was delighted that Robin's book, *White Fragility: Why It's So Hard for White People to Talk about Racism*, published by Beacon Press in 2018, had been on the *New York Times* best-seller list for 134 weeks in April 2021 (*New York Times*, 2021).

The authors of the books in the Multicultural Education Series reflect the racial, ethnic, and cultural diversity in the United States. The authors, because of their diverse cultural experiences and backgrounds, bring multiple voices and myriad perspectives to their analyses of issues related to multicultural education policy and practice and to expanding educational opportunity. Some of the authors of books in the Series who are from different ethnic and cultural groups include Gloria Ladson-Billings, Geneva Gay, and Tyrone Howard (African American); John P. Hopkins and K. Tsianina Lomawaima (American Indian); Wayne Au, Ann M. Ishimaru, and Okhee Lee (Asian American); Estela Mara Bensimon, Sonia Nieto, and Daniel G. Solórzano, (Latinx); and Paul C. Gorski, James W. Loewen, and Christine E. Sleeter (European American).

RACIAL AND SOCIAL CLASS INEQUALITY DURING THE PANDEMIC

This commemorative volume is being published at a propitious time because the devastating effects of the COVID-19 pandemic have poignantly revealed the deep racial and social-class divisions and disparities within the United States (Villarosa, 2020). During the pandemic, many middle- and upper-class professionals worked off-site and interacted virtually, sheltering safely in their homes, while most low-income and low-status essential workers had to take buses, subways, and other forms of public transportation to get to work sites where they worked directly with the public or faced the possibility of being fired from their jobs. One of the consequences of this difference was that African Americans, Latinxs, and immigrants—who were heavily concentrated in low-status jobs—became infected with the coronavirus and died at much higher rates than middle-class and upper-income workers, who were disproportionately White (Mays & Newman, 2020).

Another startling example of the racial and social-class divide in U.S. society was the several-miles-long lines of cars at food banks in different cities, depicted on national television news every evening after the U.S. economy became overwhelmed by the pandemic in late April and early May 2020. Unemployment reached its highest level since the Great Depression that began in 1929 and lasted through the 1930s (Cohen, 2020; Schwartz, Casselman, & Koeze, 2020). Food insecurity, which was also experienced by Whites, was higher among groups of color. Racial and social-class divisions during the pandemic were also manifested in the digital divide that was revealed when most school districts shuttered schools and instruction became virtual. In some city school districts, such as Chicago, Detroit, Los

Angeles, and Philadelphia, whose populations consist primarily of students of color, a large proportion of the students did not receive consistent instruction because they lacked tablets, computers, or reliable Internet connectivity (Goldstein, 2020). Nine out of 10 students in the Detroit Public Schools did not have access to tablets, computers, or the Internet until the school district was given a $23 million grant by local foundations (Williams, 2020).

The COVID-19 epidemic and its painful consequences have seriously challenged the idea of "American exceptionalism" (Grandin, 2019). On May 5, 2020, the United States had the highest number of deaths from the pandemic of the major nations. The U.S. health care system, because of its lack of preparation for the pandemic and infrastructure problems (Case & Deaton, 2020; Rosenthal, 2020), was in disarray during the early phases of the pandemic (Egan, 2020; Villarosa, 2020). The COVID-19 pandemic not only revealed the deep racial and social-class divisions within American society (Blow, 2020), but also stimulated the rise of anti-Asian racism and microaggressions (Stevens, 2020). Former President Donald Trump called COVID-19 "the Chinese virus." Some Asian Americans became victims of racial hostility and attacks. The anti-Asian events and expressions evoked, for many Asian Americans, painful and repressed memories of the Chinese Exclusion Act of 1882 and the internment of Japanese Americans during the 1940s (Stevens, 2020).

THE NEED FOR THE MULTICULTURAL EDUCATION SERIES

The books in the Multicultural Education Series are needed to help the nation's predominantly White teaching force and the increasingly diverse student population to attain the knowledge and skills needed to live and work in a pluralistic, complex nation and world stratified by race and class (Banks, 2009). The majority of students now attending American schools are students of color. During the 2015–2016 school year, 81% of the teachers in U.S. traditional public schools were White, and 71% were White in public charter schools (National Center for Education Statistics, 2019). The percentage of students of color, immigrant origin students, and students who speak a first language other than English is growing significantly in the nation's public schools.

American classrooms are experiencing the largest influx of immigrant students since the beginning of the 20th century. Approximately 12.6 million new immigrants—documented and undocumented—settled in the United States in the years from 2000 to 2016 (Zong, Batalova, & Hallock 2018). Less than 10% came from nations in Europe. Most came from Mexico, nations in South Asia, East Asia, Latin America, the Caribbean, and Central America. Although African immigrants make up a small part of the U.S. immigrant population (2,060 in 2015), they increased by 41% from 2000 to 2013 (Anderson, 2017). In 2018, the largest number of immigrants to the United States came from China (149,000 people), India (129,000), Mexico (120,000), and the Philippines (46,000). In the most recent years since 2009, more Asian immigrants have come to the United States than Hispanic immigrants (Budiman, 2020). The influence of an increasingly diverse population on U.S. schools, colleges, and universities is and will continue to be enormous.

Schools in the United States are more diverse today than they have been since the early 1900s, when a multitude of immigrants entered the United States from Southern, Central, and Eastern Europe (C. A. M. Banks, 2005). In 2017, the National Center for Education Statistics estimated that the percentage of students from ethnic minority groups made up more than 52% of the students in pre-kindergarten through 12th grade in U.S. public schools, an increase from 39.2% in 2001 (National Center for Education Statistics, 2017). Latinxs made up 25% of the children in the United States in 2017, African Americans 15%, Asian and Pacific Island children 6%, and American Indians 1% (Annie E. Casey Foundation, 2019).

Language and religious diversity is also increasing in the U.S. student population. A Center for Migration Studies publication estimated that, in 2016, 21.6% of Americans aged 5 and above (65.5 million) spoke a language other than English at home (Camarota & Ziegler, 2017). This percentage has doubled since 1990, and almost tripled since 1980. The significant number of immigrants from nations such as India and China has also greatly increased religious diversity in the United States. Harvard professor Diana L. Eck (2001) calls the United States the "most religiously diverse nation on earth" (p. 4). Islam is now the fastest-growing religion in the United States, as well as in several European nations such as France, the United Kingdom, and the Netherlands (Banks, 2009; O'Brien, 2016).

CONCEPTUAL THEMES AND TOPICS IN THE MULTICULTURAL EDUCATION SERIES

The conceptual themes and topics examined by authors in the Multicultural Education Series provide preservice educators, practicing educators, graduate students, scholars, and policymakers with an interrelated and comprehensive set of books that summarizes and analyzes important research, theory, and practice related to the education of ethnic, racial, cultural, and linguistic groups in the United States and the education of mainstream students about diversity. The dimensions of multicultural education, developed by Banks and described in Chapter 2 of this book as well as in the *Handbook of Research on Multicultural Education* (Banks, 2004), *The Routledge International Companion to Multicultural Education* (Banks, 2009), and the *Encyclopedia of Diversity in Education* (Banks, 2012), provide the conceptual framework for the development of the publications in the Series.

The dimensions are content integration, the knowledge construction process, prejudice reduction, equity pedagogy, and an empowering institutional culture and social structure.

The books in the Multicultural Education Series provide research, theoretical, and practical knowledge about the behaviors and learning characteristics of students of color, language minority students, low-income students, multiracial youth, LGBTQ+ students, and other minoritized population groups, such as students who speak different varieties of English. A number of major themes and topics characterize the books published in the Series. I will describe these categories as discrete, although in reality they overlap. For example, the book by Gorski (2018) focuses on social class but includes a cogent analysis of culturally responsive teaching.

Major themes in the Series and some of the books that exemplify them are structural and institutional racism (Sensoy & DiAngelo, 2017; Solórzano & Pérez Huber, 2020; Leonardo, 2013); culturally responsive and culturally sustaining teaching (Au, 2011; Gay, 2010; Howard, 2020); bilingual education and second-language teaching and learning (Gándara & Hopkins, 2010; García, 2005; Stillman & Anderson, 2017; Valdés, 2001); social class and education (Cookson, 2013; Gorski, 2018); and school reform that increases educational equality (Cuban, 2008; Darling-Hammond, 2010; Ishimaru, 2020).

Some books in the Multicultural Education Series focus on specific topics and population groups. Several describe educating specific ethnic groups such as African Americans (Howard, 2014), Native Americans (Hopkins, 2020; Lomawaima & McCarty, 2006), and Mexican Americans (Delgado Bernal & Aleman, 2017). The ways in which the curriculum can be reformed in various school subjects is the focus of these books: mathematics (Nasir et al, 2014; Nasir & Cobb, 2007); science (Lee & Buxton, 2010); music (Campbell, 2018), the social studies (Banks, 2007), and the language arts (Charity Hudley & Mallinson, 2011).

These books analyze and describe institutional and curriculum reform in higher education: Teranishi (2010); Douglas, Shockley, and Toldson (2020); Suarez-Orozco and Osei-Twumasi (2019); Dowd and Bensimon (2015); Contreras (2011); and Perez (2012). International perspectives on diversity in education are the focus of books by Moodley (2021); Osler (2016); Ball (2006); Dunn (2013); and Banks, Suárez-Orozco, and Ben-Peretz (2016). The nation's growing mixed-race population is described in books by Mahiri (2017) and Joseph and Briscoe-Smith (2021). Sexual orientation and LGBTQ+ issues are detailed in books by Dilg (2010) and Mayo (2014).

OVERVIEW OF THIS BOOK

Chapters from 12 of the most influential books published in the Multicultural Education Series since it began in 1996 are reprinted in this book.

Chapter 2 was written especially for this volume. The next section of this Introduction offers brief overviews of the five parts of this book and the 13 chapters that constitute the parts. This book closes with an Afterword by Margaret Smith Crocco, a perceptive historian, educator, and colleague with whom I had rich intellectual dialogues during summer quarters (1992 to 2009) and fall semester (2007) when I taught at Teachers College, Columbia University.

Part I: History and Foundations of Intergroup and Multicultural Education

The two chapters that constitute Part I discuss and analyze the history and foundations of intergroup education and multicultural education. In Chapter 1, Cherry A. McGee Banks describes how intergroup educators responded to European immigrants settling in the United States during the early decades of the 20th century. The foundation for the intergroup education movement—also called the intercultural movement—originated in the early 1920s and is a predecessor to the ethnic studies and multicultural movement that emerged in the 1960s and 1970s. Southern and Eastern European immigrants were harshly criticized by the nativists in ways similar to how Mexican immigrants and immigrants from predominantly Muslim nations are disparaged today. The intergroup educators challenged the nativists and developed teaching materials and training programs that recognized and affirmed the cultures of immigrant students and helped non-immigrant students to develop more positive attitudes toward them.

Intergroup educators also challenged the dominance of assimilationism and argued that cultural pluralism could make important contributions to American life. Investigations designed to determine the effects of curricular interventions on students' racial attitudes were an important part of the intergroup education movement. Most of these studies support the postulate that multicultural lessons, activities, and teaching materials, when used within a democratic classroom atmosphere and implemented for a sufficiently long period, help students to develop democratic racial attitudes and values.

Chapter 2, by James A. Banks, provides a brief historical overview of the development and rise of the multicultural education movement during the 1960s and 1970s. Black studies, a predecessor to ethnic studies and multicultural education (Banks, 1992), arose during the 1960s and was stimulated by the civil rights movement of the late 1950s and 1960s that was led by African Americans. Black studies gave rise to the ethnic studies movement, developed in response to the demands of African Americans and other racial and ethnic groups such as Mexican Americans, American Indians, and Asian Americans. These groups insisted that the schools incorporate their histories and cultures into the curriculum and hire more teachers and school administrators of color. Multicultural education developed during the 1970s as other marginalized groups, such as women and people with disabilities, demanded that the school, university, and college curricula be revised to incorporate their cultures, identities, and historical journeys. This chapter also explicates the *dimensions of multicultural education* that Banks conceptualized and developed, which have had a significant influence on multicultural education programs in schools, colleges, and universities in the United States as well as in other nations (Banks, 2009).

Part II: Structural and Institutional Racism in Schools

The two chapters in Part II describe how structural and institutionalized racism is embedded within all institutions in the United States, including the schools, colleges, and universities. These chapters also describe actions that teachers and other educational practitioners can take to reduce racism within in their own lives, worldviews, and practices with students and colleagues. In 2020, the killings of George Floyd and Breonna Taylor by police, and of Ahmaud Arbery by two White men when he was jogging near his home, forced the nation to reckon seriously with the widespread racism that is institutionalized within all of its institutions, including schools, colleges, and universities.

Özlem Sensoy and Robin DiAngelo, the authors of Chapter 3, provide knowledge to help educators understand the nature of oppression and institutionalized racism. They also describe vivid and compelling examples, thought experiments, and anecdotes that will help readers to master complex concepts related to diversity, social justice, and equity. Sensoy and DiAngelo draw upon their years of experiences working with predominantly White teachers and their deep knowledge of diversity issues to construct explicit definitions of complex concepts such as racism, classism, and internalized oppression.

Gary R. Howard, in Chapter 4, draws upon his experience growing up in a predominantly White community to help readers understand and reflect on institutionalized racism and White dominance. Howard asks White readers to engage in the challenging and sometimes painful process of "understanding, decoding, and dismantling the dynamics of White dominance" and to engage in personal transformation. Howard enables readers to participate in this transformation process by sharing his personal journey of transformation, presenting a conceptual framework that illuminates White dominance, and explicating the journey of White identity development. Howard ingeniously enables White readers to deeply examine race and racism within their lives and to develop a commitment to act in ways that will create just schools and communities.

Part III: Culture, Teaching, and Learning

The three chapters in Part III describe insightful and useful definitions of culture and its implications for teaching. In Chapter 5, Sonia Nieto incisively describes how culture is dynamic, multifaceted, embedded in context, and influenced by social, economic, and political factors. She also details how culture is created and socially constructed, learned, and dialectical. This chapter contains informative descriptions of language as culture, and the links among culture, language, and learning. Nieto explains the discontinuities between home and community and how the cultural gap between home and community presents learning challenges for students. She also describes ways in which teachers can respond to the cultural discontinuities between home and school by helping students bridge these two cultural communities.

In Chapter 6, Tyrone Howard gives a comprehensive overview of culturally responsive teaching and pedagogy. Howard describes the complexity of culturally responsive pedagogy and how simplistic approaches to it can be detrimental. He states, "Culturally responsive pedagogy is situated in a framework that recognizes the rich and varied cultural wealth, knowledge, and skills that students from diverse groups bring to schools, and seeks to develop dynamic teaching practices, multicultural content, multiple means of assessment, and a philosophical view of teaching that is dedicated to nurturing student academic, social, emotional, cultural, psychological, and physiological well-being" (p. 137). Howard explains why culturally responsive pedagogy, if it is not mediated by a deep understanding of the ways in which cultures are fluid, changing, multifaceted, contextual, and complex, can lead to stereotypic thinking about cultures and the essentialization of the cultures of students from diverse groups.

Chapters 5 and 6 describe the conceptual and theoretical aspects of culturally responsive teaching. Carol D. Lee, in Chapter 7, illustrates and details two examples of culturally responsive teaching in high school English classrooms using what Lee calls "cultural data sets," which are "texts from students' everyday experience that pose a problem of interpretation similar to what students will meet in the canonical texts they will read. It is important that students experience the cultural data sets as a part of their routine practices outside of school" (p. 164). The first unit described in Chapter 7 is on "symbolism." The second unit was taught by Lee to a senior class at a high school in Chicago. Lee's work builds upon, extends, and deepens the research and theory on culturally responsive and culturally sustaining teaching (Au, 2011; Gay, 2010; Ladson-Billings, 1995; Paris & Alim, 2017) by illustrating how teachers can skillfully use the funds of knowledge (Moll & González, 2004) that students bring to the classroom to enrich the teaching of academic subjects. Many of the teaching examples that Lee describes in her book are derived from her 3 years of teaching low-income African American high school students to do sophisticated analyses of complex literacy works such as Toni Morrison's (1987) novel *Beloved*.

Part IV: Curriculum Reform: History, Ethnic Studies, and English Language Learners

The three chapters in Part IV focus on curriculum reform and issues. Chapter 8 by James W. Loewen, reprinted from his book in the Multicultural Education Series, echoes some of the themes in his highly popular book, *Lies My Teacher Told Me: Everything Your American History Teacher Got Wrong* (Loewen, 2018), which has sold over two million copies. In Chapter 8, Loewen describes how instructors can teach students to use history as a tool to create their own version of the past and present, to understand how history reflects the contexts and times in which people live, and to learn how a deep understanding of the nation's past—including blatant violations of human rights such as the enslavement of African Americans, Indian removal, and the internment of Japanese Americans—can be used to help students learn how to take action that will make our nation more just and humane. As Loewen states, "There is a reciprocal relationship between justice in the present and honesty about the past "(p. 204). This chapter describes how instructors can teach students to construct their own versions of history. The chapter also helps students to understand that history is written by the winners, not by the victims. Consequently, for many years in school students learned views of American history sympathetic to President Andrew Jackson rather than to the Cherokee Indians who were forced to move from their homes during 1838–1839 to "Indian Territory" across the Mississippi River in what became known as the "Trail of Tears."

In Chapter 9, Christine E. Sleeter and Miguel Zavala summarize research that describes the effects of ethnic studies courses on the academic achievement and racial attitudes of students. The requirement for teaching ethnic studies in public schools has become a widely discussed and contentious topic since 2000. Several cities, such as Seattle, Los Angeles, Portland (Oregon), San Francisco, Chicago, and Philadelphia, have adopted ethnic studies requirements for high schools. The push for requiring the teaching of ethnic studies in the schools is coming primarily from communities of color and their allies.

In 2010, the Arizona State Department of Education banned the teaching of ethnic studies in the Tucson Public Schools. In 2017, a federal judge struck down the Arizona law after a 7-year battle. The ban was a Pyrrhic victory for ethnic studies advocates in Tucson because during the 7-year battle most of the teachers and leaders of the program had engaged in other endeavors. In March 2021, the California State Board of Education, chaired by Linda Darling-Hammond—the author of Chapter 13 in this book— adopted a statewide ethnic studies curriculum requirement after a long and contentious battle. Sleeter and Zavala concluded, after reviewing the research, that ethnic studies courses increase the academic achievement of racial and ethnic group students and help all students to attain positive racial and ethnic attitudes.

In Chapter 10, Guadalupe Valdés describes issues and research related to teaching Academic English to Mexican American students whose first language is Spanish. The assimilationist language policies in the United States evoke highly politicized and polarizing debates about bilingual education and second-language learning. The debates and controversies about bilingual education have generated more heat than light and resulted in the enactment of restrictive language policies in California, Arizona, and Massachusetts that have made it more difficult for teachers to create and implement effective practices that build upon the cultural and linguistic knowledge, skills, and strengths of language-minority students (Gándara & Hopkins, 2010; Moll & González, 2004).

Chapter 10 describes a research project that builds upon and extends Valdés's (2001) previous research and work. Valdés, Capitelli, and Alvarez (2011) conceptualized and implemented an ingenious "design experiment" to provide English language learners (ELLs) most in need of English more access to English speakers in an after-school program. They identified a "linguistically hyper-segregated" school in which Latinx students have very limited access to English. Most of the adults in the children's homes and communities spoke Spanish, and a majority of the children spoke Spanish when they interacted in school. In the design experiment, *One-on-One English*, each college undergraduate or community volunteer had rich interactions with one child about stories. An important principle that underlines this research, as well as previous work by Valdés (2001), is that non-English speakers must hear and interact with English speakers in order to learn and become competent speakers and writers of English.

Part V: School Reform

The three chapters in Part V describe ways to transform the cultures of schools so that students from diverse racial, ethnic, cultural, and language groups will have an equal opportunity to experience academic success, cultural empowerment, and recognition in schools. In Chapter 11, Noguera and Syeed describe how structural racism causes racial disparities in schools and suggest actions that teachers and school administrators can take to reduce inequality and increase the academic achievement of low-income and marginalized students such as African Americans and Latinxs. A prerequisite to taking effective action to reform low-income city schools is for educators to understand that many of the problems experienced by students in these schools are caused by the *structures* in which the schools are embedded rather than by cultures of the students and their families. Cultural explanations, such as those constructed by anthropologist John U. Ogbu

(2004), blame the problems of inner-city students on their cultures rather than on institutional structures such as racism and low teacher expectations.

Noguera and Syeed maintain that race-conscious policies as well as culturally responsive and sustaining teaching must be implemented in inner-city schools to reduce the effects of institutional and structural racism. They also advocate reconstructing existing paradigms about race and stratification, deconstructing domination, and creating new possibilities by teaching for racial justice. Noguera and Syeed believe that school transformation is facilitated by listening to communities, families, and students; implementing ethnic studies; applying intersectionality as an organizing conceptual framework; and respecting and incorporating students' cultural capital into teaching and learning. Trust, collaboration, and support are also vital components of an effective school transformation strategy.

Paul C. Gorski, in Chapter 12, challenges existing conceptions of low-income communities, families, and students and argues why it is essential for educators to embrace structural conceptions of impoverished families and communities and to discard deficit conceptions. In the 1960s most books that dealt with educating low-income students described their cultural deficits and the ways in which their family and community values and behaviors caused their low academic achievement (Bereiter & Engelmann, 1966; Riessman, 1962). A number of books published in the 2000s also describe the deficits and problems of low-income families and students (Payne, 2013; Thernstrom & Thernstrom, 2003). Gorski's work is refreshing and empowering because it emphasizes the resilience of impoverished students and families and explains why educators need to identify and examine their attitudes, beliefs, and behaviors toward low-income students in order to change their perceptions of them and to create equitable classrooms and schools in which poverty-stricken students can learn and flourish.

In Chapter 13, the final chapter in this book, Linda Darling-Hammond argues that today's expectation that schools will enable all students—rather than just a small minority—to learn challenging knowledge and skills at high levels is a new mission for schools. To accomplish this new mission, schools must be reformed and major changes must be made in school organizations and systems in which they are embedded. In other words, a major *redesign* of schools must take place for them to attain this goal. Darling-Hammond details specific changes and innovations that schools need to implement in order to be transformed and redesigned so that students from all racial, ethnic, social-class, and language groups can reach high levels of academic achievement. These changes include constructing and implementing small units within schools, creating structures for personalization, and implementing intellectually challenging and relevant instruction. Redesigned and transformative schools will also be characterized by performance-based assessment and professional learning and collaboration among school faculty and leaders. This chapter also describes ways in which successful innovation can be supported and sustained.

In her book in the Multicultural Education Series in which Chapter 13 was first published, Darling-Hammond (2010) presents indisputable and chilling statistics that document the extent to which the United States faces a national crisis because students in other nations such as South Korea, Finland, Japan, and the United Kingdom are outperforming U.S. students in math and science achievement. She also presents compelling evidence that the United States will be unable to meet its scientific and technical needs in the present and future unless it makes a national commitment to improve schools and teacher education for the nation's most vulnerable and neglected students. Darling-Hammond points out that the significant gap in the academic achievement of students in the United States and in other developed nations is widening rather than closing. Because low-income and minoritized students are a large and significant part of the student population in the United States, increasing the academic achievement of these population groups is essential for the United States to increase its median achievement levels.

TRANSFORMING MULTICULTURAL EDUCATION POLICY AND PRACTICE: EXPANDING EDUCATIONAL OPPORTUNITY

The title of this book, *Transforming Multicultural Education Policy and Practice: Expanding Educational Opportunity,* epitomizes the books that have been published in the Multicultural Education Series during its 25 years. Multicultural education, as it was conceptualized and implemented—especially in K–12 schools during the late 1960s and 1970s—often focused on discrete elements of cultures such as the foods and holidays of different racial, ethnic, cultural, and language groups. Men and women from marginalized groups who made outstanding contributions to society were also highlighted in many early programs. Problematic and oversimplified concepts of learning styles and culturally responsive teaching were and sometimes still are some of the ways in which multicultural education policy and practice are conceptualized and implemented.

The books published in the Multicultural Education Series challenge static conceptions of race and culture and present complex conceptions of these constructs. They describe race as a social construction that is contextual, fluid, and reflective of its social, political, and economic context. The books in the Multicultural Education Series also detail ways in which race is institutionalized within American society and deeply embedded within its culture, including in schools, colleges, and universities. The concepts of culturally responsive and culturally sustaining teaching are described in ways that illustrate how culture is changing, fluid, and contextual. For example, it is difficult to characterize a particular learning style for African Americans or American Indians because both groups are complex groups characterized by significant social-class, regional, language, gender, and sexual orientation differences and complexities, although each group shares a group identity, and the experience of being victims of institutionalized racism, regardless of their social-class and educational status. An important aim of the books in the Multicultural Education Series since its inception is to substantially *change and transform* the ways that multicultural education policy and practice are conceptualized and implemented, to problematize policy and practice, and consequently to expand educational opportunity for all of the nation's students.

REFERENCES

Anderson, M. (2017, February 14). African immigrant population in the U.S. steadily climbs. Pew Research Center. Retrieved from www.pewresearch.org/fact-tank/2017/02/14/african-immigrant-population-in-u-s-steadily-climbs

Annie E. Casey Foundation (2019). *2019 kids count data book: State trends in child well-being.* Author.

Au, K. H. (2011). *Literacy achievement and diversity: Keys to success for students, teachers, and schools.* Teachers College Press.

Ball, A. F. (2006). *Multicultural strategies for education and social change: Carriers of the torch in the United States and South Africa.* Teachers College Press.

Banks, C. A. M. (2005). *Improving multicultural education: Lessons from the intergroup education movement.* Teachers College Press.

Banks, J. A. (1992). African American scholarship and the evolution of multicultural education. *The Journal of Negro Education, 61*(3), 273–286.

Banks, J. A. (Ed.) (1996). *Multicultural education, transformative knowledge, and action: Historical and contemporary perspectives.* Teachers College Press.

Banks, J. A. (2004). Multicultural education: Historical development, dimensions, and practice. In J. A. Banks & C. A. M. Banks (Eds.). *Handbook of research on multicultural education* (2nd ed., pp. 3–29). Jossey-Bass.

Banks, J. A. (2007). *Educating citizens in a multicultural society* (2nd ed.). Teachers College Press.

Banks, J. A. (Ed.). (2009). *The Routledge international companion to multicultural education.* Routledge.

Banks, J. A. (2012). Multicultural education: Dimensions of. In J. A. Banks (Ed). *Encyclopedia of diversity in education* (vol. 3, pp. 1538–1547). Sage Publications.

Banks, J. A., & Banks, C. A. M. (Eds.) (1995). *Handbook of research in multicultural education.* Macmillan.

Banks, J. A., & Banks, C. A. M. (Eds.) (2004). *Handbook of research in multicultural education* (2nd ed). Jossey-Bass.

Banks, J. A., Suárez-Orozco, M. M., & Ben-Peretz, M. (Eds.). (2016). *Global migration, diversity, and civic education: Improving policy and practice.* Teachers College Press.

Bereiter, C., & Engelmann, S. (1966). *Teaching disadvantaged children in the preschool.* Prentice-Hall.

Blow, C. (2020, May 3). Covid-19's race and class warfare. *New York Times*. http://www.nytimes.com/2020/05/03/opinion/coronavirus-race-class.html

Budiman, A. (2020). Key findings about U.S. immigrants. *Factank News in numbers*. Pew Research Center. https://www.pewresearch.org/fact-tank/2020/08/20/key-findings-about-u-s-immigrants

Camarota, S. A., & Ziegler, K. (2017, October). 65.5 million U.S. residents spoke a foreign language at home in 2016. *The Center for Immigration Studies*. Retrieved from https://cis.org/Report/655-Million-US-Residents-Spoke-Foreign-Language-Home-2016

Campbell, P. S. (2018). *Music, education, and diversity: Bridging cultures and communities*. Teachers College Press.

Case, A., & Deaton, A. (2020). *Deaths of despair and the future of capitalism*. Princeton University Press.

Charity Hudley, A. H., & Mallinson, C. (2011). *Understanding English language variation in U.S. schools*. Teachers College Press.

Cohen, P. (2020, April 17). Straggling in a good economy, and now struggling in a crisis. *New York Times*. Retrieved from www.nytimes.com/2020/04/16/business/economy/coronavirus-economy.html?searchResultPosition=1

Conchas, G. Q., & Vigil, J. D. (2012). *Streetsmart schoolsmart: Urban poverty and the education of adolescent boys*. Teachers College Press.

Contreras, F. (2011). *Achieving equity for Latino students: Expanding the pathway to education through public policy*. Teachers College Press.

Cookson, P. W. Jr. (2013). *Class rules: Exposing inequality in American high schools*. Teachers College Press.

Cuban, L. (2008). *Frogs into princes: Writings on school reform*. Teachers College Press.

Darling-Hammond, L. (2010). *The flat world and education: How America's commitment to equity will determine our future*. Teachers College Press.

Delgado Bernal, D., & Aleman, E. (2017). *Transforming educational pathways for Chicana/o students: A critical race feminista praxis*. Teachers College Press.

DiAngelo, R. (2018). *White fragility: Why it's so hard for White people to talk about racism*. Beacon Press.

Dilg, M. (2010). *Our worlds in our words: Exploring race, class, gender, and sexual orientation in multicultural classrooms*. Teachers College Press.

Douglas, T.-R. M. O., Shockley, K. G., & Toldson, I. (Eds.). (2020). *Campus uprisings: How student activists and collegiate leaders resist racism and create hope*. Teachers College Press.

Dowd, A. C., & Bensimon, E. M. (2015). *Engaging the "race question": Accountability and equity in U.S. higher education*. Teachers College Press.

Dunn, A. H. (2013). *Teachers without borders? The hidden consequences of international teachers in U.S. schools*. Teachers College Press.

Eck, D. L. (2001). *A new religious America: How a "Christian country" has become the world's most religiously diverse nation*. HarperSanFrancisco.

Egan, T. (2020, May 8). The world is taking pity on us: Will American prestige ever recover? *New York Times*. Retrieved from www.nytimes.com/2020/05/08/opinion/coronavirus-trump.html

Ford, D. Y. (1996). Review: Handbook of research on multicultural education. *The Journal of Negro Education*, 65(4), 472–476.

Gándara, P., & Hopkins, M. (Eds.). (2010). *Forbidden language: English language learners and restrictive language policies*. Teachers College Press.

García, E. E. (2005). *Teaching and learning in two languages: Bilingualism and schooling in the United States*. Teachers College Press.

Gay, G. (2010). *Culturally responsive teaching: Theory, research, and practice* (3rd ed.). Teachers College Press.

Goldstein, D. (2020, May 9). The class divide: Remote learning at 2 schools, private and public. *New York Times*. Retrieved from www.nytimes.com/2020/05/09/us/coronavirus-public-private-school.html?searchResultPosition=1

Gorski, P. C. (2018). *Reaching and teaching students in poverty: Strategies for erasing the opportunity gap* (2nd ed.). Teachers College Press.

Grandin, G. (2019). *The end of the myth: From the frontier to the border wall in the mind of America*. Henry Holt & Company.

Hopkins, J. P. (2020). *Indian education for all: Decolonizing indigenous education in public schools*. Teachers College Press.

Howard, G. R. (1981). Multiethnic education in monocultural schools. In J. A. Banks (Ed.), *Education in the 80s: Multiethnic education* (pp. 117–128). National Education Association.

Howard, G. R. (1993). Whites in multicultural education: Rethinking our role. *Phi Delta Kappan, 75*(1), 36–41.

Howard, G. R. (1999). *We can't teach what we don't know: White teachers, multiracial schools*. Teachers College Press. (Third edition published in 2016.)

Howard, T. C. (2014). *Black Male(d): Peril and promise in the education of African American males*. Teachers College Press.

Howard, T. C. (2020). *Why race and culture matter in schools: Closing the achievement gap in America's classrooms* (2nd ed.). Teachers College Press.

Ishimaru, A. M. (2020). *Just schools: Building equitable collaborations with families and communities*. Teachers College Press.

Joseph, R. L., & Briscoe-Smith, A. (2021). *Generation mixed goes to school: Radically listening to multiracial kids*. Teachers College Press.

Ladson-Billings, G. (1995). Toward a theory of culturally relevant pedagogy. *American Educational Research Journal, 32*(3), 465–491.

Ladson-Billings, G. (1996). Lifting as we climb: The womanist tradition in multicultural education. In J. A. Banks (Ed.), *Multicultural education, transformative knowledge, and action: Historical and contemporary perspectives* (pp. 179–200). Teachers College Press.

Lee, C. D. (2007). *Culture, literacy, and learning: Taking bloom in the midst of the whirlwind*. Teachers College Press.

Lee, O., & Buxton, C. A. (2010). *Diversity and equity in science education: Research, policy, and practice*. Teachers College Press.

Leonardo, Z. (2013). *Race frameworks: A multidimensional theory of racism and education*. Teachers College Press.

Loewen, J. W. (2018). *Lies my teacher told me: Everything your American history teacher got wrong*. The New Press.

Lomawaima, T., & McCarty, T. L. (2006). *"To remain an Indian": Lessons in democracy form a century of Native American education*. Teachers College Press.

Mahiri, J. (2017). *Deconstructing race: Multicultural education beyond the color-bind*. Teachers College Press.

Mayo, C. (2014). *LGBTQ youth and education: Policies and practices.* Teachers College Press.

Mays, J. C., & Newman, A. (2020, April 8). Virus is twice as deadly for Black and Latino people than Whites in N.Y.C. *New York Times.* Retrieved from www.nytimes.com/2020/04/08/nyregion/coronavirus-race-deaths.html?searchResultPosition=2

Moll, L., & González, N. (2004). Engaging life: A funds-of-knowledge approach to multicultural education. In J. A. Banks & C. A. M. Banks (Eds.), *Handbook of research on multicultural education* (2nd ed., pp. 699–715). Jossey-Bass.

Moodley, K. (2021). *Race, culture, and politics in education: A journey from South Africa.* Teachers College Press.

Morrison, T. (1987). *Beloved.* Knopf.

Nasir, N. S., Cabana, C., Shreve, B., Woodbury, E., & Louie, N. (Eds.). (2014). *Mathematics for equity: A framework for successful practice.* Teachers College Press.

Nasir, N. S., & Cobb, P. (Eds.). (2007). *Improving access to mathematics: Diversity and equity in the classroom.* Teachers College Press.

National Center for Education Statistics. (2017). *Enrollment and percentage distribution of enrollment in public elementary and secondary schools, by race/ethnicity and region: Selected years, fall 1995 through fall 2025.* https://nces.ed.gov/programs/digest/d15/tables/dt15_203.50.asp

National Center for Education Statistics (2019). *Status and trends in the education of racial and ethnic groups. Spotlight: Characteristics of public school teachers by race/ethnicity.* https://nces.ed.gov/programs/raceindicators/spotlight_a.asp

New York Times (2021, April 11). Paperback nonfiction. *New York Times Book Review*, p. 25.

O'Brien, P. (2016). *The Muslim question in Europe: Political controversies and public philosophies.* Temple University Press.

Ogbu, J. U. (2004). Collective identity and the burden of "acting White" in Black history, community, and education. *The Urban Review*, 36, 1–35.

Osler, A. (2016). *Human rights and schooling: An ethical framework for teaching social justice.* Teachers College Press.

Ovando, C. J., & Gourd, K. (1996). Knowledge construction, language maintenance, revitalization, and empowerment. In J. A. Banks (Ed.), *Multicultural education, transformative knowledge, and action: Historical and contemporary perspectives* (pp. 297–322). Teachers College Press.

Paris, D., & Alim, H. S. (Eds.) (2017). *Culturally sustaining pedagogies: Teaching and learning for justice in a changing world.* Teachers College Press.

Payne, R. K. (2013). *A framework for understanding poverty* (5th ed.). aha! Process.

Perez, W. (2012). *Americans by heart: Undocumented Latino students and the promise of higher education.* Teachers College Press.

Riessman, F. (1962). *The culturally deprived child.* Harper & Row.

Rivers, S. W., & Lomotey, K. (1996). Book Review: Handbook of research on multicultural education. *Journal of Education for Students Placed at Risk*, 1(2), 193–200.

Rosenthal, E. (2020, May 6). We knew the coronavirus was coming, yet we failed. *New York Times.* Retrieved from https://www.nytimes.com/2020/05/06/opinion/coronavirus-health-care-market.html?searchResultPosition=1

Schwartz, N. D., Casselman, B., & Koeze, E. (2020, May 8). How bad is unemployment? "Literally off the charts." *New York Times*. Retrieved from www. nytimes.com/interactive/2020/05/08/business/economy/april-jobs-report.html?-searchResultPosition=2

Semel, S. F. (1996). "Yes, but . . .": Multiculturalism and the reduction of educational inequality. *Teachers College Record, 98*(1), 153–177.

Sensoy, Ö., & DiAngelo, R. (2017). *Is everyone really equal? An introduction to key concepts in social justice education* (2nd ed.). Teachers College Press.

Solórzano, D. G., & Pérez Huber, L. (2020). *Racial microaggressions: Using critical race theory to respond to everyday racism*. Teachers College Press.

Stevens, M. (2020, March 29). How Asian-American leaders are grappling with xenophobia amid coronavirus. *New York Times*. Retrieved from www.nytimes.com/2020/03/29/us/politics/coronavirus-asian-americans.html?searchResultPosition=1

Stillman, J., & Anderson, L. (2017). *Teaching for equity in complex times: Negotiating standards in a high-performing bilingual school*. Teachers College Press.

Suárez-Orozco, C., & Osei-Twumasi, O. (Eds.). (2019). *Immigrant-origin students in community college: Navigating risk and reward in higher education*. Teachers College Press.

Teranishi, R. T. (2010). *Asians in the ivory tower: Dilemmas of racial inequality in American higher education*. Teachers College Press.

Thernstrom, A., & Thernstrom, S. (2003). *No excuses: Closing the racial gap in learning*. Simon and Schuster.

Valdés, G. (2001). *Learning and not learning English: Latino students in American schools*. Teachers College Press.

Valdés, G., Capitelli, S., & Alvarez, L. (2011). *Latino children learning English: Steps in the journey*. Teachers College Press.

Vavrus, M. (2006). Book review: Handbook of research on multicultural education. *Urban Education, 22*(10), 1–11.

Villarosa, L. (2020, May 3). Who lives? Who dies? How Covid-19 has revealed the deadly realities of a racially polarized America. *New York Times Magazine*, pp. 34–39, ff. 50–51.

Williams, C. (2020, April 23). $23M to get Detroit students tablets, internet amid pandemic. Associated Press. Retrieved from https://apnews.com/cb984f50631e-4a35c17418182c63f94e

Zong, J., Batalova, J., & Hallock, J. (2018, February). *Frequently requested statistics on immigrants and immigration in the United States*. The Migration Policy Institute. Retrieved from www.migrationpolicy.org/article/frequently-requested-statistics-immigrants-and-immigration-united-states#Demographic

PART I

HISTORY AND FOUNDATIONS OF INTERGROUP AND MULTICULTURAL EDUCATION

CHAPTER 1

Responding to Diversity in the 21st Century

Lessons from the Intergroup Education Movement

Cherry A. McGee Banks

Between 1881 and the beginning of World War I, almost 22 million immigrants settled in the United States (Hutchinson, 1949). Immigration continued at an unprecedented rate throughout the early 20th century, peaking in 1914 when 1,218,480 immigrants entered the United States. (U.S. Bureau of the Census, 1975). Between 1860 and 1930, more people emigrated to the United States than the entire U.S. population in 1860. An overview of U.S. immigrants at the turn of the 20th century is included in Table 1.1.

The new immigrants were ethnically and religiously diverse. Before 1880 most U.S. immigrants came from Northern and Western Europe and were primarily Protestant. After 1880 most of the new immigrants came from southern and eastern Europe and were Catholics, Jews, Muslims, and members of the Greek and Russian Orthodox Church. Over half a million of the immigrants who arrived in 1914 came from Russia, the Baltic States, and Italy (U.S. Census Bureau, 1975). By 1910, communities known as "Little Russia," "Little Poland," "Little Hungary," and "Little Italy" could be found in large cities throughout the nation.

Most immigrants who came to the United States stayed, but some returned home. Before 1920 about 30% of U.S. immigrants returned home. Some of those returning to their homelands were sojourners who had never intended to stay in the United States. Their plan was to come to the United States to work, save their money, and then return to their homelands. Others intended to stay but eventually returned to their homelands because their experience in the United States wasn't what they had expected. Of those who returned to their homelands, some resented the way they were treated. Others couldn't adjust to life in the United States. Still others preferred the familiarity of life in their country of origin where they understood the

Table 1.1. Immigration to the United States at the Turn of the 20th Century

Region	1880–1889[1]	1890–1899[2]	1900–1909	1910–1919
Northern Europe	3,982,722	1,826,717	1,811,616	1,112,638
Central Europe	357,697	641,904	2,036,027	1,181,907
Eastern Europe	189,920	460,456	1,620,479	1,191,713
Southern Europe	298,718	629,701	2,165,849	1,570,302
Asia	6,986	57,738	237,980	198,587
South and Central America	524,826	37,350	277,809	1,070,535

1. Before 1880, most of the immigrants who came to the United States were from northern and western Europe. Following the potato famine of 1845–1849 in Ireland, thousands of Irish immigrated to the United States. They were followed by Germans and Scandinavians, who came primarily between 1840 and 1860. During that same time period, thousands of Chinese immigrated to California during the 1849 Gold Rush. They were joined during the 1860s by almost 200,000 of their brethren who helped build the Union Pacific railroad. In 1869, the Central and Union Pacific railroads linked the country from the Atlantic Ocean to the Pacific.

2. Pogroms against Jews in Russia resulted in Russian Jews immigrating to the United States. Many arrived at the new immigration center, which was opened on Ellis Island in 1892.

Source: Ziegler, B. M. (Ed.). (1953). *Immigration: An American dilemma.* D. C. Heath & Company.

language, customs, and values of their fellow countrymen (Fleming, 1970; Seller, 1977).

NATIVISTS DEFINE WHO IS AND WHO IS NOT AN AMERICAN

The new immigrants, many of whom were Italian and Jewish, did not enjoy the privilege of being seen as White and were frequently viewed with suspicion by old stock Americans (Jacobson, 1998). They spoke alien languages and had political beliefs, religious practices, and cultural characteristics that were viewed as un-American. As immigration increased, antialien sentiments and fears escalated (Hutchinson, 1949). The new immigrants were seen as a drain on American society in much the same way as the Germans and Irish had been viewed in earlier years. The new immigrants, however, were not viewed sympathetically by the Germans and Irish. Even though they themselves had been victims of prejudice and discrimination when they first arrived in the United States, many Germans and Irish embraced nativist perspectives and spoke out against the new immigrants.

Nativists argued that the new immigrants from southern and eastern Europe were threatening American values and institutions and jeopardizing the White race (Grant, 1918). Woodrow Wilson captured the anti-immigration sentiment of his day when he said, "The immigrant newcomers of recent years are men of the lowest class from the south of Italy, and men of the meaner sort out of Hungary and Poland, men out of the ranks where there was neither skill nor energy, nor any initiative of quick intelligence" (quoted in Kessner, 1977, pp. 25–26). In addition, the Bolshevik Revolution, which overthrew the Russian czar, increased concerns about the extent to which immigrants embraced revolutionary ideologies, as well as their ability to understand and appreciate American democracy (Ross, 1914). Nativists exploited fears about the stability of American institutions and their vulnerability to outside radical forces as they argued for restrictions on immigration. The American Protective Association, a nativist organization, used the availability of newer and less expensive forms of transatlantic transportation to raise fears about immigration. The association's leaders argued that unrestricted immigration would flood American institutions with "$9.60 steerage slime" (Ziegler, 1953). Nativism reached its zenith in the early 1900s in organizations such as the Ku Klux Klan, which was anti-Catholic, anti-Jewish, antiforeigner, and anti-Black.

Nativist Perspectives in Academic Texts and School Curricula

In addition to politicians and opportunists, academic and school leaders also embraced nativist sentiments. Henry Pratt Fairchild, a well-known sociologist, expressed nativist sentiments in two books—*The Melting Pot Mistake* and *Immigration: A World Movement and Its American Significance* (Fairchild, 1913, 1926). Fairchild argued that immigrants were responsible for lowering the American standard of living, increasing crime, burdening society with a disproportionate number of people in insane asylums, and for the declining quality of American life. Commenting on crime, he noted that two forms of crime, the Mafia and White slave traffic, were connected to immigration. He associated the Mafia with Italians and White slave traffic with Jewish, French, and Belgian immigrants. He was particularly concerned about the native-born children of immigrants. He used statistics to argue that they had a much higher inclination toward criminal behavior than mainstream native Whites. Although he acknowledged the complex causes of juvenile delinquency, he concluded, "Whatever the cause, this tendency toward lawlessness among the second generation of immigrants is indisputable, and is one of the most disturbing elements in the whole situation" (Fairchild, 1953, p. 49).

Nativists' perspectives, such as those articulated by Fairchild, were incorporated into school textbooks, materials, and curricula. The following statement from a 1931 curriculum guide for social studies teachers in Houston, Texas, is an example of nativist ideas in the curriculum:

Migration from the foreign countries has become a problem. The immigrants who were so freely welcomed as long as land was abundant became a menace to our higher standards of living when they remained in cities where already there were more persons than jobs. Consequently, the number of immigrants that may enter our country in any one year has been cut to a very small fraction of the number of persons from any given country who were in the U.S. in 1890. This regulation has tended to lessen the immigration from southern Europe. Before 1890 most of our immigrants had come from England, Germany, Sweden, and other countries of northern Europe. (Houston Curriculum Guide, 1931, p. 7)

The Houston Curriculum Guide provided teachers with a rationale for explaining why immigration was restricted and a way to draw a distinction between mainstream Americans, whose ancestors were drawn to the rich prairie land in the West where they started small family farms, and the new immigrants, who settled in cities, lived in ethnic communities, and took jobs in mines and factories. Interestingly, the distinctions made in the Houston Curriculum Guide between old and new immigrants were essentially the same as those used by nativists to justify immigration restrictions.

The Houston Curriculum Guide illustrates the extent to which concerns about immigration weren't limited to people on the East Coast. Houston and Galveston, Texas, were two important stopping points for immigrants moving west. Large numbers of immigrants arrived in those cities in the early 1900s. Many stayed in Texas and established homes there, while others moved on to other cities in the West.

The Move to Curb Immigration

In 1924, Congress passed the Johnson-Reed Bill. This far-reaching bill shaped U.S. immigration policy into the 1960s. A chronology of U.S. immigration laws from 1917 to 1990 is included in Table 1.2. The Johnson-Reed Bill was the culmination of years of concentrated effort to stem the flow of new immigrants. Senator Ellison DuRant Smith voiced a nativistic perspective on immigration when in 1924 he delivered an impassioned plea to the 68th Congress to "shut the door" on immigration to the United States. He asked his colleagues in the U.S. Senate to think about who they would like to represent as a typical American:

If you were to go abroad and someone were to meet you and say, "I met a typical American," what would flash into your mind as a typical representative of that new Nation? Would it be the son of an Italian immigrant, the son of a German immigrant, the son of any of the breeds from the Orient, the son of the denizens of Africa? . . . Thank God we have in America perhaps the largest percentage of any country in the world of the pure, unadulterated Anglo-Saxon stock; certainly the greatest of any nation in the Nordic breed. It is for the preservation of that splendid stock that has characterized us that I would make this

Table 1.2. A Chronology of U.S. Immigration Laws From 1917–1990

The 1917 Immigration Act	This act prevented most Asians from immigrating to the United States. However, since the Philippines was an American territory, Asians living there could immigrate to the United States. This act also required immigrants to be able to read.
The National Origins Act of 1924	This act established a total quota limiting immigration to the United States to about 150,000 immigrants per year. The law provided for a disproportionate number of people from England and Northern Europe to immigrate to the United States. Very few slots were allotted to people from southern and eastern Europe. None was given to Asians.
1952 McCarran-Walter Act	This act allowed small numbers of Asians to immigrate to the United States.
1965 Immigration Act	This act opened up immigration to the United States to people in Third World nations. It allowed 20,000 people per country to immigrate to the United States. Spouses, dependent children, and parents of U.S. citizens were exempt from the country limits.
Immigration and Control Act of 1986	This act provides for sanctions against employers who hire illegal immigrant workers. However, provisions are made for employers to hire "guest workers" who can work in the United States but are not given the same rights and benefits as U.S. citizens. It also provided amnesty for undocumented aliens who could prove that they had lived in the United States since January 1982.
Immigration Act of 1990	This act reaffirmed the importance of family reunification.

not an asylum for the oppressed of all countries. . . . The time has come when we should shut the door and keep what we have for what we hope our own people to be. (Smith, 1924, pp. 5961–5962)

While many Americans did not embrace Smith's vitriolic views, he was not an isolated, lone individual voicing an opinion that did not have strong support. Smith represented North Carolina in the U.S. Senate from 1909 until his death in 1944. Like many others who wanted to limit immigration, Smith used Madison Grant's (1918) popular theories about race to add intellectual credibility to his arguments. In his book *The Passing of the Great Race*, Grant argued that liberal immigration policies were essentially "suicidal ethics, which are exterminating his own race" (p. 81). He believed that the United States could absorb only a small number of Slavs, Jews, and members of the Iberian races. According to Grant, the idea of America as a great melting pot was flawed and race-mixing would ultimately weaken the bloodline of old-stock Americans. Grant's ideas about racial hierarchies not only provided an intellectual rationale for the Johnson-Reed Bill, they also legitimized racist depictions of White ethnics and minorities in the popular culture. Movies such as *The Birth of a Nation* and *The Jazz Singer* helped shape the way Americans thought about race then and continue to think about it today (Jacobson, 1998).

Only six senators voted against the Johnson-Reed Bill. The forces against immigration, which included the Ku Klux Klan and labor organizations, were stronger than the American Jewish Congress and other organizations and individuals who supported immigration (Congressional Record, 1924). The Johnson-Reed Bill restricted immigration to 2% of a group's population in the United States in 1890. The national origins quotas in the Johnson-Reed Bill, which were essentially a proxy for racial and ethnic quotas, ensured that future U.S. immigrants would primarily come from northern and western Europe.

A NEW BEGINNING:
INTERCULTURAL EDUCATORS CHALLENGE NATIVIST PERSPECTIVES

Nativist ideas like those articulated by Smith, Grant, and Fairchild were not universally accepted by Americans. They were challenged by academics such as Horace Kallen (1924), Julius Drachsler (1920), and Randolph Bourne (1920). They and other like-minded scholars argued that it was possible for immigrants to assimilate into American society while maintaining important elements of their ethnic cultures. Kallen (1924) and his colleagues called this idea *cultural pluralism*. They believed that cultural and ethnic diversity would enrich American society.

European immigrants challenged nativist perspectives through ethnic societies like the Knights of Columbus, the Polish National Alliance, and the Serb National Federation, as well as through ethnic newspapers. In addition to advocating for changes in immigration policies, they advocated for changes in school curricula. White ethnics wanted their children to see themselves reflected in the school curriculum. They wanted their voices, perspectives, and heroes to be visible in school texts and materials (Zimmerman, 1999). The growth of parochial schools was in part a response by White ethnic parents to public school curricula and texts that did not reflect their values, concerns, and histories.

Rachel Davis DuBois (1928), a teacher at Woodbury High School in Woodbury, New Jersey, also rejected the idea that the new immigrants were inferior to mainstream Americans. In the late 1920s she began developing school assembly programs on ethnic groups in her local community. DuBois worked with parents and members of the community to organize the assembly programs, identify artifacts that could be displayed at school, and solicit speakers who could present information on ethnic groups. The assembly

programs were designed to affirm the values, customs, and contributions
of ethnic students in the school, improve intergroup relations, and dispel
negative images of the new immigrants (DuBois, 1928). DuBois's assembly
programs at Woodbury High School served as a prototype for what later
became known as intercultural education.

Major Characteristics of Intercultural Education

Intercultural educators developed and implemented projects and programs
in schools, colleges, and teacher training institutions through the Service
Bureau for Intercultural Education in New York City directed by Rachel
Davis DuBois (DuBois, 1930); the Springfield Plan, under the leadership of
John Granrud (Alland & Wise, 1945; Bresnahan, 1971; Chatto & Halligan, 1945); the Intergroup Education in Cooperating Schools Project, led by
Hilda Taba (1953); and the College Study in Intergroup Relations Project
organized by Lloyd Cook (Cook, 1951; Cook & Cook, 1954). These and
other intercultural education projects and programs were based on the assumption that there were more similarities than differences among people
and that when people from different racial, ethnic, and religious groups had
an opportunity to get to know each other they would learn to accept and respect each other (Kilpatrick & VanTil, 1947; Taba & Elkins, 1950). William
Heard Kilpatrick and William VanTil (1947), two influential scholars who
were involved in intercultural education, defined intercultural education as
follows:

> Intercultural education aims at the best possible achievement of the values of
> participation with, acceptance of, and respect for others. It is an effort to bring
> education to bear as constructively as possible on actual and possible intercul-
> tural tensions and on the evils of any and all bias, prejudice, and discrimination
> against minority groups. In short, the effort of intercultural education is to en-
> sure to all the adequate realization of these social values and to remove and cure
> the bias and prejudice leading to such discriminations. This is the fundamental
> meaning of intercultural education, and it explains the presence of intercultural
> education as an integral part and aspect of modern democratic education. (p. 4)

Intercultural education was a broadly conceptualized movement that
wasn't limited to schools. Intercultural educators recognized that education
took place in the community as well as the classroom (Cook, 1938). Mount-
ing effective programs to reduce intergroup tension and increase the self-
esteem of the second generation required work in the community as well as
in schools. Intercultural education programs were implemented in community organizations such as the Young Men's Christian Association (YMCA)
and the Young Women's Christian Association (YWCA) as well as entire
cities such as Springfield, Massachusetts, where the Springfield Plan was
initiated.

Another important characteristic of intercultural education was the way that it linked theory and practice. Even though intercultural education was an applied field, it wasn't limited to classroom practice. It also involved research. Intergroup educators researched ways to help teachers gain the skills and knowledge they needed to work with students from diverse groups (Cook, 1950; Cook & Cook, 1954; Taba, 1953) and to reduce student prejudice (Trager & Yarrow, 1952).

Intercultural education had many variations representing different populations, sites, strategies, and activities. There were, however, several common threads that linked intercultural educators together. They included a clear focus on education as a means to address intergroup tensions, the centrality of democratic values and responsibilities in American life, and the recognition that education took place in the community as well as in schools.

Intercultural Educators Offer an Alternative to Nativism

By 1945, over 200 organizations were working in intercultural education (Giles, 1945). The number of intercultural organizations mushroomed after riots in Detroit and Los Angeles in 1943. Many of these organizations were national in scope, but a large number of them were local or regional. In a survey identifying intercultural organizations throughout the United States, H. Harry Giles (1945) found that 60 were located in the Northeast, 51 in the South, 44 in the Midwest, and 20 in the West. The number and location of intercultural organizations was consistent with the population distribution of immigrants, the second generation, and people of color. Intercultural education programs were implemented throughout the United States, but were primarily and most extensively implemented in New York City. Population demographics in New York City made it a logical center for intercultural education. Millions of immigrants landed at Castle Garden in New York Harbor, and later at Ellis Island. Castle Garden, the country's first immigration station, opened in New York City in 1855. The Ellis Island station operated in New York Harbor from 1892 to 1954. Prior to the mid-1800s, Philadelphia was the nation's chief port of entry for immigrants.

As in New York City, intergroup education was popular in Chicago, Philadelphia, Syracuse, Los Angeles, San Diego, and other cities that had large immigrant and minority populations (Committee on the Study of Teaching Materials in Intergroup Relations, 1949; Taba et al., 1949). However, intergroup education was not implemented for as long a period or as comprehensively in other cities as it was in New York City.

Intercultural Education in New York City. The New York City schools provided intercultural training for teachers, developed intercultural curricula, and purchased intercultural materials for teachers to use in their classrooms. The implementation of intergroup education in New York City, however, was not steady. It had peaks and valleys reflecting the politics of diversity in New York, teacher indifference and resistance, and the school board's concerns about the quality and impact of intergroup education (Chase, 1940; Zitron, 1968).

New York City educators' ideas and perspectives about immigrants largely mirrored those that were prevalent in U.S. society. Political concerns about ethnic diversity were among the most important factors that influenced the readiness of teachers to embrace intercultural education. Intercultural education came into being when the memory of loyalty oaths and attacks on teachers who were critical of the United States were still fresh in the minds of educators. When the United States entered World War I, anti-immigrant forces raised concerns about the possibility that teachers and university professors were subversives. People who were pacifists or critics of the war were viewed with suspicion. Concerns about the extent to which educators were patriotic supporters of the United States led to the requirement that teachers take loyalty oaths. In 1917, New York State passed a law that called for teachers to be dismissed for using seditious words or engaging in seditious acts. The New York City Board of Education required teachers to take the following loyalty oath:

> We the teachers in public schools of the City of New York declare our unqualified allegiance to the government of the United States of America and pledge ourselves by word and example to teach and impress on our pupils the duty of obedience and patriotic service as the highest ideal of American citizenship. (cited in Zitron, 1968, p. 163)

Community groups also influenced the speed and scope of the implementation of intercultural education in New York. A broad range of ethnic groups and organizations supported intercultural education, but concerns were widespread about how to present ethnic groups in the curriculum and about who could legitimately speak for a group. The American Jewish Committee clashed with intercultural educators over content on Jews. Jews were frequently presented as an ethnic group in intercultural education materials and programs. The American Jewish Committee insisted that Jews be presented as a religious group (Montalto, 1982). During the 1930s, the committee gradually withdrew its support for intercultural programs that persisted in identifying Jews as an ethnic group. Catholics and Protestants also had concerns about the way their religious groups were presented in intercultural education programs and materials (Zimmerman, 1999). When Mary L. Riley, who worked for the New York City Board of Education, received a list of speakers for an upcoming intercultural education program, she protested the inclusion of Bishop G. Bromley Oxnam. In a letter to Mrs. Lily Edelman of the East and West Association, the organization sponsoring the intercultural education program, Riley noted that Oxnam had made offensive remarks about the Roman Catholic Church and that he should be removed from the program. Riley went on to recommend other speakers who were more acceptable to the Catholic Church. These and other conflicts reflected how ethnic and religious groups jockeyed for power by using their connections with school and political leaders to exert pressure on intercultural educators, and when necessary, by withholding their support for intergroup programs.

DIVERGENT VIEWS WITHIN THE MOVEMENT

Despite consensus among intergroup educators that discrimination and hostility toward immigrant groups should be kept in check and that immigrants should be assimilated into mainstream American society, leaders in the intergroup education movement did not speak with a single voice (Montalto, 1982; Olneck, 1990). Beyond consensus on several broad goals, leaders in the intergroup education movement embraced different ideological perspectives and points of view on the direction and philosophy that should guide the movement. The movement was marked from its inception with internal conflict about how to achieve racial harmony and assimilation.

Americanization

Americanization was one of the most salient and visible ideological perspectives to influence the education of immigrant groups. However, Americanizers did not have a uniform perspective on diversity. Their perspectives ranged from conservative to moderate. Americanizers included individuals who were intolerant of diversity and believed that immigrants from northern Europe were superior to immigrants from southeastern Europe. They also included moderates. Montalto (1982) uses the term *Scientific Americanizer* to describe moderate Americanizers. Scientific Americanizers, according to Montalto, supported a limited program of ethnic and cultural education, mostly in the form of folk art performances and handicraft displays. Such programs were intended to raise the status of immigrant parents in the eyes of their children and reestablish the social control function of the immigrant family. They were not, however, designed to divert immigrant children from recognizing the importance of becoming Americans. In an effort to reduce the burden of marginality for immigrants and their children, scientific Americanizers set up classes to teach English to immigrants and provide other forms of support to help them adjust to U.S. society. Montalto (1982) concluded that "their goal was to instill an identity without substance, a sentimental attachment to the superficial aspects of cultures" (p. 54). Despite differences among Americanizers, they shared the belief that ethnic and religious diversity could potentially fracture U.S. society and that schools should work to assimilate immigrants into mainstream society as soon as possible.

Cultural Pluralism

Another important ideological strand in intercultural education was cultur-al pluralism. Rachel Davis DuBois, Leonard Covello, and other cultural plu-ralists believed that schools should be linked to students' communities and that students should be taught to appreciate their parents' culture and their ethnic heritage. Cultural pluralists also believed that all students should be taught to appreciate cultural diversity and to recognize that ethnic and religious diversity were an important part of being an American (DuBois, 1945). Because of her zeal in promoting the cultural heritage of immigrants, Americanizers accused Rachel Davis DuBois of trying to turn intercultural education into a social movement. DuBois rejected that criticism. From her perspective, it was essential that all students understand the values, beliefs, customs, and other important characteristics of American ethnic and racial groups.

During the 1930s, members of the second generation began to assume leadership roles in the intercultural movement. Second-generation intercul-tural educators were born in the United States and spoke English as their first language. With members of the second generation in leadership posi-tions, the movement began to focus more directly on the school's role in in-stilling all students with a sense of pride and appreciation for ethnic culture. Even though second-generation intercultural educators had many of the cultural characteristics of mainstream Americans, they were not strangers in ethnic communities. They understood and identified with ethnics as a re-sult of their early socialization in immigrant communities and through their ongoing contacts with family members who remained in the communities.

Cultural pluralists created educational programs that went beyond tol-erance. Their programs called for positive appreciation of immigrant culture and for incorporating ethnic cultural characteristics into the U.S. national identity (DuBois, 1945). Americanizers challenged cultural pluralists with the following question: "Are you not, by singling out first one culture group and then another for special attention in assembly programs and classroom discussions, developing rather than reducing a sense of separateness among groups?" Rachel Davis DuBois responded by pointing out that many mem-bers of cultural groups were already compartmentalized in people's minds in a negative way. Since members of culture groups are already viewed in a negative way, DuBois asked, "Shouldn't we set them off in a positive way in order to counteract that negative influence?" (DuBois, 1945, p. 158).

Cultural pluralists saw American culture as dynamic and open enough to embrace the values, beliefs, and other cultural characteristics of immi-grant groups. They believed that both old as well as new immigrants would need to make adjustments as a more authentic American identity was con-structed. Cultural pluralism, however, never gained widespread acceptance. Even though it was consistent with liberal ideology, cultural pluralism was unacceptable to many liberals. Intercultural educators who embraced cultural pluralism ultimately found themselves on the margins of a movement that they helped to create.

Variations in Intergroup Programs

In addition to ideological differences, intercultural education programs varied in their scope, target population, and content. This is somewhat understandable given the location of ethnic population centers. The content of intercultural education curricula, like multicultural education curricula today, frequently focused on local ethnic and racial groups and local intergroup tensions and concerns. Intercultural programs in New York City and other East Coast cities generally focused their attention on White ethnics from southern and eastern Europe and on religious groups. Many of the Italian immigrants who entered the United States through Ellis Island remained on the East Coast. Approximately 97% of the Italian immigrants who arrived in the United States after 1880 settled in New York City (Nelli, 1983). The remaining 3% spread out to other cities such as Philadelphia, New Castle, and Chicago in search of job opportunities (Allen & Turner, 1988).

Intercultural education programs in San Diego, California, and other cities on the West Coast included more content on ethnic minorities such as Japanese Americans and Chinese Americans. People of Asian descent primarily entered the United States through Angel Island and settled in cities on the West Coast. Many of their early settlements were in San Francisco, Los Angeles, Seattle, and Portland. However, Chinese and Japanese settlements existed in New York City as early as the 1920s and significant numbers of Chinese lived in Chicago and Boston in the early 1900s (Allen & Turner, 1988).

The organization and content of intercultural programs also varied. For example, some programs looked more like international education than intercultural education. Intercultural education programs that had an international focus were often affiliated with organizations such as the East and West Association. Pearl Buck founded the association in 1942 and dedicated its work to cultural exchange and understanding between Asia and the West. Other intercultural education programs sought to educate the "whole child" and borrowed key ideas from progressive education. Leonard Covello (1942), the principal at Benjamin Franklin High School, reflected that perspective when he said, "Life and learning in school should be continuous with those experiences out of school, with free interplay between the two" (p. 4). Many of the people involved in intergroup education were also actively involved in progressive education. Covello was a frequent speaker at Progressive Education Association conferences. William Heard Kilpatrick, well known for his seminal contributions to progressive education, also served on the board of the Bureau for Intercultural Education. This is an example of another link between progressive education and intercultural education.

SOCIAL SCIENTISTS PROVIDE INTELLECTUAL ARGUMENTS FOR INTERCULTURAL EDUCATION

Intergroup educators such as Rachel Davis DuBois, Leonard Covello, and Hilda Taba were deeply influenced by social science knowledge. They studied with the leading social scientists of their day and completed their doctorates at institutions where new ideas and key social science concepts were being discussed and researched. Social science concepts such as culture, assimilation, cultural pluralism, discrimination, and prejudice were woven into their thinking and provided an intellectual foundation for their work.

During the early 20th century, biological determinism, which claimed that racial minorities and certain White ethnics were inferior to northern Europeans, was widely accepted and used to explain status differentials between old and new immigrants (Gould, 1981). It also provided a rationale to justify the unequal treatment of particular ethnic and racial groups. Differences in the status and attainments of old and new immigrants could be explained by the fact that people of Northern and Western European ancestry were superior (Gould, 1981). Social scientists, many of whom were racial minorities and White ethnics, began to develop knowledge that challenged biological determinism and offer alternative explanations for White dominance.

African American scholars such as W. E. B. Du Bois and Carter G. Woodson were among the first scholars to challenge biological determinism. Du Bois's (1899/1973) study of African Americans in Philadelphia challenged the idea that Blacks were poor because of their inherent deficiencies. His work illustrated how the social context in which Blacks lived influenced their life chances and attainments. Du Bois's work not only provided an alternative explanation for differences among groups, it also served as a model of social science research.

Research on Assimilation

Some of the most troubling questions faced by intergroup educators were related to assimilating southern and eastern European immigrants and racial minorities into mainstream U.S. society. Social science knowledge provided insights into those questions. It suggested that culture was a much more persistent psychological and social reality than many people had previously thought and that assimilation could not be accomplished overnight. It could take several generations (Park, 1935). Some social scientists such as Robert Ezra Park believed that the second generation would never completely become Americanized (Park & Miller, 1921). Instead, they would serve as a bridge between the older unassimilated generation and the younger assimilated generations.

Park (1928) used the term *marginal man* to discuss the psychosocial conflicts experienced by many second-generation immigrants. He believed that when society opened up opportunities for minorities and immigrants, they would leave the geographical, social, and psychological boundaries of their ethnic communities. However, even though they were attempting to embrace a new way of life, they would remain psychologically tied to their ethnic communities and to the old ways of their mothers and fathers. According to Park, the dilemma for the *marginal man* is that he would never be able to fully return to his ethnic community and old way of life because he would see the community and people living there from a more detached and rational perspective. Sadly, having given up his old ways, he would never be fully accepted into his new cultural group because he could not or would not change his values, perspectives, or his fundamental sense of himself. Consequently, the *marginal man* would be destined to live in the borderlands in between two cultures, unable to be fully integrated into either. Over time, the term *marginal man* became a synonym for the second generation. However, Park used the term in a more limited way. The Jewish intellectual and the educated mulatto were used by Park as prime examples of *marginal man* when he coined the term (Cahnman, 1978).

Park and his students—who included eminent social scientists such as E. Franklin Frazier, Pauline Young, Frederick Thrasher, and Louis Wirth—developed knowledge that revealed that culture had both positive and negative effects. Culture restrained antisocial behavior and supported group cooperation but also stifled creativity and individuality (Park & Miller, 1921). Park (1928) saw the disappearance of ethnic cultures as an advance rather than a setback. He believed that race relations could be characterized by a cycle of four inevitable phases: "contact, conflict, accommodation, and eventual assimilation" (Park, 1950, p. 150). He warned that even though it may take many years, coercive attempts to speed the process of assimilation could backfire (Park, 1955).

Park's work on assimilation reflected a long-term interest in race relations and immigration. Nine years before joining the faculty at the University of Chicago, he worked with Booker T. Washington at Tuskegee Institute. From 1905 to 1914, Park served as Washington's assistant, advisor, and ghostwriter (Cahnman, 1978). In 1921, he published an extensive study of American immigration entitled *Old World Traits Transplanted* in which he discussed the theoretical framework for his understanding of the assimilation cycle (Park & Miller, 1921). Park's work on European immigrants was followed in 1924 with a major survey of race relations on the Pacific Coast, which focused on Asians. Park, along with his colleagues Emory Bogardus, Roderick McKenzie, and William Carlson, used the term *Oriental* to describe Chinese and Japanese immigrants and the term *Oriental problem* to describe "the shared experiences of Chinese and Japanese in being excluded from the White experience of successful assimilation" (Yu, 1996, p. 157). Park ended his career by retiring to Fisk University, where one of his former students, Charles S. Johnson, was president. At Fisk, he engaged in research on intercultural relations and taught courses on sociology and human ecology.

Research on Self-Esteem

The second generation was often in the peculiar position of helping their parents mediate the language, values, and other cultural characteristics of their adopted country. While playing the role of cultural translator, the second generation commonly saw their parents humiliated by people outside their communities. School was no different. There they frequently experienced humiliation and a lack of understanding and appreciation of their parents and their ancestral homeland. In movies and in other forms of popular culture the language, values, and customs of their parents were frequently ignored, dismissed, or denigrated. Nearly everywhere the second generation turned, they were tacitly encouraged to reject their parents' "old ways" and become American. Consequently, it wasn't uncommon for the second generation to see their parents as hopelessly old-fashioned. Their parents' opinions could easily be dismissed as being the response of someone who was ignorant of American culture.

If parents are not seen as respected authorities, the role that they traditionally play in directing and controlling their children's behavior is muted. When members of the second generation skipped school or engaged in petty criminal activity, many of their parents were not in a position to intervene with the traditional moral authority of a parent. The social fabric of immigrant communities and families was undermined by widespread negative images of immigrants and their cultures as being at best inferior and at worst dangerous. As family control broke down and traditional values were undermined, delinquent behaviors among the second generation increased. Over time these behaviors became widely associated with the second generation and eventually became a stereotype of it (Seller, 1977).

Research by Alfred Adler (1929) and other psychologists suggested that the antisocial behavior associated with the second generation was a reflection of their low self-esteem. Adler and his colleagues provided an intellectual basis for intergroup educators to think about the relationship between society's rejection of immigrant culture and immigrant children's rejection of their parents and ultimately themselves. Intergroup educators hypothesized that increasing the status of immigrants and ethnic groups could ameliorate the second-generation problem. Rachel Davis DuBois and other intergroup educators used Adler's transformative ideas about the relationship between societal image and self-esteem as a rationale for creating materials, activities, and programs to enhance students' self-esteem and for changing societal attitudes about immigrants. One of the strategies that intercultural educators used to help establish a positive link between self-esteem and societal image was to acknowledge publicly the accomplishments of immigrant groups and praise symbols of their cultures, such as their songs, dances, and foods (Adamic, 1934, 1940, 1944; DuBois, 1930).

Research on Culture

Franz Boas (1928) and his students at Columbia University, who included Otto Klineberg (1955), Melville J. Herskovits (1938, 1958), and Ruth Benedict (1934), created knowledge that encouraged people to think more deeply about the role ethnic cultures could play in improving United States society. Boas challenged the idea of racial purity and a superior race. He and his students promoted a sophisticated understanding of culture not as tangible artifacts but as a group's way of adapting to its environments. Boas (1928) argued that people were not bound together by blood or language, but rather by "the community of emotional life that rises from our every-day habits, from the forms of our thoughts, feelings, and actions which constitute the medium in which every individual can unfold freely his activities" (p. 9).

The new field of anthropology, founded by Boas and his students, developed concepts, ideas, and theories that suggested that culture wasn't unique to one society. Moreover, from the perspective of other cultures, United States society had limitations and could be improved. Anthropologists argued that contact with different peoples and cultures was characteristic of all great civilizations. Intergroup educators used that and other ideas from anthropology to argue that cultures should be blended in U.S. society (Benedict, 1934; Boas, 1928). Editors Alain Locke and Bernard J. Stern (1942) captured that perspective in an insightful book, *When Peoples Meet: A Study in Race and Culture Contacts*. This book was widely read by intergroup educators and used to help justify their work (Montalto, 1982).

Research on Prejudice

During World War II and the period immediately following, racial and religious tensions increased. Minorities became a focal point for frustrations born out of irritations with gas shortages, rationing, separation from loved ones, and anxiety about the future. Additionally, organizations such as the German-American Bund, the Christian Front, and the Christian Mobilizers exacerbated fears about Jewish educators radicalizing young people. Those fears were reflected in newspapers, magazines, and journal articles. Zitron (1968) reports that a 1939 issue of *Social Justice* contained an article entitled "Are Reds in Control of New York City Schools?" The members of the Teachers Union were listed in the article with the notation "Jew," "Jewess," "Undetermined," and "Gentile" beside each name (cited in Zitron, 1968, p. 193).

Intergroup tensions continued to develop throughout and after the war years. In June 1943, a major race riot in Detroit, Michigan, called national attention to the deep interracial tensions that existed between Whites and Blacks. The Detroit riot was the first of several that occurred in what came to be known as the "bloody summer" of 1943. African Americans who had left the South during the Great Migration were experiencing discrimination in a wide range of areas, including housing, education, and employment. Other ethnic minorities also had a difficult time. Mexicans who had been invited to the United States to work in bracero programs were seen as taking jobs from Whites and were unwelcome. People of Japanese descent who had been put into internment camps returned to western cities to reestablish themselves after the war. They experienced prejudice and discrimination as they returned to their homes. African Americans, Jews, Japanese, Mexicans, and other ethnic minorities were easy and visible targets for prejudice and discrimination.

To combat Hitler's focus on racial purity in Nazi Germany, social scientists began to develop new explanations for group differences. Before World War II social scientists had focused primarily on measuring the attitudes of Whites toward racial and ethnic groups. For example, in the 1920s Emory Bogardus (1925a, 1925b, 1933) developed an attitude scale to measure ethnic prejudice by measuring *social distance*, the feelings of acceptance or rejection for different racial and ethnic groups. In the 1940s and 1950s researchers began developing and testing a broader range of theories about prejudice. Social psychologists such as Theodor Adorno and Gordon Allport offered thoughtful explanations about the origin of prejudice and ways to reduce it. In *The Authoritarian Personality*, Adorno and his colleagues (1950) argued that prejudice stemmed from certain personality dispositions. Their theory about the authoritarian personality, which was very popular and widely accepted after World War II, was later regarded by social scientists to be a useful but limited theory about the origin of prejudice.

Noting that public opinion polls indicated that 85% of the U.S. population was psychologically prepared to scapegoat another group, Allport (1944) began to analyze the psychology of the bigot. He defined a bigot as "a person who, under the tyranny of his own frustrations, tabloid thinking, and projection, blames a whole group of people for faults of which they are partially or wholly innocent" (p. 2). Allport's theory not only offered explanations of prejudice but also provided ideas for improving intergroup relations. His theory is called the *contact hypothesis*. Allport stated that contact between members of different social groups could improve intergroup relations if the following four conditions were met:

1. there was equal status among the groups;
2. the activities the groups engaged in reinforced a sense of common interests and humanity between the two groups;
3. the groups shared mutual goals; and

4. the groups' activities were sanctioned by institutional authorities (Allport, 1954).

Allport's ideas on how to structure intergroup contact were used by intergroup educators to bring members of different ethnic groups together. His theory has been widely researched and in its revised form serves as the basis of many intergroup interventions today (Pettigrew, 2004; Stephan & Stephan, 2004).

Research Highlights American Creed Values

Myrdal's (1944) study on intergroup relations in the United States entitled *An American Dilemma: The Negro Problem and Modern Democracy* revealed a gap between American Creed Values such as freedom, justice, and equality, and the reality of those values in the daily lives of African Americans. By both law and custom African Americans and other people of color were denied equal rights and subjected to various forms of exclusion, segregation, and discrimination. Myrdal argued that the consequences of racism and discrimination were at odds with the nation's ideals. Intergroup educators were encouraged by Myrdal's finding that although the reality of American life was at odds with its ideal values, these values had not been forgotten and still defined what Americans believed they should and could be. Ideals associated with democracy became a major focus of intergroup education during World War II and were used as a justification for prejudice reduction activities in the schools. Intercultural educators argued that prejudice reduction had a legitimate and necessary place in the school curriculum of democratic societies.

LINKING TRANSFORMATIVE KNOWLEDGE TO SCHOOL KNOWLEDGE

The transformative knowledge created by Robert Park (1928), Franz Boas (1928), Alfred Adler (1929), Gordon Allport (1944), and other scholars was critically important to the intercultural education movement. It challenged mainstream knowledge about immigrant groups and prepared the public for receiving new ideas about the role that immigrants could play in American society. Most importantly, it provided an intellectual platform from which intercultural educators could challenge perceptions of new immigrants as individuals who didn't have a culture, had little to offer American society, and were inferior to old immigrants. Intercultural educators used transformative social science knowledge to argue for changes in textbooks, materials, curricula, and other forms of school knowledge so that the ancestral homelands and cultures of immigrants could be acknowledged and celebrated. They also used transformative knowledge to develop in-service training materials and programs for teachers who were responsible for implementing intercultural education in schools.

Intercultural educators increased their legitimacy by using transformative research to justify their work and to develop their programs and materials. Their association with transformative scholars and scholarship allowed them to speak with authority when they argued that intercultural education was an effective way to respond to the problems of second-generation children and youth.

REFERENCES

Adamic, L. (1934, November). Thirty million new Americans. *Harper's Magazine, 169*, 684–694.

Adamic, L. (1940). *From many lands*. Harper.

Adamic, L. (1944). *A nation of nations*. Harper.

Adler, A. (1929). *The science of living*. Garden City Publishing.

Adorno, T. W., Frenkel-Brunswick, E., Levinson, D., & Sanford, R. (1950). *The authoritarian personality*. Harper Press.

Alland, A., & Wise, J. W. (1945). *The Springfield Plan*. Viking Press.

Allen, J. P., & Turner, E. J. (1988). *We the people: An atlas of America's ethnic diversity*. Macmillan.

Allport, G. W. (1944). The bigot in our midst. *The commonweal*. (Found in Covello's files MSS40; Covello; 53/21.)

Allport, G. W. (1954). *The nature of prejudice*. Addison-Wesley.

Benedict, R. (1934). *Patterns of culture*. Houghton Mifflin.

Boas, F. (1928). *Anthropology and modern life*. W. W. Norton.

Bogardus, E. S. (1925a). Social distance and its origins. *Journal of Applied Sociology, 9*, 216–225.

Bogardus, E. S. (1925b). Measuring social distances. *Journal of Applied Sociology, 9*, 299–308.

Bogardus, E. S. (1933, January–February). A social distance scale. *Sociology and Social Research*, 265–271.

Bourne, R. S. (Ed.). (1920). *History of a literary radical and other essays*. B. W. Huebsch.

Bresnahan, D. (1971). *The Springfield Plan in retrospect*. Unpublished doctoral dissertation, Teachers College, Columbia University, New York.

Cahnman, W. J. (1978). Robert E. Park at Fisk. *Journal of the History of the Behavioral Sciences, 14*, 328–336.

Chase, G. (1940). *Report of the committee for evaluation of the work of the Service Bureau for Intercultural Education*. New York City School Board.

Chatto, C. I., & Halligan, A. L. (1945). *The story of the Springfield Plan*. Barnes & Noble.

Committee on the Study of Teaching Materials in Intergroup Relations. (1949). *Intergroup relations in teaching materials: A survey and appraisal*. American Council on Education.

Congressional Record. (1924). *Congressional Record, 65*, 68th Congress, 1st Session, Washington, DC: Government Printing Office. 5965–5969.

Cook, L. A. (1938). *Community backgrounds of education*. McGraw-Hill.

Cook, L. A. (Ed.). (1950). *College programs in intergroup relations: A report by twenty-four colleges participating in the college study in intergroup relations, 1945–49.* The American Council on Education.

Cook, L. A. (1951). *Intergroup relations in teacher education.* American Council on Education.

Cook, L. A., & Cook, E. (1954). *Intergroup education.* McGraw-Hill.

Covello, L. (1942). Unpublished report on Benjamin Franklin High School. (Found in Covello's files MSS40, Covello 34/11.)

Drachsler, J. (1920). *Democracy and assimilation: The blending of immigrant heritages in America.* Macmillan.

DuBois, R. D. (1928). *Education in world mindedness: A series of assembly programs given by students at Woodbury High School, Woodbury, New Jersey, 1927–1928.* [Publisher unknown]

DuBois, R. D. (1930). *The contributions of racial elements to American life* (2nd ed.). Women's International League for Peace and Freedom.

DuBois, R. D. (1945). *Build together Americans.* Hinds, Hayden, & Hildredge.

Du Bois, W. E. B. (1973). *The Philadelphia Negro: A social study.* Millwood, NY: Kraus-Thompson. (Original work published 1899)

Fairchild, H. P. (1913). *Immigration: A world movement and its American significance.* Macmillan.

Fairchild, H. P. (1926). *The melting-pot mistake.* Little, Brown.

Fairchild, H. P. (1953). Conditions in America as affected by immigration. In B. M. Ziegler (Ed.), *Immigration: An American Dilemma* (pp. 34–49). D. C. Heath.

Fleming, T. J. (1970). *The golden door.* Grosset, Dunlap.

Giles, H. H. (1945). Organizations in the field of intercultural relations. *Harvard Educational Review, 15*(2), 87–92.

Gould, S. J. (1981). *The mismeasure of man.* Norton.

Grant, M. (1918). *The passing of the great race.* Charles Scribner's Sons.

Herskovits, M. J. (1938). *Acculturation: The study of culture contact.* J. J. Augustin.

Herskovits, M. J. (1958). *The myth of the Negro past.* Beacon Press.

Houston Curriculum Guide (1931). *Life on the American frontier, a study of the westward movement in American history.* Unit III. Houston Public Schools.

Hutchinson, E. P. (1949). *Immigration policy since World War I. The Annals,* 262, 15–21.

Jacobson, M. F. (1998). *Whiteness of a different color: European immigrants and the alchemy of race.* Harvard University Press.

Kallen, H. M. (1924). *Culture and democracy in the United States.* Boni & Liveright.

Kessner, T. (1977). *The golden door: Italian and Jewish immigrant mobility in New York City, 1880–1915.* Oxford University Press.

Kilpatrick, W. H., & VanTil, W. (Eds.). (1947). *Intercultural attitudes in the making, ninth yearbook of the John Dewey Society.* Harper & Brothers.

Klineberg, O. (1955). *Race differences.* Harper & Brothers.

Locke, A., & Stern, B. J. (Eds.). (1942). *When peoples meet: A study in race and culture contacts.* New York: Progressive Education Association.

Montalto, N. V. (1982). *A history of the intercultural education movement, 1924–1941.* Garland Publishing.

Myrdal, G. (1944). *An American dilemma.* McGraw-Hill.

Nelli, H. S. (1983). *From immigrants to ethnics: The Italian Americans.* Oxford.

Olneck, M. R. (1990). The reoccurring dream: Symbolism and ideology in intercultural education and multicultural education. *American Journal of Education, 98*, 147–174.

Park, R. E. (1928). Human migration and the marginal man. *American Journal of Sociology, 33*, 881–893.

Park, R. E. (1935). Assimilation. In *Encyclopedia of the social sciences, II* (pp. 281–283). Macmillan.

Park, R. E. (1950). *Race and culture.* Free Press.

Park, R. E. (1955). *Society: Collective behavior, news, and opinion, sociology and modern society.* Free Press.

Park, R. E., & Miller, H. E. (1921). *Old world traits transplanted.* New York: Macmillan.

Pettigrew, T. F. (2004). Intergroup contact: Theory, research and new perspectives. In J. A. Banks & C. A. M. Banks (Eds.), *Handbook of research on multicultural education* (pp. 770–781). Jossey-Bass.

Ross, E. A. (1914). *Immigrants in politics: The political consequences of immigration. In B. M. schooling, and the acceptance of her educational ideas in Estonia. In Jubilee conference: Hilda Taba-90* (pp. 51–59). Tartu University Press (Estonia).

Seller, M. (1977). *To seek America: A history of ethnic life in the United States.* Jerome S. Ozer.

Smith, E. D. (1924, April 9). *Congressional Record, 65,* 68th Congress, 1st Session. Government Printing Office. pp. 5961–5962.

Stephan, W., & Stephan, C. (2004). Intergroup relations in multicultural education programs. In J. A. Banks & C. A. M. Banks (Eds.), *Handbook of research on multicultural education* (pp. 782–798). Jossey-Bass.

Taba, H. (1953). *Leadership training in intergroup education.* American Council on Education.

Taba, H., Brady, E. H., Jennings, H. H., Robinson, J. T., & Dolton, F. (1949). *Curriculum in intergroup relations: Case studies in instruction for secondary schools.* American Council on Education.

Taba, H., & Elkins, D. (1950). *With focus on human relations.* American Council on Education.

Trager, H. G., & Yarrow, M. R. (1952). *They learn what they live: Prejudice in young children.* Harper & Brothers.

U.S. Census Bureau (1975). *Historical statistics of the United States, colonial times to 1970, bicentennial edition, Part 2.* U.S. Government Printing Office.

Yu, H. (1996). Constructing the "Oriental Problem" in American thought, 1920–1960. In J. A. Banks (Ed.), *Multicultural education, Transformative knowledge and action* (pp. 156–175). Teachers College Press.

Ziegler, B. M. (Ed.). (1953). *Immigration: An American dilemma* (pp. 71–77). D. C. Heath & Co.

Zimmerman, J. (1999). Storm over the schoolhouse: Exploring popular influences upon the American curriculum, 1890–1941. *Teachers College Record, 100*(3), 602–626.

Zitron, C. L. (1968). *The New York City teachers union, 1916–1964: A story of educational and social commitment.* Humanities Press.

CHAPTER 2

Multicultural Education

History and Dimensions

James A. Banks

Multicultural education grew out of the ferment of the civil rights move-ment of the 1960s. During this decade, African Americans embarked on a quest for their rights that was unprecedented in the United States. A major goal of this movement was to eliminate discrimination in public accommo-dations, housing, employment, and education. Its consequences had a sig-nificant influence on educational institutions as ethnic groups—first African Americans and then other groups—demanded that the schools and other ed-ucational institutions reform curricula to reflect their experiences, histories, cultures, and perspectives. Ethnic groups also demanded that the schools hire more Black and Brown teachers and administrators so that their chil-dren would have more successful role models. Ethnic groups pushed for community control of schools in their neighborhoods and for the revision of textbooks to make them reflect the diversity of peoples in the United States.

The first responses of schools and educators to the ethnic movements of the 1960s were hurried (Banks, 2006, 2016). Courses and programs were developed without the thought and careful planning needed to make them educationally sound or to institutionalize them within the educational sys-tem. Holidays and other special days, ethnic celebrations, and courses that focused on one ethnic group were the dominant characteristics of school reforms related to ethnic and cultural diversity during the 1960s and early 1970s. Grant and Sleeter (2013) call this approach "single-group studies." The ethnic studies courses developed and implemented during this period were usually electives and were taken primarily by students who were mem-bers of the group that was the subject of the course.

The visible success of the civil rights movement, plus growing rage and a liberal national atmosphere, stimulated other marginalized groups to take actions to eliminate discrimination against them and to demand that the ed-ucational system respond to their needs, aspirations, cultures, and histories. The women's rights movement emerged as one of the most significant social reform movements of the 20th century (Brewer, 2012). During the 1960s and 1970s, discrimination against women in employment, income, and education was widespread and often blatant. The women's rights movement articulated and publicized how discrimination and institutionalized sexism limited the opportunities of women and adversely affected the nation. The leaders of this movement, such as Betty Friedan and Gloria Steinem (2015), demanded that political, social, economic, and educational institutions act to eliminate sex discrimination and provide opportunities for women to actualize their talents and realize their ambitions. Major goals of the women's rights movement included offering equal pay for equal work, eliminating laws that discriminated against women and made them second-class citizens, hiring more women in leadership positions, and increasing the participation of men in household work and child rearing.

When *feminists* (people who work for the political, social, and economic equalities of the sexes) looked at educational institutions, they noted problems similar to those identified by ethnic groups of color. Textbooks and curricula were dominated by men; women were largely invisible. Feminists pointed out that history textbooks were dominated by political and military history—areas in which men had been the main participants (Trecker, 1973). Social and family history and the history of labor and ordinary people were largely ignored. Feminists pushed for the revision of textbooks to include more history about the important roles of women in the development of the United States and the world. They also demanded that more women be hired for administrative positions in the schools. Although most teachers in the elementary schools were women, most administrators were men.

Other marginalized groups, stimulated by the social ferment and the quest for human rights during the 1970s, articulated their grievances and demanded that institutions be reformed so they would face less discrimination and acquire more human rights. People with disabilities, senior citizens, and LGBTQ+ (Lesbian, Gay, Bisexual, Transgender, and Questioning) people formed groups that organized politically during this period and made significant inroads in changing institutions and laws. Advocates for citizens with disabilities attained significant legal victories during the 1970s. The Education for All Handicapped Children Act of 1975 (PL 94-142)—which required that students with disabilities be educated in the least restricted environment and institutionalized the word *mainstreaming* in education—was perhaps the most significant legal victory of the movement for the rights of students with disabilities in education.

HOW MULTICULTURAL EDUCATION DEVELOPED

Multicultural education emerged from the diverse courses, programs, and practices that educational institutions devised to respond to the demands, needs, and aspirations of the various groups. Consequently, multicultural education in actual practice is not one identifiable course or educational program. Rather, practicing educators use the term *multicultural education* to describe a wide variety of programs and practices related to educational equity, women, ethnic groups, language minorities, low-income groups, LGBTQ+ people, and people with disabilities. In one school district, multicultural education may mean a curriculum that incorporates the experiences of ethnic groups of color; in another, a program may include the experiences of both ethnic groups and women. In a third school district, this term may be used the way it is by authors such as Banks (2020), Nieto and Bode (2020), and Grant and Sleeter (2013)—that is, to mean a total school reform effort designed to increase educational equity for a range of cultural, ethnic, and income groups. This broader and more comprehensive notion of multicultural education differs from the limited concept of multicultural education in which it is viewed only as curriculum reform.

Multicultural education is at least three things: an *idea or concept*, an *educational reform movement*, and a *process*. Multicultural education incorporates the idea that all students—regardless of gender, sexual orientation, social class, or ethnic, racial, or cultural characteristics—should have an equal opportunity to learn in school. Another important idea in multicultural education is that some students, because of these characteristics, have a better chance to learn in schools as they are currently structured than do students who belong to other groups or who have different cultural characteristics.

THE DIMENSIONS OF MULTICULTURAL EDUCATION

I have developed a comprehensive conceptualization of multicultural education that consists of five dimensions (Banks, 2004): (1) *content integration*; (2) *knowledge construction*; (3) *prejudice reduction*; (4) *equity pedagogy*; and (5) an *empowering school culture and social structure*. The dimensions are frequently used by educational practitioners in both schools and colleges and universities to assist them in implementing multicultural education comprehensively rather than in a limited way by only adding content to the curriculum related to diverse racial, ethnic, and cultural groups. I will discuss each of the dimensions in turn.

Content Integration

Content integration deals with the extent to which teachers use examples and content from a variety of cultures and groups to illustrate key concepts, principles, generalizations, and theories in their subject area or discipline.

The infusion of ethnic and cultural content into the subject area should be logical, not contrived. More opportunities exist for the integration of ethnic and cultural content in some subject areas than in others. In the social studies, the language arts, and music, frequent and ample opportunities exist for teachers to use ethnic and cultural content to illustrate concepts, themes, and principles. There are also opportunities to integrate multicultural content into math and science. However, the opportunities are not as ample as they are in the social studies (Loewen, 2018), the language arts (Paris & Alim, 2017), and music (Campbell, 2018).

silos

When many teachers think of multicultural education, they think only or primarily of content related to ethnic, racial, and cultural groups. Conceptualizing multicultural education exclusively as content related to various ethnic and cultural groups is problematic for several reasons. Teachers who cannot easily see how their content is related to cultural issues will easily dismiss multicultural education with the argument that it is not relevant to their disciplines. This is done frequently by secondary math and science teachers.

The irrelevant-of-content argument can become a legitimized form of resistance to multicultural education when it is conceptualized primarily or exclusively as content. Math and science teachers often state that multicultural education is fine for social studies and literature teachers but that it has little to do with their subjects. Furthermore, they say, math and science are the same regardless of the culture or the kids. Multicultural education needs to be more broadly defined and understood, as is done in the dimensions of multicultural education, so that teachers from a wide range of disciplines can respond to it in appropriate ways and resistance to it can be minimized.

The Knowledge Construction Process

The knowledge construction process relates to the extent to which teachers help students to understand, investigate, and determine how the implicit cultural assumptions, frames of reference, perspectives, and biases within a discipline influence the ways in which knowledge is constructed within it (Banks, 1996).

Students can analyze the knowledge construction process in science by studying how racism has been perpetuated in science by genetic theories of intelligence, Darwinism, and eugenics. In his important book *The Mismeasure of Man*, Gould (1996) describes how scientific racism developed and was influential in the 19th and 20th centuries. Scientific racism has had and continues to have a significant influence on the interpretations of mental ability tests in the United States.

The publication of *The Bell Curve* (Herrnstein & Murray, 1994), its widespread and enthusiastic public reception, and the social context out of which it emerged provide an excellent case study for discussion and analysis by students who are studying knowledge construction (Kincheloe, Steinberg, & Gresson, 1996). Herrnstein and Murray contend that low-income groups and African Americans have fewer intellectual abilities than do other groups and that these differences are inherited. Students can examine the arguments made by the authors, their major assumptions, and how their conclusions relate to the social and political context.

Gould (1994) contends that Herrnstein and Murray's arguments reflect the social context of the times, "a historical moment of unprecedented ungenerosity, when a mood for slashing social programs can be powerfully abetted by an argument that beneficiaries cannot be helped, owing to inborn cognitive limits expressed as low I.Q. scores" (p. 139). Students should also study counterarguments to *The Bell Curve* made by respected scientists. Two good sources are *The Bell Curve Debate: History, Documents, Opinions*, edited by Jacoby and Glauberman (1995), and *Measured Lies: The Bell Curve Examined*, edited by Kincheloe, Steinberg, and Gresson (1996).

Students can examine the knowledge construction process in the social studies when they study such units and topics as the European discovery of America and the westward movement. The teacher can ask the students the latent meanings of concepts such as the "European discovery of America" and the "New World." The students can discuss what these concepts imply or suggest about the Native American cultures that had existed in the Americas for about 40,000 years before the Europeans arrived. When studying the westward movement, the teacher can ask students these questions: Whose point of view or perspective does this concept reflect, that of the European Americans or the Lakota Sioux? Who was moving west? How might a Lakota Sioux historian describe this period in U.S. history? What are other ways of thinking about and describing the westward movement? James W. Loewen's *Teaching What Really Happened: How to Avoid the Tyranny of Textbooks and Get Students Excited About Doing History* (2018) contains excellent examples of lessons that teachers can use to help students understand the ways in which the perspectives and points of view of authors influence the writing and construction of history.

Prejudice Reduction

Prejudice reduction describes lessons and activities teachers use to help students develop positive attitudes toward different racial, ethnic, and cultural groups. Research indicates that children come to school with many negative attitudes toward and misconceptions about different racial and ethnic groups (Aboud, 2009; Levy & Killen, 2008). Research also indicates that lessons, units, and teaching materials that include content about different racial and ethnic groups can help students to develop more positive intergroup attitudes if certain conditions exist in the teaching situation (Bigler & Hughes, 2009). These conditions include positive images of the ethnic groups in the materials and the use of multiethnic materials in a consistent and sequential way.

Allport's (1954) contact hypothesis provides several useful guidelines for helping students to develop positive interracial attitudes and actions in contact situations. He states that contact between groups will improve intergroup relations when the contact is characterized by these four conditions: (1) equal status, (2) common goals, (3) intergroup cooperation, and (4) support of authorities such as teachers and administrators (Schofield, 2012).

An Equity Pedagogy

Teachers in each discipline can analyze their teaching procedures and styles to determine the extent to which they reflect multicultural issues and concerns. An equity pedagogy exists when teachers modify their teaching in ways that will facilitate the academic achievement of students from diverse racial, cultural, gender, and social-class groups. This includes using a variety of teaching styles and approaches that are consistent with the wide range of learning styles within various cultural and ethnic groups, being demanding but highly personalized when working with groups such as Native American and Alaskan students, and using cooperative learning techniques in math and science instruction in order to enhance the academic achievement of students of color (Cohen & Lotan, 2014; Slavin, 2012). What I call equity pedagogy means essentially the same as what Gloria Ladson-Billings (1995) calls "culturally relevant pedagogy" and what Geneva Gay (2018) calls "culturally responsive pedagogy."

An Empowering School Culture and Social Structure

Another important dimension of multicultural education is a school culture and organization that promote gender, racial, and social-class equity. The culture and organization of the school must be examined by all members of the school staff. They all must also participate in restructuring it. Grouping and labeling practices, sports participation, disproportionality in achievement, disproportionality in enrollment in gifted and special education programs, and the interaction of the staff and the students across ethnic and racial lines are important variables that need to be examined in order to create a school culture that empowers students from different racial, ethnic, language, and gender groups.

Figure 2.1 summarizes the dimensions of multicultural education. The next section identifies the major variables of the school that must be changed in order to institutionalize a school culture that empowers students from diverse cultural, racial, ethnic, gender, and social-class groups.

Figure 2.1. The Dimensions of Multicultural Education

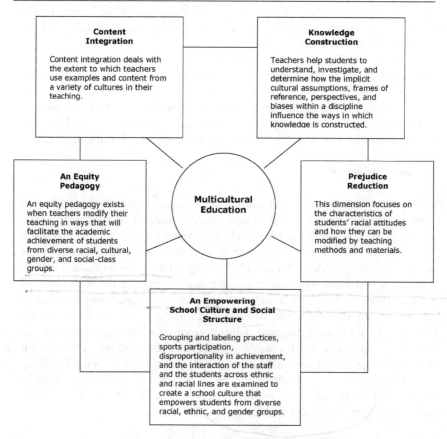

THE SCHOOL AS A SOCIAL SYSTEM

To implement multicultural education successfully, we must think of the school as a social system in which all major variables are closely interrelated. Thinking of the school as a social system suggests that educators must formulate and initiate a change strategy that reforms the total school environment to implement multicultural education. The major school variables that must be reformed are presented in Figure 2.2.

Reforming any one of the variables in Figure 2.2, such as the formalized curriculum or curricular materials, is necessary but not sufficient. Multicultural and sensitive teaching materials are ineffective in the hands of teachers who have negative attitudes toward different racial, ethnic, language, and cultural groups. Such teachers are rarely likely to use multicultural materials or are likely to use them detrimentally. Thus, helping teachers and other members of the school staff to gain knowledge about diverse groups and

Figure 2.2. The School as a Social System

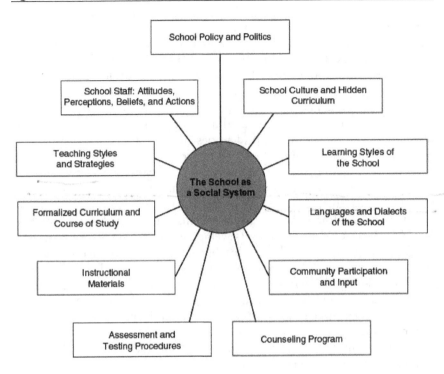

The total school environment is a system consisting of a number of major identifiable variables and factors, such as a school culture, school policy and politics, and the formalized curriculum and course of study. Any of these factors may be the focus of initial school reform, but changes must take place in each of them to create and sustain an effective multicultural school environment.

democratic attitudes and values is essential when implementing multicultural programs.

To implement multicultural education in a school, we must reform its power relationships, verbal interaction between teachers and students, culture, curriculum, extracurricular activities, attitudes toward minority languages (Romaine, 2009), testing and assessment practices, and grouping practices. The school's institutional norms, social structures, cause-belief statements, values, and goals must be transformed and reconstructed.

Major attention should be focused on the school's hidden curriculum and its implicit norms and values. A school has both a manifest and a hidden curriculum. The manifest curriculum consists of such factors as guides, textbooks, bulletin boards, and lesson plans. These aspects of the school environment are important and must be reformed to create a school culture that promotes positive attitudes toward diverse cultural groups and helps students from these groups experience academic success. However, the school's hidden, or latent, curriculum is often more important than its manifest or overt curriculum. *The latent curriculum* has been defined as the one that no teacher explicitly teaches but that all students learn. It is that powerful part of the school culture that communicates to students the school's attitudes toward a range of issues and problems, including how the school views them as human beings, as exceptional students, as students from various religious, cultural, racial, and ethnic groups, and as individuals with different sexual orientations and identities (Mayo, 2014). Jackson (1992) calls the latent curriculum the "untaught lessons."

When formulating plans for multicultural education, educators should conceptualize the school as a culture that has norms, values, statuses, and goals like other social systems. The school has a dominant culture and a variety of microcultures. Almost all classrooms in the United States are multicultural because White students as well as Black and Brown students are socialized within diverse cultures. Teachers also come from many different groups. As Erickson (2012) points out, all individuals—including students and teachers—are also *multicultural* because components of more than one culture or group influence their behavior. Each individual belongs to an ethnic or culture group, has a sexual orientation and identity, and is religious or nonreligious.

Many teachers were socialized in cultures other than the Anglo mainstream, although these may be forgotten and repressed. Teachers can get in touch with their own cultures and use the perspectives and insights they acquired as vehicles for helping them relate to and understand the diverse cultures of their students.

Multicultural education is an idea stating that all students, regardless of the groups to which they belong, such as those related to gender, ethnicity, race, culture, language, social class, religion, sexual orientation, or exceptionality, should experience educational equality in the schools. Some students, because of their particular characteristics, have a better chance to succeed in school as it is currently structured than students from other groups. Multicultural education is also a reform movement designed to bring about a transformation of the school so that students from different genders and from diverse cultural, language, and ethnic groups will have an equal chance to experience school success. Multicultural education views the school as a social system that consists of highly interrelated parts and variables. Therefore, in order to transform the school to bring about educational equality, all major components of the school must be substantially changed. A focus on any one variable in the school, such as the formalized curriculum, will not implement multicultural education.

Multicultural education is a continuing process because the idealized goals it tries to actualize—such as educational equality and the eradication of all forms of discrimination—can never be fully achieved in human society. Multicultural education, which was born during the social protest of the 1960s and 1970s, is an international movement that exists in nations throughout the world (Banks, 2009). A major goal of multicultural education is to help students develop the knowledge, attitudes, and skills needed to function within their own home and community cultures, other minoritized cultures, the U.S. mainstream culture, and the global community.

REFERENCES

Aboud, F. E. (2009). Modifying children's racial attitudes. In J. A. Banks (Ed.), *The Routledge international companion to multicultural education* (pp. 199–209). Routledge.

Allport, G. W. (1954). *The nature of prejudice.* Addison-Wesley.

Banks, J. A. (Ed.). (1996). *Multicultural education, transformative knowledge, and action: Historical and contemporary perspectives.* Teachers College Press.

Banks, J. A. (2004). Multicultural education: Historical development, dimensions, and practice. In J. A. Banks & C. A. M. Banks (Eds.), *Handbook of research on multicultural education* (2nd ed., pp. 3–29). Jossey-Bass.

Banks, J. A. (2006). *Race, culture, and education: The selected works of James A. Banks.* Routledge.

Banks, J. A. (Ed.). (2009). *The Routledge international companion to multicultural education.* Routledge.

Banks, J. A. (2016). *Cultural diversity and education: Foundations, curriculum, and teaching* (6th ed.). Routledge.

Banks, J. A. (2020). *Diversity, transformative knowledge, and civic education: Selected essays.* Routledge.

Bigler, R. S., & Hughes, J. M. (2009). The nature and origins of children's racial attitudes. In J. A. Banks (Ed.), *The Routledge international companion to multicultural education* (pp. 186–198). Routledge.

Brewer, R. M. (2012). Feminist movement. In J. A. Banks (Ed.), *Encyclopedia of diversity in education* (vol. 2, pp. 896–901). Sage.

Campbell, P. S. (2018). *Music, education, and diversity: Building cultures and communities.* Teachers College Press.

Cohen, E. G., & Lotan, R. (2014). *Designing groupwork: Strategies for the heterogeneous classroom* (3rd ed.). Teachers College Press.

Erickson, F. (2012). Culture and education. In J. A. Banks (Ed.), *Encyclopedia of diversity in education* (vol. 1, pp. 559–568). Sage.

Gay, G. (2018). *Culturally responsive teaching: Theory, research, and practice* (3rd ed.). Teachers College Press.

Gould, S. J. (1994). Curveball. *The New Yorker, 70*(38), 139–149.

Gould, S. J. (1996). *The mismeasure of man* (rev. & exp. ed.). Norton.

Grant, C. A., & Sleeter, C. E. (2013). Race, class, gender, and disability in the classroom. In J. A. Banks & C. A. M. Banks (Eds.), *Multicultural education: Issues and perspectives* (8th ed., pp. 43–60). Wiley.

Herrnstein, R. J., & Murray, C. (1994). *The bell curve: Intelligence and class structure in American life.* Free Press.

Jackson, P. W. (1992). *Untaught lessons.* Teachers College Press.

Jacoby, R., & Glauberman, N. (Eds.). (1995). *The bell curve debate: History, documents, opinions*. Times Books/Random House.

Kincheloe, J. L., Steinberg, S. R., & Gresson, A. D., III (Eds.). (1996). *Measured lies: The bell curve examined*. St. Martin's Press.

Ladson-Billings, G. (1995). Toward a theory of culturally relevant pedagogy. *American Educational Research Journal, 32*(3), 465–491.

Levy, S. R., & Killen, M. (Eds.) (2008). *Intergroup attitudes and relations in childhood through adulthood*. Oxford University Press.

Loewen, J. W. (2018). *Teaching what really happened: How to avoid the tyranny of textbooks and get students excited about doing history* (2nd ed.). Teachers College Press.

Mayo, C. (2014). *LGBTQ youth and education: Policies and practices*. Teachers College Press.

Nieto, S., & Bode, P. (2020). School reform and student learning: A multicultural perspective. In J. A. Banks & C. A. M. Banks (Eds.), *Multicultural education: Issues and perspectives* (10th ed., pp. 267–283). Wiley.

Paris, D., & Alim, H. S. (Eds.). (2017). *Culturally sustaining pedagogies: Teaching and learning for justice in a changing world*. Teachers College Press.

Romaine, S. (2009). Language, culture, and identity across nations. In J. A. Banks (Ed.), *The Routledge international companion to multicultural education* (pp. 373–384). Routledge.

Schofield, J. W. (2012). Contact theory. In J. A. Banks (Ed.), *Encyclopedia of diversity in education* (vol. 1, pp. 445–447). Sage.

Slavin, R. E. (2012). Cooperative learning. In J. A. Banks (Ed.), *Encyclopedia of diversity in education*, (vol. 2, pp. 451–458). Sage.

Steinem, G. (2015). *My life on the road*. Random House.

Trecker, J. L. (1973). Teaching the role of women in American history. In J. A. Banks (Ed.), *Teaching ethnic studies: Concepts and strategies* (43rd Yearbook, pp. 279–297). National Council for the Social Studies.

PART II

STRUCTURAL AND INSTITUTIONAL RACISM IN SCHOOLS

CHAPTER 3

Understanding the Structural Nature of Oppression Through Racism

Özlem Sensoy and Robin DiAngelo

"I was really lucky. I grew up in a good neighborhood and went to good schools. There were no problems with racism, I didn't learn anything negative about different races. My family taught me that everyone is equal."

In this chapter we examine racism. One note before we begin: Race is a deeply complex sociopolitical system whose boundaries shift and adapt over time. As such, *White* and *peoples of Color* are not discrete categories, and within these groupings are other levels of complexity and difference based on the various roles assigned by dominant society at various times. For example, Asians and Blacks, while both identified as peoples of Color, have very different experiences under racism based on the roles dominant society assigns to each of these groups, as do Indigenous and multiracial peoples. When we use the term *peoples of Color,* we realize that not everyone would accept this term because (a) it conflates very complex dynamics among and between groups and (b) it does not deal adequately with the experiences of Indigenous and multiracial peoples. However, at the introductory level, we use this terminology because it is most widely understood as capturing the overall dynamics of White-settler dominance over Indigenous groups and groups of Color, and people perceived as belonging to those groups. The term *peoples* is used (rather than *people*) to signal the heterogeneity of groups' experiences under this umbrella term. These terms indicate the two broad, socially recognized divisions of the racial hierarchy in the United States and Canada. Thus, when we use the terms *White* and *peoples of Color,* we are speaking in general terms about dynamics that occur at the group level and are pervasive throughout U.S. and Canadian societies. When we use the pronouns "we" and "us," we are speaking specifically as White authors about ourselves and other White people.

Racism is among the most charged issues in society and is challenging to discuss for many reasons: pervasive miseducation about what racism is and how it works; a lack of productive language with which to discuss racism; institutional and economic interests in upholding racism; ideologies such as individualism and colorblindness; and an emotional attachment to commonsense opinions that protect (rather than expand) our worldviews. In order to meet these challenges, we offer the following reminders:

- A strong opinion is not the same as informed knowledge.
- There is a difference between agreement and understanding: When discussing complex institutional dynamics such as racism, consider that "I don't agree" may actually mean "I don't understand."
- We have a deep interest in denying those forms of oppression that benefit us.
- We may also have an interest in denying forms of oppression that harm us. For example, peoples of Color can deny the existence of racism and even support its structures. However, this still benefits Whites at the group level, not peoples of Color.
- Racism goes beyond individual intentions to collective group patterns.
- We don't have to be aware of oppression in order for it to exist.
- Our racial position (whether we are perceived as White, a person of Color, Indigenous, or multiracial) will greatly affect our ability to see racism. For example if we swim against the current of racial privilege, it's often easier to recognize, while harder to recognize if we swim with it.
- Putting our effort into protecting rather than expanding our current worldview prevents our intellectual and emotional growth.

Many of the dynamics of racism that we explain here will be familiar to peoples of Color. However, they may find this discussion useful in that it provides language and a theoretical framework for everyday experiences that often go unacknowledged by dominant culture.

WHAT IS RACE?

In order to understand racism, we first need to address our ideas about race itself. Many of us believe that race is biological—in other words, that there are distinct genetic differences between races that account for differences in traits such as sexuality, athleticism, or mathematical ability. This idea of race as biology makes it easy to believe that many of the divisions we see in society are natural. But race, like gender and disability, is socially constructed (Brzuzy, 1997; López, 2000; Weber, 2010). The differences we see with our eyes, such as hair texture and eye color or shape, are superficial and emerged over time as humans adapted to geography (Cavalli-Sforza, Menozzi, & Piazza, 1994). However, *race as a social idea* has profound significance and impacts every aspect of our lives. This impact includes where we are most likely to live, which schools we will attend, who our friends and partners will be, what careers we will have, and even how long we can expect to live (Adelman, 2003; Johnson & Shapiro, 2003).

Race as we commonly understand it is a relatively modern concept (Gossett, 1997). Humans have not been here long enough to evolve into separate species and we are, in fact, among the most genetically similar of species on Earth. External characteristics we attribute to race, such as skin color, are not a reliable indicator of internal variation between any two people (Cooper, Kaufman, & Ward, 2003). To challenge deep-seated ideas about racial difference and genetics, we need to understand the early social investment in race science that was used to organize society and its resources along racial lines.

A BRIEF HISTORY OF
THE SOCIAL CONSTRUCTION OF RACE IN THE UNITED STATES

Ancient societies did not divide people into racial categories, although other categories of organization (such as religious affiliation or class status) were common. When the United States was formed, freedom and equality—regardless of religion or class status—were radical new ideas. At the same time, the United States' economy was based on the enslavement of African peoples and the displacement and genocide of Indigenous North American peoples. There were enormous economic interests in justifying these practices. To reconcile the tension between the noble ideology of equality and the cruel reality of genocide and enslavement, Thomas Jefferson (who owned hundreds of enslaved Africans) and others turned to science. Jefferson suggested that there were natural differences between the races and set science on the path to find them (Jefferson, 1787/2002). These social and political interests shaped race science (for example, in the early to mid-1800s, skulls were measured in an attempt to prove the existence of a natural racial hierarchy). In less than a century these studies enabled Jefferson's suggestion of racial difference to become commonly accepted scientific fact (Stepan, 1982).

But while race has no biological foundation, it has developed as a social idea with very real consequences. In the late 1600s the term *White* first appeared in colonial law. By 1790 people were asked to claim their race on the census, and by 1825 the degree of blood determined who would be classified as "Indian." In the late 1800s through the early 20th century, as waves of immigrants entered the United States, the idea of Whiteness became more and more concrete (Gossett, 1997; Ignatiev, 1995; Jacobson, 1998).

> ✋ **STOP:** Remember, we are addressing racism at the group, not individual, level. At the group level, all of us navigate the current of dominant culture. In the United States and Canada, if we are White, we swim *with* that current, and if we are a person of Color, we must swim *against* it. While this is the racial reality at the group level, how we respond individually may vary.

While slavery was abolished overall in 1865, Whiteness remained profoundly important as legal racist exclusion and violence continued. To gain citizenship and other rights, one had to be legally classified as White. Individuals seeking these rights began to challenge their classifications and petitioned the courts to be reclassified as White. These legal challenges put the courts in the position to decide who was White and who was not. In fact, in 1923 the court stated that Whiteness was based on the common understanding of the White man. In other words, people already seen as White got to decide who was White (Tehranian, 2000).

While they may have initially been divided in terms of ethnic or class status, over time European immigrants were united in Whiteness. For example, early Irish, Italian, and Jewish immigrants were not considered White, but they "became" White as they assimilated into the dominant culture (Brodkin, 1998; Ignatiev, 1995; Jacobson, 1998; Roediger, 1999). Reflecting on the social and economic advantages of Whiteness, critical race scholar Cheryl Harris (1993) coined the phrase "Whiteness as property." This phrase captures the reality that being perceived as White carries more than a mere racial classification. It is a social and institutional status and identity imbued with legal, political, economic, and social rights and privileges that are denied to others.

A BRIEF HISTORY OF THE SOCIAL CONSTRUCTION OF RACE IN CANADA

Like the United States, Canada is a nation built on the genocide and forced removal of Indigenous peoples who had been living on the territory for several thousands of years before the arrival of Europeans (Dickason, 2002; Thobani, 2007). The Indigenous peoples of Canada (also referred to as Aboriginal) were living in all regions of the territory when first contact occurred in the 15th century, and had very well-developed social, political, and economic structures. Today, Canada recognizes three main groups of Indigenous peoples: First Nations, Inuit, and Métis. In the 2006 Census, one million people self-identified as Aboriginal—approximately 4% of Canada's total population (Statistics Canada, 2006).

There was a very complex relationship between French and English colonial powers and the various Indigenous communities during the process of colonization. In some cases the colonizers forced relocation and even genocide, while in other cases colonizers pursued strategies to coexist. These strategies included "civilizing" processes whereby the government and religious organizations set out to reform the "savage Indian" and help him assimilate into colonial society (Milloy, 2000). A major part of this strategy was the Gradual Civilization Act of 1857, and one of its mechanisms was the system of residential schools (Haig-Brown, 1998; Hare, 2007). The mission of these schools was primarily to "civilize" Indigenous children. By the late 1800s, attendance in residential schools for Indigenous children aged 7 to 15 was compulsory. These children were forcibly removed from their homes, taken to residential schools, forbidden (and punished) for speaking their native languages, forced to convert to Christianity, and prevented from seeing their families for long periods; in many cases they were physically, sexually, and emotionally abused. The mortality rate at some schools was over 50% (Milloy, 1999). Most of the schools were closed by the 1960s, but the last school didn't close until 1996. The psychic trauma is still a part of the Indigenous community's collective memory and has resulted in a generational gap within Indigenous communities. Scholars who study the history and legacy of residential schools contend that this trauma is deeply connected to the higher rates of alcoholism, drug abuse, and suicide among Indigenous people (Haskell & Randall, 2009; Kirmayer & Valaskakis, 2009).

The race science being conducted and disseminated in the United States was adopted into government programs and policies in Canada as well. Blacks and Indigenous people were enslaved (Winks, 1971/1997), Chinese workers were excluded from citizenship (Li, 1988; Mar, 2010), and extremist hate groups have long flourished in Canada (Lund, 2006). But since the 1970s one of the key strategies for managing racial diversity has been the policy of multiculturalism. The "melting pot" ideology of the United States was not useful in Canada, in part because it pressures the so-called two founding, colonizing nations (France and England) to assimilate. It would have meant an end to official bilingualism, on which Quebec would not compromise. The ongoing challenges to sustain the Canadian federation (and prevent Quebec from seceding) required an ideology that represented Canada as a tolerant, pluralistic, multicultural society. For these reasons, the "mosaic" (rather than "melting pot") became the dominant image used to describe Canadian racial and ethnic diversity (Joshee, 1995, 2004). In 1985 the government passed the Act for the Preservation and Enhancement of Multiculturalism in Canada. These policies promote the idea that all groups are positioned equally in Canadian society (the colonizer nations of England and France and their respective languages, people of Aboriginal heritage, and the multitude of immigrant communities in the nation) while leaving structural inequality unaddressed.

📖 **Racism:** White racial and cultural prejudice and discrimination, supported by institutional power and authority, used to the advantage of Whites and the disadvantage of peoples of Color. Racism encompasses economic, political, social, and institutional actions and beliefs that systematize and perpetuate an unequal distribution of privileges, resources, and power between Whites and peoples of Color.

WHAT IS RACISM?

Racism is a form of oppression in which one racial group dominates others. In the United States and Canada, Whites are the dominant group and peoples of Color are the minoritized group; therefore, racism here is White racial and cultural prejudice and discrimination, supported intentionally or unintentionally by institutional power and authority, used to the advantage of Whites and the disadvantage of peoples of Color (Hilliard, 1992). In other nations the dominant and minoritized racial groups will not be the same because of the difference in their social and political histories. From here forward, we will be speaking of racism only as it plays out in the United States and Canada.

Racism is not fluid in that it does not move back and forth, one day benefiting Whites and another day (or even era) benefiting peoples of Color. The direction of power between Whites and peoples of Color is historic, traditional, normalized, and deeply embedded in the fabric of U.S. and Canadian societies (Henry & Tator, 2006; James, 2007; Wise, 2005). The critical element that differentiates *racism* from *racial prejudice* and *discrimination* is the historical accumulation and ongoing use of institutional power and authority that supports discriminatory behaviors in systemic and far-reaching ways. Peoples of Color may hold prejudices and discriminate against Whites, but do not have the social and institutional power backing their prejudice and discrimination that transforms it into racism; the impact of their prejudice on Whites is temporary and contextual. Peoples of Color may also hold prejudices and discriminate against their own and other groups of Color, but the impact of their prejudice and discrimination ultimately serves to hold them down and in this way reinforces the system of racism and serves White interests. From a critical social justice perspective, the term *racism* refers to this system of collective social and institutional White power and privilege.

TWO KEY CHALLENGES TO UNDERSTANDING RACISM

Dominant society teaches us that racism consists of individual acts of meanness committed by a few bad people. The people who commit these acts are considered racists; the rest of us are not racist. These ideas construct racism as an individual binary: racist/not-racist (Trepagnier, 2010). As we have discussed, a binary is an either/or construct that positions a social dynamic into two distinct and mutually exclusive categories. As with the gender binary, virtually all people know how to fill in the two sides of the race binary: If you *are* a racist, the discourse goes, you are ignorant, prejudiced, mean-spirited, and most likely old, southern, and drive a pickup truck (working class). If you are *not* a racist, you are nice, well-intentioned, open-minded, progressive, and "don't have a prejudiced bone in your body." Most of us understand, at this moment in our cultural history, which is the right side of this binary to be on. But these categories are false, for all people hold prejudices, especially across racial lines in a society deeply divided by race.

So the first problem with the binary is that it is a false division. It reinforces the idea that racism only occurs in specific incidences, and is only done by specific (bad) people. Of course, racism can certainly manifest as individual acts of meanness, ignorance, and violence. However, the focus on individual *incidents*, rather than on racism as an all-encompassing *system*, prevents the personal, interpersonal, cultural, historical, and structural analysis that is necessary in order to challenge it.

The second problem with the binary concerns the impact of such a worldview on our actions. If, as a White person, I conceptualize racism as a binary and I see myself on the "not racist" side, what further action is required of me? No action is required at all, *because I am not a racist.* Therefore racism is not my problem; it doesn't concern me and there is nothing further I need to do. This guarantees that as a member of the dominant group, I will not build my skills in thinking critically about racism, or use my position to challenge racial inequality. Further, if I conceptualize racism as an either/or proposition, then any suggestion that I have racist thoughts or feelings places me on the wrong side of the binary. As a result, all of my energy will go to denying and negating this possibility rather than trying to understand what these thoughts and feelings are and how they are manifesting. If you are White and have ever been challenged to look at an aspect of yourself related to racism—perhaps you told a joke or made an assumption that someone pointed out to you was racially problematic—it is common to feel very defensive. This defensiveness reveals the binary that informs our understanding of racism; we interpret the feedback to mean that we have done something bad and are thus being told that we are bad people. This binary, which is the foundation of how Whites conceptualize racism (Trepagnier, 2010), and the defensiveness it triggers are primary obstacles preventing us from moving forward in our understanding.

As a person of Color, you may also be invested in denying racism for a range of complex reasons, including these: (1) You have also been socialized to see racism in binary terms. (2) You have been socialized to see peoples of Color as "just as racist" as Whites. (3) Denying racism helps you to cope with its overwhelming dynamics. (4) You have had some measure of success in mainstream society and rationalize that members of minoritized racial groups just need to work harder. (5) You have an immigrant experience that is different from that of some other racial groups. (6) You do not carry the weight of internalized racial oppression because you have not grown up in the U.S. or Canadian contexts. (7) Whites are more comfortable with your racial group, with the shade of your skin, social class expression, or other aspects of your identity. Yet there are costs for this denial, including a disconnection from one's cultural roots and separation from other minoritized racial groups. Ultimately, this denial supports the dominant group.

The racist/not-racist binary illustrates the role that ideology plays in holding oppression in place, and the ideology of individualism in particular. Individualism is a storyline or narrative that creates, communicates, reproduces, and reinforces the concept that each of us is a unique individual and that our group memberships, such as our race, class, or gender, are not important or relevant to our opportunities. This narrative causes a problematic tension because the legitimacy of our institutions depends upon the concept that all citizens are equal. At the same time, we each occupy distinct race, gender, class, and other positions that profoundly shape our life chances in ways that are not natural, voluntary, or random; opportunity is not equally distributed across race, class, and gender (Flax, 1998). Individualism helps manage this tension by claiming that there are no intrinsic barriers to individual success, and that failure is not a consequence of social structures but of individual character. According to the ideology of individualism, race is irrelevant. Specifically, individualism obscures racism because it does the following things (DiAngelo, 2016):

- Denies the significance of race and the advantages of being White
- Hides the collective accumulation of wealth over generations
- Denies the historical context of our current positions
- Prevents a macro analysis of the institutions and structures of social life
- Denies collective socialization and the power of dominant culture (such as media, education, and religion) to shape our perspectives and ideology
- Maintains a false sense of colorblindness
- Reproduces the myth of meritocracy, the idea that success is the result of hard work alone

Let us be clear—we are not arguing against individualism *in general*. Rather, we are arguing that White insistence on individualism *in regard to race* prevents cross-racial understanding and denies the salience of race and racism in White people's lives. Further, being viewed as an individual is a privilege available only to the dominant group. In other words, peoples of Color are almost always seen as "having a race" and described in racial terms (e.g., "a *Black* man," "an *Aboriginal* director"), whereas Whites are rarely defined by race (e.g., "a man," "a director"), thereby allowing Whites to move through society as "just people," while peoples of Color are seen as part of a racial group (DiAngelo, 2016; Dyer, 1997). This dynamic also allows Whites to see themselves as objective and peoples of Color as having "special" or biased interests and agendas.

Of course to see oneself as an individual is a very different dynamic for peoples of Color. While for White people insisting that one is an individual is often a strategy for *resisting* acknowledging that their race has meaning, for peoples of Color it can be a strategy for *coping* with always being seen in racial terms. Since peoples of Color are denied individuality by dominant society, individualism can actually be a way to challenge racism and an important counter to the relentless imposition of racial identity on them. Because the social and institutional positions are not the same between Whites and peoples of Color, the dynamics of how ideologies are used are not the same.

Thus to challenge a particular form of oppression requires different tasks based on one's position. If we fall into the dominant group, one of our tasks is to look past our sense of ourselves as individuals and examine our group history and socialization. If we fall into the minoritized group, one of our tasks is to claim individual complexity. That is, to challenge the way in which society has focused solely on our minoritized identity and denied us a sense of individuality.

RACISM TODAY

Contrary to the opinions of many Whites, we are not living in a postracial society. Racial disparity between Whites and peoples of Color exists in every institution across society. Here we give brief examples of how racism plays out within a few social institutions.

Health. According to the UN ranking of the standard of living of the world's nations (the Human Development Index or HDI), Indigenous people in Canada and the United States have a lower HDI score when compared to the general population (Mikkonen & Raphael, 2010):

 STOP: While they may be difficult to see and thus are often denied, racial disparities and their effects on overall quality of life have been extensively documented by a wide range of agencies, including federal (such as Statistics Canada, U.S. Census Bureau, United Nations), university (such as UCLA Civil Rights Project, Metropolis Project), and nonprofit (such as Canadian Centre for Policy Alternatives, Canadian Anti-Racism Education and Research Society, NAACP, AntiDefamation League).

- U.S. general population HDI: ranks 7th internationally
- Canadian general population HDI: ranks 8th internationally
- U.S. American Indian/Alaska Native population HDI: ranks 31st internationally
- Canadian Aboriginal population HDI: ranks 33rd internationally

In 2015 the average life expectancy for a U.S. citizen was 79.3 years, and for a Canadian citizen was 82.2 years, which are both higher than the average global life expectancy of 71.4. While Canada overall ranks 13 of 38 OECD nations, the U.S. ranks 26 of 38 nations for life expectancy (https://www.americashealthrankings.org/learn/reports/2016-annual-report/comparison-with-other-nations).

At birth, the life expectancy in the United States is as follows (Arias, Heron, & Xu, 2016):

White males—76.7   Black males—72.3
White females—81.4   Black females—78.4

Economy. In the United States in 2014, the median household income was $53,657 (DeNavas-Walt & Proctor, 2015), broken down as:

- Black household—$35,398
- Hispanic (any race) household—$42,491
- White (not Hispanic) household—$60,256
- Asian household—$74,297

The 2014 poverty rate in the United States was 14.8% (46.7 million people in poverty). The 2014 rate was 2.3% higher than the 2007 rate (De-Navas-Walt & Proctor, 2015). By race:

- Non-Hispanic Whites—10.1%
- Asians—12%
- Hispanics—23.6%
- Blacks—26.2%

Racialized Canadians are at greater risk of living in poverty. The 2006 Canada Census (the last stats available) show the overall poverty rate in Canada was 11% but 22% for racialized persons, and 9% for non-racialized persons (Government of Canada, 2013).

For every dollar earned by a non-racialized man, a racialized woman in Canada will earn 55.6 cents (Block & Galabuzi, 2011).

Criminal justice. When broken down by race and gender, incarceration rates in the United States are as follows (Mauer & King, 2007; Sakala, 2014):

- White (non-Hispanic) men: 64% of U.S. population, 39% of incarcerated population—450 per 100,000
- Hispanic men: 16% of U.S. population, 19% of incarcerated population—831 per 100,000
- Black men: 13% of U.S. population, 40% of incarcerated population—2,306 per 100,000

In Canada, the 2014 federal incarceration rate was 54 per 100,000 (Statistics Canada, 2015a). Aboriginal people account for a disproportionate percentage of the prison population. Although they make up approximately 3% of the national adult population, adult Aboriginal people made up 26% of correctional admissions, with Aboriginal females accounting for a higher proportion of female admissions (36%) than Aboriginal males for male admissions (25%) (Statistics Canada, 2015a). This gap is more pronounced for Aboriginal youth, who accounted for 41% of corrections admissions while representing 7% of the youth population. Aboriginal girls accounted for 53% of female youth admitted to corrections, whereas Aboriginal male youth accounted for 38% of males admitted (Statistics Canada, 2015b).

These disparities are an important reminder about the role of theory in explaining data. Theory is the way we make sense of what we see. Reflect for a moment on how you explain racial disparities. This is an important exercise because our explanations reveal our meaning-making frameworks and thus are a great entry point into deeper racial self-knowledge. We can explain these statistics with cultural deficit theory (in other words, there is something wrong with the culture of communities of Color that results in these disparities). However, cultural deficit theory blames peoples of Color for their struggles within a racist society while obscuring larger structural barriers. Cultural deficit theory also exempts dominant culture from the need to play any role in the eradication of racism.

If we consider historical, institutional, and cultural racism, the explanation looks very different. Many incarcerated peoples of Color have attended underfunded and deteriorating schools, have had poor access to health care, have historically been denied mortgages and other wealth-building programs, and have received inequitable treatment in every other major institution that would have given them and their children an equal starting point in life (Alexander, 2010). These are examples of institutional racism, not a personal lack of responsibility or a cultural flaw.

The way that we explain (or theorize) a problem determines how we respond to the problem. If we perceive the problem as one of a violent and criminal people, we might build more prisons and create more sophisticated mechanisms to monitor them. And in fact, although crime has actually *decreased* over the last 30 years, this is the view we have taken, and in response

PERSPECTIVE CHECK: If some of these questions do not apply to the cultural context you grew up in, try the following: Adjust the questions to capture how you learned about racial difference, for example how you saw people from racial groups residing outside of your nation-state or perhaps people from ethnic groups different from your own residing within your nation-state. Use socioeconomic class to think through the questions. For example, how did class differences shape where you lived and how you learned your "place" in society? Consider the impact of Whiteness as a global phenomenon. What did you learn it meant to be White? What did you learn it meant to be a member of a racial group that is not White?

the United States has built more and more prisons and incarcerated more and more peoples of Color, so that the United States now has the highest number of people incarcerated in the world, and the vast majority of them are Black and Latino, a rate that is way out of proportion with their numbers in the wider population (Alexander, 2010). But if we perceive the problem as one of structural racism, we might change the way we fund schools, ensure that every family has affordable access to health care and social services, work to decrease racial profiling, and change the policies that allow wealth to be ever more concentrated into fewer hands.

Both Canada and the United States are nations built on the labor of peoples of Color: the labor of Indigenous peoples who were enslaved, served in military capacities, and helped early colonizers navigate the land; the labor of enslaved Africans who fueled high-value agricultural industries such as cotton, tobacco, sugar, and coffee; the labor of Chinese and Japanese workers who did the backbreaking work of building the railways that formed the major transportation portals for the early period of the nation-state. All of this labor was given for very little if any financial remuneration, authority, or ownership of the national infrastructure and wealth that was built on it.

While we might acknowledge that these were unfair practices of the past, consider the division of labor along race lines in the United States and in Canada today. Who are the people picking the fruit we buy, cleaning our homes, hotels, and workplaces, providing at-home child care or elder care, and sewing the clothes that come to our local department and box stores at remarkably cheap prices? Backbreaking, low-wage, low-reward work is still performed primarily by peoples of Color (Marable, Ness, & Wilson, 2006; Schoenfish-Keita & Johnson, 2010; Sharma, 2002).

There have been some protections put in place to guard against the most blatant and intentional manifestations of racism from the past, but racism still operates in new and modified ways. Colorblind racism is a cogent example of this adaptation. This is the belief that pretending that we don't notice race will end (or has already ended) racism. This idea comes out of the civil rights movement of the 1960s and Martin Luther King's "I

Have a Dream" speech. King's speech symbolized a turning point in the adaptation of racism in dominant culture. Before the period leading up to his speech, many White people felt quite comfortable to admit to their racial prejudices and sense of racial superiority. But once the civil rights movement took root and civil rights legislation was passed, a significant change occurred in mainstream culture; it was no longer as acceptable for White people to admit to racial prejudice.

White racism didn't disappear, of course; Whites just became somewhat more careful in public space (Picca & Feagin, 2007). Seizing on one part of King's speech—that one day he might be judged by the content of his character and not the color of his skin—dominant culture began promoting the idea of "colorblindness" as a remedy for racism. King's speech was given at a march for economic justice—the March on Washington for Jobs and Freedom—and he was there to advocate for the elimination of poverty, but few people today know what his cause was fully about (Bonilla-Silva, 2006).

While colorblindness sounds good in theory, in practice it is highly problematic. We *do* see the race of other people, and that race has meaning for us. Everyone receives racist messages that circulate in society; they are all around us. While some of these messages are blatant (racist jokes, for example), we must understand that most of the messages we receive are subtler and are often invisible, especially to Whites. We know that while we learn very early about race, much of what we learn is below the level of our conscious awareness, and colorblind ideology makes it difficult for us to address these unconscious beliefs. While colorblindness started out as a well-intended strategy for interrupting racism, in practice it has served to deny the reality of racism and thus hold it in place.

To get a sense of what might be below the surface of our conscious racial awareness, try the following thought experiment:

At what point in your life were you aware that people from racial groups other than your own existed (most peoples of Color recall a sense of "always having been" aware, while most White people recall being aware by at least age 5). If you were aware of the existence of people from racial groups other than your own, where did they live? If they did not live in your neighborhood, what kind of neighborhood did they live in? Were their neighborhoods considered "good" or "bad"? What images did you associate with these other neighborhoods? What about sights and smells? What kind of activities did you think went on there? Where did your ideas come from? Were you encouraged to visit their neighborhoods? Or were you discouraged from visiting their neighborhoods? If you attended a school considered "good," what made it good? Conversely, what made a school "bad"? Who went to "bad" schools? If the schools in your area were racially segregated, were their schools considered equal to, better, or worse than yours? Why didn't you attend school together? If this is because you lived in different r.s project hourly

> **STOP:** Not all our messages are as *implicit* (under the surface) as de facto segregation. We are also surrounded by friends and family who make direct comments and jokes about people of other races.

neighborhoods, why did you live in different neighborhoods? If you were told by your parents and teachers that "all people are equal regardless of the color of their skin," yet you lived separately from people who had a different skin color, what message did that contradiction send? If you lived and went to school in racial segregation you had to make sense of this incongruity. In other words, what does it mean to say that all people are equal but live separately from them? Our lived separation is a more powerful message than our words of inclusion because the separation is manifested in action, while inclusion is not.

DYNAMICS OF WHITE RACIAL SUPERIORITY

If we are White we receive constant messages that we are better and more important than peoples of Color, regardless of our personal intentions or beliefs (Fine, 1997). These messages operate on multiple levels and are conveyed in a range of ways, such as (1) our centrality in history textbooks and other historical representations; (2) our centrality in media and advertising; (3) our teachers, role models, heroes, and heroines all reflecting *us*; (4) everyday discussions about "good" neighborhoods and schools and the racial makeup of these favored locations; (5) popular TV shows centered on friendship circles that are all White, even when they take place in racially diverse cities such as New York (*Friends, Seinfeld, Sex and the City, Gossip Girl, Girls*); (6) religious iconography that depicts Adam and Eve, other key Christian figures, and even God as White; (7) newscasters referring to any crime than occurs in a White neighborhood as "shocking"; and (8) the lack of a sense of loss about the absence of peoples of Color in most White people's lives. These are examples of implicit (indirect) rather than explicit (direct) messages, all telling us that it's better to be White. Although we can attempt to notice and block out each one, they come at us collectively and so relentlessly that blocking them out is virtually impossible. While we may explicitly reject the notion that we are inherently better than peoples of Color, we cannot avoid internalizing the message of White superiority below the surface of our consciousness because it is ubiquitous in mainstream culture.

Let's look a little more closely at the increase in racial segregation as an example. Whites are the racial group that lives the most racially segregated lives (Johnson & Shapiro, 2003), and Whites are most likely to be in the economic position to choose this segregation (rather than have it imposed

on them). <u>In the United States we are actually returning to pre-integration</u>
<u>levels of racial segregation; schools and neighborhoods are becoming *more*</u>
<u>racially separated</u>, not less (Frankenberg, Lee, & Orfield, 2003). In fact, racial segregation is often what defines schools and neighborhoods as "good" for Whites; we come to understand that a "good school" or "good neighborhood" is often coded language for "White," while "urban" is code for "not-White" and therefore less desirable (Johnson & Shapiro, 2003; Watson, 2011). At the same time, although we prefer segregation, most Whites profess to be colorblind and claim that race does not matter (Bonilla-Silva, 2006). Even when Whites live in physical proximity to peoples of Color (and this is exceptional outside of a lower-class urban neighborhood), segregation is occurring on many other levels in the culture (and often in the school itself), including images in media and information in schools. <u>Because Whites choose to live primarily segregated lives within</u>
<u>a White-dominated society, we receive little or no authentic information</u>
<u>about racism and are thus unprepared to think about it critically.</u>

Stereotypical media representations compound the impact of racial segregation on our limited understanding of peoples of Color. Most people understand that movies have a profound effect on our ideas about the world. Concepts of masculinity and femininity, sexuality, desire, adventure, romance, family, love, and conflict are all conveyed to us through the stories told in films. Anyone who is around children—even as young as 2—will see the power of movies to shape children's interests, fantasies, and play. <u>Now consider that the vast majority of all mainstream films</u>
<u>are written and directed by White men, most often from the middle and</u>
<u>upper classes.</u> In fact, worldwide, the top 25 highest-grossing films of all time were all directed by men (with one woman as co-director for *Frozen*), and nearly all of them White (James Wan, a man of Color, directed *Furious 7*) (Box Office Mojo, 2017). Of the top 100 films worldwide, 99 were directed entirely by men. Of these top 100 films, 95 were directed by White people. Because of the racial segregation that is ubiquitous throughout society, these men are very unlikely to have gone to school with, lived nearby, been taught by, or been employed by or with peoples of Color. Therefore they are very unlikely to have meaningful or egalitarian cross-racial relationships. Yet these men are society's "cultural authors"— their dreams, their desires, their conceptions of "the other" become ours. Consider the implications of this very privileged and homogenous group essentially telling all of our stories.

The life and work of Jay Silverheels (Figure 3.1) illustrates the challenges peoples of Color have dealing with racism in Hollywood.

Because we all share the same socialization through the wider culture (the frames in our glasses metaphor), familiar images are an effective way to quickly communicate a storyline. For example, consider a director making

Figure 3.1. Jay Silverheels (1919–1980)

Silverheels was an elite athlete competing in high-level wrestling, lacrosse, and boxing events and playing on Canada's national lacrosse team before he developed an interest in acting. Like many Indigenous actors, early in his career he was credited in bit parts simply as "Indian." But many of us remember him in the role that made him famous, playing the Lone Ranger's companion, Tonto. Silverheels himself recognized the difficulty of portraying a character that was described by some as the Uncle Tom of Indigenous peoples. However, with this role Silverheels would be the first Native American actor to star in a leading role on a television show.

Like many minoritized actors, Silverheels found it difficult to break out of the stereotypical characters he was asked to play. He was also an activist for improving the portrayal of Native American peoples in media. He was very aware of the problems of Hollywood's representation of Indigenous peoples but felt that working Indigenous actors could influence the films and shows in which they appeared. In 1966 he helped found the Indian Actors Workshop to offer free classes to aspiring Native American actors to work in film, theater, and television.

Source: www.poorwilliam.net/pix/silverheels-jay.jpg

---

a film about a White teacher who is courageous enough to teach in an "inner-city" school and, in so doing, teaches the children valuable lessons that it is assumed they wouldn't otherwise receive. The director will very likely pan the camera down a street to show houses and apartments in disrepair, graffiti, and groups of Blacks, Latinos, or Southeast Asians hanging out on street corners. The audience, because it has seen this association many times before, immediately knows that we are in a dangerous neighborhood, and the context has been set. Over and over, White male directors depict peoples of Color and their neighborhoods in narrow, limited, and stereotypical ways. Not having many (if any) cross-racial friendships, most Whites come to rely on these images for their understanding of peoples of Color, reinforcing the idea of a positive "us" versus a negative "them."

In addition to a wide range of film roles, Whites see their own images reflected back in virtually any situation or location deemed valuable in dominant society (e.g., academia, politics, management, art events, popular magazines, the Academy Awards). Indeed, it is a rare event for most Whites to experience a sense of *not* belonging racially, and these situations are usually temporary and easily avoidable. Thus racial belonging and "rightness" become deeply internalized and taken for granted.

A key dynamic of the relationship between dominant and minoritized groups is to name the minoritized group as different, while the dominant group remains unnamed. For example, when we say "American" we do not mean "any and all Americans," we mean White Americans but are not naming White because it is assumed unless otherwise noted. Just as when we say "soccer game" we do not mean "any and all soccer games," we mean men's soccer game but are not naming men because it is already assumed unless otherwise noted. We would have to make the point that it was a Chinese American or women's soccer game that we are referring to. We are comfortable with this pattern because we are socialized to name the minoritized groups (*Chinese* American, *women's* soccer) and assign a universal neutrality to dominant groups.

This naming/not-naming dynamic sets race up as something *they* have, not *us*. Whites tend to see race only when peoples of Color are present, but see all-White spaces as neutral and nonracial. Because racial segregation for most Whites is normal and unremarkable, we rarely, if ever, have to think about race and racism. Conversely, peoples of Color must always bear the mark of race as they move about their daily lives. The psychic burden that peoples of Color must carry to get through a day is often exhausting, while Whites are freed from carrying this racial burden. Race becomes something for peoples of Color to think about—it is what happens to them. This allows Whites much more energy to devote to other issues and prevents us from developing the stamina to sustain attention on an issue as charged and uncomfortable for us as race.

DYNAMICS OF INTERNALIZED RACIAL OPPRESSION

All of the messages that White people receive about their value, both explicitly and implicitly, are also received by peoples of Color (Mullaly, 2002; Tatum, 1997). In other words, peoples of Color are also told, in myriad ways, that to be White is better than to be a person of Color. And similar to the mixed messages that White parents send to their children by saying that everyone is equal while simultaneously living in segregation, children of Color also get mixed messages. Their parents may tell them that they are good, strong, and beautiful, but the society around them is still conveying that they are of lesser value.

Internalized racial oppression occurs when a person of Color, consciously and subconsciously, accepts the negative representation or invisibility of peoples of Color in media, education, medicine, science, and all other aspects of society. Over time, the person comes to believe that they are less valuable and may act this out through self-defeating behaviors and sometimes by distancing themselves from others of their own or other non-White racial groups. Although there are important differences in how

various racialized groups experience internalized racial oppression, groups
of Color are collectively shaped by the following:

- Historical violence and the ongoing threat of violence
- Destruction, colonization, dilution, and exoticization of their
  cultures
- Division, separation, and isolation from one another and from
  dominant culture
- Forced changes in behaviors to ensure psychological and physical
  safety and to gain access to resources
- Having individual behaviors redefined as group norms
- Denied individuality and held up as representative of (or
  occasionally as exceptions to) their group
- Being blamed for the effects of long-term oppression by the
  dominant group, and having the effects of that oppression used to
  rationalize further oppression

The internalization of and adaptation to dominant culture's messages
can cause a kind of self-defeating cycle. Carter Woodson, writing in 1933,
powerfully captures the dynamics of internalized racial oppression when he
writes:

> If you can control a man's thinking, you don't have to worry about his actions.
> If you can determine what a man thinks, you do not have worry about what
> he will do. If you can make a man believe that he is inferior, you don't have to
> compel him to seek an inferior status, he will do so without being told, and if
> you can make a man believe that he is justly an outcast, you don't have to order
> him to the back door, he will go to the back door on his own, and if there is no
> back door, the very nature of the man will demand that you build one. (p. xiii)

Woodson is speaking to one of the more profound and painful dynamics of oppression; once people believe that they deserve their position in
society, external force is not needed. As can be seen in several important
studies discussed below, this internalization occurs at a very early age. It
is important to note, however, that peoples of Color have always resisted
internalized racial oppression, but this resistance has costs and can be very
dangerous; resistance has historically been used to further rationalize violence against peoples of Color.

Claude Steele's (1997) work on stereotype threat demonstrates the impact of internalized racial oppression. *Stereotype threat* refers to a concern
that you will be evaluated negatively due to stereotypes about your racial
group, and that concern causes you to perform poorly, thereby reinforcing
the stereotype. Because there is a powerful stereotype in mainstream culture that Blacks are less intelligent than Whites and other racial groups,

Steele and his colleagues examined the effects of this stereotype on test performance. They found that the mere threat of the stereotype can diminish the performance of Black students. Their research shows that when Black students are told that their racial group tends to do poorly on a test, they score lower when taking that test. When the stereotype is not raised, they perform better.

In light of Steele's work, consider how much attention is given in schools to the so-called achievement gap and other disparities in outcome between Whites and some groups of Color (Black, Latino, and Indigenous students in particular), and how often these disparities are formally and informally explained as a function of genetics or inferior cultural morals that do not value education. Concerns and assumptions about their abilities constantly surround students of Color. It is important to remember that these stereotypes are not just "in their heads"; Whites do hold these stereotypes and they do affect the way Whites evaluate peoples of Color (Bertrand & Mullainathan, 2004; Picca & Feagin, 2007). White teachers, for example, who comprise over 90% of K–12 teachers (Picower, 2009), are in a particularly powerful position to evaluate students of Color. Thus, Steele's research captures the relationship between internalized oppression and internalized superiority.

Another powerful illustration of internalized racial oppression was demonstrated through the work of psychologists Kenneth Clark and Mamie Clark (1950). The Clarks used dolls to study children's attitudes about race. The Clarks testified as expert witnesses in *Briggs v. Elliott*, one of the cases connected to the 1954 *Brown v. Board of Education* case in the United States, which ruled that enforced racial segregation in schools was illegal. The Clarks found that Black children often preferred to play with White dolls over Black dolls and that when asked to fill in a human figure with the color of their own skin, they frequently chose a shade lighter than their skin actually was. Black children also described the White doll as good and pretty, but the Black doll as bad and ugly. The Clarks offered their results as evidence that the children had internalized racism. Chief Justice Earl Warren delivered the opinion of the Court: "To separate [some children] from others of similar age and qualifications solely because of their race generates a feeling of inferiority as to their status in the community that may affect their hearts and minds in a way unlikely ever to be undone" (*Brown v. Board of Education*, 1954). This is an important quote to remember as we watch schools in the United States return to pre–civil rights era levels of racial segregation.

In 2005, Kiri Davis, an African American teen, repeated the Clarks' experiment to see what had changed in Black children's attitudes over the past 50 years. In her documentary film *A Girl Like Me*, 15 out of the 21 children she interviewed (71%) preferred the White dolls for the same reasons as children cited in the 1940s; the White doll was "good" and the Black doll was "bad." While many people believe that children are innocent and un-aware of racial messages, research has shown that children of all races and as young as 3 have internalized the societal message that White is superior to Black (Doyle & Aboud, 1995; Van Ausdale & Feagin, 2001). The effect of this on White children is internalized racial superiority; the effect on children of Color is internalized racial inferiority. Internalized racial inferiority has devastating impacts on all aspects of a person's life.

This brief discussion of some of the dynamics of internalized racial oppression is not meant to blame the victim for the effects of racism. Rather, it is meant to briefly highlight the damaging effects of White racism and White supremacy on peoples of Color.

RACISM AND INTERSECTIONALITY

While we have discussed racism in general terms, our other social group memberships, such as class, gender, sexuality, and ability, greatly affect how we will experience race. For example, one of the key limitations of second wave feminism was that the movement addressed women as though they were a cohesive group and assumed they had shared experiences and interests. Actually, the women we think of as at the forefront of the women's movement of the 1960s were White middle-class women (Frankenberg, 1993; Moraga & Anzaldúa, 1981). In many key areas, their interests were not the same as other groups of women. For example, while White middle-class women may have been eager to break their domestic confinement and enter the workplace, women of Color had long been in the workplace. Women of Color's interests may have been better served by fighting for the economic and social conditions that would allow them to stay home to raise their children without being seen as lazy or bad mothers.

Intersectionality is the term scholars use to acknowledge the reality that we simultaneously occupy both oppressed and privileged positions and that these positions intersect in complex ways (Collins, 2000; Crenshaw, 1995). For example, poor Whites, while oppressed through classism, are also elevated by race privilege, so that to be poor and Asian, for example, is not the same experience as being poor and White. Further, because of sexism, to be a poor White female will create barriers that a poor White male will not face due to gender privilege. However, while the poor White female *will* have to deal with sexism, she will not have to deal with the racism that a poor Asian female will face. Indeed, race privilege will help a poor White female cope with poverty, for example, when looking for work or navigating social services such as welfare and health care. Facing oppression in one area of social life does not "cancel out" your privilege in another; these identities will be more or less salient in different situations. The challenge is to identify how our identities play out in shifting social contexts.

We return now to the student quote that opened this chapter: "I was really lucky. I grew up in a good neighborhood and went to good schools There were no problems with racism. I didn't learn anything about different races. My family taught me that everyone is equal." This quote is a powerful illustration of how White people make sense of race and the invisibility of racism to us.

First, the term "good neighborhood" is usually code for "predominately White." To believe that one learned nothing about racism and that there were "no problems" with racism in a White environment positions Whites as outside of race; Whites are "just human," with no racial experience of their own. Race becomes what peoples of Color have. If peoples of Color are not present, race is not present. Further, if peoples of Color are not present, not only is race absent, so is that terrible thing: *racism*. Ironically, this positions racism as something peoples of Color bring to Whites, rather than a system that Whites control and impose on peoples of Color. To place race and racism on peoples of Color and to see race and racism as absent in an all-White space is to construct Whiteness as neutral and innocent. We need to ask ourselves why a neighborhood is seen as good if it's segregated.

Second, a predominately White neighborhood is not the product of luck, a natural preference to be with one's "own," or a fluke; all-White neighborhoods are the end result of centuries of racist policies, practices, and attitudes that have systematically denied peoples of Color entrance into White neighborhoods (Conley, 1999). In the past this was done legally. Today this is accomplished through mechanisms such as discrimination in lending, real estate practices that steer homebuyers into specific neighborhoods, funding roads but not public transportation that could make suburbs more accessible, and White flight. All-White neighborhoods and schools don't just happen.

Contrary to her claims, this student learned quite a bit about race in her White neighborhood and schools. As we noted earlier, there is a contradiction in saying to our children, "Everyone is the same," while raising them in all-White spaces. Conveying to our children that living in a White neighborhood makes them lucky, rather than conveying to them that they have lost something valuable by not having cross-racial relationships, is to teach them a great deal about race.

REFERENCES

Adelman, L. (Executive Director & Producer). (2003). *Race: The power of an illusion*. California Newsreel.

Alexander, M. (2010). *The new Jim Crow: Mass incarceration in the age of colorblindness*. New Press.

Arias, E., Heron, M., & Xu, J. (2016). United States life tables, 2012. *National Vital Statistic Reports*, 65(8). Retrieved from www.cdc.gov/nchs/data/nvsr/nvsr65/nvsr65_08.pdf

Bertrand, M., & Mullainathan, S. (2004). Are Emily and Greg more employable than Lakisha and Jamal? A field experiment on labor market discrimination.

The American Economic Review, 94(4), 991–1013.

Block, S., & Galabuzi, G.-E. (2011). *Canada's colour-coded labour market: The gap for racialized workers.* Wellesley Institute and Canadian Centre for Policy.

Bonilla-Silva, E. (2006). *Racism without racists: Color-blind racism and the persistence of racial inequality in the United States* (2nd ed.). Rowman & Littlefield.

Box Office Mojo. (2017). All time box office worldwide grosses. Retrieved from www.boxofficemojo.com/alltime/world

Brodkin, K. (1998). *How Jews became White folks and what that says about race in America.* Rutgers University Press.

Brzuzy, S. (1997). Deconstructing disability: The impact of definition. *Journal of Poverty 1*, 81–91.

Bureau of Labor Statistics (2016). *Characteristics of minimum wage workers, 2015.* BLS Reports. Retrieved from www.bls.gov/opub/reports/minimum-wage/2015/home.htm

Cavalli-Sforza, L. L., Menozzi, P., & Piazza, A. (1994). *The history and geography of human genes.* Princeton University Press.

Clark, K. B., & Clark, M. P. (1950). Emotional factors in racial identification and preference in Negro children. *The Journal of Negro Education, 19*(3), 341–350.

Collins, P. H. (2000). It's all in the family: Intersections of gender, race, and nation. In U. Narayan & S. Harding (Eds.), *Decentering the center: Philosophy for a multicultural, postcolonial, and feminist world* (pp. 156–176). Indiana University Press.

Conley, D. (1999). *Being Black, living in the red: Race, wealth, and social policy in America.* University of California Press.

Cooper, R. S., Kaufman, J. S., & Ward, R. (2003). Race and genomics. *New England Journal of Medicine, 348*(12), 1166–1170.

Crenshaw, K. (1995). Mapping the margins: Intersectionality, identity politics, and violence against women of color. In K. Crenshaw, N. Gotanda, G. Peller, & K. Thomas (Eds.), *Critical race theory: The key writings that formed the movement* (pp. 357–383). New Press.

Davis, K. (Director). (2005). *A girl like me* [Documentary]. Reel Works Teen Filmmaking. https://vimeo.com/59262534

DeNavas-Walt, C., & Proctor, B. D. (2015). Income and poverty in the United States: 2014. U.S. Government Printing Office. Retrieved from www.census.gov/content/dam/Census/library/publications/2015/demo/p60-252.pdf

DiAngelo, R. (2016). *What does it mean to be White? Developing White racial literacy* (2nd ed.). New York: Peter Lang.

Dickason, O. P. (2002). *Canada's first nations: A history of founding peoples from earliest times* (3rd ed.). Oxford University Press.

Doyle, A. B., & Aboud, F. E. (1995). A longitudinal study of White children's racial prejudice as a social-cognitive development. *Merrill-Palmer Quarterly, 41*(2), 209–228.

Dyer, R. (1997). *White.* Routledge.

Fine, M. (1997). Witnessing Whiteness. In M. Fine, L. Weis, C. Powell, & L. Wong (Eds.), *Off White: Readings on race, power, and society* (pp. 57–65). Routledge.

Flax, J. (1998). *American dream in Black and White: The Clarence Thomas hearings.* Cornell University Press.

Frankenberg, E., Lee, C., & Orfield, G. (2003). *A multiracial society with segregated* schools: Are we losing the dream? Civil Rights Project.

Frankenberg, R. (1993). *The social construction of Whiteness: White women, race matters*. University of Minnesota Press.

Gossett, T. E. (1997). *Race: The history of an idea in America*. Oxford University Press.

Government of Canada (2013). *Poverty profile: A snapshot of racialized poverty in Canada*. Retrieved from www.canada.ca/content/dam/esdc-edsc/migration/documents/eng/communities/reports/poverty_profile/snapshot.pdf

Haig-Brown, C. (1998). *Resistance and renewal: Surviving the Indian residential school*. Arsenal Pulp Press.

Hare, J. (2007). First Nations education policy in Canada: Building capacity for change and control. In R. Joshee & L. Johnson (Eds.), *Multicultural education policies in Canada and the United States* (pp. 51–68). University of British Columbia Press.

Harris, C. I. (1993). Whiteness as property. *Harvard Law Review, 106*(8), 1707.

Haskell, L., & Randall, M. (2009). Disrupted attachments: A social context complex trauma framework and the lives of Aboriginal peoples in Canada. *Journal of Aboriginal Health, 5*(3), 48–99.

Henry, F., & Tator, C. (2006). *The colour of democracy: Racism in Canadian society*. Thomson Nelson.

Hilliard, A. (1992, January). *Racism: Its origins and how it works*. Paper presented at the meeting of the Midwest Association for the Education of Young Children, Madison, Wisconsin.

Ignatiev, N. (1995). *How the Irish became White*. Routledge.

Jacobson, M. F. (1998). *Whiteness of a different color: European immigrants and the alchemy of race*. Harvard University Press.

James, C. E. (2007). "Reverse racism?" Students' responses to equity programs. In T. D. Gupta, C. E. James, R. C. A. Maaka, G. E. Galabuzi, & C. Andersen (Eds.), *Race and racialization: Essential readings* (pp. 356–362). Canadian Scholars' Press.

Jefferson, T. (2002). *Notes on the state of Virginia: With related documents*. (D. Waldstreicher, Ed.). Bedford/St. Martin's. (Original work published 1787)

Johnson, H. B., & Shapiro, T. M. (2003). Good neighborhoods, good schools: Race and the "good choices" of White families. In A. W. Doane & E. Bonilla-Silva (Eds.), *White out: The continuing significance of racism* (pp. 173–187). Routledge.

Joshee, R. (1995). An historical approach to understanding Canadian multicultural policy. In T. Wotherspoon & P. Jungbluth (Eds.), *Multicultural education in a changing global economy: Canada and the Netherlands* (pp. 23–40). Waxmann.

Joshee, R. (2004). Citizenship and multicultural education in Canada: From assimilation to social cohension. In J. A. Banks (Ed.), *Diversity and citizenship education: Global perspectives* (pp. 127–156). Jossey-Bass.

Kirmayer, L. J., & Valaskakis, G. G. (Eds.). (2009). *Healing traditions: The mental health of Aboriginal peoples in Canada*. Vancouver, Canada: University of British Columbia Press.

Li, P. S. (1988). *The Chinese in Canada*. Toronto, Canada: Oxford University Press.

López, I. F. H. (2000). The social construction of race. In R. Delgado & J. Stefancic (Eds.), *Critical race theory: The cutting edge* (2nd ed., pp. 163–175). Temple University Press.

Lund, D. E. (2006). Social justice activism in the heartland of hate: Countering extremism in Alberta. *The Alberta Journal of Educational Research*, 52(2), 181–194.

Mar, L. R. (2010). *Brokering belonging: Chinese in Canada's exclusion era, 1885–1945*. Oxford University Press.

Marable, M., Ness, I., & Wilson, J. (2006). *Race and labor matters in the new U.S. economy*. Rowman & Littlefield.

Mauer, M., & King, R. S. (2007). *Uneven justice: State rates of incarceration by race and ethnicity*. The Sentencing Project. Retrieved from advancabag.com/documents/rd_stateratesofincbyraceandethnicity.pdf

Mikkonen, J., & Raphael, D. (2010). *Social determinants of health: The Canadian facts*. Retrieved from www.thecanadianfacts.org

Milloy, J. S. (1999). *A national crime: The Canadian government and the residential school system, 1879–1986*. University of Manitoba Press.

Milloy, J. S. (2000). The early Indian Acts: Developmental strategy and constitutional change. In I. A. L. Getty & A. S. Lussier (Eds.), *As long as the sun shines and water flows: A reader in Canadian Native studies* (pp. 56–64). University of British Columbia Press.

Moraga, C., & Anzaldúa, G. (Eds.). (1981). *This bridge called my back: Writings by radical women of color*. Persephone Press.

Mullaly, R. (2002). *Challenging oppression: A critical social work approach*. Oxford University Press.

Picca, L., & Feagin, J. (2007). *Two-faced racism: Whites in the backstage and frontstage*. Routledge.

Picower, B. (2009). The unexamined Whiteness of teaching: How White teachers maintain and enact dominant racial ideologies. *Race Ethnicity and Education*, 12(2), 197–215.

Roediger, D. R. (1999). *The wages of Whiteness: Race and the making of the American working class*. Verso.

Sakala, L. (2014). Breaking down mass incarceration in the 2010 census: State-by-state incarceration rates by race/ethnicity [Brief]. Prison Policy Initiative. Retrieved from www.prisonpolicy.org/reports/rates.html

Schoenfish-Keita, J., & Johnson, G. S. (2010). Environmental justice and health: An analysis of persons of color injured at the work place. *Race, Gender, and Class*, 17(1/2), 270–304.

Sharma, N. (2002). Immigrant and migrant workers in Canada: Labour movements, racism and the expansion of globalization. *Canadian Woman Studies*, 21/22(4/1), 18–25.

Statistics Canada. (2006). *Aboriginal identity population, 2006 counts*. Retrieved from www12.statcan.ca/census-recensement/2006/dp-pd/hlt/97-558/pages/page.cfm?Lang=E&Geo=PR&Code=01&Table=3&Data=Count&Sex=1&StartRec=1&Sort=2&Display=Page

Statistics Canada (2015a). *Adult correctional statistics in Canada, 2013/2014*. Retrieved from www.statcan.gc.ca/pub/85-002-x/2015001/article/14163-eng.htm

Statistics Canada (2015b). *Youth correctional statistics in Canada, 2013/2014*. Retrieved from www.statcan.gc.ca/pub/85-002-x/2015001/article/14164-eng.htm#a6

Steele, C. M. (1997). A threat in the air: How stereotypes shape intellectual identity and performance. *American Psychologist, 52*(6), 613–629.

Stepan, N. (1982). *The idea of race in science.* Macmillan.

Tatum, B. (1997). *"Why are all the Black kids sitting together in the cafeteria?" And other conversations about race.* Basic Books.

Tehranian, J. (2000). Performing Whiteness: Naturalization litigation and the construction of racial identity in America. *Yale Law Journal, 109*(4), 817–848.

Thobani, S. (2007). *Exalted subjects: Studies in the making of race and nation in Canada.* University of Toronto Press.

Trepagnier, B. (2010). *Silent racism: How well-meaning White people perpetuate the racial divide* (2nd ed.). Paradigm.

Van Ausdale, D., & Feagin, J. (2001). The first R: How children learn race and racism. Rowman & Littlefield.

Watson, D. (2011). "Urban, but not too urban": Unpacking teachers' desires to teach urban students. *Journal of Teacher Education, 62*(1), 23–34.

Weber, L. (2010). *Understanding race, class, gender, and sexuality: A conceptual framework* (2nd ed.). Oxford University Press.

Winks, R. W. (1997). *The Blacks in Canada: A history* (2nd ed.). McGill-Queen's University Press. (Original work published 1971)

Wise, T. (2005). *Affirmative action: Racial preference in Black and White.* Routledge.

Woodson, C. G. (1933). *The mis-education of the Negro.* Tribeca Books.

CHAPTER 4

White Dominance and the Weight of the West

Gary R. Howard

Deference to the physical superlative, a preference for the scent of our own clan: a thousand anachronisms dance down the strands of our DNA from a hidebound tribal past, guiding us toward the glories of survival, and some vainglories as well. If we resent being bound by these ropes, the best hope is to seize them out like snakes by the throat, look them in the eye, and own up to the venom.

—Barbara Kingsolver, *High Tide in Tucson*

During a multicultural workshop in Austin, Texas, a White elementary teacher, with a tone of intense frustration in her voice, said to the group, "I don't understand all of this talk about differences. Each of my little kindergarten kids comes to me with the same stuff. It doesn't matter whether they're Black, Hispanic, or White, they each have a brain, a body, and a family. They each get the same curriculum. I treat them all the same. And yet, by the end of the year, and as I watch them move up through the grades, the Blacks and Hispanics fall behind and the White kids do better. What happens?"

I wondered how best to respond to the complexities underlying this teacher's naive assumptions. There is so much that needs to be said about the notion that all children come to us with "the same stuff." I wanted to engage her in a discussion of the personal and cultural histories that each of her students brings to the classroom. These histories are not the same, yet they profoundly influence the educational process. I wanted to discuss the institutional practices that systematically favor certain racial, economic, and language groups, while negatively influencing others. I wanted to explore with her the 500-year history of racism, slavery, and cultural genocide, which has had a devastating impact on the lives of many of her students and their families. I wanted to share with her the many lessons of race privilege and oppression I had learned from my Black and Latino neighbors in New Haven during the 1960s. In short, I wanted to abandon the "Introduction to Multicultural Curriculum" presentation I had been asked to deliver and shift to a deeper and more fundamental focus related to the history of White social dominance in the United States and around the globe.

REFLECTIONS IN THE EYE OF A SNAKE

As a White educator, I find it difficult to approach the topic of White dominance. I know that many of my White colleagues are tired of hearing about it. The litany of past and present sins committed by Whites against people of other races and cultures echoes in our ears, and we resist yet another recitation of this old and damning chant. We are tempted to cry out, "Enough! I know this story and I don't need to hear it again." Even those of us who are actively engaged in the work for racial justice, and committed to more equitable educational outcomes for all of our students, still tire of being seen as the demons of history and the omnipresent oppressors of those who are not White.

Yet, I also know that the naiveté evidenced by the teacher in Texas represents too many of my White colleagues. In my 40 years of working with educators in the United States and Australia, I have often heard sentiments similar to those expressed by this teacher. I continue to ask: How is it possible, with so much research and information available about race issues today, that prospective educators can complete their entire teacher education and certification program without gaining a deeper grasp of social reality?

Even though we sometimes may be tempted to avoid the discussion of White racial dominance, we have a responsibility to our students to assure that we remain open to ever-deeper levels of awareness. It is the unexamined nature of White dominance that is often our problem (Fine, Weis, Powell, & Wong, 2004). If our examination and understanding of the root causes of social inequality are too shallow, then our approach to corrective action will necessarily be superficial and ineffective (Grant & Sleeter, 2011). If we do not face dominance, we are predisposed to perpetuate it.

Students, parents, and colleagues of color have repeatedly called for greater racial and cultural awareness on the part of White educators. Their voices challenge us to catch up with our own history by acknowledging the reality of past and present racism and dominance. As I seek to address this challenge in the present chapter, a single question looms large: How do I be antiracist without appearing anti-White?

I have found in my work that most White educators want to overcome the effects of dominance. We want to end racism rather than perpetuate it. Yet I have also found that many White educators, like the naive teacher in Texas, have not engaged in a sufficiently deep analysis of the root causes and dynamics of dominance. Using Kingsolver's imagery from the opening quote to this chapter, many of my colleagues have never looked directly into the eyes of the snake of White dominance, and when invited to do so, they feel frightened rather than enlightened, and resist exploring a topic they believe will lead only to blame. And even those of us who have tried to stare down that viper are often uncomfortable with the reflection of ourselves we discover there, and we shy away from further confrontations or deeper learning. As Levine (1996) pointed out decades ago, "The quest to understand the past and the present in their full complexity and ambiguity can be discomfiting and even threatening" (p. xvii).

It is important to remember as we embark on this complex and sometimes uncomfortable journey into greater understanding that the "enemy" is dominance itself, not White people. This distinction becomes blurred at times precisely because of the overwhelming convergence of Whiteness and dominance in Western nations. Education in the West is the focus of this chapter, and in this context the overarching presence of dominance has been related to the establishment of European hegemony. If we were to broaden the focal point and look at the universal history of human suffering caused by arrangements of dominance and racism, there are many stories to be told, and the villains have not always been White. My intent here is to encourage meaningful discourse about Whiteness and social dominance in Western educational settings without becoming lost in the cycles of blame, guilt, anger, and denial that have so often in the past prevented honest engagement of these issues (Chavez Chavez & O'Donnell, 1998; Nagda & Gurin, 2007; Zúñiga et al., 2007).

SOCIAL DOMINANCE IN RESEARCH AND THEORY

A broad range of educational and social science research converges on the issue of social dominance. The study of dominance is related to research on issues such as prejudice, stereotyping, discrimination, racism, sexism, neoclassical elitism theory, social identity theories, and work in the field of political socialization (Sidanius & Pratto, 2012). Although a full review of the literature related to social dominance is beyond the scope of this chapter (Carmines, Sniderman, & Easter, 2011; Sniderman, Tetlock, & Carmines, 1993), my interest here is to introduce those concepts and findings that relate most directly to preparing White educators for the work of understanding and unraveling racial dominance in educational settings.

Minimal Group Paradigm

Early research by Tajfel (1970) suggests that even superficial and seemingly meaningless distinctions between individuals can become the basis for prejudicial attitudes and discriminatory behaviors. Using Tajfel's minimal group paradigm, Howard and Rothbart (1980) conducted studies with college students wherein artificial and arbitrary distinctions were manufactured by the experimenters, informing each subject of his or her identity as either an "overestimator" or "underestimator" of the number of dots projected briefly on a screen. Observing their colleagues in a series of tasks, subjects were asked to allocate rewards to pairs of individuals, who were also labeled by their group status. When the pairs included one in-group member and one out-group member, the subjects consistently favored their own group.

The minimal group paradigm suggests that human beings tend to demonstrate discriminatory in-group and out-group dynamics even when there is an extremely limited basis for drawing distinctions between members of the groups. As teachers, we often witness this process in our classrooms. In one of my student workshops, which included young people from two neighboring high schools in the same rural, predominantly White town in upstate New York, the lesson of minimal group distinctions was brought home to me in a rather humorous way. Even though the two schools were virtually indistinguishable demographically, the students from one seemed to invest a great deal of energy in perpetuating a stereotype of students from the other school as a "bunch of hicks." During the workshop this issue of "degrees of hickness" was vigorously debated by students from both schools, with the tension and volume in the room rising as each new attack or counterattack further denigrated the members of the opposing group. Determined not to lose the workshop to the heat of such a seemingly insignificant battle, my co-facilitator and I finally called a break and discussed how we might use the "hick" issue as an entree into our intended discussion of race and gender stereotypes. The perfect teachable moment came when one of the few African American students in the workshop, a young woman who had recently moved to this small town from an urban and highly multicultural neighborhood, said to me, "Mr. Howard, I don't see what all this hassle is about. As far as I'm concerned, they're *all* a bunch of hicks."

This story illustrates two basic lessons of minimal group theory: (1) As human beings we tend to draw distinctions between ourselves as individuals and groups, even if the distinctions are essentially meaningless in a larger context, and (2) having drawn these distinctions, we then ascribe values of superiority and inferiority to the various in-groups and out-groups we ourselves have created. When we add to this process the existence of a powerful "visible marker" such as race, we are left with patterns of intergroup relations that are extremely resistant to change (Gaertner & Dovidio, 2014; Rothbart & John, 1993).

The implications of minimal group theory are burdensome for those of us concerned with achieving more equitable interactions and outcomes in the classroom. If human beings are by nature predisposed to categorize and negatively discriminate against perceived out-groups, even when the basis for that differentiation is trivial and meaningless, then it might appear overwhelmingly difficult to reduce group-based biases related to more significant issues of human difference such as race, gender identity, social class, religion, ability, and sexual orientation. Although intergroup tensions are not always a bad thing, and have sometimes been the catalysts for confronting issues of injustice (see Saguy et al., 2011), the minimal group paradigm does raise a cautionary flag for us as educators, signaling both the difficulty and the necessity of working toward greater intergroup harmony (C. A. M. Banks, 2005).

Social Positionality

Researchers in the area of social positionality have provided additional clarification regarding the issue of dominance. They have demonstrated that human beings tend to draw distinctions not only in terms of in-group and out-group but also in terms of dominance and subordination. How we view the world, how we construct reality, and how we ascribe meaning and value to our lives are intimately connected to our position within social and historical hierarchies of dominance and subordination (Rosaldo, 1993). Social positionality has both subjective and objective dimensions. The subjective dimension relates to how I see myself and how others see me. The objective dimension relates to my social position in terms of more quantitative and observable measures, such as income, education level, or job status. The issue of positionality helps clarify the discussion of White collective identity. From the perspective of those members of society who are *not* White, it is quite clear, both subjectively and objectively, that Whites have been collectively allocated disproportionate amounts of power, authority, wealth, control, and dominance. However, for me as an individual White person, subjectively experiencing my own reality, I may or may not feel dominant. I may or may not perceive myself as belonging to a collective group defined by Whiteness.

It is from the conceptual frame of social positionality and collective identity that we can better understand and deconstruct typical comments from White participants in race awareness workshops, such as "I never owned slaves" or "I didn't kill Indians." As White people experiencing the world from our social position of dominance, we often fail, on an individual level, to identify with the collective group history that has been the foundation for establishing our dominance. For example, a White male bank president in one of my corporate diversity workshops was having trouble understanding the relationship between White collective identity and dominance. After listening to several stories from Black, Hispanic, and Asian participants in the workshop, who described their direct experiences related to racism and White dominance, he gradually began to grasp the powerful impact of his own social positionality. His comment to the group was, "I feel like I'm a fish who just discovered water. I've been swimming so long in dominance that I wasn't aware of it." His personal revelation is echoed by Sleeter's (1996) assessment of her social positionality as a White woman: "The racism I was raised with was grounded in taken-for-granted acceptance of White people as the center of the universe" (p. 19).

Social positionality for Whites in Western societies has afforded us a personal sense of invisibility related to the unfolding drama of dominance (McIntosh, 1988). This invisibility was clearly illustrated in a workshop I led for a group of senior-level administrators at a large university in Australia. In this university the student population was highly diverse, yet the upper-level managers were exclusively White and predominantly male. From previous work with Aboriginal students, international students, and diverse members of the faculty and staff, I knew that racial inequities were being inadequately addressed by this group of senior administrators. I began my half-day session with a discussion of European hegemony and social dominance in educational settings. I wanted to introduce a basic conceptual framework for understanding dominance and then spend most of our time developing strategies for more equitable policies and practices. It soon became clear, however, that these senior managers did not accept my beginning premise regarding White dominance. And without acknowledging the reality of dominance, we could not engage in a meaningful discussion of strategies for change.

Swimming in White dominance, these university administrators were unable or unwilling to critically analyze their own social positionality. They were each in his own right highly accomplished and respected scholars and administrators, but they remained profoundly ignorant of the dynamics of social dominance relative to their position of power within the university. I realized that my brief workshop should have been preceded by a more lengthy and remedial course on the history of intergroup relations, racist practices, and White social dominance in Australia.

For White educators, it is especially important that we lift the curtain of ignorance and denial that has protected us from understanding our location on the broader stage of hierarchical social arrangements. We need to see how the lives of our students have been scripted by their membership in groups differing in degrees of social dominance and marginality. In the case of the teacher in Texas, who saw all her students coming into her classroom with "the same stuff," it is clear that she, like the university administrators in Australia, had not learned the skills to adequately and critically assess her own role in the larger social drama of dominance. As James Banks (1996) reminded us many years ago:

If we fail to recognize the ways in which social location produces subjectivity and influences the construction of knowledge, we are unlikely to interrogate

Counter
said dopir

established knowledge that contributes to the oppression of marginalized and victimized groups. (p. 65)

Social Dominance Theory

Social dominance theory offers a third research strand that can help inform educational practitioners who are concerned with issues of racial equity and social justice. The four basic assumptions of social dominance theory (Sidanius & Pratto, 1993, 2012) are the following:

1. Human social systems are predisposed to form social hierarchies, with hegemonic groups at the top and negative reference groups at the bottom.
2. Hegemonic groups tend to be disproportionately male, a phenomenon that social dominance theorist call the "iron law of andrancy."
3. Most forms of social oppression, such as racism, sexism, and classism, can be viewed as manifestations of group-based social hierarchy.
4. Social hierarchy is a survival strategy that has been selected by many species of primates, including *Homo sapiens*.

By way of definition within social dominance theory, "hegemonic groups" are those that tend to be disproportionately represented at the higher positions of authority within social institutions, whereas "negative reference groups" are those that are least likely to be represented there (Sidanius & Pratto, 2012).

Social dominance theorists take the notion of social positionality and cast it in a historical and evolutionary context of survival and immutability. There is a deterministic tone to their assumptions and conclusions regarding human social systems. Similar to the minimal group paradigm, social dominance theorists suggest that human beings are inherently predisposed to create group-based systems of categorization and discrimination. Sidanius and Pratto (2012) propose that an "oppression equilibrium" must be established to stabilize any society, wherein there is enough oppression to keep the hierarchical arrangements in place, but not so much as to cause either outright rebellion or the total destruction of negative reference groups, that is, genocide. Social hierarchies are maintained through a combination of individual and institutional discrimination, which also must be limited to prevent social destabilization and to avoid excessive conflict with the expressed values and beliefs of the social system. These theorists rather cynically maintain that the most stable societies are those in which negative reference groups accept the legitimacy of the hierarchical structure, thus internalizing their oppression by rationalizing to themselves their place in the scheme of things.

Early work in social dominance theory was based on a functional approach to the study of individual attitudes, values, and beliefs (D. Katz, 1960). From this point of view, individuals develop belief structures that support and rationalize their social position and their collective reality. Social dominance theorists maintain that the functional role of values and beliefs applies not only to individuals but also to social systems. Thus, within hierarchical systems, most social institutions are supported by a set of "legitimizing myths" that serve to explain and rationalize the differential distribution of power and rewards in favor of the dominant group. In her earlier work, Appleby (1992) drew a similar conclusion from an analysis of the founding of the colonial system in North America:

> Being the true heirs of European culture, the American colonists had perpetuated the invidious distinction between the talented few and the vulgar many, making status an important feature of all their institutional arrangements. (p. 425)

Social dominance theorists argue that hierarchical systems of group-based preference are inevitable, immutable, and universal in human experience. In this they seem more concerned with issues of social equilibrium and stability than with the achievement of equity and social justice. Because of their fixed and deterministic perspective, and in light of their pessimism regarding the possibility of change, it might be argued that social dominance theorists have actually created their own grand legitimizing myth for the perpetuation of White dominance.

Privilege and Penalty

In addition to the minimal group paradigm, social positionality, and social dominance theory, a fourth direction in the literature looks at dominance as a system of "privilege and penalty" (Hankivsky et al., 2012; McIntosh, 1988; Nieto, 2005; M. Weinberg, 1991). From this perspective, social arrangements of dominance cause privileges to flow to certain groups whether or not those privileges are earned. Likewise, penalties, punishments, and inequities flow to other groups through no fault of their own other than their group membership. Like the Iowa banker who experienced his dominance as a "fish discovering water," many of these privileges flow to Whites without our awareness or intent, and they continue to flow to us even if we consciously desire *not* to be dominant (McIntosh, 1988; Pennington, Brock, & Ndura, 2012; Sleeter, 1996; Wise, 2003). The privilege-and-penalty analysis echoes in many ways the notions of hegemonic and negative reference groups in social dominance theory. Both approaches are descriptive of the actual history of interaction between dominant and subordinate groups, wherein group-based inequalities are intrinsically linked to the very foundations of personal and institutional behavior. Systems of privilege and penalty are also consistent with the minimal group paradigm, in that both conceptual frameworks are based on the dynamics of group-based categorization and discrimination.

Critical Race Theory

Critical race theory takes much of the above research on dominance and focuses it particularly on issues of race and whiteness (Delgado & Stefancic, 2012). Critical race theory emerged in the 1980s when legal scholars began to examine how the arrangements of racism continued to manifest throughout our society in spite of the gains made during the civil rights movement. The early work by legal scholars, including Derrick Bell (1987) and Lani Guinier (1994), demonstrated how the dynamics of White privilege and social dominance are deeply embedded in all institutions, particularly within the legal system. Scholars in the field of education later extended this critical analysis to show how race-based biases and structures of White dominance are built into the processes, policies, and outcomes of schooling (Apple, 2009; Gillborn, 2008; Howard, 2008; Ladson-Billings & Tate, 1995; Mc-Laren, 1997). For those of us involved in the early multicultural education movement, critical race theory brought a much-needed challenge to the superficial "foods, fairs, and festivals" approach to diversity, reminding us that our simplistic focus on "cultural awareness" was in many ways masking the deeper structural issues of racism and White privilege.

Research Implications

Taken together, research findings in the areas of minimal group paradigm, social positionality, social dominance theory, systems of privilege and penalty, and critical race theory form a strong foundation for understanding White dominance. First, the minimal group paradigm suggests that all human beings are predisposed to form in-groups and out-groups and to respond to other human beings based on these self-created, and sometimes trivial, distinctions. Second, work in the area of social positionality reminds us that our place in the social hierarchy of dominance determines how we construct knowledge, how we come to determine what is real and true. Third, social dominance theory places systems of dominance and subordination in an evolutionary context, arguing that such group-based arrangements have been ever-present, and perhaps even inevitable, in human experience. Fourth, work in the area of privilege and penalty demonstrates that systems of social dominance are characterized by the differential distribution of rewards and punishments to individuals and groups not on the basis of worth but solely as a function of group membership. And finally, the development of critical race theory over the past few decades has given

Social Dominance They are
Waves of Resistance in
How Study ...

White Dominance and the Weight of the West   89

a specific race-based focus to all of the other strands in the literature, providing the language and the analysis for a clearer understanding of privilege, power, and systems of White social dominance.

The research literature clearly demonstrates that social dominance is a common human phenomenon, not a uniquely White issue. As I stated in the introduction to this chapter, the viper of social dominance comes in all colors. We need look no further than our history texts and daily newspapers for continual reminders of social dominance as evidenced by widely varied peoples and cultures. Realities such as the Chinese occupation of Tibet, the Japanese oppression of the Ainu in Hokkaido, the Turkish genocide against the Armenians, the Black-on-Black acts of genocide in Rwanda and Darfur, the deadly Sunni versus Shi'ite conflicts in the Middle East, and many other ethnic power struggles around the world clearly establish that the drive for social dominance is not a peculiarly "White thing."

However, when we consider social dominance in the context of Western education, and in light of the broad-based expansion of European influence throughout the world, it is important to explore the particular nature of White dominance. Precisely because our White forebears had both the means and the will to establish racial dominance in many corners of the world, we as White educators ought to understand how our inherited hegemonic position continues to influence the educational process today. Because European dominance has been so broadly and effectively established, it is important to ask ourselves as White educators how our own social positionality and history of dominance might be implicated in the disproportionate distribution of privilege and penalty in contemporary educational systems, which is so clearly evidenced by the persistence of race-based disparities in the outcomes of schooling. We ought to seek this understanding not because we stand accused of the sins and excesses of our ancestors, but because those dynamics of dominance are still functioning today and we are committed to equitable opportunities and outcomes for all of our students.

In seeking this understanding, however, it must be acknowledged that it is often difficult for the members of any hegemonic group to see their own dominance. Because of our social positionality as Whites in Western settings, the arrangements of dominance may appear "normal" to us (Gillborn, 2008), part of the assumed and natural fabric of reality, deeply ingrained inequities, which I refer to in my workshops as "historically normalized oppression." For this reason, I have often found it difficult, as with the university administrators in Australia, to engage my White colleagues in an authentic dialogue about White dominance. This difficulty is partly a function of denial and defensiveness, but it also relates to the lack of an adequate lens for viewing our own dominance, a lens that allows us to see beyond the rarified blinders of our social positionality.

THE LENS OF INDIGENOUS EXPERIENCE

In my work with White educators I have found it helpful to use the lens of "otherness" as a vehicle for understanding dominance. Learning from the experiences of those groups who have been marginalized by White dominance has been the primary vehicle for my own growth in this arena. The opportunities afforded me in the Hill neighborhood in New Haven to glimpse reality through the eyes of Black children and community activists were pivotal in my development as an educator and as a human being. These experiences led me to conclude that White racial awareness must be mediated through actual engagement with "the other." Authentic engagement with the reality of those whose stories are significantly different from our own can allow us to transcend, to some degree, the limits of social positionality and help us see White racial dominance in a clearer light.

In addition to the New Haven years, profound lessons about White dominance have come through my engagement with Indigenous people from many parts of the world. Through the eyes of Indigenous people, and from the perspective of their many centuries of exposure to European dominance, I have gained a deeper understanding of whiteness in the West. For the remainder of this chapter I will review much of the information that has come to me through the lens of Indigenous people's experiences in dealing with Whites throughout the past 500 years. I share these lessons here as a way of illustrating the actual methodologies of dominance, the means by which the theoretical issues explored above have become manifested in the lives of human beings. It is a painful story to tell, and I do not recount it with the intention of casting blame or inciting guilt. The heaviness of the story is not meant to debilitate us, but rather to inspire us for renewed and intentional action. I choose to enter this discussion here because it is important that we understand White dominance in more than a theoretical way. If we are to grow in our effectiveness as White educators of diverse students, we need to understand how the issues addressed by the minimal group paradigm, social positionality, social dominance theory, privilege and penalty, and critical race theory actually influence the lives of children and the outcomes of schooling. For me, the lens of Indigenous experience has given a human face to these theoretical constructs.

The Methodologies of Dominance

I share my thoughts here from the perspective of a "non-Indigenous" person who has attended a series of four World Indigenous People's Conferences on Education. The first was held in Vancouver, Canada, hosted by Native Canadians; the second in Ngāruawāhia, New Zealand, hosted by the Maori people; the third in Wollongong, New South Wales, hosted by the Aboriginal people of Australia; and the fourth in Albuquerque, New Mexico, hosted by Native Americans.

Although these Indigenous meetings, which continue to occur every 3 years, have received little attention in the global press, I feel they are one of the more significant educational phenomena occurring in the present era of school reform. The conferences have drawn delegates from widely diverse cultures, with more than 5,000 people from 28 countries attending the Australian event. The many Indigenous nations, tribes, and cultural groups who are drawn to these conferences share a common historical experience: They all played host to Europe's "Age of Discovery."

The conferences themselves have been a vehicle for acknowledging the common suffering of the colonial experience and a means for coalescing the power and vision of colonized people. For the first time in history, Indigenous people from all parts of the planet, people who have heretofore suffered separately from the overlay of White dominance, are now coming together to share their stories, preserve their cultures, share in the healing process, and secure political empowerment. The conferences are also an attempt to ensure that the oppression, pain, and racism of the past 500 years are not continued in the future. In this way, the World Indigenous People's Conferences are attempting to shift the tide of global history by unraveling the legacy of Western White domination.

The Mapuche of Chile, the Maya of Mexico, the Cherokee of the United States, the Mohawk of Canada, the Native People of Hawai'i, the Cordillera people of the Philippines, the Aboriginal people of Australia, the Maori of New Zealand, the Masai of Kenya, and the many other groups who have attended these conferences all have similar stories to share. For each of these groups of people, being "discovered" by Europeans resulted in devastating loss and oppression through the combination of disease, warfare, land theft, discriminatory government policy, the removal of children from their homes, the introduction of alcohol, and the use of foreign religion and education as tools of forced assimilation and cultural genocide. The methods used by Westerners to colonize each of the various groups of Indigenous people are so similar that each group immediately recognizes its own experience in the stories of the others. The striking similarity in the processes employed by Europeans in establishing dominance has led me to ponder whether some sadistic 15th-century bureaucrat may have authored a handbook entitled, "The Seven Basics of Western Dominance: Bacteria, Bullets, Beads, Bureaucracy, Books, Booze, and the Bible."

I will describe briefly how these various elements in the methodology of dominance have influenced the lives of Indigenous people and cemented the foundation of White Western dominance in lands throughout the world. The discussion that follows is intended to illustrate the actual workings of

White dominance in the lives of people who have been its victims and to help us see more clearly the implications of the theoretical issues explored in the previous section. Except where otherwise noted, I base my account on information shared with me by delegates to the World Indigenous People's Conferences on Education.

Disease. Bacteria were usually the primary killer of Indigenous people unfortunate enough to be on the receiving end of European expansion. Within the first century of White contact in North America, for example, European diseases had devastated up to 90% of the population in some of the Eastern Algonquin Nations, and by 1837 the entire Mandan Nation on the banks of the Missouri River had been reduced by small-pox to only 37 survivors (Lewis, 1996). European diseases spread so fast among American Indian Nations that one-half of the Nez Perce people had died of smallpox a full quarter century before the first White person was seen in Nez Perce country (Ward, 1996). In some cases European bacteria were used as weapons of war through the intentional distribution of smallpox-infested blankets and infected barrels of whiskey to Native people who stood in the path of Manifest Destiny (Patterson & Runge, 2002; Prucha, 1975; Riley, 2010). The great irony of this tragic period is that American Indian people had no similarly devastating bacteria to pass on to the Europeans.

Warfare. Violence was often used to eliminate those Indigenous people who did not fall victim to European diseases. In Central America and Mexico, as a result of Spanish invasion, violence, and accompanying diseases, over two-thirds of the Indian population were killed between 1519 and 1650 (Jonas, 1991). In the United States, General William Tecumseh Sherman was anxious after the Civil War to find some basis to justify a major war with the Indians (Yazzie, 2000). Viewing them as "the enemies of our race and our civilization," he said in 1866, "God only knows when, and I do not see how, we can make a decent excuse for an Indian War" (cited in Lewis, 1996, p. 386).

Similarly, several of my Aboriginal colleagues in Australia share accounts of the mass organized killing of Aboriginal people carried out by European invaders in their attempt to "clear" the land for grazing and White settlement. To this end, many young men who were anxious for adventure and new opportunity in the land down under were recruited out of Wales, Scotland, and other countries to come to Australia as "shooters." Ostensibly hired to kill predatory animals, many did not know until they arrived in Australia that their targets would be human (Bob Morgan, personal communication, June 1994). On learning the truth, some refused to carry out their assigned mission. An Aboriginal friend, for example, told me that his grandfather originally came from Wales as a shooter, but when he discovered the evil for which he had been hired, he abandoned his employers, married an Aboriginal woman, and lived out the rest of his life among her family and community.

Land Theft. The imposition of European notions of private ownership and the extra-legal appropriation of Native land are perennial topics of discussion at the World Indigenous People's Conferences. In their early contact with Whites, most Indigenous people were astonished by the strange European proclivity for buying and selling pieces of the earth. As expressed by Chief Joseph (Hin-mah-too-yah-lat-kekht) of the Nez Perce, the Indigenous view of the land was much different:

> The earth was created by the assistance of the sun, and it should be left as it was. . . . The country was made without lines of demarcation, and it is no man's business to divide it. . . . I see the Whites all over the country gaining wealth, and I see their desire to give us lands which are worthless. . . . The earth and myself are of one mind. The measure of the land and the measure of our bodies are the same. (cited in McLuhan, 1971, p. 28)

Chief Joseph's sentiments are not an artifact of the past, and it is often difficult for Westerners today to comprehend the power and centrality of Indigenous people's continuing connection to the land. Aboriginal elders, for example, are bound by tradition to be personally responsible for particular sacred sites in Australia. From generation to generation, specific caretaker roles are passed on, requiring an individual to watch over an important place or feature of the land, to keep its stories and its songs, and to be a protector of that location (Lorraine Mafi-Williams, personal communication, January 1991). If these places are desecrated through mining or other forms of economic development, the Aboriginal caretakers may be so disturbed by the violation of the land that they themselves will die along with the spirit of the land they were pledged to defend (Erica Hampton, personal communication, January 1991). This Aboriginal view of the land has always stood in stark contrast to the utilitarian view of the early British settlers, as evidenced by Sir Thomas Mitchell's (1839) reflections on his "discovery" of the plains of Western Victoria in Australia:

> The scene was different from anything I had ever before witnessed, either in New South Wales or elsewhere, a land so inviting yet without inhabitants. As I stood, the first intruder on the sublime solitude of these verdant plains as yet untouched by flocks of herds, I felt conscious of being the harbinger of mighty changes, and that our steps would soon be followed by the men and animals for whom it seemed to have been prepared. (p. 159)

Indigenous people on many continents today are waging continuing political battles to protect, recover, and preserve their lands from the kind of proprietary hubris expressed by Mitchell (Solidarity Foundation, 1996; Weinberg, 1996; Wittstock & Salinas, 2010). In Guatemala, for example, it was not until 1996 that the Mayan people were able to return from exile in Mexico to reclaim homelands taken from them in a 1954 CIA-sponsored coup that opened their land for takeover by the U.S.-based United Fruit Company (Jonas, 1991). In another case, a participant I met at the Indigenous conference in Australia wrote in a letter to me that his people are facing "torture, rape, extrajudicial execution, arbitrary arrest, and disappearances" because of their efforts to protect their land and preserve their culture. For his protection and privacy I choose not to identify his name or specific Indigenous group, but my friend speaks for many peoples of the world who are suffering today from the continuing encroachment of Western dominance.

In the United States, of course, we have a long tradition of taking Native land, even that which was once guaranteed by treaty to remain in American Indian hands "for as long as the rivers shall run" (Deloria, 1974; Townsend, 2009). President Andrew Jackson, chief architect of the "Trail of Tears," justified one such program of theft, the Indian Removal Act of 1830, with the following words:

> These tribes cannot exist surrounded by our settlements and continual contact with our citizens. They have neither the intelligence, the industry, the moral habits, nor the desire of improvement. They must necessarily yield to the force of circumstance and, ere long, disappear. (cited in Ward, 1996, p. 83)

Having once accomplished, through Jackson's policies, the task of removing most of the American Indians east of the Mississippi, a young nation hungry for land then proceeded to take the American West as well. The "legitimizing myth" for this relentless acquisition of American Indian land was well articulated in 1843 by Missouri Congressman Thomas Hart Benton: "The White race went for the land and they will continue to go for it . . . the principle is founded in God's command and it will continue to be obeyed" (*Congressional Globe*, 1846, pp. 917–918).

Unfortunately, this twisted and racist theological rationale is still alive even among educators today. In 2014, a White workshop participant came to me after my talk on land theft and genocide as the basis for the "Founding Father's" wealth and power, and said, "Gary, I disagree with your critique of the origins of our nation. God meant for White people to occupy and control this continent." With a teacher who still worships at the altar of Manifest Destiny, I fear for students of color in that classroom.

For comparative purposes, it is interesting to also look at the process of land appropriation in Australia. By the time the British began to invade

Australia in 1788, they had learned many lessons in the Americas. According to the doctrine of discovery, which had been established in Europe by the early 1500s, when explorers of new lands found people living there, they could not claim those lands directly for their home countries (Johnson, 2007; Williams, 1990). They could legitimately claim only the right to negotiate for the land with its prior inhabitants. The doctrine of discovery was the foundation for the entire treaty-making process in the Americas, forcing European nations to acknowledge, however disingenuously, the legitimacy of Native title.

Having found the doctrine of discovery to be a cumbersome and inefficient process in the Americas, necessitating the continual making and breaking of treaties and the constant creation of justifications for illegal practices, the British in Australia decided to avoid the entire ordeal. They did so by declaring Australia *terra nullius*, which means "empty land," land without human occupants. In this way the British established a "legal" justification for taking the entire continent. They then proceeded to bring *terra nullius* into reality by disposing with treaties and going directly to bullets, thus enacting a program of genocide that would leave many Aboriginal language groups extinct by the 20th century (Broome, 1982; Short, 2008). It was not until the 1990s, following the Australian High Court decision in the landmark *Mabo* case, that the Australian Parliament finally recognized the legitimacy of Native title (*Mabo v. Queensland*, No. 2, 1992), yet Aboriginal people today are still fighting for full access to these rights.

Religion. In addition to the devastating loss of life and land, the use of the Bible and Christianity as tools of oppression has been a particularly tragic chapter in the establishment of White dominance. In the early 1500s, while Europeans were launching their frenzy of discovery and encountering new lands and cultures around the world, a major debate took place among the Christian hierarchy in Europe regarding the spiritual status of Indigenous people (Stevens, 2004; Williams, 1990). Because these people were not Christians, they were seen by Europeans as "infidels." The central question of church debate became, "Are the infidels human?" If Indigenous people were not fully human, then by church doctrine they did not possess souls and could not be converted to Christianity. If, however, they were determined to be human, it would become the church's obligation to bring their souls into the "one true faith." This debate was carried on as part of the discussion regarding the doctrine of discovery, wherein European nations considered possible justifications for claiming new lands and depriving the original inhabitants of life, liberty, and property (Miller, 2011; Williams, 1990).

Ultimately, of course, the existence of Indigenous souls was decided in the affirmative by the White church fathers, opening the way for Christianity to play a key role in the expansion of European hegemony. The Age of Discovery was thereby granted a holy mission—not only to claim new wealth and real estate for the nobles back home but also to bring the "heathens" to Jesus. Those Indigenous people who had not fallen victim to European bacteria or bullets would now be subjected to the invaders' view of spiritual truth. Many Indigenous leaders foresaw what was coming, as is clear in these words of warning delivered by Sweet Medicine to his fellow Cheyenne prior to White encroachment on their land:

> Some day you will meet a people who are White. They will try to give you many things, but do not take them. At last, I think you will take these things and they will bring sickness to you. . . . Your ways will change. You will leave your religion for something new. You will lose respect for your leaders and start quarrelling with one another. . . . You will take the new ways and forget the good things by which you have lived and in the end you will become worse than crazy. (cited in Ward, 1996, p. 30)

In most countries invaded by Europeans, missionaries became the advanced guard for the "civilizing" process. Good Christians made compliant subjects. Traditional Indigenous spiritual practices were made illegal, and people who chose to continue practicing them were punished and/or forced to go underground. The Makah, for example, who are a whaling people on the northwestern tip of Washington State, would canoe across the treacherous waters off Cape Flattery to Tatoosh Island, where they could celebrate their spiritual longhouse traditions out of sight of their White overseers, who were afraid to venture across the rough seas (personal communication, John Ides, 1985). Changes in these policies of spiritual repression have been slow in coming. In the United States, it was not until 1978 (Bogen & Goldstein, 2009; Harvey & Harjo, 1994) that Congress finally passed the Indian Religious Freedom Act, and even today some groups of traditional practitioners, such as the Native American Church, are continually harassed.

Missionaries and Bureaucrats. The oversight and administration of Indigenous communities in the United States and Australia were often delegated to missionaries (Dolan, 1985; Reyhner & Eder, 1989). Governments in both countries parceled out communities of Indigenous people to different Christian denominations. As part of the "peace policy" in the United States, the Catholics, Baptists, Lutherans, Congregationalists, Anglicans, Dutch Reform, and most other major Christian bodies received an allocation of Indigenous souls to place under the care of their particular doctrine. In his annual report of 1872, the Commissioner of Indian Affairs, Francis A. Walker, spoke highly of this "extra-official" relationship between the U.S. government and the churches, and he summoned the missionaries "to assume charge of the intellectual and moral education of the Indians" (cited in Prucha, 1975, p. 142).

Enormous power was given to these "mission managers," as they came to be called in Australia (Rowley, 1970). The Christian overseers were responsible for the distribution of food rations, the allocation of jobs, and the granting of permission to travel off the mission or the reservation. These faith-based bureaucrats administered a system of privilege and penalty designed for the control and compliance of Native people. Conversion to Christianity was often a necessary survival strategy for Indigenous people who wished to feed, clothe, and house their families (Fuchs & Havinghurst, 1973). Thus the Bible joined with the bureaucracy in the paternalistic control of Indigenous people's lives.

Education. The removal of Indigenous children from their homes to attend boarding schools is another tragic story in the history of White dominance. Education was often used as a tool for reinforcing the colonial policies of forced assimilation (Battiste, 2012; Robinson-Zañartu, 2003). In the United States, American Indian children were usually taken so far from their parents that they would not be able to run home. Administered under the euphemistic intention of "civilizing the Indian," the boarding schools were, in fact, a severe system of cultural genocide (Reyhner & Singh, 2010). Evincing both the misguided idealism and the blind racism of the boarding school policy, the Commissioner of Indian Affairs in 1889 laid out the following "principles for Indian education":

> Education is to be the medium through which the rising generation of Indians are to be brought into fraternal and harmonious relationship with their White fellow-citizens, and with them enjoy the sweets of refined homes, the delights of social intercourse, the emoluments of commerce and trade, the advantages of travel, together with the pleasures that come from literature, science and philosophy, and the solace and stimulus afforded by a true religion. (cited in Prucha, 1975, p. 178)

In spite of this flowery pronouncement, neither delight nor pleasure came to American Indian people as a result of the boarding school policy (Jacobs, 2009). Children were removed from their families at a young age and kept for many years. Their hair was cut in Western style. Traditional clothing, regalia, spirituality, and language were forbidden. Punishments for violation of rules in the boarding schools were harsh, painful, and humiliating (Gone, 2009; Robinson et al., 2004). Christian indoctrination was an integral part of the process of deculturing Native children, an attempt to "bring the infidels and savages living in those parts to human civility" (Vogel, 1972, pp. 45–46). The stated intention of the policy was to "kill the Indian and save the man" (O'Brien, 1889, cited in Harvey & Harjo, 1994, p. 134). The "educational" value of these schools was limited, with the curriculum being primarily geared to training for menial labor and domestic servitude.

Similar policies were instituted in Australia, creating a "stolen generation" of Aboriginal children who did not have the benefit of growing up in their own families and communities (Jacobs, 2009; Reed, 1982). An Aboriginal friend shared with me her memories of being taken from her parents at the age of 12, never to see them again until she was 21 years old. The officers of the "Aboriginal Protection Board" came into the homes of her friends and neighbors on the mission and forcibly removed children from their parents. As in the United States, these Aboriginal children were often taken to boarding schools far from home where they would receive Christian indoctrination and training as domestic workers. My friend spent many years as a menial laborer in White homes before she was finally able in her late 40s to demonstrate her considerable academic and intellectual skills by completing a university degree and becoming a noted writer and filmmaker. It would be impossible to adequately describe or quantify the extent to which the intellectual and creative potential of young Indigenous students has been either derailed or destroyed through the coercive assimilation of the boarding school policies in both Australia and the United States (Dupris, 1979; Robinson-Zañartu, 2003). For purposes of classroom discussion of this process, the Australian film *Rabbit Proof Fence* (Noyce, Winter, & Noyce, 2002) is an excellent and historically accurate resource.

Alienation and Alcohol. The tragic impact of education as a tool for forced assimilation continues into the present. Even into the late 1960s, American Indian students at boarding schools were being coerced into religious training, with various Christian denominations given direct access to captive audiences of Indigenous children (Carlson, 1997). The ongoing process of humiliation and deculturalization is in the memory of American Indian people living today. Those who experienced years of mistreatment in the boarding schools often returned to their families as broken and lost individuals (Locust, 1988). Forced assimilation left them too White to be accepted by their relatives back on the reservation, and yet they remained too Indian to be accepted into White society (Reyhner & Singh, 2010). Many turned to alcohol to ease the pain of their alienation from their own identity (Emerson, 1997; Gone, 2009; Yates, 1987). A Turtle Mountain Cree colleague, Ken LaFountaine, who created a program at Shoreline Community College in Washington State for educating White students about Indian history, attributes a major portion of American Indian alcoholism and suicide today to the long-term devastating effects of the boarding school policy (personal communication, 1997).

Dominance Continues

Even today it is difficult for many non-Indian teachers to work effectively with American Indian students (Deloria, 1991; Peshkin, 2008). This was made clear to me when the rural school district where I taught received a new influx of Indian families. The Stillaguamish tribe won federal recognition and reclamation of traditional lands in our community, and in the course of one year Indian students became a significant new presence in our classrooms. Almost immediately on their arrival, however, teachers began complaining that these students "didn't fit in well" and that Indian parents "showed little interest in their children's education."

Many of my colleagues didn't realize that the trauma of the boarding school experience is a very present memory for the parents and the grandparents of today's American Indian students, often creating considerable tension and cultural discontinuity between the home and the school (Gone, 2009; Joe, 1994; Secada, 1991). Although most Indian families want the same positive educational outcomes for their children as other parents do, the emotional legacy of cultural genocide is not easily overcome. For generations of Indian people, schooling has not been a positive experience, and it will take much work on the part of educators to regain their trust.

This trust was not easily developed in my local school district. Most of our teachers, like their peers nationwide, had little experience or understanding of the culture and learning characteristics of Indigenous children (Greenfield & Cocking, 2014; Reynolds, 2005). From their social positionality of whiteness, teachers described Indian students as "withdrawn, shy, quiet, inattentive, and unmotivated." Consequently, our school psychologist soon became overwhelmed with teacher requests for special education testing of Indian students. According to teachers and other White workers in the schools, these students were "unresponsive" in the classrooms, "causing problems" on the playground, truant at the high school, and receiving inordinate numbers of discipline tickets on the school buses. Ironically, the same students described by teachers as being passive and withdrawn in the classrooms were accused by others of being overly aggressive outside the classroom. Consistent with our earlier discussion of social dominance, Indian students were being viewed as a negative reference group within the school culture, and school district personnel were imposing diagnostic assumptions based on the legitimizing myths underlying their position of power (Fryberg et al., 2013).

Teacher misperceptions and assumptions about Indian students in our school district reflected a broad national trend that often places Indian students as a group at the highest risk of school failure, dropping out, and over-representation in special education (Faircloth & Tippeconnic, 2010; Hebbeler et al., 2001; Pecora et al., 2010; Robinson-Zañartu, 2003).

Realizing that the actual deficiency lay more with us as educators than with American Indian students or their families, my wife, Lotus Linton-Howard, and I launched an educational program for teachers and other employees, which we called "The Indian Child in the Classroom." Experts in the field of Indian education, who were also members of various Indian communities in our state, came to share their perspectives and strategies with our faculty and staff. Participants gained an Indian historical perspective, an understanding of the long-lasting effects of dominance, and an introduction to features of Indian culture that related directly to their work with American Indian students. Indian parents were pleased that the school district cared enough to provide this education for the teachers and staff. The process resulted in considerable change in the school district. We didn't solve all the problems that have evolved over centuries of dominance and cultural conflict, but we did manage to shift the focus away from a deficit approach to Indian students and their parents. Working together, we gradually began to take mutual responsibility for creating a more positive educational environment for American Indian children.

WHITE DOMINANCE IN THEORY AND PRACTICE

The experience of Indigenous people relative to European expansion over the past 500 years graphically demonstrates the methodologies of White dominance. Through the lens of Indigenous experience, the theoretical issues of dominance discussed earlier can be viewed in the living context of the past and the present. Consistent with research findings related to the minimal group paradigm, Native peoples throughout the world have been categorized as "the other." From the perspective of the European invaders, Indigenousness, in itself, became a powerful marker for defining the "we" and the "they" of the colonial experience, creating a basis for discrimination against an out-group that the Europeans had defined as inferior. As would be predicted by the theory of social positionality, European colonialists constructed social reality through education, religion, and government policy in such a way as to justify and perpetuate their position of power. Consistent with social dominance theory, Whites in the colonialized world established a set of legitimizing myths that characterized Indigenous people as infidels, heathens, savages, and uncivilized, thus deepening the divide of social positionality between themselves and those whom they had designated as a negative reference group. White hegemony then became embedded in systems of privilege and penalty that further legitimized and exacerbated the subordinate position of Indigenous people. All of this is consistent with critical race theory, which provides an overarching analysis of the historical and contemporary construction of privilege, power, and systems of White dominance.

It is clear from this brief review of Indigenous experience that the methodologies of dominance have been intentional, targeted, consistent across diverse and distant settings, and highly effective in establishing White social hegemony. It is also clear, as I discovered in my own school district and see reflected today in schools throughout the nation, that White dominance is not a relic of the past but continues to have direct and deleterious influence in the lives of children today.

It is also important to point out that many marginalized groups have experienced White dominance in ways similar to Indigenous people. The political and economic abandonment of Black and Latino families that I witnessed in 1960s New Haven is clearly present in places like Ferguson and Baltimore, where police brutality has ignited the fires of racial unrest once again in the 21st century. The weight of White dominance still lies heavy across our nation and our schools.

The generational trauma created in the American Indian boarding schools is not dissimilar from the trauma presently experienced by Black and Hispanic students in their inner-city schools (Carlson, 1997; Leary, 2005; McCarty, 2009). Similar elements of colonialism and White social dominance are present in both. We cannot improve the quality of education for any group of racial and cultural "others" in Western nations today without first understanding the extent to which our educational practices and institutions continue to be influenced by colonial beliefs and race-based power relations. Kozol's (1991, 2005, 2012) work in inner-city schools, such as those in East St. Louis, where he witnessed Black children living and attending school under abominable conditions, documents similar conclusions. As Todorov (1982) discovered from his extensive study of the colonial process, "it is in fact the conquest of America that heralds and establishes our present identity" (p. 5). If we are serious about addressing issues of educational inequality for Blacks, Latinos, Native Americans, and other oppressed people, West (1993) and Sue (2006) remind us that we must begin not with the "deficiencies" of marginalized groups but with the fundamental social flaws that have been created by White dominance.

The lens of Indigenous experience provides one vehicle for helping White educators see the consequences of social dominance. Through the eyes of the "other" we are able to penetrate the barrier of social positionality and see ourselves from a more realistic perspective. When we expand the focal point to include other marginalized groups, it becomes clear that the shadow of dominance is not merely a theoretical construct but a living reality that continues to occlude the clear light of opportunity for many of our students today.

THE POSSIBILITY OF CHANGE

Before closing this chapter, it must be emphasized that the exploration of White dominance presented here is not intended to incite blame, shame, or guilt on the part of White educators. As I stated at the beginning of this chapter, the beast of dominance comes in many colors and guises, and Whites alone do not hold a monopoly on the imposition of human suffering. I have engaged the issue of White dominance here because it has had such a broad impact throughout the world. It is not the only form of dominance, but it has been the most pervasive in Western educational settings. Also, I have recognized in my 40 years of work in schools that many White educators, like fish immersed in the normalcy of water, have been swimming unaware in the medium of our own dominance. Only when we begin to see ourselves through a different lens, as we did through the perspective of Indigenous people above, does the image of our social position come more clearly into focus.

I am hopeful that White educators in racially diverse schools can come to see the broader context of our work and begin to understand the significant and varying impact of dominance in the lives of the students we serve. It is from this perspective that we can finally approach the teacher in Texas who was mystified by her observation of differential student outcomes based on race and culture. Our children, as we have seen so clearly through the lens of White dominance and Indigenous experience, do *not* come to us with "the same stuff." Many of the negative influences of history have been disproportionately distributed across the lives of our students, and these "savage inequalities" remain with us today (Kozol, 1991, 2012).

Neither the pains nor the privileges of history have been allocated fairly in the lives of children. The realities of group membership in terms of race, culture, language, economics, and social positionality are inextricably tied to educational outcomes. Like the teachers of American Indian students in my school district, we too often attribute failure to the culture and characteristics of the child rather than to the inherent structures of dominance programmed into the larger society, and into our personal and professional psyches. In our lack of awareness we can become mere pawns of dominance, perpetuating the legitimizing myths that have kept Whites in control for centuries. If we do not understand dominance, we cannot hope to transcend it.

I believe that most White educators want schooling to become more than a mechanism of social control that favors White children. Those of us who share this conviction must choose to become more aware—to open our eyes, our minds, and our hearts to the realities of White dominance. In making this choice, we are challenged to embark on a great journey. It is a difficult journey down a river of healing, through many whitewater rapids and the treacherous currents of self-examination and personal change. In accepting this challenge, we are called to transform both ourselves and the social arrangements of positionality and dominance that have favored us as White people. The tide of our own past history is against us on this journey, but the force of the river and the future of our students require that we join the quest. As a participant in one of my workshops stated, "We are a world in need of healing, but healing can begin only when we acknowledge the depth of our pain."

Too much human energy has already been expended in perpetuating the cycles of dominance, oppression, blame, guilt, and denial. As a nation, we have danced around the edges of democracy for over two centuries, but rarely have we committed ourselves to realizing its deepest vision of justice and liberty. We have talked incessantly about racial inequality, but seldom have we engaged the conversation around healing and reconciliation. If we can face the painful truths of White dominance, and not fall victim to the enervating cycles of blame and guilt, there is some hope that we might then be able to engage our hearts, our minds, and our hands in the healing work of social transformation.

REFERENCES

Apple, M. W. (2009). Is racism in education an accident? *Educational Policy, 23*(4), 651–659.

Appleby, J. (1992). Recovering America's historic diversity: Beyond exceptionalism. *Journal of American History, 79*(2), 419–431.

Banks, C. A. M. (2005). *Improving multicultural education: Lessons from the intergroup education movement.* Teachers College Press.

Banks, J. A. (1996). The historical reconstruction of knowledge about race: Implications for transformative teaching. In J. A. Banks (Ed.), *Multicultural education, transformative knowledge, and action* (pp. 64–87). Teachers College Press.

Battiste, M. (2012). Enabling the autumn seed: Toward a decolonized approach to Aboriginal knowledge, language, and education. In S. Z. Burke & P. Milewski (Eds.), *Schooling in transition: Readings in Canadian history of education* (pp. 275–286). University of Toronto Press.

Bell, D. (1987). *And we are not saved: The illusive quest for racial justice.* Basic Books.

Bogen, D. S., & Goldstein, L. (2009). Culture, religion, and Indigenous people. *Maryland Law Review, 69*(1), 48–65.

Broome, R. (1982). *Aboriginal Australians: Black response to white dominance, 1788–1980.* Allen & Unwin.

Carlson, D. (1997). Stories of colonial and postcolonial education. In M. Fine, L. Weis, L. Powell, & L. Wang (Eds.), *Off White: Readings on race, power, and society* (pp. 137–148). Routledge.

Carmines, E. G., Sniderman, P. M., & Easter, B. C. (2011). On the meaning, measurement, and implications of racial resentment. *The Annals of the American Academy of Political and Social Science, 634*(1), 98–116.

Carter, R. T. (1995). *The influence of race and racial identity in psychotherapy: Toward a racially inclusive model*. Wiley.

Chavez Chavez, C. R., & O'Donnell, J. (1998). *Speaking the unpleasant: The politics of (non)engagement in the multicultural education terrain*. State University of New York Press.

Congressional Globe. (1846). Washington, DC.

Delgado, R., & Stefancic, J. (2012). *Critical race theory: An introduction* (2nd ed.). NYU Press.

Deloria, V., Jr. (1974). *Behind the trail of broken treaties: An Indian declaration of independence*. Delacorte.

Deloria, V., Jr. (1991). *Indian education in America*. American Indian Science and Engineering Society.

Dolan, J. P. (1985). *The American Catholic experience: A history from colonial times to the present*. Doubleday & Company.

Dupris, J. C. (1979). The national impact of multicultural education: A renaissance of Native American culture through tribal self-determination and Indian control of education. In *Multicultural education and the American Indian* (pp. 43–54). University of California, American Indian Studies Center.

Emerson, L. (1997, March 7). *Traditional views on Native American retention in schools*. Paper presented to the Cultural Advocates for Nations at Risk Project, San Diego State University.

Faircloth, S. C., & Tippeconnic, J. W. III. (2010). The dropout/graduation crisis among American Indian and Alaska Native students. Retrieved from https://escholarship.org/uc/item/4ps2m2rf

Fine, M., Weis, L., Powell, L., & Wong, L. (Eds.). (2004). *Off white: Readings on race, power, and society* (2nd ed.). Routledge.

Fryberg, S. A., Troop-Gordon, W., D'Arrisso, A., Flores, H., Ponizovskiy, V., Ranney, J. D., et al. (2013). Cultural mismatch and the education of Aboriginal youths: The interplay of cultural identities and teacher ratings. *Developmental Psychology, 49*(1), 72–79.

Fuchs, E., & Havinghurst, R. J. (1973). *To live on this earth: American Indian education*. Doubleday.

Gaertner, S. L., & Dovidio, J. F. (2014). *Reducing intergroup bias: The common ingroup identity model*. Routledge.

Gillborn, D. (2008). *Racism and education: Coincidence or conspiracy?* Routledge.

Gone, J. P. (2009). A community-based treatment for Native American historical trauma: Prospects for evidence-based practice. *Journal of Consulting and Clinical Psychology, 77*(4), 751–762.

Grant, C. A., & Sleeter, C. E. (2011). *Doing multicultural education for achievement and equity* (2nd ed.). Routledge.

Greenfield, P. M., & Cocking, R. R. (2014). *Cross-cultural roots of minority child development*. Psychology Press.

Guinier, L. (1994). *The tyranny of the majority: Fundamental fairness in representative democracy*. Free Press.

Hankivsky, O., Grace, D., Hunting, G., Ferlatte, O., Clark, N., Fridkin, A., Giesbrecht, M., Rudrum, S., & Laviolette, T. (2012). Intersectionality-based policy analysis. In O. Hankivsky (Ed.), *An intersectionality-based policy analysis framework* (pp. 33–45). Institute for Intersectionality Research and Policy, Simon Fraser University.

Harvey, K. D., & Harjo, L. D. (1994). *Indian country: A history of native people in America.* North American Press.

Hebbeler, K., Wagner, M., Spiker, D., Scarborough, A., Simeonsson, R., & Collier, M. (2001). *A first look at the characteristics of children and families entering early intervention services.* SRI International.

Howard, L., & Rothbart, M. (1980). Social categorization and memory for in-group and outgroup behavior. *Journal of Personality and Social Psychology, 38,* 301–310.

Howard, T. C. (2008). Who really cares? The disenfranchisement of African American males in PreK–12 schools: A critical race theory perspective. *Teachers College Record, 110*(5), 954–985.

Jacobs, M. D. (2009). *White mother to a dark race: Settler colonialism, maternalism, and the removal of indigenous children in the American west and Australia, 1880–1940.* University of Nebraska Press.

Joe, J. R. (1994). Revaluing Native American concepts of development and education. In P. M. Greenfield & R. R. Cocking (Eds.), *Cross-cultural roots of minority child development* (pp. 107–113). Erlbaum.

Johnson, T. R. (2007). *Red power: The Native American civil rights movement.* Infobase Publishing.

Jonas, S. (1991). *The battle for Guatemala: Rebels, death squads, and U.S. power.* Westview.

Katz, D. (1960). The functional approach to the study of attitudes. *Public Opinion Quarterly, 24,* 163–204.

King, J. E. (2004). Dysconscious racism. In D. Gillborn & G. Ladson-Billings (Eds.), *The Routledge Falmer reader in multicultural education* (pp. 71–83). Routledge Falmer.

Kingsolver, B. (1995). *High tide in Tucson.* HarperCollins.

Kozol, J. (1991). *Savage inequalities.* Crown.

Kozol, J. (2005). *The shame of the nation: The restoration of apartheid schooling in America.* Crown.

Kozol, J. (2012). *Fire in the ashes: Twenty-five years among the poorest children in America.* Broadway Books.

Ladson-Billings, G., & Tate, W., IV. (1995). Toward a critical race theory of education. *Teachers College Record, 97*(1), 4768.

Leary, J. D. (2005). *Post traumatic slave syndrome: America's legacy of enduring injury and healing.* Uptone Press.

Levine, L. (1996). *The opening of the American mind.* Beacon.

Lewis, J. E. (1996). *The West: The making of the American West.* Carroll & Graf.

Locust, C. (1988). Wounding the spirit: Discrimination and traditional American Indian belief systems. *Harvard Educational Review, 58*(3), 315–330.

Mabo v. Queensland (No. 2). (1992). *Australian Commonwealth Law Report No. 1.* Australia Government Publishers.

McCarty, T. L. (2009). The impact of high-stakes accountability policies on Native American learners: Evidence from research. *Teaching Education, 20*(1), 7–29.

McIntosh, P. (1988). White privilege and male privilege: A personal account of coming to see correspondences through work in women's studies. In M. L. Andersen & P. Hill-Collins (Eds.), *Race, class, and gender: An anthology* (pp. 70–81). Wellesley College Center for Research on Women.

McLaren, P. (1997). *Revolutionary multiculturalism: Pedagogies of dissent for the new millennium*. Westview Press.

McLuhan, T. C. (1971). *Touch the earth: A self-portrait of Indian existence*. Promontory Press.

Miller, R. J. (2011). American Indians, the doctrine of discovery, and manifest destiny. *Wyoming Law Review, 11*(2), 329.

Mitchell, T. L. (1839). *Three expeditions into the interior of eastern Australia* (Vol. II.). T & W Boone.

Nagda, B. R. A., & Gurin, P. (2007). Intergroup dialogue: A critical-dialogic approach to learning about difference, inequality, and social justice. *New Directions for Teaching and Learning, 2007* (111), 35–45.

Nieto, S. (2005). Social justice in hard times: Celebrating the vision of Dr. Martin Luther King, Jr. *Multicultural Perspectives, 7*(1), 3–7.

Noyce, P., Olsen, C., & Winter, J. (Producers), & Noyce, P. (Director). (2002). *Rabbit-proof fence* [Motion picture]. Miramax.

Patterson, K. B., & Runge, T. (2002). Smallpox and the Native American. *American Journal of the Medical Sciences, 323*(4), 216–222.

Pecora, P. J., Whittaker, J. K., Maluccio, A. N., & Barth, R. P. (2010). *The child welfare challenge: Policy, practice, and research* (3rd ed.). Transaction Publishers.

Pennington, J. L., Brock, C. H., & Ndura, E. (2012). Unraveling the threads of White teachers' conceptions of caring: Repositioning White privilege. *Urban Education, 47*(4), 747–775.

Peshkin, A. (2008). *Places of memory: Whiteman's schools and Native American communities*. Routledge.

Prucha, F. P. (1975). *Documents of United States Indian policy*. University of Nebraska Press.

Reed, P. (1982). The stolen generations: The removal of Aboriginal children in N.S.W., 1883–1969. New South Wales Ministry of Aboriginal Affairs.

Reyhner, J., & Eder, J. (1989). *A history of Indian education*. Native American Studies, Eastern Montana College.

Reyhner, J., & Singh, N. K. (2010). Cultural genocide in Australia, Canada, New Zealand, and the United States. *Indigenous Policy Journal, 21*(4), 1–26.

Reynolds, R. J. (2005). The education of indigenous Australian students: Same story, different hemisphere. *Multicultural Perspectives, 7*(2), 48–55.

Riley, J. C. (2010). Smallpox and American Indians revisited. *Journal of the History of Medicine and Allied Sciences, 65*(4), 445–477.

Robinson, M., Robinson-Zañartu, C., Honanie, E., Hunt, T., & Zamora, E. (2004, June). *Decolonizing issues in the education of Native American students*. Invited presentation to the 9th Annual Conference on Gifted/Talented and Exceptional Education for Native People, San Diego, California.

Robinson-Zañartu, C. (2003). *Native American scholars and collaborators*. U.S. Department of Education, Office of Special Education.

Rosaldo, R. (1993). *Culture and truth: The remaking of social analysis*. Beacon Press.

Rothbart, M., & John, O. P. (1993). Intergroup relations and stereotype change:

A social-cognitive analysis of some longitudinal findings. In P. M. Sniderman, P. E. Tetlock, & E. G. Carmines (Eds.), *Prejudice, politics, and the American dilemma* (pp. 32–59). Stanford University Press.

Rowley, C. D. (1970). *The destruction of Aboriginal society.* Penguin.

Rushdie, S. (1997, August 11). India at five-O. *Time*, pp. 40–42.

Saguy, T., Tausch, N., Dovidio, J. F., Pratto, F., & Singh, P. (2011). Tension and harmony in intergroup relations. In P. R. Shaver & M. Mikulincer (Eds.), *Understanding and reducing aggression, violence, and their consequences* (pp. 333–348). American Psychological Association.

Secada, W. G. (1991). Selected conceptual and methodological issues for studying the mathematics education of the disadvantaged. In M. S. Knapp & P. M. Shields (Eds.), *Better schooling for children of poverty: Alternatives to conventional wisdom* (pp. 61–84). McCutchan.

Short, D. (2008). *Reconciliation and colonial power: Indigenous rights in Australia.* Ashgate Publishing, Ltd.

Sidanius, J., & Pratto, F. (1993). The inevitability of oppression and the dynamics of social dominance. In P. M. Sniderman, P. E. Tetlock, & E. G. Carmines (Eds.), *Prejudice, politics, and the American dilemma* (pp. 173–211). Stanford University Press.

Sidanius, J., & Pratto, F. (2012). Social dominance theory. *Handbook of Theories of Social Psychology, 2,* 418–438.

Sleeter, C. E. (1996). *Multicultural education as social activism.* State University of New York Press.

Sniderman, P. M., Tetlock, P., & Carmines, E. G. (1993). *Prejudice, politics, and the American dilemma.* Stanford University Press.

Solidarity Foundation. (1996, Spring). Pulling the land out from under Brazil's Indigenous peoples. *Native Americans, 13*(1), 12–13.

Stevens, L. M. (2004). *The poor Indians: British missionaries, Native Americans, and colonial sensibility.* University of Pennsylvania Press.

Sue, D. W. (2006). The invisible Whiteness of being: Whiteness, White supremacy, White privilege, and racism. In C. Madonna & S. Derald Wing (Eds.), *Addressing racism: Facilitating cultural competence in mental health and educational settings* (pp. 15–30). John Wiley & Sons.

Tajfel, H. (1970). Experiments in intergroup discrimination. *Scientific American, 233*(5), 96–102.

Todorov, T. (1982). *The conquest of America: The question of the other.* HarperCollins.

Townsend, C. (Ed.). (2009). *American Indian history: A documentary reader.* Wiley-Blackwell.

Vogel, V. J. (1972). *This country was ours: A documentary history of the American Indian.* Harper & Row.

Ward, G. C. (1996). *The West: An illustrated history.* Little, Brown.

Weinberg, B. (1996, Summer). Land and sovereignty in Hawai'i: A native nation re-emerges. *Native Americans, 13*(2), 30–41.

Weinberg, M. (1991). *Racism in the United States: A comprehensive classified bibliography.* Greenwood.

West, C. (1993). The new cultural politics of difference. In C. McCarthy & W. Crichlow (Eds.), *Race, identity, and representation* (pp. 11–23). Routledge.

Williams, R. A. (1990). *The American Indian in western legal thought: The discourses of conquest.* Oxford University Press.

Wise, T. (2003, July 8). *White supremacy: No one is innocent.* Tolerance.org. Retrieved from www.tolerance.org/news/article_tol.jsp?id=800

Wittstock, L. W., & Salinas, E. J. (2010). *A brief history of the American Indian movement.* Retrieved from www.aimovement.org/ggc/history.html

Yates, A. (1987). Current status and future directions of research on the American Indian child. *American Journal of Psychiatry, 144,* 1135–1142.

Yazzie, R. (2000). Indigenous peoples and postcolonial colonialism. In M. Battiste (Ed.), *Reclaiming indigenous voice and vision* (pp. 39–49). UBC Press.

Zúñiga, X., Nagda, B. R. A., Chesler, M., & Cytron-Walker, A. (2007). *Intergroup Dialogue in Higher Education: Meaningful Learning about Social Justice.* John Wiley & Sons.

PART III

CULTURE, TEACHING, AND LEARNING

CHAPTER 5

Culture and Learning

Sonia Nieto

> [We] are not simply bearers of cultures, languages, and histories, with a duty to reproduce them. We are the products of linguistic-cultural circumstances, actors with a capacity to resynthesize what we have been socialized into and to solve new and emerging problems of existence. We are not duty-bound to conserve ancestral characteristics which are not structurally useful. We are both socially determined and creators of human futures.
>
> —Mary Kalantzis, Bill Cope, and Diana Slade, *Minority Languages*

The term *culture* can be problematic because it can mean different things to different people in different contexts. For instance, *culture* is sometimes used as if it pertained only to those with formal education and privileged social status, implying activities such as attending the opera once a month. Today, most people acknowledge that culture is not just what an elite group of people do in their spare time, yet various and conflicting ideas persist as to what culture actually means in everyday life. Among many Whites in the United States, for instance, culture is thought to be held exclusively by those different from them. As a consequence, it is not unusual to hear people, especially those of European background, lament that they do not "have" culture in the same way that African Americans, Asian Americans, Native Americans, or other groups visibly different from the dominant group "have" it. In other cases, culture is used interchangeably with ethnicity, as if both simply were passed down constant and eternal from one generation to the next. At still other times, culture can mean the traditions one celebrates within the family, in which case culture is reduced to foods, dances, and holidays. Less often is culture thought of as the values one holds dear, or the way one looks at and interacts with the world.

In this chapter, I explore the complex relationship between culture and learning. First, I define culture through a number of interrelated characteristics that make it clear that culture is more than artifacts, rituals, and traditions. In fact, it is becoming increasingly indisputable that culture and cultural differences, including language, play a discernible although complicated role in learning. I will consider how culture and language influence learning by looking at some of the cultural discontinuities between school and home expectations of students from various backgrounds.

DEFINING CULTURE

Elsewhere, I have defined culture as "the ever-changing values, traditions, social and political relationships, and worldview created, shared, and transformed by a group of people bound together by a combination of factors that can include a common history, geographic location, language, social class, and religion" (Nieto, 2000, p. 139). As is clear from this definition, culture is complex and intricate; it includes content or product (the *what* of culture), process (*how* it is created and transformed), and the agents of culture (*who* is responsible for creating and changing it). Culture cannot be reduced to holidays, foods, or dances, although these are, of course, elements of culture. This definition also makes it clear that everyone has a culture because all people participate in the world through social and political relationships informed by history as well as by race, ethnicity, language, social class, gender, sexual orientation, and other circumstances related to identity and experience.

At least two issues need to be kept in mind if culture is to have any meaning for educators who want to understand how it is related to learning. First, culture needs to be thought of in an unsentimental way. Otherwise, it is sometimes little more than a yearning for a past that never existed, or an idealized, sanitized version of what exists in reality. The result may be an unadulterated, essentialized "culture on a pedestal" that bears little resemblance to the messy and contradictory culture of real life. The problem of viewing some aspects of culture as indispensable attributes that must be shared by all people within a particular group springs from a romanticized and uncritical understanding of culture. For instance, I have heard the argument that poetry cannot be considered Puerto Rican unless it is written in Spanish. Thus, the Spanish language becomes a *constitutive characteristic* of being Puerto Rican. While there is no argument that speaking Spanish is an important and even major aspect of Puerto Rican culture, it is by no means a prerequisite for Puerto Ricanness. There are hundreds of thousands of Puerto Ricans who live in the United States and identify themselves first and foremost as Puerto Rican but who do not speak Spanish due to the historical conditions in which they have lived.

The second consideration to be kept in mind is that the sociopolitical context of culture needs to be acknowledged. That is, cultures do not exist in a vacuum but rather are situated in particular historical, social, political, and economic conditions, and therefore they are influenced by issues of power. The claim of Whites that they do not have a culture is a case in point.

Whites frequently do not experience their culture as a culture because as the officially sanctioned and high-status culture, it "just is." Therefore, when Whites say they do not "have" a culture, they in effect relegate culture to no more than quaint customs or colorful traditions. This stance is disingenuous at best because it fails to observe that Whites as a group participate disproportionately in a *culture of power* (Delpit, 1988) simply based on their race, although access to this power is not available to those who are not White (nor, it should be stressed, is it shared equally among Whites).

In what follows, I describe a set of attributes that are key to understanding how culture is implicated in learning, and how these notions of culture complicate a facile approach to multicultural education. These characteristics are complementary and interconnected to an extent that they are difficult to disentangle from one another. I do so here only for purposes of clarity, not to suggest that they exist in isolation. The characteristics I review here include culture as *dynamic; multifaceted; embedded in context; influenced by social, economic, and political factors; created and socially constructed; learned;* and *dialectical.*

Culture Is Dynamic

Culture does not exist outside of human beings. This means that cultures are not static relics, stagnant behaviors, or sterile values. Steven Arvizu's (1994) wonderful description of culture as a *verb* rather than a noun captures this essence of culture beautifully. That is, culture is dynamic, active, changing, always on the move. Even within their native contexts, cultures are always changing as a result of political, social, and other modifications in the immediate environment. When people with different backgrounds come in contact with one another, such change is to be expected even more.

But cultural change is not simply a one-way process. The popular conception of cultural change is that it is much like a transfusion: As one culture is emptied out of a person, a new one is poured in. In this conception, each culture is inert and permanent, and human beings do not influence the process to any significant degree. But the reality is that cultures are always hybrids, and that people select and reject particular elements of culture as suitable, or not, for particular contexts. Cultural values are not gotten rid of as easily as blood, nor are new ones simply infused. For instance, ample ethnographic evidence shows that in spite of the enormous political, social, and economic changes among American Indians in the past 100 years, their child-rearing practices, although they have, of course, changed, have also remained quite stable (Deyhle & Swisher, 1997). Likewise, among immigrants to the United States, ethnic values and identities appear to be preserved to some extent for many generations (Greenfield, 1994; McGoldrick, Pearce, & Giordano, 1982).

In some ways, we can think of culture as having both *surface* and *deep structure*, to borrow a concept from linguistics (Chomsky, 1965). For instance, in previous research (Nieto, 2000), when interviewing young people of diverse backgrounds I was initially surprised by the seeming homogeneity of the youth culture they manifested. That is, regardless of racial, ethnic, or linguistic background, or time in the United States—but usually intimately connected to a shared urban culture and social class—the youths often expressed strikingly similar tastes in music, food, clothes, and television viewing habits. Yet, when I probed more deeply, I also found evidence of deeply held values from their ethnic heritage. For example, Marisol, a young Puerto Rican woman I interviewed, loved hip hop and rap music, pizza, and lasagna. She never mentioned Puerto Rican food, and Puerto Rican music to her was just the "old-fashioned" and boring music her parents listened to. Nonetheless, in her everyday interactions with her parents and siblings, and in the answers she gave to my interview questions, she reflected deep aspects of Puerto Rican culture such as respect for elders, a profound kinship with and devotion to family, and a desire to uphold important traditions such as staying with family rather than going out with friends on important holidays. Just as there is no such thing as a "pure race," there is likewise no "pure culture." That is, cultures influence one another, and even minority cultures and those with less status have an impact on majority cultures, sometimes in dramatic ways. Rap music, with its accompanying style of talk, dress, and movement, is a notable example among young people of diverse backgrounds in urban areas.

In terms of schooling, the problem with thinking of culture as static is that curriculum and pedagogy are designed as if culture were unchanging indeed. This issue was well expressed by Frederick Erickson (1990), who argued that when culture is thought of as fixed, or simply as an aesthetic, the educational practice derived from it supports the status quo. This is because reality itself can then be perceived as inherently static. Erickson goes on to say, "When we think of culture and social identity in more fluid terms, however, we can find a foundation for educational practice that is transformative" (p. 22). The view of culture as dynamic rather than fixed is unquestionably more befitting a conception of multicultural education as liberating pedagogy based on social justice.

Culture Is Multifaceted

Closely related to the dynamic nature of culture is that cultural identifications are multiple, eclectic, mixed, and heterogeneous. This means, for one thing, that culture cannot be conflated with just ethnicity or race. As an example, Mexican or Mexican American culture may be familiar to us because it concerns an identity based primarily on ethnicity, the best-known site of culture. But one also can speak, for instance, of a lesbian culture because as a group lesbians share a history and identity along with particular social and political relationships. Thus, one can be culturally Mexican American and a lesbian at the same time. But having multiple cultural identities does not imply that each identity is claimed or manifested equally. A wealthy light-skinned Mexican American lesbian and a working-class Mexican American lesbian may have little in common other than their ethnic heritage and sexual orientation, and the oppression that comes along with these identities. People create their identities in different ways: While one Mexican American lesbian may identify herself first and foremost ethnically, another may identify herself as a lesbian, a third as both, and a fourth primarily as a member of the working class.

Because culture is not simply ethnicity, even within particular cultural groups identities are diverse and often conflicting. Skin color, time of arrival in the United States, language use, level of education, family dynamics, place of residence, and many other differences within groups may influence how one interprets or "lives" a culture. Further, the intersection of ethnicity and social class, or what Milton Gordon (1964) termed *ethclass*, is a key factor in defining culture. For instance, as a young girl I was surprised to meet middle-class Puerto Ricans when I spent a summer in Puerto Rico. Given my experiences up to that time as a member of an urban U.S. Puerto Rican family that could best be described as working poor, I had thought that only Whites could be middle class. Although I spoke Spanish fairly well and thought of myself as Puerto Rican, I discovered that in some ways I had more in common with my African American peers in my Brooklyn neighborhood and school than with the middle-class Puerto Ricans I met on the island. I began to see that my Puerto Rican culture was in fact quite different from Puerto Rican culture as defined on the island. Years later I understood that these differences involved location, experience, and social class.

Another important aspect of identity has to do with how interactions with people of other cultural groups may influence culture and identity. This is certainly the case in urban areas, where the identities of young people of many diverse ethnic and racial backgrounds defy easy categorization. Shirley Brice Heath (1995) has suggested that young urban dwellers in the United States are creating new cultural categories based on shared experiences because, according to her, these young people "think of themselves as a *who* and not a *what*" (p. 45). They engage not only in border crossings but also in what Heath called "crossings and crisscrossings" (p. 48). Given the growing presence of people in the United States who claim a biracial, multiracial, or multiethnic identity, ethnicity alone is unable to fully define culture. The multiple identities of youth have important and far-reaching implications for the development and implementation of multicultural education: It is evident that simplistic and bounded conceptions that focus just on specific racial or ethnic groupings fail to capture the realities of many urban youths who live with complicated and heterogeneous realities.

Culture Is Embedded in Context

To say that culture is embedded in context is to say that it invariably is influenced by the environment in which it exists. The culture of Japanese students in Japan is of necessity different from that of Japanese immigrant students in the United States or of Japanese immigrant students in Peru or Brazil. When culture is presented to students as if it were context-free, they learn to think of it as quite separate from the lives that people lead every day. It is what Frederick Erickson (1990) has described as the fragmenting of people's lives "as we freeze them outside time, outside a world of struggle in concrete history" (p. 34). Culture is commonly decontextualized. In the United States, decontextualization typically occurs in the school curriculum and in media images outside of school. A notable case is that of American Indians, who customarily have been removed from their cultural and historical rootedness through images that eternalize them as either noble heroes or uncivilized savages, and typically as a combination of the two (Churchill, 1992). On the other hand, the history of oppression, dehumanization, resistance, and struggle of the many Indigenous nations rarely is studied in schools. If any doubt remains regarding the image of American Indians held by most non-Indian children in the United States, ask even 6-year-olds and they will provide in precise detail the most stereotypical and ahistorical portrait of Indians, as Erickson (1990) noted, "outside time" (p. 34). If these children happen to live in a geographic region where there are no reservations or other large concentrations of Indians, they often are shocked to learn that Indians are still around today and that they are teachers, or truck drivers, or artists. Even when American Indians are included in the curriculum as existing in the present, the idyllic images of them tend to reinforce common stereotypes. For instance, while we may be happy to show students pictures of powwows, we are less likely to discuss how reservations have been used as toxic dumping sites.

   A further example of how culture is influenced by context will suffice. Puerto Ricans generally eat a great deal of rice in many different manifestations. Rice is a primary Puerto Rican staple. There is even a saying that demonstrates how common it is: "Puertorriqueños somos como el arroz blanco: Estamos por todas partes" (Puerto Ricans are like white rice: We are everywhere), an adage that says as much about rice as it does about the diaspora of the Puerto Rican people, over half of whom live outside the island. As a rule, Puerto Ricans eat short-grained rice, but I prefer long-grained rice, and other Puerto Ricans often made me feel practically like a cultural traitor when I admitted so. I remember my amazement when a fellow academic, a renowned Puerto Rican historian, explained the reason behind the preference for short-grained rice. This preference did not grow out of the blue, nor does any particular quality of the rice make it inherently better. On the contrary, the predilection for short-grained rice was influenced by the historical context of Puerto Ricans as a colonized people.

Apparently, near the beginning of the twentieth century when Puerto Rico was first taken over by the United States as spoils of the Spanish-American War, the United States had a surplus of short-grained rice. Since colonies were the common destination for unwanted or surplus goods from the metropolis, Puerto Rico became the dumping ground for short-grained rice, which in the United States had lower status than long-grained rice. Over time, a preference for short-grained rice thus became part of Puerto Rican culture. As is true of all cultural values, however, this particular preference was influenced by history, economics, and power, as we will see in what follows.

Culture Is Influenced by Social, Economic, and Political Factors

Intimately related to the fact that culture is bound to a particular context is that it is influenced significantly by political, historical, and economic conditions. Elements of culture exist not in isolation but through concrete relationships characterized by differential access to power. As a result, dominant social groups in a society often determine what counts as culture. This is why, for example, a dominant cultural group such as Whites in America can unabashedly designate itself as "the norm" and others as "culturally deprived" (Lewis, 1965; Reissman, 1962). Those designated as deprived may not see themselves this way, but naming by others can take on great power; over time, some of those called "culturally deprived" may come to believe it's true. Yet "culturally deprived" means simply that the group in question does not share all elements of the culture of the dominant group. Nor do they often share in the power of that group. A paradox is that while Whites see themselves as culturally neutral or "cultureless," at the same time they insist, through constant messages in the dominant ideology, that theirs is the valued and valuable culture. Everyone else is thus culturally deprived.

The theories of sociologist Pierre Bourdieu (1986) are significant here. According to Bourdieu, it is not simply money, or *economic capital*, that determines one's standing in the social structure; equally important are what he has termed *social capital* and *cultural capital*. Social capital is made up of social obligations and networks that are convertible into economic capital. Cultural capital, which is more immediately important to us here, can be defined as the acquired tastes, values, languages, and dialects, or the educational qualifications, that mark a person as belonging to a privileged social and cultural class. Just as in the case of learning one's native culture and language, cultural capital is acquired in the absence of any deliberate or explicit teaching; it is therefore unconsciously learned. The initial accumulation of cultural capital, in the words of Bourdieu (1986), is "the best hidden form of hereditary transmission of capital" (p. 246).

In essence, then, culture is deeply entangled with economic and political privilege. That is, the tastes, values, languages, and dialects that have the greatest status are associated with the dominant social class *not because these tastes, values, languages, or dialects are inherently better but because they have higher social prestige as determined by the group with the greatest power.* As a case in point, for many years linguists have proposed that Black English is a rich and creative variety of English, as logical and appropriate as standard English for purposes of communication (Labov, 1972; Smitherman, 1977). Yet the conventional wisdom still common among teachers is that Black English is simply "bad English." Thus, rather than building on students' native discourse—what has been termed *additive bilingualism* (Lambert, 1975)—most teachers simply attempt to eradicate Black English and replace it with Standard English, a *subtractive* form of bilingualism. On the other hand, when expressions from Black English make their way into Standard English because they are used by middle-class Whites, they immediately take on a higher social status and thus become acceptable.

The example of Black English underscores the impact that culture may have on learning and academic achievement. Most schools are organized to reflect and support the cultural capital of privileged social and cultural groups; in the United States, that group is middle- and upper-class English-speaking Whites. As a result of their identity and upbringing, some children arrive at the schoolhouse door with a built-in privilege because they have learned this cultural capital primarily in the same way as they have learned to walk, that is, unconsciously and effortlessly. Their culture—in this case, the variety of English they speak—seems both natural and correct. Yet, as suggested by Carol Lee and Diana Slaughter-Defoe (1995), because of the low prestige of Black English, "the influences of language on learning for African Americans are both complex and problematic" (p. 357).

This example also places in bold relief the arbitrary nature of cultural capital. Paulo Freire (Shor & Freire, 1987) captured the frivolous essence of such designations when he asked, "When did a certain form of grammar become 'correct'? Who named the language of the elite as 'correct,' as the standard?" He answered his own question by stating, "They did, of course. But, why not call it 'upper-class dominating English' instead of 'Standard English.' That authentic naming would reveal, instead of obscure, the politics of power and language in society" (p. 45). Further on, in discussing the same topic, he added, "This so-called 'standard' is a deeply *ideological* concept, but it is necessary to teach correct usage while also criticizing its political implications" (p. 71).

One could envision another, quite different, scenario. If, for instance, through some extraordinary turn of events, working-class African Americans were to become the esteemed social group in the United States, Black English would probably become the new standard. In turn, schools would ensure that the curriculum, texts, and other materials reflected this new form of cultural capital; in addition, only those teachers who were intimately familiar with Black English and who considered it an innately superior variety of English would be hired. Accordingly, the children of working-class African American homes would enter school with a built-in advantage over

other children, who would be considered "culturally deprived" because they
lacked the cultural capital of Black English. As far-fetched as this scenario
sounds given the current economic and political realities in the United States,
it serves as a graphic example of the capricious nature of determining whose
culture becomes highly valued.

Culture Is Created and Socially Constructed

As discussed earlier, culture is often thought of as a product-in-place, and
as something handed down that must be kept the way it is. Not only does
this result in a static view of culture, it also implies that culture is already
finished. As we have seen, culture is constantly evolving, and the reason it
evolves is because *human beings change it*. The action of people on culture
takes place in big ways and small, by everyday people and by those who
have power. When Jonathan Kozol (1978) went to Cuba to research the
successful massive literacy campaign that had just taken place, he spoke
with young people in schools, many of whom had been the teachers of the
peasants who learned to read. He was awed by the young people's responses
when he asked them what was meant by history. He recounted that when
he had asked that same question of students in Schenectady, New York, the
answers had been fairly uniform: "History is everything that happened in
the past and is now over. . . . History is what is done by serious and important people" (p. 176). In contrast, when he asked young people in Cuba the
same question, their answers were starkly different: "It is the past, but there
are things that we do now which will be part of history someday" (p. 176).
These young people saw that history was not just what was written in history books, or the actions of "important people" in conquest, war, or politics.
What they had done in the literacy campaign was also history.

In the same way, culture is what we do every day. Cultures change as a
result of the decisions that we, as cultural agents, make about our traditions,
attitudes, behaviors, and values. Were it not so, we would forever be mere
pawns or victims of the actions of others. Sometimes, of course, cultural values develop as a result of victimization. The earlier example of short-grained
rice is a case in point. But even here, people took what they were given and
made it a positive value. Without such valuing, short-grained rice would not
have become part of the culture. The cuisine of poor people throughout the
world is another illustration of how culture is created. Poor people often get
nothing but leftovers, the parts of animals or plants that nobody else wants.
What they have done with these remains has sometimes been nothing short
of extraordinary. This is cultural creation in action. Put another way, in
the words of Frederick Erickson (1997): "Culture can be thought of as a
construction—it constructs us and we construct it" (p. 39). Culture, then, is
not a passive legacy, but an active operation that takes place through contact and interactions with others. Culture is a social construction because it
cannot exist outside of social contact and collaboration.

Culture Is Learned

Closely related to the fact that culture is created and socially constructed is that it is *learned*. That is, culture is not handed down through our genes; nor is it inherited. This is very clear to see, for example, when children from a particular ethnic group (for instance, Korean) are adopted by families from another ethnic group (usually European American). Although the children may still be considered ethnically and racially Korean, they will in all likelihood be culturally European American, unless their parents make a conscious and determined effort to teach them the culture and history of their heritage while raising them, or the children themselves later decide to do so.

Culture, especially ethnic and religious culture, is learned through interactions with families and communities. It usually is not consciously taught, or consciously learned. That is why it seems so natural and effortless. Although this process does not hold true of all cultures—for example, deaf or gay culture—we predictably learn culture while sitting on our mothers' or grandmothers' laps, standing by our fathers, listening to the conversations of family members around us, and modeling our behavior on theirs. In fact, most people do not even think about their culture unless it is in a subordinate position to another culture or—if they belong to a majority culture—when they leave the confines of home and are no longer part of the cultural norm.

That culture is learned is also apparent in the very concept of *biculturalism*. Bilingual education, for instance, very often is called *bilingual/bicultural education* because it is based on the principle that one can learn two languages and two cultural systems in order to function and even to succeed in different linguistic and cultural contexts. This point was made in research by Gloria Ladson-Billings (1994). Of the eight teachers she identified as successful with African American youths, three were White, and of those, one had a White culture of reference, another a bicultural culture of reference, and the third an African American culture of reference. However, becoming bicultural is not as simple as discarding one set of clothes for another. Because culture is complex, "learning" a culture that is not one's native culture is an exceedingly difficult task, one accomplished only through direct, sustained, and profound involvement with it. Because most teachers in the United States have not been through this process, it can be difficult for them to understand how excruciating the process is for their students. Furthermore, it is difficult to become bicultural in an untroubled sense because it means internalizing two cultural systems whose inherent values may be diametrically opposed.

In the United States, it is generally only students from dominated cultures who need to become bicultural as a requirement for academic and societal success. That they do so is a testament to great strength and resiliency.

The fact that these students, in spite of being young, feeling isolated, and facing what can be terrifying situations in unfamiliar environments, nonetheless can incorporate the cultural motifs of disparate values and behaviors says a great deal about human tenacity. What they accomplish might best be thought of as critical biculturalism, a biculturalism that is neither facile nor uncomplicated, but full of inconsistencies and challenges.

Culture Is Dialectical

Culture often is thought of as a seamless web of interrelated and mutually supportive values and behaviors. Nothing could be further from the truth. Because they are complex systems created by people and influenced by social, economic, and political factors, cultures are also dialectical, conflicted, and full of inherent tensions. A culture is neither "good" nor "bad" in general, but rather embodies values that have grown out of historical and social conditions and necessities. As individuals, we may find elements of our own or others' cultures uplifting or repugnant. That culture is dialectical does not mean that we need to embrace all of its contradictory manifestations in order to be "authentic" members of the culture.

Young people whose cultures are disparaged by society sometimes feel they have to accept either one culture or the other wholly and uncritically. This was found to be the case, for instance, among Romani (Gypsy) youth in research carried out in Hungary (Forray & Hegedüs, 1989). Prevalent gender expectations of Romani boys and girls tend to be fairly fixed and stereotypical. Yet because the family is often the only place where culturally dominated young people can positively strengthen their self-image, Romani girls may correctly perceive that breaking free of even limited expectations of their future life options also results in giving up their ethnic identity and abandoning their families. Through questionnaires collected from elementary school teachers of Romani children, it became clear that teachers' negative attitudes and behaviors concerning the fixed gender roles in the Romani culture were at least partly responsible for strengthening the expected gender-based behavior among girls in school. Had teachers been able to develop a more culturally balanced and sensitive approach, it is conceivable that the Romani girls might have felt safe to explore other options without feeling they were cultural traitors.

That culture is dialectical also leads to an awareness that there is no special virtue in preserving particular elements of culture as if they existed outside of social, political, and historical spaces. Kalantzis, Cope, and Slade (1989) have described this contradiction eloquently:

> Preserving "communities" is not a good for its own sake, as if peoples should be preserved as museum pieces, so that they are not lost to posterity. "Communities" are always mixed, contradictory, conflict-ridden and by no means socially

isolated entities. Active cultural re-creation, if people so wish, might involve consciously dropping one language in preference for another or abandoning some cultural tradition or other—such as sexism. (p. 12)

The work of Puerto Rican sociologist Rafael Ramirez (1974) is particularly relevant here. Ramirez has suggested that we can think of every culture as a coin that has two contradictory faces or subsystems. He calls these the *culture of survival* and the *culture of liberation*, and each is important in defining the complexity of culture. The culture of survival embodies those attitudes, values, traditions, and behaviors developed in response to political, economic, or social forces, some of which may be interpreted as a threat to the survival of the culture in some way. They can either limit (e.g., the unequal treatment of women) or expand (e.g., mutual cooperation) people's perspectives within a particular culture. In the case of the role of women, values and behaviors of both males and females grew out of the necessity to view women, because of their unique biology, as primary caregivers. The need to survive is thus manifested in many cultures in perfectly understandable ways—though not always ethical or equitable—given the history of the species. According to Ramirez:

> The culture of survival is characterized mainly by the contradiction that it sustains, affirms, and provides certain power but, at the same time, does not confront or alter the oppressive elements and institutions nor affect the structure of political and economic power that controls the system. (p. 86)

In contrast, for Ramirez the culture of liberation consists of the values, attitudes, traditions, and behaviors that embody liberatory aspects of culture. This face of culture is part of the process of decolonization, and of questioning unjust structures and values, and it "comprises those elements that promote a new social order in which the democratization of the sociopolitical institutions, economic equality and cooperation and solidarity in interpersonal relations predominate" (p. 88). In this way, Ramirez says, authoritarianism is contrasted with democracy, racism with consciousness of racial and ethnic identity, and sexism with gender equality. Human rights that are generally accepted by most societies can be included in the framework of the culture of liberation. Understanding the contradictory nature of culture is important if students and teachers are to develop a critical, instead of a romantic, perspective of their own and other people's cultures.

LANGUAGE AS CULTURE

As we have seen, language is deeply implicated with culture and an important part of it. That is, the language, language variety, or dialect one speaks is culture made manifest, although it is not, of course, all there is to culture. This explains why, for instance, so many assimilationist movements both inside and outside of schools—from the forced removal of American Indian children to boarding schools beginning in the 19th century, to the recent English-Only Movement—have had native-language devaluation and elimination as major goals. In a very real sense, language is power, and this truth has been at the core of such movements. In the words of Richard Ruiz (1991), "A major dimension of the power of language is the power to define, to decide the nature of lived experience" (p. 218). Doing away with a language, or prohibiting its use, tears away at the soul of a people. Consequently, it is not surprising that language often has served as a powerful symbol and organizing tool for language-minority groups. For instance, using the example of four indigenous minority cultures (Navajo, Huala Pai, Maori, and Hawaiian), Carlos Ovando and Karen Gourd (1996) have shown how language maintenance and revitalization movements have been used by marginalized groups as major vehicles to attain power within society, to create a sense of peoplehood, and to challenge officially sanctioned structures and languages.

In the United States, attitudes about languages and language varieties other than the mainstream language have oscillated between grudging acceptance and outright hostility. These attitudes have been rationalized as necessary for political and social cohesion and for academic success (Crawford, 1992). Laws as well as school policies have reflected for the most part negative attitudes about native-language maintenance: Examples include the virtual disappearance of native-language instruction between the two world wars, recent court cases involving workers who dared to speak their native language among themselves, and even mothers who, in the privacy of their own homes, speak with their children in their own language, the language that reflects their nurture and love. This was the case of a young mother chastised by a judge for speaking Spanish to her child (cited in Cummins, 1996). Marta Laureano, who was involved in a child custody case in Texas, was admonished by Judge Samuel Kiser that she was relegating her daughter to a future as a housemaid if she continued speaking Spanish to her. He also charged that speaking Spanish to her was "bordering on abuse" and ordered her to speak only English at home (Cummins, 1996, p. 21).

If research were to prove that maintaining native-language use was a detriment to learning, there might be some reason to consider assimilation as a positive process. This has not proven to be the case, however. David Dolson's (1985) research on the home language use and academic performance of Latino students, for instance, found that those from *additive* bilingual home contexts—that is, homes where Spanish continued to be used even after children learned English—significantly outperformed their peers from *subtractive* homes—where the Spanish was replaced by English. Moreover, he discovered that more Spanish at home usually resulted in better

English skills as well, supporting the idea that Spanish language use in the home fosters improved academic performance. Lourdes Díaz Soto's (1993) research among 30 Hispanic families of young children with low and high academic achievement found that parents of the higher-achieving children inevitably favored a native-language environment to a greater extent than those of lower-achieving youngsters. Her findings, rather than suggesting the suppression or elimination of native language use at home and school— an attitude all too common in schools—support just the opposite.

Similar conclusions have been reached by researchers using the case of Black English or Black dialect. In one study, for example, dialect-speaking 4-year-olds enrolled in a Head Start program were able to recall more details with greater accuracy when they retold stories in their cultural dialect rather than in Standard English (Hall, Reder, & Cole, 1979). A more recent research study by Geneva Smitherman (1994) concerning the impact of Black English Vernacular (BEV) on the writing of African American students echoed this finding among older students. Using essays written by African American students for the National Assessment of Educational Progress (NAEP), Smitherman demonstrated that the use of African American discourse style correlated positively with higher scores.

There is even some evidence to support the hypothesis that speaking only English may act as a *barrier* to academic success for bicultural students. Research in five cities by David Adams and his colleagues (Adams et al., 1994), examining the predictive value of English proficiency, Spanish proficiency, and the use of each at home relative to the academic achievement of Latino students, found that recent immigrants who were *more* fluent in Spanish performed better than did second- or third-generation Latinos. They also found a small but negative influence of English-language proficiency on the academic performance of the Mexican American students in the sample; that is, better English proficiency meant lower academic performance among Mexican American youths. How to analyze this finding? The researchers conjectured that there might be what they called a "counterforce" against the traditional relationship between English proficiency and academic performance. They continued, "This counterforce may very well be the peer pressure students experience which works against school achievement, in spite of the students' English-language proficiency" (Adams et al., 1994, pp. 11–12).

This research confirms that simply speaking English is no guarantee that academic success will follow. There appear to be several reasons for this. First, when children are able to keep up with their native language at home, they develop *metalinguistic awareness*, that is, a greater understanding of how language itself works, and of how to use language for further learning. Based on her extensive research concerning second language acquisition, Virginia Collier (1995) has suggested that practicing English at home among students who are more proficient in another language actually can slow down cognitive development because it is only when parents and their children speak the language they know best that they are working at their "level of cognitive maturity" (p. 14). Furthermore, given the negative attitudes we have seen among teachers about languages and language varieties other than standard English, and especially about languages they consider to have a low status, children who speak these languages may become further alienated from school and what it represents. In essence, students may disidentify with school. For example, the research by Adams and colleagues (1994) supports the hypothesis that the identification of second- and third-generation Americans with school and academic achievement is weak owing to the repeated and consistent school failure among some groups (Ogbu, 1987). Knowing English may not be sufficient to defy the weak identification with schooling.

LINKS AMONG CULTURE, LANGUAGE, AND LEARNING

Given the preceding discussion, it is indisputable that culture, language, and learning are connected. In what follows, some of the links will be made more explicit, beginning with a discussion of child-rearing practices.

Child-Rearing Practices and Learning

Child-rearing is above all a teaching and learning process, making the home the first context for learning. The earliest and most significant socialization of children takes place within their families and communities. Just as they learn to walk and talk, children also learn *how to learn* as defined within their particular cultural contexts. Children's interactions with parents or other caregivers thus pave the way for how they will fare in school. That is, where students' cultural values and behaviors "fit" with school policies and practices, learning can take place in a fairly straightforward manner; where they clash, learning may be experienced in a negative way.

Early research on child-rearing practices often focused on maladaptive responses to school and helped explain the relative lack of success of children from nonmainstream families. A more positive approach was proposed by Manuel Ramirez and Alfredo Castañeda (1974). While granting that families of different cultural groups employ different child-rearing practices and that these practices influence children's learning in school, Ramirez and Castañeda suggested that, rather than expect families to do all the changing, schools too needed to change by responding to the different ways of learning that children bring to school. The child-rearing styles of caregivers from diverse cultures, according to these researchers, resulted in different learning styles, or diverse ways of receiving and processing information. They concluded that the only appropriate response of schools in a pluralistic and democratic society was to develop learning environments that were, in their words, "culturally democratic," that is, environments that reflect the learning styles of all students within them. This perspective was radically different from the usual expectation that all children arrive at school with the same ways of learning. Given the notion that schools create and perpetuate inequality through policies and practices, including the pressure to assimilate, the perspective suggested by Ramirez and Castañeda makes a good deal of sense.

Ramirez and Castañeda were among the first researchers to suggest that all learning styles, not just the analytic style generally favored by majority-group students and practiced in most schools, are suitable for academic work. They built on the theories of Herman Witkin (1962) that people have either a *field independent* learning style (usually defined as preferring to learn in an analytic matter with materials devoid of social context) or a *field dependent* learning style (understood as favoring highly social and contextualized settings). Based on their research with children of various cultural backgrounds, they concluded that European American children tend to be field independent, and Mexican American, American Indian, and African American children tend to be field *sensitive*, the term they substituted for the more negatively charged *dependent*. They suggested that students need to be provided environments where they can learn according to their preferred style, while also becoming *bicognitive*, that is, comfortable and proficient in both styles.

The proposition that students from diverse backgrounds use various approaches to learning and that schools need to make accommodations for them represented a considerable advance in both the theory and practice of education. Nevertheless, much of the learning style research can be criticized on a number of grounds. First, there is no agreement on the number or range of learning styles that actually exist. Second, this research has inclined toward overdetermination, basing students' learning styles almost exclusively on their culture when in fact we know that learning is a much more complex matter. Third, some assessment and instructional strategies and adaptations developed as a result of the learning style research have been overly mechanical and technical, although they might never have been intended to be used as such. For instance, one of the few reviews that looked seriously at the outcomes of adapting instruction to the visual learning style presumably favored by American Indian children concluded that virtually no evidence supported the idea that such adaptations resulted in greater learning (Kleinfeld & Nelson, 1991).

An example of how this kind of research has been poorly used can be found in professional development workshops or education texts that provide lists of "attributes" of students of particular cultural backgrounds based on the learning styles they are reputed to have ("Vietnamese children are . . ." or "African American children learn best when . . ."). All too often, the effect of such categorizations is that the existing stereotypes of children from particular backgrounds become even more rigid. Moreover, categorizing students' learning styles based on race or ethnicity can veer dangerously close to the racist implications drawn from distinctions on IQ tests (Herrnstein & Murray, 1994; Jensen, 1969). For instance, Asa Hilliard (1989) voiced grave reservations about the use of the term "learning style" as an excuse for low expectations on the part of teachers, and on poor instruction based on these expectations. In this case, the remedy can be worse than the illness itself.

In spite of the theoretical and implementation problems with learning style research, Donna Deyhle and Karen Swisher (1997) suggest that ethnographic studies can prove to be insightful in providing evidence concerning the significance of child-rearing values on learning styles. In these studies, students' learning styles are gleaned from many hours of observation and analysis. Deyhle and Swisher believe that becoming aware of students' preferred ways of learning can be useful, although it is by no means sufficient to guarantee that appropriate environments are created for student learning. Their reasonable conclusion is: "Knowledge of group tendencies presents a framework through which to observe and understand individual behaviors" (p. 151). Cross-cultural psychologists have developed a more conceptually sophisticated explanation for how families of diverse cultural backgrounds influence learning and the cognitive development of their children through their child-rearing practices and interactions, and based on the kind of ecological system in which they live (Greenfield, 1994).

Although research in learning styles has brought the issue of culture and its possible impact on learning to the forefront, the field is fraught with conflict due to criticisms such as those mentioned above, among others. One way to ameliorate what can be the overly deterministic tone of this research is to speak of *learning preferences* instead of *styles*. In this case, the implication is that numerous factors influence how people learn, and that in fact all individuals differ in some ways from one another in how they learn. In any event, learning styles or preferences by themselves, although providing an important piece of the puzzle for understanding student learning, do not adequately explain the vastly different outcomes of student achievement. Others have suggested a shift in focus from *learning style* to *cultural style* or *teaching style* (Hilliard, 1989; Ladson-Billings, 1992).

Cultural, Linguistic, and Communication Discontinuities Between Home and School

The discontinuities experienced by students whose cultures and/or languages differ substantially from the mainstream, and how these might interfere with learning, are questions that have gained enormous significance in the past 2 decades, especially by educators using an anthropological perspective.

One such theory, the *communication process explanation* (Erickson, 1993), is based on the fact that although students may be socialized to learn in particular ways at home, these cultural and communication patterns may be missing in the school setting. The research undergirding this argument has generally been ethnographic in nature, and based on months, and sometimes years, of extensive fieldwork and analysis.

Two significant early studies were groundbreaking in the field and serve as examples of this theory. Susan Philips's (1982) ethnographic research among American Indian schoolchildren on the Warm Springs Reservation in Oregon concluded that the core values with which the children were raised—including harmony, internal locus of control, shared authority, voluntary participation, and cooperation—often were violated in the school setting. For instance, she found that the children did poorly in classroom contexts that demanded individualized performance and emphasized competition. However, they became motivated learners when the context did not require them to perform in public and when cooperation was valued over competition, as in student-directed group projects. Given the assessment practices of most schools, these students were at a disadvantage because their learning was not always demonstrated in the kinds of behaviors expected of them, such as individual performance and recitation.

Philips's insights were a powerful challenge to previous deficit-based conclusions that American Indian children were "slow," "inarticulate," or "culturally deprived," and that they were therefore incapable of learning. Her research provided an alternative, culturally based explanation for the apparent discontinuities between home and school. In a similar vein, Shirley Brice Heath's (1983) research in a working-class African American community she called "Trackton" is a compelling example of cultural and communication discontinuities. In her research, she discovered that the questioning rituals in which parents and other adults in the community engaged with children were not preparing them adequately for the kinds of activities they would face in schools. Further, when Heath observed White middle-class teachers in their own homes, she found that their questions, both to their own children and to their students, differed a great deal from the kinds of questions that the parents of children in Trackton asked. Teachers' questions invariably pulled attributes such as size, shape, or color out of context and asked children to name them. Hugh Mehan (1991) has called these questions "mini-lessons" that prepare children from middle-class homes for the kinds of questions they will hear in school.

On the other hand, the parents of the children from Trackton asked them questions about whole events or objects, and about their uses, causes, and effects. Parents often asked their children questions that were linguistically complex and that required analogical comparisons and complex metaphors rather than "correct" answers out of context. The result of these differences was a lack of communication among teachers and students in the school. Students who at home were talkative and expressive would become silent and unresponsive in school because of the nature of the questions that teachers asked; this behavior led teachers to conclude that the children were slow to learn or deficient in language skills. It was only through their fieldwork as ethnographers of their own classrooms that the teachers became aware of the differences in questioning rituals and of the kinds of questions that their students' families and other adults in the community asked. Teachers were then able to change some of their questioning procedures to take advantage of the skills that the children already had, building on these skills to then ask more traditional "school" questions. The results were striking, as students became responsive and enthusiastic learners, a dramatic departure from their previous behavior.

A. Wade Boykin (1994) also has reviewed the implications of cultural discontinuities for African American students. According to Boykin, Black students in the United States generally practice a cultural style that he calls *Afrocultural expression*. This style emphasizes spirituality, harmony, movement, verve, communalism, oral tradition, and expressive individualism, elements either missing, downplayed, or disparaged in most mainstream classrooms. As a result, there are often incompatibilities between Black students' cultural styles and the learning environment in most schools, and Black students may end up losing out. The problem is not that their styles are incompatible with learning, but rather that these styles are not valued in most classrooms as legitimate conduits for learning.

These examples provide evidence that home cultures and native languages sometimes get in the way of student learning not because of the nature of the home cultures or native languages themselves, but rather because they do not conform to the way that schools define learning. On the other hand, this cultural mismatch is not inevitable: Much research in the past 2 decades has concluded that culture and language can work in a mutual and collaborative manner to promote learning rather than obstruct it. Teachers and schools, not only students, need to accommodate to cultural and linguistic differences. According to Margaret Gibson (1991), schooling itself may contribute unintentionally to the educational problems of bicultural students by pressuring them to assimilate against their wishes. Maintaining their language and culture is a far healthier response on the part of young people than adopting an oppositional identity that may effectively limit the possibility of academic achievement.

Other research has confirmed the benefits of maintaining a cultural identification. For instance, in her research among Navajo students, Donna Deyhle (1992) found that those who came from the most traditional Navajo homes, spoke their native language, and participated in traditional religious and social activities were among the most academically successful students in school. Similar findings have been reported for students of other cultural groups. A study of Cambodian refugee children by the Metropolitan Indochinese Children and Adolescent Service found that the more they adapted their behavior to fit in with mainstream U.S. culture, the more their emotional adjustment suffered (National Coalition, 1988). Another study of Southeast Asian students found a significant connection between grades and culture; that is, higher grade point averages correlated with the maintenance of traditional values, ethnic pride, and close social and cultural ties with members of the same ethnic group (Rumbaut & Imo, 1987). Likewise, based on her extensive research with adolescent students of color of diverse ethnic backgrounds, Jean Phinney (1993) determined that adolescents who have explored their ethnicity and are clear about its importance in their lives are more likely to be better adjusted than those who have not.

Responses to Cultural Discontinuities

Because many children from diverse cultural backgrounds experience school failure, we need to address how cultural discontinuities between students' homes and their schools affect learning. Many attempts have been made to adapt learning environments to more closely match the native cultures of students. Responding to cultural discontinuities takes many forms and can mean anything from developing specific instructional strategies to providing environments that are totally culturally responsive.

Culturally responsive education, an approach based on using students' cultures as an important source of their education, can go a long way in improving the education of students whose cultures and backgrounds have been maligned or omitted in schools. This approach offers crucial insights for understanding the lack of achievement of students from culturally subordinated groups. One of the best known of these is KEEP (the Kamehameha Elementary Education Program) in Hawaii (Au, 1980). KEEP was established because cultural discontinuities in instruction were identified as a major problem in the poor academic achievement of Native Hawaiian children. Educational modifications in KEEP included changing from a purely phonics approach to one emphasizing comprehension, from individual work desks to work centers with heterogeneous groups, and from high praise to more culturally appropriate practices, including indirect and group praise. The KEEP culturally compatible K–3 language arts approach has met with great success in student learning and achievement. Similar positive conclusions have been reached when the cultures of students of diverse backgrounds have been used as a bridge to the dominant culture (Abi-Nader, 1993; Hollins, King, & Hayman, 1994; Irvine, 1997; Ladson-Billings, 1994).

In spite of the promising approaches highlighted by this research, a number of serious problems remain. For one, culturally responsive pedagogy sometimes is based on a static view of culture that may even verge on the stereotypical. Students of particular backgrounds may be thought of as walking embodiments of specific cultural values and behaviors, with no individual personalities and perspectives of their own. An unavoidable result is that entire cultures are identified by a rigid set of characteristics.

High Context   Low Context

Culturally congruent approaches, applied uncritically and mechanistically, fall into the same trap as monocultural education; that is, they may be based on an essentialist notion of culture that assumes that all students from the same cultural background learn in the same way. If this is the case, pedagogy and curriculum become, in the words of Erickson (1990), "cosmetically relevant" rather than "genuinely transformative" (p. 23).

A result of essentialist notions is that the diversity of individual students' experiences and identities may be overlooked, and their culture may be used to homogenize all students of the same group. This happens, for instance, when teachers make comments such as, "Korean children prefer to work on their own," as such statements deny the individual idiosyncrasies, preferences, and outlooks of particular students and their families. All cultures operate in synergy, creating new and different forms that borrow from and lend substance to one another. In other words, the multifaceted, contested, and complex nature of culture sometimes is not taken into consideration in culturally responsive pedagogy. Because cultures never exist in a pristine state, untouched by their context, any approach to meaningful and effective pedagogy needs to take into account how students' languages, cultures, and other differences exist within, and are influenced by, mainstream U.S. culture as well as by other subcultures with which they come into contact.

A culturally responsive stance sometimes considers those of nonmajority backgrounds to exist in complete contrast to the majority population, but this is rarely true. I recall, for example, the reaction of a young African American student after he visited an American Indian community in the Northeast: "They have VCRs!" he exclaimed in surprise tinged with disappointment. This young man attended a progressive alternative school with a multicultural curriculum with which I was associated many years ago. The school was a wonderful place in many ways, and the curriculum emphasized positive and liberatory aspects of the histories and cultures of people of color. Nevertheless, we were not immune from falling victim to developing our own static, albeit more positive, romanticized vision of what people of diverse cultures were like. In this case, in preparing students for the trip, we somehow had managed to remove all vestiges of materialistic contemporary life from Indigenous people, and the result was that the children developed an unrealistic and partial view of an entire group of people.

These caveats concerning cultural discontinuities also were explored in research with a Mexicano community by Olga Vasquez, Lucinda Pease-Alvarez, and Sheila Shannon (1994). In a number of case studies of children from this community, they found that a great deal of *convergence* existed between the children's home and school language interaction patterns. Although these researchers did not question that cultural discontinuities exist, they rejected the suggestion that home–school discontinuity can predict the success or failure of an entire cultural group. Instead, based on research in which they saw firsthand the students' multiple linguistic and cultural skills, they urged educators to consider "the complexity of their students' experiences in a multilayered network of cultures and reference groups" (p. 187).

Finally, a focus on cultural discontinuities alone may hide the structural inequalities with which so many students, especially those who live in poverty, contend on a daily basis. It is therefore necessary to look beyond cultural responsiveness alone to help explain student academic success.

CONCLUSION: IMPLICATIONS

What are the implications for teachers and schools concerning the links among language, culture, and learning? I would suggest that at least three issues need to be emphasized.

1. *Students' identification with, and maintenance of, their native culture and language can have a positive influence on learning.* The judgment that cultural identification and maintenance are important for academic achievement is not new, but it bears repeating because it is still far from accepted in most schools and classrooms. Research in the past 2 decades consistently has found that students who are allowed and encouraged to identify with their native languages and cultures in their schools and communities can improve their learning. This finding is also a direct and aggressive challenge to the assimilationist perspective that learning can take place only after one has left behind the language and culture of one's birth. Research in this area has made it clear that students' cultures are important to them and their families. However, maintaining them is also problematic because the identities of bicultural students may be disparaged or dismissed by schools.

2. *The role of the teacher as cultural accommodator and mediator is fundamental in promoting student learning.* In much of the research reviewed, it has become apparent that teachers have a great deal to do with whether and how students learn. Consequently, teachers' role as cultural mediators in their students' learning becomes even more urgent. In many cases, teachers need to teach children how to "do school" in order to be academically successful. This kind of mediation may not be necessary for the children of middle-class and culturally mainstream families, but very often it is required for students whose families do not have the high-status cultural capital required for academic success. Teachers need to support this kind of learning while at the same time affirming the cultures and languages that children bring to school as viable and valuable resources for learning.

3. *A focus on cultural differences in isolation from the broader school and societal context will likely not lead to increased learning or empowerment.* Personal

and institutional accommodations to student differences need to be in place in order for students to become successful learners. Obviously, these accommodations require drastic shifts in teachers' beliefs and attitudes, and in schools' policies and practices: Instead of simply tinkering with a few cultural additions to the curriculum or adopting a new teaching strategy, a wholesale transformation of schools is in order if we are serious about affording all students an equal chance to learn.

REFERENCES

Abi-Nader, J. (1993). Meeting the needs of multicultural classrooms: Family values and the motivation of minority students. In M. J. O'Hair & S. J. Odell (Eds.), *Diversity in teaching: Teacher education yearbook 1* (pp. 212–236). Harcourt Brace Jovanovich.

Adams, D., Astone, B., Nuñez-Wormack, E., & Smodlaka, I. (1994). Predicting the academic achievement of Puerto Rican and Mexican-American ninth-grade students. *The Urban Review, 26*(1), 1–14.

Arvizu, S. F. (1994). Building bridges for the future: Anthropological contributions to diversity and classroom practice. In R. A. DeVillar, C. J. Faltis, & J. P. Cummins (Eds.), *Cultural diversity in schools: From rhetoric to reality* (pp. 75–97). State University of New York Press.

Au, K. (1980). Participation structures in a reading lesson with Hawaiian children. *Anthropology and Education Quarterly, 11*(2), 91–115.

Bourdieu, P. (1986). The forms of capital. In J. G. Richardson (Ed.), *Handbook of theory and research for the sociology of education* (pp. 241–248). Greenwood Press.

Boykin, A. W. (1994). Afrocultural expression and its implications for schooling. In E. R. Hollins, J. E. King, & W. C. Hayman (Eds.), *Teaching diverse populations: Formulating a knowledge base* (pp. 225–273). State University of New York Press.

Chomsky, N. (1965). *Aspects of the theory of syntax.* MIT Press.

Churchill, W. (1992). *Fantasies of the master race: Literature, cinema and the colonization of American Indians* (M. A. Jaimes, Ed.). Common Courage Press.

Collier, V. E. (1995). *Promoting academic success for ESL students: Understanding second language acquisition at school.* New Jersey Teachers of English to Speakers of Other Languages-Bilingual Educators, Elizabeth, NJ.

Crawford, J. (1992). *Hold your tongue: Bilingualism and the politics of "English only."* Addison-Wesley.

Cummins, J. (1996). *Negotiating identities: Education for empowerment in a diverse society.* California Association for Bilingual Education.

Delpit, L. D. (1988). The silenced dialogue: Power and pedagogy in educating other people's children. *Harvard Educational Review, 58,* 280–298.

Deyhle, D. (1992). Constructing failure and maintaining cultural identity: Navajo and Ute school leavers. *Journal of American Indian Education, 31,* 24–47.

Deyhle, D., & Swisher, K. (1997). Research in American Indian and Alaska Native education: From assimilation to self-determination. In M. W. Apple (Ed.),

Review of research in education (vol. 22, pp. 113–194). American Educational Research Association.

Dolson, D. P. (1985). The effects of Spanish home language use on the scholastic performance of Hispanic pupils. *Journal of Multilingual and Multicultural Education, 6*(2), 135–155.

Erickson, F. (1990). Culture, politics, and educational practice. *Educational Foundations, 4*(2), 21–45.

Erickson, F. (1993). Transformation and school success: The politics and culture of educational achievement. In E. Jacob & C. Jordan (Eds.), *Minority education: Anthropological perspectives* (pp. 27–51). Ablex.

Erickson, F. (1997). Culture in society and in educational practices. In J. A. Banks & C. A. M. Banks (Eds.), *Multicultural education: Issues and perspectives* (3rd ed.; pp. 32–60). Allyn & Bacon.

Forray, K. R., & Hegedüs, A. T. (1989). Differences in the upbringing and behavior of Romani boys and girls, as seen by teachers. *Journal of Multilingual and Multicultural Development, 10*(6), 515–528.

Gibson, M. A. (1991). Minorities and schooling: Some implications. In M. A. Gibson & J. U. Ogbu (Eds.), *Minority status and schooling: A comparative study of immigrant and involuntary minorities* (pp. 357–381). Garland.

Gordon, M. (1964). *Assimilation in American life: The role of race, religion, and national origins.* Oxford University Press.

Greenfield, P. M. (1994). Independence and interdependence as developmental scripts: Implications for theory, research, and practice. In P. M. Greenfield & R. R. Cocking (Eds.), *Cross-cultural roots of minority child development* (pp. 1–37). Erlbaum.

Hall, W. S., Reder, S., & Cole, M. (1979). Story recall in young Black and white children: Effects of racial group membership, race of experimenter, and dialect. In A. W. Boykin, A. J. Franklin, & Y. F. Yates (Eds.), *Research directions of Black psychologists* (pp. 253–265). Russell Sage Foundation.

Heath, S. B. (1983). *Ways with words.* Cambridge University Press.

Heath, S. B. (1995). Race, ethnicity, and the defiance of categories. In W. D. Hawley & A. W. Jackson (Eds.), *Toward a common destiny: Improving race and ethnic relations in America* (pp. 39–70). Jossey-Bass.

Herrnstein, R. J., & Murray, C. (1994). *The bell curve: Intelligence and class structure in American life.* Free Press.

Hilliard, A. (1989). Teachers and cultural style in a pluralistic society. *NEA Today, 7*(6), 65–69.

Hollins, E. R., King, J. E., & Hayman, W. C. (1994). *Teaching diverse populations: Formulating a knowledge base.* State University of New York Press.

Irvine, J. J. (1997). (Ed.). *Critical knowledge for diverse teachers and learners.* American Association of Colleges for Teacher Education.

Jensen, A. R. (1969). How much can we boost I.Q. and scholastic achievement? *Harvard Educational Review, 39*(2), 1–123.

Kalantzis, M., Cope, B., & Slade, D. (1989). *Minority languages.* Falmer Press.

Kleinfeld, J., & Nelson, E. (1991). Adapting instruction to Native Americans' learning styles: An iconoclastic view. *Journal of Cross-Cultural Psychology, 22,* 273–282.

Kozol, J. (1978). *Children of the revolution: A Yankee teacher in the Cuban schools.* Delacorte Press.

Labov, W. (1972). *Language in the inner city: Studies in the Black English vernacular.* University of Pennsylvania Press.

Ladson-Billings, G. (1992). Culturally relevant teaching: The key to making multicultural education work. In C. A. Grant (Ed.), *Research and multicultural education: From the margins to the mainstream* (pp. 106–121). Falmer Press.

Ladson-Billings, G. (1994). *The dreamkeepers: Successful teachers of African American children.* Jossey-Bass.

Lambert, W. F. (1975). Culture and language as factors in learning and education. In A. Wolfgang (Ed.), *Education of immigrant students* (pp. 55–83). Ontario Institute for Studies in Education.

Lee, C. D., & Slaughter-Defoe, D. T. (1995). Historical and sociocultural influences on African American education. In J. A. Banks & C. A. M. Banks (Eds.), *Handbook of research on multicultural education* (pp. 348–371). Macmillan.

Lewis, G. (1965). *La vida: A Puerto Rican family in the culture of poverty—San Juan and New York.* Random House.

McGoldrick, M., Pearce, J. K., & Giordano, J. (Eds.). (1982). *Ethnicity and family therapy.* Guilford Press.

Mehan, H. (1991). *Sociological foundations supporting the study of cultural literacy* (Research Report No. 1). University of California, National Center for Research on Cultural Diversity and Second Language Learning, Santa Cruz.

National Coalition of Advocates for Students. (1988). *New voices: Immigrant students in U.S. public schools.* National Coalition of Advocates for Students.

Nieto, S. (2000). *Affirming diversity: The sociopolitical context of multicultural education* (3rd ed.). Longman.

Ogbu, J. U. (1987). Variability in minority school performance: A problem in search of an explanation. *Anthropology and Education Quarterly, 18*(4), 313–334.

Ovando, C. J., & Gourd, K. (1996). Knowledge construction, language maintenance, revitalization, and empowerment. In J. A. Banks (Ed.), *Multicultural education, transformative knowledge, and action: Historical and contemporary perspectives* (pp. 297–322). Teachers College Press.

Philips, S. U. (1982). *The invisible culture: Communication in classroom and community on the Warm Springs Indian Reservation.* Longman.

Phinney, J. S. (1993). A three-stage model of ethnic identity development in adolescence. In M. E. Bernal & G. P. Knight (Eds.), *Ethnic identity: Formation and transmission among Hispanics and other minorities* (pp. 61–79). State University of New York Press.

Ramirez, M., & Castañeda, A. (1974). *Cultural democracy, bicognitive development, and education.* Academic Press.

Ramirez, R. (1974). Culture of liberation and the liberation of culture. In Centro de Estudios Puertorriqueños, *Taller de cultura: Cuaderno 6, Conferencia de historiografía* (pp. 81–99). City University of New York, Puerto Rican Studies Research Center.

Reissman, F. (1962). *The culturally deprived child.* Harper & Row.

Ruiz, R. (1991). The empowerment of language-minority students. In C. E. Sleeter

(Ed.), *Empowerment through multicultural education* (pp. 217–227). State University of New York Press.

Rumbaut, R. G., & Imo, K. (1987). *The adaptation of Southeast Asian refugee youth: A comparative study*. Office of Refugee Resettlement, San Diego, CA.

Shor, I., & Freire, P. (1987). *A pedagogy for liberation: Dialogues on transforming education*. Bergin & Garvey.

Smitherman, G. (1977). *Talkin and testifyin: The language of Black America*. Houghton Mifflin.

Smitherman, G. (1994). The blacker the berry, the sweeter the juice: African American student writers. In A. H. Dyson & C. Genishi (Eds.), *The need for story: Cultural diversity in classroom and community* (pp. 80–101). National Council of Teachers of English.

Soto, L. D. (1993). Native language school success. *Bilingual Research Journal, 17*(1–2), 83–97.

Vasquez, O. A., Pease-Alvarez, L., & Shannon, S. M. (1994). *Pushing boundaries: Language and culture in a Mexicano community*. Cambridge University Press.

Witkin, H. A. (1962). *Psychological differentiation*. Wiley.

CHAPTER 6

Culturally Responsive Pedagogy

Tyrone C. Howard

This chapter will examine culturally responsive pedagogy, which has gained increased attention over the past decade as a way to rethink instructional practice in an effort to improve the educational performance of African American, Latinx, Native American, and various Asian American students (Gay, 2000). The merger of culture and pedagogy is a more complex and intricate set of processes than many practitioners and researchers have suggested. While it may improve student learning, researchers continue to evaluate its effectiveness for helping culturally diverse students improve academically. The marriage of culture and pedagogy is built upon a comprehensive and informed set of knowledge and skills that many practitioners often lack in their attempts to engage diverse students in the teaching and learning process.

Culturally responsive pedagogy is more than just a way of teaching or a simple set of practices embedded in curriculum lessons and units. It seeks to move away from the "methods fetish" (Bartolome, 1994) that has become far too commonplace in teacher education as being the most useful way to teach certain types of students—especially low-income and students of color. Practitioners who seek to reduce culturally responsive teaching to a simple act or who ask, as one preservice teacher once asked me in a class, "Can you just show me how to do it?" fail to recognize the intricacies of the concept. Culturally responsive pedagogy embodies a professional, political, cultural, ethical, and ideological disposition that supersedes mundane teaching acts; it is centered in fundamental beliefs about teaching, learning, students, their families, and their communities, and an unyielding commitment to see student success become less rhetoric and more of a reality. Culturally responsive pedagogy is situated in a framework that recognizes the rich and varied cultural wealth, knowledge, and skills that students from diverse groups bring to schools, and seeks to develop dynamic teaching practices, multicultural content, multiple means of assessment, and a philosophical view of teaching that is dedicated to nurturing student academic, social, emotional, cultural, psychological, and physiological well-being.

Culturally responsive teaching is a response to the ongoing achievement disparities between African American and Latinx students, and their White and certain Asian American counterparts. A plethora of school reform initiatives, research agendas, and school intervention programs have been designed to eradicate chronic differences in the educational outcomes of students (Ferguson, 2000). A host of explanations have been offered to explain the differences in academic performance and outcomes among underachieving groups. One of the more troubling explanations for disparate educational outcomes that culturally responsive teaching attempts to disrupt is deficit-based explanations of low-income students and students of color. These explanations usually are centered on low-income students and students of color lacking or being devoid of culture, coming from a culture of poverty that is not suited for academic success, possessing an oppositional culture, having a disdain for academic achievement, or having parents who lack concern for their children's academic aspirations (McWhorter, 2000; Ogbu, 1987; Steele, 1990; Valencia, 1997). These deficit-based explanations also have derided students' language as being deficient because of its variation from Standard English (Alim & Baugh, 2007). Some scholars have maintained that academic achievement outcomes are caused by innate differences in intelligence between racial groups (Herrnstein & Murray, 1994), a belief not as prevalent as it was half a century ago, but still present. Ryan (1971) asserted that accounts of deficit thinking are essentially *victim blaming*, or a way of shifting deep-seated structural inequities to individual, family, and community deficits. Deficit theorists have advocated changing student knowledge, language, culture, and behavior to be more consistent with mainstream ways of being (Olson, 1997; Pearl, 1970; Valenzuela, 1999). These efforts typically have been met with student resistance, disengagement, and ultimately educational disenfranchisement for millions of low-income and culturally diverse students (Kohl, 1995; Solórzano & Delgado Bernal, 2001).

A number of scholars respond to cultural deficit theory by stating that students from diverse backgrounds are not deficient in their ways of being, but are different (Ford, 1996; Irvine, 2003; Lee, 2007). These scholars describe different ways of thinking about students, their families, and communities, and offer different ways of thinking about closing the achievement gap. Table 6.1 briefly describes how deficit and difference theorists view fundamental aspects of diverse students and their families.

In response to the deficit explanations offered for the chronic academic underachievement of culturally diverse and low-income students, some scholars have asserted that the performance discrepancies are a result of cultural discontinuity that exists between culturally diverse students and their teachers. Cultural discontinuity has generated increased attention to culturally responsive pedagogy. A growing number of scholars have posited that teacher beliefs and practices should recognize and respect the intricacies and complexities of culture, and the differences that come with it, and

Table 6.1. Deficit and difference viewpoints

Cultural Deficit Theory	Cultural Difference Theory
Culture is nonexistent or abnormal	Culture is rich, unique, and complex
Language is a deficit	Language is an asset
Home environment is pathological	Home environment has capital
Genetics matter	Environment matters
Solution: Transform the Child	*Solution: Transform the School*

that pedagogical practices and ideological stances should be structured in ways that are culturally recognizable and socially meaningful (Foster, 1989, 1993; Howard, 2001b, 2003; Lee, 2007; Nasir, 2000). A significant increase in professional works concerned with culturally responsive teaching occurred between 1999 and 2009. Culturally responsive pedagogy assumes that if teachers are able to make connections between the cultural knowledge, beliefs, and practices that students bring from home and the content and pedagogy that they use in their classrooms, the academic performance and overall schooling experiences of learners from culturally diverse groups will improve (Gay, 2000; Hollie, 2001; Howard, 2001a; Irvine, 1990; Ladson-Billings, 1995; Lee, 1995, 1998; Lipman, 1995; Lynn, 2006; Parsons, 2005; Pierce, 2005; Sheets, 1995; Tate, 1995; Wortham, 2002).

SEEKING CLARITY IN CULTURE AND PEDAGOGY

A perusal of the works concerned with culturally responsive pedagogy reveals that it continues to grow as both scholars and practitioners recognize the potential of rethinking pedagogy in a way that belies traditional approaches to content, instruction, and assessment. A multitude of terms have been used in the professional literature to describe culturally responsive teaching, including *culturally embedded, culturally relevant, culturally congruent, culturally mediated, culturally sensitive,* and *culturally synchronized teaching.* Because there are at least 3 decades of theoretical and empirical work on culturally responsive teaching, it is important to determine what we know about the concept and where gaps exist in the knowledge base. It is also crucial to assess whether sufficient evidence indicates that culturally responsive teaching contributes to students' performance in schools. We must also examine where we have observed success, because this knowledge will help to inform future research, theory, and practice, as well as areas that may need to be reexamined and reconceptualized. Gay (2000) asserts that culturally responsive teaching is a "very different pedagogical paradigm" (p. 24). An examination of research and theory on culturally responsive pedagogy reveals that it is based on five key principles.

- The eradication of deficits-based ideologies of culturally diverse students
- The disruption of the idea that Eurocentric or middle-class forms of discourse, knowledge, language, culture, and historical interpretations are normative
- A critical consciousness and sociopolitical awareness that reflects an ongoing commitment to challenge injustice and disrupt inequities and oppression of any group of people
- An authentic and culturally informed notion of *care* for students, wherein their academic, social, emotional, psychological, and cultural well-being is adhered to
- A recognition of the complexity of culture, in which educators allow students to use their personal culture to enhance their quest for educational excellence

These principles are informed by the growing body of research that examines the utility and complexity of culturally responsive pedagogy and serves as a critical blueprint upon which all students can be educated, particularly in multicultural schools.

Varying questions and objections have been raised about the appropriateness of culturally responsive pedagogy. Some scholars have suggested that cultural instantiations are lacking in depth and rigor, while others have claimed that the emphasis on culture denies students access to core academic skills such as reading, writing, and math, which are purported to be culturally neutral (Hirsch, 1987; Ravitch, 2003). Another commonly cited critique is that culturally responsive pedagogy seems appropriate only for students of color. Irvine and Armento (2001) respond to this critique by stating that culturally responsive teaching is not a novel or transformative approach to teaching. In fact, they maintain that culturally responsive teaching has been a staple in U.S. schools for centuries, but that it has been most responsive to only one group of students—U.S.-born, middle-class, English-speaking White students.

Irvine and Armento (2001) assert that curriculum, instruction, and assessment that are responsive primarily to one group (middle-class White students) is one of the fundamental reasons why, historically, middle-class White students have performed better than all other student groups. The epistemological origin of school knowledge is heavily steeped in a Eurocentric worldview and ideology that largely omit the experiences, histories, contributions, and cultures of people of color, the poor, and women. Banks's (1996) typology of the types of knowledge is as an important exemplar of how different types of knowledge inform school content. Juxtaposing Banks's typology within a K–12 school framework cogently highlights the way in which academic and school knowledge most frequently taught in U.S. public schools can conflict with the cultural knowledge that students bring from home and can contribute to cultural confusion, disconnects, and misunderstandings that frequently occur in classrooms across the United States. Culturally responsive pedagogy seeks to offer the same types of educational opportunities, personal enhancements, school structures, and experiences in schools that have been in place for dominant groups since the establishment of U.S. public schools. Gay (2000) reaffirms this contention by suggesting that "the fundamental aim of culturally responsive pedagogy is to empower ethnically diverse students through academic success, cultural affiliation, and personal efficacy" (p. 111). Django Paris (2012) coined the term *culturally sustaining pedagogy* as an approach to extend the work of other scholars:

> Relevance and responsiveness do not guarantee in stance or meaning that one goal of an educational program is to maintain heritage ways and to value cultural and linguistic sharing across difference, to sustain and support bi- and multilingualism and bi- and multiculturalism. They do not explicitly enough support the linguistic and cultural dexterity and plurality. (p. 95)

Paris contends that educators must remain intensely mindful of the complexities of language, literacy, culture, and identities in the process of teaching and learning. To that end, he has suggested that culturally sustaining pedagogy is a more enduring approach:

> More than responsive of or relevant to the cultural experiences and practices of young people—it requires that they support young people in sustaining the cultural and linguistic competence of their communities while simultaneously offering access to dominant cultural competence. Culturally sustaining pedagogy, then, has as its explicit goal supporting multilingualism and multiculturalism in practice and perspective for students and teachers. That is, culturally sustaining pedagogy seeks to perpetuate and foster—to sustain—linguistic, literate, and cultural pluralism as part of the democratic project of schooling. (p. 95)

Another exemplary work on the marriage between culture, teaching, and learning has been Zaretta Hammond's (2014) work on culturally responsive teaching and the brain. Hammond offers an important and desperately needed neuroscience-based teaching framework that goes beyond surface changes to really build cognitive capacity in students from diverse backgrounds. Her contention is that cultural stereotyping is quite dangerous and that educators who seek to create cultural connections can do more damage than assistance in this process. To that end, she offers a framework that offers practitioners a way to see how structuring pedagogy in a manner that taps into students' cultural archetypes can create more viable pathways for learning. Moreover, her framework connects cognition, culture, teaching, and learning in a manner that speaks to the assets that diverse students bring to the classroom that are often unseen or misunderstood by teachers not familiar with the depth, breadth, and complexity of cultural norms, knowledge, and variation.

EMPIRICAL AND CONCEPTUAL
WORK ON CULTURALLY RESPONSIVE PEDAGOGY

Culturally responsive pedagogy is becoming more comprehensive and more concrete as it shifts from conceptual theory to grounded practice. Gay (2000) suggests that culturally responsive pedagogy recognizes the uniqueness of student culture by using "the cultural knowledge, prior experiences, frames of reference, and performance styles of ethnically diverse students to make learning more relevant to and effective for them. It teaches *to and through* the strengths of these students. It is culturally *validating and affirming*" (p. 29, emphasis in original). Ladson-Billings (1994) describes the concept, which she calls culturally relevant, as one that "empowers students intellectually, socially, emotionally, and politically by using cultural referents to impart knowledge, skills, and attitudes" (p. 18).

Ladson-Billings (1994) explained how teachers influence students' literacy development through the incorporation of culturally recognizable content. Her work also stresses how teachers' conception of self, ethic of care, and clear and deliberate instructional focus are important components of developing culturally relevant teaching practices. Culturally responsive teaching has been criticized because few studies examine the concept in mathematics. A number of studies have attempted to address this void. For example, Tate (1995) examined culturally relevant teaching in mathematics and discovered teachers who used community issues as a framework for improving math proficiency. Other scholars have examined culturally relevant approaches to mathematics (Gutstein, Lipman, Hernandez, & de los Reyes, 1997; Nasir & Cobb, 2006; Nelson-Barber & Estrin, 1995). Nasir's (2000) research investigated the construction of identity, culture, and learning. In her work, she found the relationship between identity and schooling to be an integral one in the area of mathematics proficiency for African American adolescents. Building on the students' knowledge of dominoes, Nasir's qualitative and quantitative findings revealed that, in dominoes, mathematical goals were reached in the context of activity when math concepts became a normalized and mandatory part of a particular activity.

Civil and Khan (2001) studied teachers who used students' home experiences in planting gardens to develop important math concepts. Ensign (2003) documented how one teacher used students' experiences within their local stores and price comparisons as a conduit to build better comprehension of math concepts. Martin (2000) examined mathematical proficiency of African American students and suggests that the history and context of the African American experiences are crucial for improved mathematical

proficiency and reasoning; he recommends that educators develop an awareness of the socioeconomic issues that influence African American students'
educational experiences.

E. C. Parsons (2005) studied how teachers disrupt cultural hegemony
in school curriculum and discourse. She examined how a teacher used the
approach of affirming students' best qualities and challenged dominant discourses that silenced African American students and privileged White students as a form of culturally sensitive teaching. Powell (1997) investigated
how White teachers teach in diverse school settings and discovered that the
teachers used biographies to examine their own backgrounds and as a result
developed a critical consciousness that helped them develop a more inclusive and affirming form of pedagogy that increased student engagement.
Powell's work builds on one of the key tenets in Ladson-Billings's (1995)
framework that identifies teachers' conception of self as an integral element
of culturally responsive teaching.

Beauboeuf-Lafontant (1999) investigated teachers' construction of
self-concept by studying six African American teachers and discovered that
the teachers' "psychological worldviews" had a significant influence on the
way in which their culturally relevant teaching approaches were carried out.
She also asserted that teachers who used culturally embedded approaches
were explicitly aware of the political nature of their work. She suggested
that *politically relevant teaching* might be a more appropriate term for this
approach to teaching than culturally relevant teaching, because teachers in
her study were acutely aware of the political context in which their work
was situated. By problematizing the salience of gender in his study, Lynn
(2006) looked at culturally relevant teaching by analyzing the role of African American male teachers and discovered that they placed an important
premium on students' lived experiences. Lynn also noted that the teachers
adopted an activist orientation in their teaching that examined critical issues
in the local context, which engaged students.

Each of these studies highlighted the multifaceted way in which culturally responsive teaching is implemented. Much like Ladson-Billings's (1995)
seminal work, the studies stressed teachers' conception of self; this means
self-examination is instrumental in recognizing the importance of racial and
ethnic identity for students. There is an explicit commitment to improving student academic performance. Teachers view their roles as pedagogues
who teach in a way that helps students improve in core academic areas such
as reading, language arts, mathematics, and writing.

In addition to enhancing academic performance, culturally responsive
pedagogy seeks to develop a critical consciousness and commitment to social justice, wherein students understand the social, historical, and political
issues within an historical and contemporary context and seek to identify
and address inequities that exclude marginalized groups. Another contribution of these studies of culturally responsive pedagogy is the much-needed
attention they have placed on key subject areas such as English language

arts, mathematics, and social studies. Teachers use the students' cultural knowledge (through family, community, personal, and home experiences) as starting points to engage them in academic content. Several of these studies identify White teachers who use culturally responsive teaching with students of color. One of the frequent comments I hear from White teachers is that these approaches can be used only by teachers of color because "they understand" students' culture in ways that White teachers do not. I am quick to challenge and refute such assertions by stating that one of the essential elements of culturally responsive teaching is getting to know and understand students, their cultures, their families, and their communities. A teacher's ability to know and understand students is not restricted by her or his race; it is tied to a willingness of educators to know and understand the complexities of race and culture, develop a healthy sense of their own racial identity and privilege, develop a skill set of instructional practices that tap into cultural knowledge, reject deficit views of students of color, and possess an authentic sense of students' ability to be academically successful.

Another significant element these studies reveal is the importance of care. Gay (2000) elaborates on the importance of care to culturally responsive teaching:

> Caring is one of the major pillars of culturally responsive pedagogy for ethni-
> cally diverse students. It is manifested in the form of teacher attitudes, expecta-
> tions, and behaviors about students' human value, intellectual capability, and
> performance responsibilities. . . . This is expressed for their psychoemotional
> well-being and academic success; personal, morality, and social actions, ob-
> ligations and celebrations; community and individuality; and unique cultural
> connections and universal human bonds. (pp. 45–46)

These studies acknowledge the political nature of teaching. Reflecting on Freire's (1970) notion of reading the *word* and the *world*, these studies highlight teachers who view their work as not just a job but as a specialized craft, a unique calling, a moral endeavor embedded in a cultural context that seeks to defy conventional thinking about culturally diverse and low-income students. These teachers are informed by a genuine desire to empower students, and see themselves as transformative agents in that process.

While the knowledge base of culturally responsive teaching has grown, in order for the area to continue to advance in depth and breadth, additional studies are needed that will continue to inform both researchers and practitioners. Culturally responsive teaching can be strengthened if research answers these questions:

1. What means of assessment are best suited to measure the effectiveness of culturally responsive teaching?

2. What are the best methods to prepare teachers to develop culturally responsive teaching approaches?

3. How do practitioners develop culturally appropriate methods of teaching in classroom settings where there are students from various cultures?

4. How can culturally responsive teaching methods disrupt essentializing accounts of students' cultures?

5. How can researchers document the wide variations of culturally mediated teaching when tacit knowledge of student culture is possessed by teachers?

One of the challenges in moving culturally responsive teaching forward is to continue to disrupt the static notions of culture that dominate educational discourse. The challenge of static notions of culture is tied to the idea that practitioners must be able to move beyond cultural fairs, ethnic celebrations, and multicultural feasts in order to diversify their curricula. For further explanations on how to move beyond these superficial accounts of students' culture, see J. A. Banks's (1989) work on the five levels of multicultural content.

THE IMPORTANCE OF PEDAGOGY

After developing a clear and complex understanding of culture, teachers must develop a conception of what Shulman (1987) refers to as pedagogical content knowledge. Shulman states that pedagogical content knowledge is a form of practical knowledge used by teachers to guide their actions in classroom settings. Shulman bases the concept of pedagogical knowledge on three key areas: (1) knowledge of how to structure and represent academic content for direct teaching to students; (2) knowledge of the common conceptions, misconceptions, and difficulties that students encounter in the learning process; and (3) knowledge of specific teaching skills that can be used to address students' learning needs in the learning context. Constructing pedagogy in meaningful ways is important in culturally responsive teaching. An in-depth understanding of each of Shulman's principles is fundamental, especially when situated within a culturally specific manner. The mere understanding of culture cannot translate into effective teaching strategies. Far too often I have seen practitioners who possess a solid grasp of students' backgrounds, families, and cultural practices fall short in assisting students to become optimal learners because they do not know how to teach concepts or to structure instructional practices, and have an overall lack of pedagogical knowledge.

Some researchers and theorists have called for effective teaching that recognizes the complexities of teaching and the need for teachers to develop breadth and depth of pedagogy, content, and students' backgrounds in order to enhance learning. Dalton (2008) sets forth five pedagogical standards that she maintains are essential for transformative teaching:

1. Teacher and students producing together through joint activity
2. Developing language and literacy competence across the curriculum
3. Connecting school to students' lives by linking teaching and curriculum to students' experiences at home and in their communities
4. Teaching complex thinking
5. Teaching through conversation, in particular engaging students in instructional conversation

Teachers must have a firm grasp of how students learn and the types of pedagogical knowledge and skills that can be used to tap into students' prior knowledge in ways that will pique their interest in learning, increase their levels of engagement, and encourage them to feel a part of the learning process. Hess (2009) describes effective ways to facilitate discussion, including incorporation of multiple perspectives around a particular topic or issue. Knowledge is not viewed as a static entity not open to multiple interpretations. The multiple vantage point perspective is stimulated by instructional approaches that encourage students to think critically about information, analyze various sources of information, contemplate opposing viewpoints, gather additional information, and make informed decisions. Culturally responsive teaching values different viewpoints about topics and encourages students to offer insights and perspectives that may not be those of the majority but are nonetheless equally respected by teachers and students. Culturally responsive teaching asks students to question, deconstruct, and then reconstruct knowledge. Culturally responsive teaching is also a mutual exchange of knowledge and information, wherein educators are learning from students, and vice versa. Ladson-Billings (1995) states that for culturally relevant teachers, knowledge is not static but is viewed critically from multiple vantage points. Knowledge should be viewed as a mechanism for developing a critical consciousness in students, wherein they acquire information that allows them to critique social inequities locally, nationally, and globally (Banks, 2009). The development of critical consciousness is a domain where subject areas such as history, sociology, language arts, English literature, biology, and business can be taught in transformative ways that seek to incorporate culturally responsive teaching approaches that encourage students to go beyond surface-level comprehension of course content. Social studies and language arts content in particular allow teachers to use concepts, issues, themes, literature, and events (historical and contemporary) as contexts to help students think democratically and develop decisionmaking and social action skills (Banks, 1990).

An additional component I would add to the importance of pedagogy is relationship building. Evidence is growing on the importance of relationship building between teachers and students as a way to enhance learning (Howard, McCall, & Howard, 2020; Milner, 2018). The work on relationship building operates from a framework of teachers who take time to know students personally outside of school. Through learning about their interests, dreams, hopes, and aspirations, teachers can build trust, rapport, and connections with students that can lead to better school experiences and outcomes. To that end, it is important to note that relationship building can occur across racial, cultural, and linguistic categories. Hence, it is important for teachers who come from White, middle-class backgrounds to know that the ability to connect with racially and culturally diverse backgrounds is not necessarily from being members of those groups, but from cultivating relationships that can build personal connections between teachers and students. Among the recommendations that teachers might consider to build relationships are the following:

- Talk to students.
- Develop assignments that allow students to share relevant experiences.
- Attend an extracurricular activity of a student.
- Greet students daily and know their names.
- Share stories about yourself.
- Create one-on-one meetings with students.
- Connect to caregivers.
- Ask questions.

Note that relationship building of any type takes time. Educators must be aware that relationship connections with students is not an overnight process; it can take time and lots of effort to connect to students. For a much more detailed account of the benefits of relationship building and strategies that educators can use to connect to students see Howard et al. (2020).

PROGRAMS WITH CULTURALLY RESPONSIVE TEACHING

While considerable attention has been placed on the conceptual understanding of culturally responsive pedagogy, a number of school districts have implemented action plans, mission statements, and teacher training designed to translate theoretical principles of culturally responsive teaching into classroom practice and school culture. One example of this implementation is in the Los Angeles Unified School District. In 2001, concerned about the persistent failure of its African American student population, the district developed a program called the African American Learners Initiative (AALI), a resolution committed to improving the academic performance of African American students. One of the essential components

of the AALI is the Academic English Mastery Program (AEMP, 2008).
According to its website:

> AEMP is a comprehensive, research-based program designed to
> promote equity in access to the District's core language, literacy,
> and mathematics curriculums for Standard English Learners (SEL's).
> AEMP's program's mission is to eliminate disparities in educational
> outcomes for African American and other underachieving students.
> Working in alignment with the District's instructional initiatives
> the Program advances the acquisition of school language, literacy,
> and learning in SEL through culturally and linguistically responsive
> pedagogy, and forwards the Superintendents priority to close the
> achievement gap.

AEMP's framework classifies SELs as students for whom Standard English is not native and whose home language differs in structure and form
from standard academic English. These students often are classified as "English only" because their home language generally incorporates English vocabulary but embodies phonology, grammar, and sentence structure rules
borrowed from indigenous languages other than English. The AEMP mission expands on the idea of distinguishing English language learners (ELLs)
from Standard English learners by stating that the former are students for
whom English is not native and the latter are students for whom Standard
English is not native.

The AEMP assumes that both ELLs and SELs are considered linguistically diverse, but SELs generally can understand Standard English when
it is spoken, whereas ELLs may have language comprehension difficulties.
Languages spoken by SELs may include African American language (sometimes referred to as African American English), Mexican American language
(also referred to as Chicano English), Hawaiian American language (also referred to as Hawaiian Pidgin English), and Native American language (NL)
(sometimes referred to as American Indian English or Red English). Both
ELLs and SELs need to acquire knowledge of the rules of Standard academic
English in its oral and written forms in order to be successful in U.S. schools.
In their work with schools, AEMP teachers stress that language acquisition
is a highly complex, structured, and dynamic process that students engage
in varying ways. Even for students whose only language is English, there
is a need to recognize the richness in linguistic diversity, yet provide them
with assistance to master the acquisition of Standard English without having to sacrifice the unique nuances, structures, and patterns of their use of
English, which is a fundamental attribute of culturally relevant teaching.
AEMP's work has been most effective when teachers have fully embraced
the rich linguistic differences and cultural knowledge students bring from
home. Teachers from AEMP classrooms have reported significant improvement in students' reading proficiency, Standard English acquisition, literary

interpretations, and vocabulary. Consequently, these teachers reported decreases in behavior problems and student absences, and increases in overall self-efficacy, engagement, and problem-solving skills.

Teaching in Action

Part of the work I have been involved in over the past several years has examined teacher practice with students from culturally diverse groups. One of the aims of this work has been to investigate how teachers may use students' cultural knowledge in ways that increase student engagement, improve learning, and enhance students' levels of comprehension of academic content. This work has been done across elementary and secondary schools in Los Angeles County. The makeup of these classrooms was predominantly African American and Latinx, and each of the schools was located in a low-income neighborhood and classified as a Title I school, meaning they had high numbers of low-SES students, high numbers of students qualifying for free and reduced-price lunch, and a growing number of students who spoke English as their second language. To highlight culturally responsive pedagogy in action, I will discuss different episodes of teaching, learning, people, and programs that exemplify how the idea of culture and instruction can be used to foster student learning and critical thinking, and thereby improve educational outcomes.

In the city of Inglewood, California, the charter school Culture and Language Academy of Success (CLAS) places an explicit emphasis on African American culture to help students master academic success. CLAS focuses on incorporating African and African American cultural knowledge as part of the professional development of teachers to help them acquire a deeper understanding of how to structure pedagogical practices that can build on African American culture. A wide range of instructional practices defy traditional teacher–student interactions in this K–8 school. Teachers are rarely in their seats as they actively interact with students, providing a wide range of instructional strategies. Students are engaged in hands-on problem solving, and there is a palpable sense of energy and excitement about teaching and learning that is rarely seen or felt in most schools.

In Mrs. Johnston's 5th-grade classroom, the methods incorporated were directly tied to the ideas and principles associated with the Gifted and Talented Education Program (GATE). She never referred to her teaching as culturally responsive, but she made several references to the idea of "knowing what my students know, and understanding how they see the world," as the general premise that guided her work. As a former GATE teacher, she stated that classrooms in most schools assume two types of curriculum and instruction: the type received by students in GATE classes, and the type provided to the rest of the students. She found these distinctions most disturbing because the quality of teaching that students in non-GATE classes received was "downright appalling."

The use of gifted principles is critical in that it offers students important opportunities for learning that frequently are missing from schools where low-income students and students of color are present. VanTassel-Baska (1992) identifies five goals essential to gifted education and cognitive development, which all teachers should help students develop: (1) increasing high-level proficiency in all core subject areas; (2) becoming independent investigators; (3) appreciating the world of ideas; (4) enhancing higher-level thinking skills; and (5) encouraging the spirit of inquiry.

The belief that all students are capable learners is essential to culturally responsive teaching, and was clearly evident in Mrs. Johnston's classroom. One of the approaches that Mrs. Johnston used in her 5th-grade classroom from day 1 was to have students write often. The students wrote in their daily journals about their experiences on a multitude of topics, such as their likes, dislikes, fears, hopes, dreams, and aspirations. Mrs. Johnston stated that the purpose of these writing activities was to learn about students' lives outside of schools, to tap into their thinking, and to try to assess how they think. She also mentioned that she used this approach to engage the students in a process that allowed her to look into students' lives outside of school and "take a walk into their brains" so that she could make connections to what they knew and understood. Writing has been cited by a number of scholars as a way to engage underperforming urban youth in the learning process (Morrell & Duncan-Andrade, 2005). Culturally responsive instructional practices are implemented when teachers are able to take the personal and cultural knowledge that students bring from home and use it as a conduit to course content. Mrs. Johnston frequently would teach the writing process, introduce parts of speech, and teach key grammar and punctuation concepts using students' daily journal writing. She informed me that she was always careful not to compromise the integrity of the students' thoughts by having them change their topics or alter the essence of their content. However, she stated that she pushed her students to think about how they expressed their thoughts in writing and how they would capture a reader's attention, and she sought to make sure they developed a command of how to use Standard English in conveying their ideas.

Mrs. Johnston's approach to developing a rigorous writing program in her class offers a direct response to critics of culturally responsive teaching who have asserted that such approaches lack rigor, are devoid of depth, and essentially do not assist students to become proficient learners (D'Souza, 1995; Ravitch, 2003). Mrs. Johnston's emphasis on writing represented the ideal nexus of using cultural knowledge to promote higher-order thinking in order to engage students in rigorous reading and writing. Her approach was exemplified in her assigning students to develop persuasive speeches. The cultural relevance in this particular assignment was evident when she allowed students to identify topics they would write their speeches about. She stated that the topics should be areas that students were passionate about and really had strong conviction toward and would "fight for the right to believe." The following were topics or guided questions for persuasive speeches:

- Why gang members should be given harsher penalties
- Why city leaders should listen to students' ideas about improving the city
- The top three reasons kids join gangs and how we can stop it
- Why the neighborhood Boys and Girls Club should not have been closed
- Why drug dealers should not be given long prison sentences
- Why teachers should not give homework
- Why the government does not care about poor people

The majority of the topics that students selected had connections to issues they faced in their own experiences with their families, communities, or schools. Many of the topics dealt with what they believed to be inequities in laws and circumstances, such as one young man's topic centered on why new school-funding formulas should be established, or a young woman's topic that addressed the negative impact rap music has on young girls' self-esteem and educational performance. Requiring students to identify topics and conduct independent research using five different sources (newspaper, Internet, magazines, books, and personal conversation) challenged them to think deeply about their topics. Students also were required to identify consenting arguments to their speeches and to identify rebuttals. They had to be prepared to give a 3- to 4-minute speech on the topic, accompanied by a three-page written paper. Extra credit was offered to students for developing a plan of implementation that would consist of their taking steps to address the topic on which they had become an "expert."

Mrs. Johnston's assignment was in many ways similar to tasks that countless teachers across the country give to their students. However, the fundamental difference was the students' ability to select the topics of their choice to which they felt an emotional connection and to take what otherwise could be a mundane task and transform it into a more socially meaningful and culturally responsive task. One of the shortcomings of many traditional classroom activities is that students are expected to access only limited types of knowledge, usually dictated by teachers' experiences and preferences that are often at odds with students' backgrounds and interests. Or in some cases, the examples, concepts, and themes that students are required to use are directly from textbooks or school-sanctioned mainstream knowledge. Consequently, a key component for teachers to remain mindful of is students' ability to learn core academic proficiencies by tapping into different knowledge sources—particularly their own culturally and individually mediated knowledge. Equally important to culturally responsive teaching is the willingness of teachers to educate themselves on students' cultures, communities, and experiences.

A teacher's ability to connect with student knowledge is a concept that researchers have examined. Central to these works and integral to the concept of culturally relevant teaching is the use of what Moll and González (2004) refer to as students' *funds of knowledge*. They define the concept as "the knowledge base that underlies the productive and exchange activities of households" (p. 700). The funds of knowledge approach to teaching also entails using anthropological approaches to understand students' lives outside of school, most specifically students' roles within their families and their relationships with assets in their respective communities, and developing a more profound and holistic sense of how students interpret their world. Moll and González (2004) write:

> A major limitation of most classroom innovations is that they do not require (or motivate) teachers or students to go beyond the classroom walls to make instruction work. Consequently, sooner or later the classroom comes under the control of a restrictive status quo. Capitalizing on cultural resources for teaching allows both teachers and students to continuously challenge the status quo. (p. 711)

Challenging the status quo is a critical element of the way in which students can critique inequities by using their own worldviews. To highlight this point, one of the core ideas embedded in critical thinking, as laid out by researchers of gifted education, is that students are able to synthesize and evaluate information in one context and apply the same knowledge and skills in different contexts; this ability demonstrates higher levels of cognitive processing (Ford, 1996; VanTassel-Baska, 1992). Building on Moll and González's (2004) idea of challenging the status quo, a critical analysis of traditional or mainstream ways of knowing can be an important element of the way in which students can critique inequities by using their own worldviews. For many students of color, and from low-income backgrounds, challenging the status quo can entail evaluating harsh realities in their schools, neighborhoods, and communities, comparing these occurrences with the experiences and communities of more affluent students, and questioning the dominant script about why such inequities exist. One of the core ideas embedded in critical thinking as laid out by researchers on gifted education is that students are able to synthesize and evaluate information in one context and apply the same knowledge and skills in different contexts.

More Culturally Responsive Teaching in Action

In another classroom I observed at a Los Angeles school, Mrs. Givens, a 7th-grade math teacher, used community assets that students viewed or frequented in their respective communities to teach the concept of ratios and proportions structured within a culturally responsive framework. She asked students to pay particular attention to various businesses, buildings, parks, homes, and other structures that they observed on their daily treks to and from school. The students made note of a disproportionately high number of churches, liquor stores, abandoned buildings, and billboards in their communities. To further develop the concept of ratios and proportions, Mrs. Givens asked students to identify various buildings and billboards per square block and to develop an inventory. One student in Mrs. Givens's class documented seven stores that sold liquor on her three-block walk home. Another student described the 20 billboards he noticed on his seven-block walk home, and identified a 3:1 ratio of billboards to blocks. Most important in his assessment of billboards was what they advertised. To his dismay, 6 of the 20 billboards advertised liquor, five marketed cigarettes, and four promoted the purchase of lottery tickets. Mrs. Givens encouraged the student to make inferences about what such billboards mean in a low-income community. This project, with its origins in math concepts, contributed to the type of critical questioning that is an essential part of culturally relevant teaching.

The importance of teaching core academic concepts, while also helping students to develop a critical consciousness about issues, events, and occurrences in their own communities, is germane to culturally responsive teaching. The way in which Mrs. Givens was able to use assets or occurrences from a community standpoint was quite creative and appeared to engage students. They analyzed the number of homicides in Los Angeles from the current year to the previous year to determine the percentage increase. They tabulated demographic shifts among different ethnic groups to understand percentage, decimal, and fraction values. In her classroom, Mrs. Givens created exemplary models of rigorous, standards-based instruction, with explicit ties to community wealth, knowledge, and assets with which most of her students were familiar.

UCLA Sunnyside GEAR UP

To illustrate how the concept of culturally responsive teaching is a complex commitment and idea that can aid in improving the achievement of students at the high school level, and how it can help to reduce achievement gaps between African American and Latinx students and their White and Asian counterparts, I will describe my work with the UCLA Sunnyside GEAR UP (Gaining Early Awareness and Readiness for Undergraduate Program). For 2 years, I was fortunate enough to serve as the principal investigator of the GEAR UP program, a multiyear project at Sunnyside High School, located in Southern California. Working in conjunction with the UCLA Graduate School of Education and Information Studies, the program provided intensive academic support (e.g., in-class and after-school tutoring, study skills preparation, California High School Exit Exam preparation, and CAT 6 test preparation) for any student interested in support services for preparing for college entry. UCLA Sunnyside GEAR UP also coordinated school activities that informed parents, teachers, and students about college requirements, the college admissions process, and financial aid.

During the 2006–2007 school year, Sunnyside High School was made up of approximately 2,100 students, of whom 50% were Latinx, 48% African American, and 2% White, Pacific Islander, Filipino, or Asian. Sunnyside High School is a Title I school with a 24.6% English language learner population. Approximately 450 students participated regularly in GEAR UP activities (3–4 times a week), over a 3-year period. Approximately 85% of the students were African American. The program sought to challenge the idea that students from low-income, urban areas, where resources and access to information for academic success are frequently limited, can be high-achievers if they are given access to adequate resources, academic support, and committed and qualified personnel working toward the same goal.

The manner in which culturally responsive teaching was manifested at Sunnyside High School was not through specific teaching acts or the incorporation of culturally sensitive or inclusive learning materials. It was embedded in authentic and genuine care and concern for the students, coupled with an ongoing commitment to rigorous, high-quality, individualized and small-group tutoring and academic support for students. This care was manifested through the program's mission to increase the numbers of African American and Latinx students who would be competitively eligible for admission to the country's top universities. Care also was manifested through the hiring of a multiracial staff of more than 40 people who devoted countless hours to counseling, tutoring, and mentoring a plethora of students in a multitude of ways. Finally, culturally responsive tenets were manifested in the staff's refusal to allow historically low expectations, limited funding, and school bureaucracy to limit the types of opportunities that the students deserved, and the type of academic success that was possible as students pursued postsecondary options.

The work done by the GEAR UP staff also highlights the way in which one element of the achievement gap was ameliorated—improving the college-going rates of African American and Latinx students. Historically, Sunnyside High School was one of the more understaffed and underperforming schools in Los Angeles County. One indicator of this perennial underperformance was that less than 10% of its graduating seniors had gone on to 4-year universities prior to our work at the school. One of GEAR UP's major goals with Sunnyside High School was to implement a program that could begin to identify students during their freshman year who showed academic promise and prepare them for college by the time they graduated.

The GEAR UP office, housed in a trailer on the school's campus, became the unofficial source of information for college preparation, academic counseling, and tutoring. Critical to the development of this space was the importance of relationships built among the project's director, the program coordinator, the five full-time staff members, and the more than 40 tutors who worked with the students daily. GEAR UP staff conveyed an authentic sense of care by going out of their way to visit students' homes and meeting parents, siblings, and legal guardians; providing financial assistance for students; and conveying a steadfast message that anyone involved in the program was required to have an unyielding belief in students' academic potential. Care, rigor, and accountability became the hallmarks of the support that GEAR UP provided to Sunnyside High students.

Care was manifested through a deep-seated concern for students' academic, social, and emotional well-being. Rigor was apparent in the intense tutoring sessions that occurred every day between students and tutors in class and after school covering subjects such as AP chemistry, history, calculus, algebra, English, and Spanish. Accountability was prevalent in that students understood that if they were to benefit from the GEAR UP program, being in good academic and behavior standing in all of their courses was a prerequisite. GEAR UP staff engaged in regular dialogue with classroom teachers about students' performance. Specific recommendations frequently were offered by classroom teachers on ways to assist students in tutoring sessions. Students were required to review test preparation in tutoring sessions, to complete enrichment work with tutors, and to be accountable to tutors in addition to classroom teachers.

The initial findings from our research with students at Sunnyside High School revealed a significant improvement in academic performance during the 2005–2006 academic year, when the initial group of targeted students were in their junior year, as demonstrated by the Annual Performance Index (API) and shown in Figure 6.1. The AP Index score increased from 475 during the 2001–2002 school year (the year prior to GEAR UP arrival) to 578 during the 2005–2006 school year, an increase of 103 points.

A vital part of the success of the GEAR UP program at Sunnyside was the ongoing support of its administrative staff and the dedicated classroom teachers who played a critical role in our work. Sunnyside High School staff worked with GEAR UP staff in myriad ways to ensure student academic success. Allowing GEAR UP tutors to be in classrooms each day to support teachers was critical to improving student performance; offering space on campus for a continued presence was instrumental; and having a school leader who encouraged GEAR UP's work to help students surpass academic expectations was fundamental to the program's success. This university–school partnership revealed the way that an educational alliance with common goals, shared responsibilities, and ongoing lines of open communication can work toward improving student achievement.

Figure 6.1. Annual Performance Index Scores for Ing School

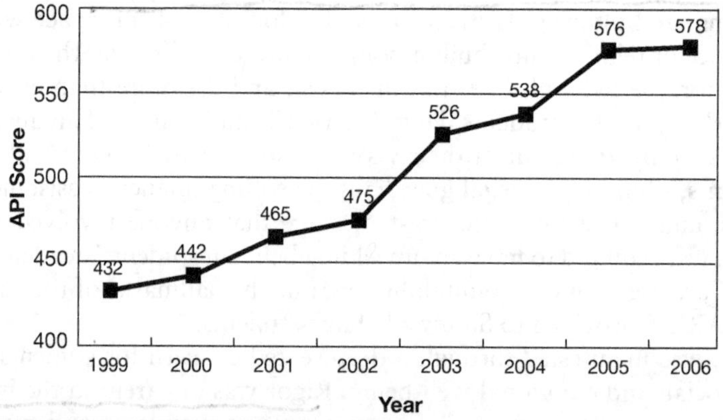

Source: California Department of Education, 2006.

As we examined our findings of the graduating class of 2007 (the group targeted as high school freshmen), the data showed that the students who were consistent participants in GEAR UP programs (meaning they attended tutoring and academic support 4–5 times a week) performed significantly better than students who did not participate in programs on a consistent basis. Our analysis identified 59 of the 385 students in the graduating class of 2007 to be consistent participants in GEAR UP programs. This group, identified as "core" students, had a mean GPA of 3.29 compared with their non–GEAR UP counterparts, who had a mean GPA of 2.51. Table 6.2 shows this breakdown across gender lines as well.

An examination of the student GPA by race and ethnicity also revealed marked improvement of students who participated in GEAR UP programs. Table 6.3 shows that the mean GPA for the core African American students at Sunnyside was close to 2.56, while the GEAR UP students' mean GPA was 3.26. Even more noteworthy is an examination of student performance across race and gender. African American males in particular showed noteworthy gains. This was meaningful given the dismal performance of Black males across the country and in Southern California, where in some districts the drop-out rate is reported to be close to 50% (Orfield, 2004).

In addition to the significant gains made by African American students in the GEAR UP program, equally impressive gains were made by Latinx students, who were frequent participants in the program as well. Table 6.4 shows the disaggregated data for Latinx student performance at Sunnyside High School during the 2006–2007 school year.

During the 2006–2007 school year, the number of students participating in advanced placement (AP) courses increased in algebra I and II, geometry, precalculus, calculus, chemistry, and physics. For example, the percentage of 10th-graders taking geometry increased from 23% during the

Table 6.2. 2006–2007 GPA breakdown

Class of 2007 Average GPAs	GEAR UP Class of 2007 Average GPAs	Difference
Graduating Class (n = 385): 2.51	2007 Core Cohort (59 students): 3.29	+ 0.78
Avg. Female GPA: 2.67	Avg. GEAR UP Female GPA (37 students): 3.26	+ 0.59
Avg. Male GPA: 2.31	Avg. GEAR UP Male GPA (22 students): 3.32	+ 1.01

Table 6.3. 2006–2007 Semester 2 GPA breakdown by ethnicity and gender: Black students

Class of 2007 Average GPAs	GEAR UP Class of 2007 Average GPAs	Difference
Entire Class: Avg. Black GPA = 2.56	2007 Core Cohort: Avg. GU Black GPA (40 students) = 3.26	+ 0.70
Avg. Black Female GPA = 2.65	Avg. GU Black Female GPA (24 students) = 3.23	+ 0.58
Avg. Black Male GPA = 2.51	Avg. GU Black Male GPA (16 students) = 3.29	+ 0.78

Table 6.4. 2006–2007 Semester 1 GPA breakdown by ethnicity and gender: Latinx students

Class of 2007 Average GPAs	GEAR UP Class of 2007 Average GPAs	Difference
Entire Class: Avg. Latinx GPA = 2.45	2007 Core Cohort: Avg. GU Latinx GPA (20 students) = 3.31	+ 0.86
Avg. Latinx Female GPA = 2.59	Avg. GU Latinx Female GPA (14 students) = 3.19	+ 0.60
Avg. Latinx Male GPA = 2.27	Avg. GU Latinx Male GPA (6 students) = 3.59	+ 1.32

2004–2005 school year to 65% during the 2005–2006 school year. In addition, of the juniors at Sunnyside, 35% were enrolled in algebra II and 40% were enrolled in chemistry during the 2005–2006 school year. Much of this work also helped students to develop the skill set and knowledge base that would enable them to compete in more academically rigorous courses.

Another major accomplishment of the GEAR UP program was the increased educational expectations participating students developed for themselves. In 2006, the Advanced Readiness in Students' Education (ARISE) program, a 2-week (12-day) academic intensive series, focused on preparing new sophomores and juniors for courses in AP geometry, algebra II, calculus, English language, and literature. The courses were selected based on the University of California's competitive eligibility formula. Along with the program's strong academic focus, the students also were able to participate in a variety of enrichment activities, which included poetry/spoken word, art, drama, nutrition, and fitness, and a computer technology program. During the 2007 academic year, we offered the ARISE program again, and it continued to help students to develop a strong educational foundation and prepare them for success in a college or university. By providing a space where students could thrive with adequate resources at hand, GEAR UP helped students to develop their confidence and mentored them to raise their own academic expectations and performance.

Even with limited funding, GEAR UP continued to provide a high level of service and intensified programs that met the needs of those who were served. As the program drew to a close after the 2006–2007 academic year because of limited funding, we celebrated many measures of success over our final year, such as seeing 85% of seniors who participated in the California High School Exit Exam tutoring program pass the exam. In addition, we witnessed the largest graduating class (385) from Sunnyside High School in nearly a decade, an approximately 25% increase in the number of graduates over the previous year (291). Furthermore, in a senior survey of 247 of the 385 (65%) graduating seniors, almost 80% reported they were going to either a 2-year or 4-year college the following year. Moreover, of the graduating class, 80 students were accepted by 4-year colleges, which meant that a little over 20% of the class entered universities the following fall. This number is double the previous year's number. Nine African American students (six of whom were males) were accepted by UCLA, typically one of the more difficult colleges to gain admission to, compared with only four students in 2006, more than doubling the number of students accepted to UCLA from Sunnyside High School.

An additional program effective at incorporating cultural content, critical consciousness, and learning in a collaborative fashion has been the UCLA Vice Provost Initiative for Precollege Scholars (VIPS) (see Howard, Tunstall, & Flennaugh, 2016). At a time when discussions about how to equitably and constitutionally achieve ethnic and racial diversity on college campuses have been plentiful, VIPS provides a more culturally informed, compassionate, and collaborative effort to provide better access and equity for postsecondary options to students of color from low-income, urban communities. The program responds to what is often referred to as the "higher education demographic imperative," which contends that not addressing the chronic under-representation of various segments of the U.S. population has potentially damaging consequences for the nation educationally, politically, economically, and technologically (Jayakumar, Vue, & Allen, 2013).

In response to the nationwide challenge to provide greater access to higher education for all students, the VIPS program is a university/K–12 school partnership that has addressed the shortage of underrepresented students on college campuses by institutionalizing a program centered on increasing the number of underserved students from Los Angeles County to gain access to competitive colleges and universities across the nation. When it comes to increasing the college admission rates of African American and Latinx students into a multitude of colleges and universities over the past 15 years, the incorporation of culturally responsive content, a focus on critical consciousness, culturally and racially connected mentorship, and an intentional spotlight on community enhancement has led to remarkable results. VIPS and their results offer researchers, university and school administrators, and practitioners important considerations for addressing the underrepresentation of African American and Latino students on university campuses. The messages from such a program are clear in that students from culturally diverse and low-income backgrounds, when provided proper support structures, are more than capable of becoming college ready. Moreover, the program demonstrates how students in this college access program develop an equity-minded and social justice orientation toward engaging their education, and ultimately improving their own communities, or communities similar to theirs. The critical consciousness that students develop from the program has led to many of them becoming change agents at their high schools, college campuses, communities, and in their career pursuits.

The knowledge base on culturally responsive teaching continues to emerge. Although this information has been critical to inform the larger educational community, there is a need to ask more questions that will help scholars and practitioners expand the concept, in particular if it is successful in improving the academic performance of underachievers. Despite arguments to the contrary, growing evidence shows that culturally responsive teaching approaches are having an influence on student outcomes, improving student learning, and engaging students who often are disengaged from teaching and learning. Culturally responsive teaching, like much of teaching, is a multifaceted, dynamic, and intellectually intense endeavor. It must be undergirded by a deep-seated commitment to the holistic development and well-being of students, their families, and their communities.

Culturally responsive teaching also can be enhanced by examining policies and large-scale programs that have been implemented and that have helped underachieving students. While individual accounts of teachers who possess the knowledge, skills, and cultural competence to assist culturally diverse learners are valuable, there are far too many teachers who still lack this viable knowledge that can enable them to implement transformative approaches to teaching and learning. Identifying and replicating effective programs will be fundamental to closing the stubborn achievement gap that continues to result in countless numbers of learners who experience school failure. In addition to identifying these programs, researchers and practitioners must engage in information exchanges about where such interventions are having success and try to replicate them. The premise of replicating effective programs is centered on the belief that many teachers want to use practices that will improve students' performance, but lack the necessary knowledge and skills about the culture–cognition connection.

REFERENCES

Academic English Mastery Program. https://lausdaea.net/aemp/

Alim, H. A., & Baugh, J. (2007). *Talkin Black talk: Language, education, and social change.* Teachers College Press.

Banks, J. A. (1989). Integrating the curriculum with ethnic content: Approaches and guidelines. In J. A. Banks & C. A. M. Banks (Eds.), *Multicultural education: Issues and perspectives* (1st ed., pp. 189–207). Allyn & Bacon.

Banks, J. A. (1990). *Teaching strategies for the social studies: Inquiry, valuing, and decision making.* (4th ed.) Longman.

Banks, J. A. (Ed.) (1996). *Multicultural education, transformative knowledge, and action: Historical and contemporary perspectives.* Teachers College Press.

Banks, J. A. (Ed.) (2009). *The Routledge international companion to multicultural education.* Routledge.

Bartolome, L. I. (1994). Beyond the methods fetish: Toward a humanizing pedagogy. *Harvard Educational Review, 64*(2), 173–194.

Beauboeuf-Lafontant, T. M. (1999). A movement against and beyond boundaries: "Politically relevant teaching" among African American teachers. *Teachers College Record, 100*(4), 702–723.

Civil, M., & Khan, L. H. (2001). Mathematics instruction developed from a garden theme. *Teaching Children Mathematics, 7*(7), 400–405.

Dalton, S. S. (2008). *Five standards for effective teaching: How to succeed with all learners.* Wiley & Sons.

D'Souza, D. (1995). *The end of racism: Principles for a multiracial society.* Free Press.

Ensign, J. (2003). Including culturally relevant math in an urban school. *Educational Studies, 34,* 414–423.

Ferguson, R. (2000). *A diagnostic analysis of Black-White SAT disparities in Shaker Heights, Ohio.* Brookings Institution.

Ford, D. Y. (1996). *Reversing the underachievement among gifted Black students: Promising practices and programs.* Teachers College Press.

Foster, M. (1989). "It's cookin' now": A performance analysis of the speech events of a Black teacher in an urban community college. *Language in Society, 18*(1), 1–29.

Foster, M. (1993). Educating for competence in community and culture. *Urban Education, 27*(4), 370–394.

Freire, P. (1970). Cultural action for freedom. *Harvard Educational Review, 8,* 26–39.

Gay, G. (2000). *Culturally responsive teaching: Theory, research, and practice* (3rd ed.). Teachers College Press.

Gutstein, E., Lipman, P., Hernandez, P., & de los Reyes, R. (1997). Culturally relevant mathematics teaching in a Mexican American context. *Journal for*

Research in Mathematics Education, 28(6), 709–737.

Hammond, Z. (2014). *Culturally responsive teaching and the brain: Promoting authentic engagement and rigor among culturally and linguistically diverse students.* Corwin Press.

Herrnstein, R., & Murray, C. (1994). *The bell curve: Intelligence and class structure in American life.* Free Press.

Hess, D. E. (2009). *Controversy in the classroom: The democratic power of discussion.* Routledge.

Hirsch, E. D. (1987). *Cultural literacy: What every American needs to know.* Houghton Mifflin.

Hollie, S. (2001). Acknowledging the language of African American students: Instructional strategies. *The English Journal, 90,* 54–59.

Howard, J. R., McCall, T., & Howard, T. C. (2020). *No more teaching without positive relationships.* Heinemann.

Howard, T. C. (2001a). Powerful pedagogy for African American students: Conceptions of culturally relevant pedagogy. *Journal of Urban Education, 36*(2), 179–202.

Howard, T. C. (2001b). Telling their side of the story: African American students' perceptions of culturally relevant teaching. *The Urban Review, 33*(2), 131–149.

Howard, T. C. (2003). Culturally relevant pedagogy: Ingredients for critical teacher reflection. *Theory Into Practice, 42*(3), 195–202.

Howard, T. C., Tunstall, J. D., & Flennaugh, T. K. (2016). *Expanding college access for urban youth: What schools and colleges can do.* Teachers College Press.

Irvine, J. J. (1990). *Black students and school failure.* Greenwood Press.

Irvine, J. J. (2003). *Educating teachers for diversity: Seeing with a cultural eye.* Teachers College Press.

Irvine, J. J., & Armento, B. (2001). *Culturally responsive teaching: Lesson planning for the elementary and middle grades.* McGraw-Hill.

Jayakumar, U. M., Vue, R., & Allen, W. R. (2013). Pathways to college for young Black scholars: A community cultural wealth. *Harvard Educational Review, 83*(4), 551–579.

Kohl, H. (1995). *I won't learn from you: And other thoughts on creative maladjustment.* The New Press.

Ladson-Billings, G. (1994). *The Dreamkeepers: Successful teaching for African-American students.* Jossey-Bass.

Ladson-Billings. G. (1995). Toward a theory of culturally relevant pedagogy. *American Educational Research Journal, 32*(3), 465–491.

Lee, C. D. (1995). Signifying as a scaffold for literary interpretation. *Journal of Black Psychology, 21*(4), 357–381.

Lee, C. D. (1998). Culturally responsive pedagogy and performance-based assessment. *The Journal of Negro Education, 67*(3), 268–279.

Lee, C. D. (2007). *Culture, literacy, and learning: Blooming in the midst of the whirlwind.* Teachers College Press.

Lipman, P. (1995). "Bringing out the best in them": The contribution of culturally relevant teachers to education. *Theory Into Practice, 34*(3), 203–208.

Lynn, M. (2006). Education for the community: Exploring the culturally relevant practices of Black male teachers. *Teachers College Record, 108*(12), 2497–2522.

Martin, D. B. (2000). *Mathematics success and failure among African-American youth: The roles of sociohistorical context, community forces, school influence and individual agency*. Erlbaum.

McWhorter, J. (2000). *Losing the race*. Free Press.

Milner, H. R. (2018). Relationship-centered teaching: Addressing racial tensions in the classrooms. *Kappa Delta Pi Record, 54*, 60–66.

Moll, L., & González, N. (2004). Engaging life: A funds-of-knowledge approach to multicultural education. In J. A. Banks & C. A. M. Banks (Eds.), *Handbook of research on multicultural education* (2nd ed., pp. 699–715). Jossey Bass.

Morrell, E., & Duncan-Andrade, J. (2005). Toward a critical classroom discourse: Promoting academic literacy through engraining hip hop culture with urban youth. *English Journal, 91*(6), 88–94.

Nasir, N. (2000). Points ain't everything: Emergent goals and average, and percent understanding in the play of basketball among African American students. *Anthropology and Educational Quarterly, 31*(3), 283–305.

Nasir, N. S., & Cobb, P. (Eds.). (2006). *Improving access to mathematics: Diversity and equity in the classroom*. Teachers College Press.

Nelson-Barber, S., & Estrin, E. T. (1995). Bringing Native American perspectives to mathematics and science teaching. *Theory Into Practice, 34*(3), 174–185.

Ogbu, J. (1987). Opportunity structure, cultural boundaries, and literacy. In J. Langer (Ed.), *Language, literacy, and culture: Issues of society and schooling* (pp. 149–177). Ablex Press.

Olson, L. (1997). *Made in America: Immigrant students in public schools*. New Press.

Orfield, G. (2004). *Dropouts in America: Confronting the graduation crisis*. Harvard Education Press.

Paris, D. (2012). Culturally sustaining pedagogy: A needed change in stance, terminology, and practice. *Educational Researcher, 41*(3), 93–97.

Parsons, E. C. (2005). From caring as a relation to culturally relevant caring: A White teacher's bridge to Black students. *Equity and Excellence, 38*, 25–34.

Pearl, A. (1970). The poverty of psychology—an indictment. In V. L. Allen (Ed.), *Psychological factors in poverty* (pp. 348–364). Markham.

Pierce, E. (2005). Culturally relevant teaching: A teacher's journey to "get it right." *Multicultural Education, 12*, 1–6.

Powell, R. (1997). Then the beauty emerges: A longitudinal case study of culturally relevant teaching. *Teaching and Teacher Education, 13*(5), 467–484.

Ravitch, D. (2003). *The language police*. Knopf.

Ryan, W. (1971). *Blaming the victim*. Random House.

Sheets, R. H. (1995). From remedial to gifted: Effects of culturally centered pedagogy. *Theory Into Practice, 34*(3), 186–193.

Shulman, L. J. (1987). Knowledge and teaching: Foundations of the new reform. *Harvard Educational Review, 57*, 1–22.

Solórzano, D. G., & Delgado Bernal, D. (2001). Examining transformational resistance through a critical race and latcrit theory framework: Chicana and Chicano students in an urban context. *Urban Education, 36*(3), 308–342.

Steele, S. (1990). *The content of our character*. St. Martin's Press.

Tate, W. (1995). Returning to the root: A culturally relevant approach to mathematics pedagogy. *Theory Into Practice, 34*(3), 166–173.

Valencia, R. R. (1997). *The evolution of deficit thinking: Educational thought and practice*. Falmer Press.

Valenzuela, A. (1999). *Subtractive schooling: U.S.-Mexican youth and the politics of caring*. State University of New York Press.

VanTassel-Baska, J. (1992). *Planning effective curriculum for gifted learners*. Love.

Wortham, S. (2002). Struggling toward culturally relevant pedagogy in the Latinx diaspora. *Journal of Latinx and Education, 1*(2), 133–144.

CHAPTER 7

Modeling with Cultural Data Sets

Carol D. Lee

In Cultural Modeling, units of instruction, organized around particular interpretive problems, begin with what I call *cultural data sets*. These are texts from students' everyday experience that pose a problem of interpretation similar to what students will meet in the canonical texts they will read. It is important that students experience the cultural data sets as a part of their routine practices outside of school. Generally, students have greater prior knowledge of such cultural data sets than teachers. Typically, cultural data sets represent practices and knowledge not only devalued by schools but viewed by schools as detrimental to academic progress. Since my work has been with African American students, cultural data sets have included R & B or rap lyrics, rap videos, stretches of signifying dialogues (a genre of talk in African American English Vernacular), as well as film clips and television programs.

The Cultural Modeling research group has made several interesting findings from using cultural data sets in this way. First, students model for each other how they reason about an interpretive problem in question. The teacher then gives a language to the strategies, a metalanguage of problem solving that applies not only to the text in question but to many kinds of texts. Second, the level of reasoning is very high from the beginning of instruction. This is because students already use such reasoning in their everyday lives, but this knowledge is tacit. Because it is tacit, when they meet similar types of problems in other contexts, such as in canonical works of literature in their English language arts classrooms, they see no connections to what they already know and therefore do not tap into the relevant schemata or organized bodies of knowledge that can help them with the problem. This is the classic difficulty of what Whitehead (1929) called "inert knowledge." Third, the power relationships between students and the teacher about who can serve as authoritative knowledge sources is restructured from the very beginning of instruction.

CULTURAL MODELING OF SYMBOLISM

In this section I describe a unit of instruction on symbolism, a Cultural Modeling unit taught to all senior English students at Fairgate High School. In each of the texts in the unit, a significant problem of symbolism arises. The symbolism in each text is not an isolated case, but rather is central to making sense of the text as a whole. The primary text is Toni Morrison's (1987) award-winning novel *Beloved*—a complex novel for many reasons. For one thing, it includes an inverted chronology: Morrison will sometimes move through two time periods in the course of a single paragraph, and the markers for such transitions are rarely explicit. In addition, the novel is clearly in the tradition of magical realism, which means supernatural events occur but are to be taken as real. They are not like events in horror movies but are representative of cultural worldviews in which the worlds of spirits and of humans intersect in real ways. It is in this sense that *Beloved* is much more than a ghost story. There are also numerous shifts in point of view. The same event—such as the story of Denver's birth—will be told from more than one point of view. This variation in point of view is not an indicator of unreliability; rather, I think Morrison is saying to the reader that truth is never objective, that it always captures multiple perspectives, each with different meanings to the people involved. Finally, the symbolism in *Beloved* is robust. Nearly every chapter poses several symbols that together intersect to carry the subtle themes of this monumental work.

Besides *Beloved*, the following texts were included in this extended unit on symbolism:

Short Stories / Chapters

- John Edgar Wideman (1998), Damballah (from the novel *Damballah*).
- Jewelle Gomez (1991), "Louisiana" (from the novel *The Gilda Stories*).
- Stephen Crane (1895), "The Open Boat" (from *The Red Badge of Courage*).
- William Faulkner (1950), "A Rose for Emily."
- William Faulkner (1950), "Wash."
- Amy Tan (1989), "Lena St. Clair: Rice Husband"; "Ying-Ying St. Clair: Waiting Between the Trees" (from the novel *The Joy Luck Club*).
- Virginia Woolf (1972), "A Haunted House."

Poems

- Robert Hayden (1966), "Runnagate."
- Frances Harper (1854), "The Slave Mother."
- Emily Dickinson (1863), "Because I Could Not Stop for Death."
- John Milton (1667), *Paradise Lost* (selections).
- Dante (1321), *Inferno* (selections).
- Robert Frost (1916),"The Road Not Taken."
- Dylan Thomas (1952), "Do Not Go Gentle Into That Good Night."

Novel

- Ralph Ellison (1933), *Invisible Man.*

These are all very demanding texts. The first text taught was Wideman's (1998) "Damballah," which shared many of the features of *Beloved*: inverted chronology, magical realism, symbolism, and one of the themes of *Beloved*, resistance to enslavement. After "Damballah," the students read *Beloved*. The texts read after *Beloved* presented not only complex problems of symbolism but also themes that students met in *Beloved*: guilt, redemption, dilemmas that try the soul, the multiplicative consequences of racism, and complexities of what happens when different worldviews meet.

Note that this is a unit of instruction taught in a high school with a history of underachievement. The vast majority of these high school seniors had reading scores on the Test of Academic Proficiency (TAP) well below the 50th percentile. All of the students were African American, most from families living in low-income communities. This unit was based on the assumptions that these students were capable of much more than their test scores and academic histories implied and that they had robust experiences in the world that were important resources on which they could draw to tackle the problems presented in this unit of instruction. The challenge was to design instruction in such a way that the heuristics and strategies as well as habits of mind needed to attack these problems could be made explicit. Since inverted chronology was an ongoing area of difficulty in *Beloved* and other texts that would follow, we provided students with additional cultural data sets that exposed signals for shifts in time. Students also read background information relevant to the setting of the novel, including selections from Lerone Bennett's (1964) *Before the Mayflower: A History of the Negro in America, 1619–1964* for background information on the historical experiences of the African Holocaust of Enslavement. Reading logs, graphic organizers, and focused questions were used throughout the unit in order to focus students' attention on making sense *while* they were reading. These efforts represent common teaching strategies used across most literature classrooms. However, what was unique was the preparation for these difficult texts through modeling strategies for detecting and interpreting symbolism through cultural data sets that came from the everyday experiences of these African American adolescents.

The cultural data sets used to teach symbolism in this unit were the following:

- Rap lyrics—"The Mask" by the Fugees (1996)
- R & B lyrics—"People Make the World Go Round" by the Stylistics (1990)
- Rap video—"I Used to Love H.E.R." by Common Sense (1994)
- Television minifilm—Julie Dash's *Sax Cantor Riff* (1997) from the HBO series *Subway Stories*

The point of cultural data sets is to provide students with support for making public and explicit the tacit knowledge they possess about how to make sense of a particular kind of problem, to provide them with a language to talk about their problem-solving processes, and to help them make connections between what they already do and what they are expected to do with canonical, school-based problems (such as the literature that would follow). Further, the work with the cultural data sets is intended to establish a culture of inquiry, of argumentation with evidence, of hypothesizing, of intellectual risk taking as norms for participation in class—a redefining of what it means to work in these classrooms. In addition to these habits of mind, the work with cultural data sets is intended to socialize students into using particular habits of mind specific to the discipline in question, the particular ways that inquiry, argumentation with evidence, hypothesizing, and risk taking are characteristic of response to literature, mathematics, history, or science.

With respect to response to literature, these habits of mind include the essential disposition of paying attention to language play as an aesthetically pleasing end in itself. It includes a willingness to enter the subjunctive world of an imaginary text. It also includes a disposition to impose coherence even when there seems to be little in the text. The coherence is a construction that readers make, and experienced readers configure that coherence based on beliefs they bring to the text. These may be dispositions to see issues of gender as important (i.e., feminist criticism), to see issues of equity in the structure of societies (i.e., Marxist criticism), to privilege a Black or African view of the world (i.e., Black Aesthetic criticism), or to privilege purely individual and personal connections with the text (i.e., Reader Response criticism). We made a conscious decision to privilege what some might view as something close to—although clearly not— a New Criticism orientation, in the sense that paying close attention to the text as a source of evidence was privileged from the beginning of instruction. We took this stance because I believe that a close reading of the text is the starting point for novices to be able to engage in other critical stances. Regardless of critical stance, good readers read closely.

In order to make tacit knowledge of problem-solving strategies public, a main focus of modeling with cultural data sets is the coordination of what I call *metacognitive instructional conversations. Metacognition* involves thinking about one's own thinking, monitoring one's understanding, and knowing what to do when comprehension breaks down (Flavell, 1981). Explaining one's thinking is difficult for most people. It is especially difficult for students whose history of schooling has been dominated by a recitation around right and wrong answers where the teacher is the primary source of authority. It is clear from early class discussions that talking about their thinking was both very unfamiliar and very difficult for these students. In addition, it was challenging for me as a teacher to learn how to coordinate such discussions.

Metacognitive discussions as a central pillar of modeling with cultural data sets require that talk addresses not so much what students know about the meaning of a text as about how students come to know. Cultural data sets are ripe for such talk because in most cases the students know more about the meaning of these texts than the teachers. Thus, to merely discuss what the texts mean is somewhat inauthentic, except as the students teach the teacher about the meaning of these texts. That does happen and is an important feature of such modeling.

To illustrate these features of metacognitive discussions, I refer to a class taught by Wilma Hayes. Mrs. Hayes (I use her real name with her permission) is an extraordinary teacher. I had the wonderful opportunity to work with her 4 years before the full Cultural Modeling project at Fairgate High School. She always said that teachers should not be asked if they taught a subject, topic, or skill, but rather what did students learn. Mrs. Hayes had an established routine in all of her classrooms of handing responsibility for thinking over to students. She would wait however long it took for students to respond rather than impose her thoughts on the group. Her most repeated question to students was always "How do you know?"

In this class the students have been reading the lyrics of "The Mask" by the Fugees (1996). Each stanza is followed by the following chorus lines:

> M to the A to the S to the K,
> Put the mask up on the face just to make the next day. Brothers be gaming, Ladies be claiming.
> I walk the streets and camouflage my identity. My posse Uptown wear the mask.
> My crew in the Queens wear the mask.
> Stick up kids with the Tommy Hil wear the mask.
> Yeah everybody wear the mask but how long will it last.

The particular stanza being discussed is about Lauryn Hill, a popular member of the Fugees, visiting a club in her old neighborhood. She is approached by a young man drinking an Amaretto sour who grabs her. She initially is prepared to rebuke the young man when she recognizes him as Tariq, someone she knew from around her grandmother's house.

I thought he was the wonder, and I was stunned by his lips,
Taking sips sipping Amaretto sour with a twist,
Shook my hips to the bass line, this joker grabbed my waistline,
Putting pressure on my spine trying to get L-Boog to wind,
I backed up off him, then caught him with five fingers to his face, I had to put him in his place,
This kids invading my space, But then I recognized the smile, but I couldn't place the style,
So many fronts in his mouth, I thought he was the Golden Child . . .

The students have been working in small groups discussing the meaning of "The Mask." Mrs. Hayes, who does not listen to rap music or attend movies because of her religious beliefs, moves from group to group. She sits with one group that is discussing the reference to the "Golden Child." The discussion of this group follows.

1   *T:* What does he mean here, "so many fronts in his mouth I thought he was the Golden Child."
2   *Ellen, Alicia, Fatima:* Gold teeth.
3   *T:* But . . .
4   *Ellen:* That's like a big front anyway, cuz he got all this gold, all up in his mouth, and he just makin it his business to smile and let it be noticed.
5   *T:* But who is "the Golden Child"?
6   *Fatima:* The golden child that little boy who . . .
7   *Ellen:* Eddie Murphy played . . .
8   *Alicia:* In that movie. (laugh)
9   *T:* So he's referring to something in a movie?
10 *Alicia:* Yeah. (pause) You know how the golden child had all the power in the movie. (waits for a response) OK. (laughs)
11 *T:* I'm listening.
12 *Alicia:* It was the movie. You ever seen the movie *The Golden Child*?
13 *T:* Umm, umm [no].
14 *Ellen:* Oh well that's . . . (laughs)
15 *Alicia:* It was the movie where this little boy he had all the power. But I don't really think that he just directly referring to it. He just indirectly. Everybody know the Golden Child had all the power.

But he said that he had all these fronts in his mouth and he's the Golden Child . . .

16 *Ellen:* Right, Golden Child, except you know he got gold teeth.

17 *Alicia:* He had all this gold in his mouth like he this Golden Child.

18 *T:* And what would you have needed to know in order to come to that conclusion? What you just said . . . ?

19 *Alicia:* I just need to know all the fronts in his mouth. When she said "mouth," I knew.

20 *Ellen:* Right. Once she said that you knew what that meant.

21 *T:* And what else would a person need to know in order to come to the conclusion that you just came to? What little bits of information would a person need? And where are you getting your answers from?

22 *Alicia:* From stuff we already knew.

23 *T:* So you're using prior knowledge.

24 *Ellen:* They say in here how they . . .

25 *Alicia:* We were usin our context clues, we were like when we see the word *mouth* then you know it's automatically it's something that got to do with, got to be in his mouth.

26 *T:* I'm saying that to you because a piece of my knowledge that's missing is, I don't know anything about the *Golden Child*. So I'm in the same position that you're in sometimes when you approach these novels. I may know what the author's talking about because I can hook it on to something, and that's why if you can prove it, instead of saying there's no right or wrong answer, you have a reason for coming up with that. And I don't know what he's talking about, to be honest with you. That's why I listen to you.

27 *Ellen:* He just talkin a lot about bringing attention to sayin he got a lot of gold in his mouth. He might not necessarily mean the Golden Child. Cuz that don't have a lot to do with his mouth.

28 *T:* So the Golden Child would be like a symbol?

29 *Ellen:* Right.

30 *T:* Representing . . .

31 *Ellen:* But not a symbol as being the Golden Child for his teeth, for having gold teeth.

32 *Alicia:* It's figurative language. It's like if I be like Ellen, you star bright something, that's another way of sayin she real light-skinned. You know, that's figurative language.

33 *T:* Umm hmm.

34 *Ellen:* (Laughs) No, It's all right, it's all right.

35 *Alicia:* I mean no, cuz you know, so she can understand this. Cuz if you called me little black star, you know . . .

This discussion reveals several important characteristics of discussions around cultural data sets as modeling. First, it is clear from the discussion that the students have more prior knowledge about this text than the teacher. Perhaps because of this, power relationships between the teacher and the students radically shift from the IRE (Initiation-Response-Evaluation) pattern of talk that is very typical in classrooms, particularly in those serving students from low-income minority backgrounds (Cazden, 2000; Mehan, 1979). Although Wells (1995) has accurately noted that the IRE pattern of talk can serve useful functions in classrooms, problems arise when it is the only pattern. The IRE pattern involves teachers having sole control over what responses are allowed in discussion and over who gets to talk. In this interchange, 37% of the turns are held by the teacher, while 63% are held and largely controlled by students. (Turns are numbered in the figures.) When Mrs. Hayes asks in turn 1 the meaning of the phrase "so many fronts in his mouth that I thought he was the Golden Child," and in turn 5, "Who is 'the Golden Child'?" she is posing genuine questions to which she does not know the answer. The students recognize that these are genuine questions. I believe it is this recognition by the students that invites them to take on the stance of teacher in relation to Mrs. Hayes and that opens up structures of talk that they control. The turns of talk after each of Mrs. Hayes's questions involve multiple responses from students and Mrs. Hayes does not control who speaks. The students' assumption of teaching roles bids them to draw actively on prior knowledge that they have and Mrs. Hayes does not.

A second feature of modeling discourse is the focus on students' problem-solving processes. Such modeling represents an interesting instantiation of Vygotsky's (1978) concept of a zone of proximal development. Vygotsky defines the *zone of proximal development* as the distance between what learners can do on their own and what they can do with assistance. It is a dynamic zone in the sense that the students are assisting the teacher and the teacher is assisting the students. Neither has full knowledge of the task. Mrs. Hayes's knowledge of the referents in the lyrics is incomplete. The students' knowledge of the task toward which Mrs. Hayes is seeking to scaffold them is incomplete, namely to articulate heuristics for detecting and interpreting symbolism. Although the students bring important prior knowledge to such tasks, their knowledge is both tacit and incomplete. The quality of reasoning that we find the students demonstrating is rarely an object of explicit conversation outside of school. Thus the quality of reasoning we see here is the extension of an emergent understanding that is a result of careful scaffolding by the teacher. The teacher's role in this process is fundamental, and Mrs. Hayes is superb in this work.

It should be noted, however, that there are expert communities of practice within youth culture. Morgan (2002), for example, describes communities of young people who engage in a practice called *wordsmithing*, a poetry-crafting process. Fisher (2003, 2004) also describes intergeneration-al communities who foster the development of young people in this art. In such communities, explication of popular texts of rap and contemporary youth poetry are a routine practice. Most students in this class are not mem-bers of such writing communities.

Most of Mrs. Hayes's turns are directed toward students' articulating their reasoning—how it is that they come to know. In turn 18, Mrs. Hayes asks "And what would you have needed to know in order to come to that conclusion?" In turn 21, she asks, "Where are you getting your answers from?" It is clear from her repeated formulations of this general question that expressing how they reason is not easy for the students. However, it is revealing to follow the refinement of communication in turns 22, 24, and 25. The first statement, "From stuff we already knew," is accurate, but in a more vernacular register. In turn 24, the student directs attention to the text itself as a source of knowledge. This is an extremely important recognition and is consistent with one of the habits of mind the modeling activities are intended to invoke, namely, that careful attention to the text is privileged. Ellen is not able to complete her sentence because Alicia completes the thought with no pause between turns. In turn 25, Alicia not only makes ex-plicit reference to the words in the text that signal special attention but also uses a teaching register, "We were usin our context clues." Certainly, Mrs. Hayes has taught them about context clues and named the phenomena. But here, students invoke it and name it without prompting from Mrs. Hayes. They have invoked the construct and see its application to their explication of these lyrics.

This is an example of students making connections between what they can do with everyday texts and what they can do with canonical texts. In this instance, the rap lyrics are being reconstructed as canonical because they are working on it as they have worked on school-based canonical texts. It represents the beginnings of what Saxe (1991) calls a "form-function shift." In a form-function shift, the form and function of a concept or tool changes from one context to be appropriated in slightly different ways to a new con-text. It is a particular way of viewing transfer. There are many examples of form-function shifts from these classrooms; I offer this example as represen-tative of a qualitative shift in reasoning in one context to another.

Mrs. Hayes is especially skillful at being explicit about turning respon-sibility for student thinking over to the students. In turn 26, she makes a powerful connection. Whereas in turn 23, she had revoiced the student's vernacular register (i.e., "from stuff we already knew") to a more disci-plinary register (i.e., "So you're using prior knowledge") (O'Connor & Mi-chaels, 1993), in turn 26, she shifts her position back to that of a learner: "I'm saying that to you because a piece of my knowledge that's missing is, I don't know anything about the Golden Child." It is within that turn that Mrs. Hayes makes the brilliant and pivotal move of making explicit how what the students are doing with these rap lyrics is like what they will be doing with the novels that follow: "So I'm in the same position that you're in. I may know what the author's talking about because I can hook it on to something, and that's why if you can prove it, instead of saying there's no right or wrong answer, you have a reason for coming up with that." She thus communicates a powerful conception of reading—that is, even expert readers can be stumped, which implies that not knowing or being confused is not a bad thing. She also labels what the students have accomplished up to this point. They have provided evidence and reasons for their claims. This epistemological stance is continuously restated across class sessions to socialize a culture of inquiry and argumentation based on evidence. It communicates to students that this is what we do here. This is the game we play.

A third feature of Cultural Modeling is the high quality of reasoning that students display from the beginning of instruction. This conversation about "The Mask" occurs very early in the instructional unit. At the conclusion of turn 26, Mrs. Hayes admits, "And I don't know what he's talking about, to be honest with you. That's why I listen to you." The students resume with vigor their mission to teach Mrs. Hayes. The reasoning is brilliant. In turn 27, Ellen articulates what Rabinowitz (1987) calls "rules of notice." These are conventions that the author uses to alert the reader to pay special attention. This heuristic has not been taught to the students. However, in order to teach Mrs. Hayes, whom the students see as a naive observer of rap, Ellen reveals that the reason the author uses the phrase "fronts in his mouth" is to bring attention to the fact that Tariq has a lot of gold in his mouth. She then goes on to make an insightful distinction between the attention to the gold in his mouth and his being the Golden Child, "cuz that don't have a lot to do with his mouth."

Mrs. Hayes takes up that assertion as implying that the reference to the Golden Child is intended to be symbolic. In a revolutionary response—something we rarely see happening in classrooms, especially in schools like Fairgate—the students correct Mrs. Hayes. Instead of being enticed to follow the reasoning of the teacher as the sole source of authoritative knowledge, the students put forth an alternative explanation. They argue that the reference to the Golden Child is not intended to be symbolic, but rather a way to emphasize the gold in his mouth. Although they do not have the language to label their reasoning, they are arguing that this is a case of hyperbole. Because so much rich reasoning emerges in these modeling discussions, it is a challenge for teachers to always understand the significance of what students are saying. This is because students are communicating their reasoning often by using a vernacular register and contextualizing their claims to the text (i.e., cultural data set) under discussion. The teacher must translate such contextualized statements by mapping them onto her understanding of core constructs, strategies, and heuristics in the discipline. In this case, Mrs. Hayes would need to have understood Alicia's statement in turn

32, "It's figurative language. It's like if I be like Ellen, you star bright something, that's another way of sayin she real light-skinned as an expression of hyperbole. Mrs. Hayes did not understand the import of Ellen's statement in turn 27 at the time. However, after reviewing the video of this class session, she saw a missed teaching opportunity.

A final feature to discuss is the ongoing presence of community-based language practices as an exciting medium of communication. In this case, students are often invoking African American English rhetorical features as the envelope for communication. In turns 32, 34, and 35, Alicia and Ellen are signifying with each other. As I have explained before, signifying is a form of ritual insult used for generations as a form of language play, often involving figurative language and double entendre. Alicia and Ellen are good friends. Ellen is light-skinned and Alicia dark-skinned. When Alicia offers the example in turn 32, she is using Ellen as her example of using figurative language to emphasize a point, "Ellen, you star bright." Students in the group laugh, and Ellen says "No, it's all right." Alicia then responds, "Cuz if you called me little black star, you know . . ." Alicia is playfully insinuating that if Ellen called her "little black star," those would be fighting words. This also reflects a longstanding conflict in the historical African American community over skin color (Hunter, 2005). It is not a serious argument here, but a playful one, a way of playing games with words (Goodwin, 1990). That such playfulness has a place in the classroom invites a level of comfort, of intimacy, of safety that invites students to engage and to take intellectual risks. It is one of the features of modeling discourse that makes connections between home/community and school real and meaningful.

RANGE OF REASONING SCAFFOLDED THROUGH CULTURAL DATA SETS

The next set of examples is taken from a senior class I taught at Fairgate High School. Students are again working in small groups and tackling the rap lyrics of "The Mask" by the Fugees as a platform for establishing classroom culture and for making explicit tacit strategies for tackling symbolism. In this example, students are discussing a different stanza:

I used to work at Burger King. A king taking orders.
Punching my clock. Now I'm wanted by the manager.
Soupin' me up sayin' "You're a nice worker,"
"How would you like a quarter raise, move up the register"
"Large in charge, but cha gotta be my spy,
Come back and tell me who's baggin' my fries,
Getting high on company time."
Hell, no sirree, wrong M.C.

Why should I be a spy, when you spying me,
And you see whatcha thought ya saw but never seen.
Ya missed ya last move, Checkmate! Crown me King.
Held my 22 pistol, whipped him in his face.
Hired now I'm fired, sold bud now I'm wired,
Eyes pitch red but da beat bop my head.

These lyrics illustrate one of the tensions in using texts from youth culture, especially hip-hop. The line "Held my 22 pistol, whipped him in his face" is clearly violent. While I can certainly understand the caution some schools may have about such lyrics, I would argue that the violence committed by Macbeth, in a play the students would read later in this unit, is far worse than that depicted in "The Mask." At one level, it may seem ironic that so much of the canonical literature we teach is extraordinarily violent and counter to accepted social norms—Oedipus has sex with his mother (Sophocles, trans. 1977); in *Crime and Punishment*, Raskolnikov commits a brutal murder (Dostoevsky, 1866/1984). Great literature is not defined by the presence of violence or sexuality or the lack thereof, but by how great writers have the ability to make us think deeply about the dilemmas of the human experience. I would not argue that "The Mask" is a profound statement on the human experience, but it is an accurate one. We all, at one time or another, wear masks to disguise our intentions. Intimate friends, government officials, the rich and famous—all wear masks. While "The Mask" may be an accurate, albeit not profound, statement, there are hip-hop lyrics that possess insights into the human experience. Wyclef Jean (1998) a member of the Fugees, communicates a philosophical statement on violence in the world with "Gunpowder." "Don't Go Chasing Waterfalls" by TLC (1994) is more than an argument against unprotected sex, offering a symbol that has many degrees of freedom, capable of being appropriated for a number of important life lessons. Thus the terrain of the canonical and the so-called vernacular is murkier than we might expect.

Jonetha offers a very literary interpretation of this passage:

1   *Jonetha:* Oh, I . . . (Class is noisy)
2. *T:* Shhh. OK, quiet down.
3. *Jonetha:* I'm saying I think he had a mask on when he was fighting, when he beat him up, because in order for him to have the mask on, he was spying on that person. He was spying on somebody. I don't know who he was spying on. But in order for him to realize that the man was spying on him, he had to take off his mask. In order to realize that the man was saying . . . I don't know! Shoot. (laughter from class).

4. *T:* Let me try to break this out a little bit. Jonetha give me the words. You're saying . . .

5. *Jonetha:* I'm saying that the man, in order for him to realize that the other man was spying on him, that he had to take off his mask.

As with the students in Mrs. Hayes's class, these insights are not the result of any explicit preparation by the teacher, no worksheets, no guiding questions, no activating prior knowledge, just discussion. Jonetha's argument is fundamentally as follows: In order for a king to work at Burger King, he must take on a mask of servility because kings don't work at fast food joints. In asking the worker to spy on his colleagues, the manager also assumes a mask to hide the fact that he is trying to use the worker. Thus in order for the king, masking himself as a worker, to recognize that the manager is trying to dupe him, the worker must remove his mask and stand as his true self. Two observations are appropriate here. First, it is clear that as the teacher I am translating Jonetha's words. That is my job. Second, in my process of translating, I am mapping the qualities of Jonetha's interpretation on to my internal representation of the domain of response to literature. Jonetha is clear that the mask is symbolic. She has no illusions that the king disguised as worker or the manager is wearing a physical mask. It is her recognition that a literal interpretation here doesn't make sense that leads her to infer a symbolic significance. She has paid careful attention to the details of the text, noting the meaning of the opening line: a king working at Burger King. She imputes significance to this contradiction and uses that attribution of significance to filter the details that follow. She uses her knowledge of the social world to impute internal states to the worker and the manager, states that must be inferred. This is precisely the kind of reasoning that I will want her to engage in when the class begins reading *Beloved* and the other texts that will follow.

Besides offering a very literary interpretation, Jonetha also demonstrates important habits of mind that are required for literary reasoning. She attends to the details of language play in the text. She does not ignore the salient detail of a king working at Burger King. Further, Jonetha is willing to put forth a hypothesis about which she is not entirely clear. Her wording in turn 3 clearly shows she is still figuring this out. Her frustration is evident when she says, "I don't know! Shoot." This willingness to take intellectual risks is absolutely necessary if the students are to wrestle with the complex canonical works that follow. When the problem is really difficult, it is rare that you can be certain of your first efforts to make sense of it. The students about whom I am concerned have generally across their school careers experienced classrooms where intellectual risk taking is not valued, where the name of the game is an immediate right answer. My efforts in turn 4 to get her to restate her claims cues Jonetha and the rest of the class that uncertainty is a good thing.

A continuing challenge in this kind of modeling is to help the students communicate abstractions. Initially, their responses are circumscribed by the immediate context of the cultural data set. The teacher's job is to revoice contextualized claims as general propositions that can be applied across similar kinds of problems. This was clear in the examples of Mrs. Hayes. Sometimes, the statement of an abstraction emerges from students' interactions with one another. Across these class sessions, students' debates were quite heated. This level of intensity transferred to the canonical texts as well. When students perceive a debate as authentic, they have a vested interest in either clarifying or contesting.

In the following example, this same class I taught is discussing the chorus that repeats across "The Mask":

1   T: OK, "my posse up town wear the mask, my crew in Queens wear the mask, stick up kids with Tommy Hil wear the mask." Who is he talking about here?

2   Carl: So they tryin to say that little kids are stickin up people too with masks on? Is that what they trying to say?

3   T: They actually have masks on?

4   Marvin: No, well basically, they tryin to hide their true identity. Even if they don't actually have a mask, it's like an illusion in a sense, because obviously they don't walk around with a mask on, but they walk around with this cover like, you know how some people try and act like they're hard, but they really not. And they, you know, but that don't mean that they have. They got like a cover, you know a shield over em, but it's not, it's an invisible shield.

It is clear that the student in turn 2 is reading the chorus as a literal statement. To try and push the student's thinking, I ask a question intended to get the student to think about the unlikelihood that a literal interpretation makes sense. Of course, it is possible if one lives in a neighborhood with much violence to imagine that someone could stick up (i.e., rob) wearing a mask. However, this student is even misinterpreting the vernacular-based, satirical comment "stick up kids with Tommy Hil," a wry commentary on poor kids on the street wearing Tommy Hilfiger clothing. Without prompting from the teacher, Marvin in turn 4 responds to the teacher's query (directed at Carl from turn 2) with a brilliant explication of why the literal should be rejected. Marvin's explication includes a wonderful abstract claim about the meaning of the mask, "it's an invisible shield." It is evident that these students have begun to play the game of literary reasoning. In fact, it is a game, and they recognize that it is playful and thus an enticing world to enter.

Another cultural data set that proved to be quite powerful in eliciting insightful reasoning from the students is the short film *Sax Cantor*

Riff, written and directed by Julie Dash (1997), who made the beautiful, award-winning film *Daughters of the Dust* (1991). This 5-minute video appeared as one of many short films—all of which take place in a New York subway station—in the HBO series *Subway Stories*. The film opens with an African American saxophonist playing a jazz riff. Then an old man (likely an Eastern European immigrant) is shown admonishing a group of young women of color for taunting him and stealing from his newsstand. All of a sudden, a young African American woman walks down the stairs of the subway, with flowers in her arms. She approaches the pay phone and calls her mother, who is in the hospital. She tells her mother that she doesn't have money for a taxi, but she wanted to talk with her before it was too late. In a voice that resonates through the subway, she begins singing the African American spiritual "Soon I will be done with the troubles of the world." The group of girls watch in amazement, first thinking the woman is crazy, but then determining that something must be wrong. The woman drops the phone, continues singing, and begins walking up the stairs to leave the subway. Meanwhile, the camera zooms in on the scarf around her neck, waving in the wind with images of flowers in its design. She drops the flowers she was carrying, and the camera zooms in on the flowers flying in the air while a train goes by. As the train passes, you see clearly a sign that says Church Avenue. As the jazz riff reappears, a Jewish man, likely a cantor, wearing the dark suit and wide brim hat of the Hassidic, comes down the stairs of the subway singing in Hebrew, "Let my prayers, O Lo-rd, be for You at a time of favor; O G-d, with Your abundant kindness, answer me with Your saving truth." Then he and the African American saxophone player face each other from separate sides of the track. They nod their heads toward each other.

This particular cultural data set is good fodder for discussion for several reasons. First, it is replete with symbolism. Student discussions of this minifilm were rich with literary reasoning even though none had seen this film. Second, it provides an opportunity to discuss authorial intent. In our discussions, the director Julie Dash was positioned as the "author" of the text because she intentionally put every image and word into the created product. This recognition of authorial intent, of the conscious craft of the "writer," transferred to discussions of the canonical texts that would come later.

The following exchange took place as part of a whole-class discussion after viewing *Sax Cantor Riff*:

1   *T:* Do you know why? You think that everything . . .
2   *Sarah:* (inaudible) Try to make money.
3   *T:* So you think that Julie Dash made this film so she could show a saxophone player make money in a subway?
4   *Job:* Yeah.
5   *T:* Remember the question, the question may be why does she, Julie Dash, she is like the author so to speak. She made a film just

to show the guy try and make money in the subway without . . . (inaudible) You think . . .

6   *Trish:* Well what else was she doing?

7   *T:* That's a good question. You think that HBO would have given her all the money it took to make that movie so they would show . . .

8   *Trish:* But that ain't all they was showing.

9   *T:* Okay so what are some of the questions?

10 *Felice:* I don't know what's going on now.

11 *T:* Well that's a question to answer. (Students are talking among themselves.) First thing you need to do is come up with the questions. What are some questions you ask yourself?

12 *Job:* Why were there roses?

13 *T:* Why were there roses on the floor of the subway? (Students were talking all at the same time.)

14 *Marion:* Were they roses or flowers?

15 *T:* Good question.

16 *Felice:* Why did it have to be Church Avenue?

17 *T:* Why did it have to be Church, ooh wow, why did it have to be Church Avenue? That's deep. Haven't noticed that. That's wonderful! David.

18 *David:* Why was the scarf blowing around in the subway?

19 *T:* Why was the scarf blowing around in the subway?

20 *Felice:* Because the wind was blowing.

21 *T:* Is there wind in the subway? (Students were talking at the same time.)

22 *Marion:* They showed it twice.

23 *T:* They showed it twice, that meant it was important right? They showed it . . . great. What other questions? Keep in mind that there can be literal questions of everything, right? It's possible that the scarf was blowing because the train was passing and there was some air blowing. But maybe there is something else. It's possible that she dropped the flowers but maybe there is something else. That's what we're looking for. What other questions do you have? (A male student was talking to another male student.) What did you say, Victor?

24 *Victor:* I was talking about the scarf because it keep you in mind of because it started off with this and went to that.

25 *T:* All right, let's put some of these questions on the board.

Turns 1–9 are about recognizing authorial intent. They are also about figuring out where one should focus attention in a literary text. It is evident at this early stage that some students do not see the relevance of this point. When Trish in turn 8 alerts the class that the saxophone player is not the only thing being shown, she shows that students have been paying attention to many details of the film. Beginning in turn 9, the teacher asks what questions students have about the film in order to make public the range of details to which they are attending and to determine what may be sources of misunderstanding. Another function is to continue to communicate to the students that asking questions and being uncertain is a good thing. This goal is reflected in turns 10 and 11 when one student says, "I don't know what's going on now," and the teacher responds, "Well that's a question to answer." Their responses indicate that they have attended to the unusual details of the film. Their ability to pay attention to such details in the absence of any direct instruction to what Rabinowitz (1987) calls "rules of notice" is evidence of their tacit knowledge of symbolism and other tropes employed in the narrativization of experience. If these details were not salient to the students, they would not have raised questions about them.

Their responses are revealing. It is important to remember that there was no prompting by the teacher about what kinds of questions were valued. Virtually all of their questions were about why some detail of the film was present. The prevalence of such "why" questions and the particular details they asked about suggest that these students already engage in a kind of literary reasoning, albeit tacit, as they listen to music, watch television and film, and themselves tell stories. They ask why there are flowers, does it make a difference whether these are just flowers or specifically roses, why the sign said Church Avenue, and why the camera zooms in on the scarf blowing in the wind. These are precisely the details that are symbolic, precisely the details that the "author" Julie Dash positioned her camera work on to draw the "reader's" attention. To recognize such details as significant is to use important rules of notice. As typically happens across the instructional unit, the students notice details that the teacher had not. For example, in turn 16, a student has noticed the sign Church Avenue. The teacher responds in turn 17 showing that she is moved by the observation, "Why did it have to be Church, ooh, wow, why did it have to be Church Avenue? That's deep. Haven't noticed that. That's wonderful!"

Besides revealing the students' attention to symbolic details, the discussion also involves descriptions of why they paid attention to particular details. Again, because the students see the discussion as authentic, they act as if it is important to clarify misconceptions that others have. This happens without prompting by the teacher. In turn 18, David asks, "Why was the scarf blowing around in the subway?" In turn 20, Felice responds, "Because the wind was blowing." This counterfactual statement, echoed by the teacher's question in turn 21, "Is there wind in the subway?" stirs a lot of talk among the students, all of whom are talking at the same time. Then in turn 22, Marion clarifies that the scarf's blowing is important because "they showed it twice." This is a very revealing response. These students have likely traveled on the subway. They know that unless a train is going by (which actually it is in the film at the point where you see the scarf blowing), there is no wind as such in a subway. Rather than responding to an obvious question posed by the teacher in turn 21, the student picks up on a device used by the director to bring attention, that is, she shows the scarf blowing twice. This device, as is the case with most cultural data sets, has an analogue in literary texts. When the author repeats a detail, that is usually an indicator that it's important, and if the other heuristics apply for rejecting a literal interpretation and defining the problem space as symbolic, the reader will read the text as symbolic.

I have mentioned before that one of the goals of modeling is for the teacher to provide a metalanguage to capture what students' responses signify. In turn 23, the teacher revoices and elaborates the student's prior observation in turn 22. Here the teacher describes some of the issues in defining the problem space. The details could simply be literal descriptions, that is, the scarf was blowing because there was wind in the subway; or there could be a meaning that goes beyond the literal, a meaning that could be symbolic. It became clear in small-group discussions that followed that these students saw the flowers, the sign, the scarf with flowers blowing, and the train passing by, all as symbolic.

The point of relating these discussions from my English class has been to reveal the quality of literary reasoning in which these students engage from the beginning of instruction without any explicit teaching about the tropes they meet. The Cultural Modeling research groups analyzed the quality of literary reasoning in modeling discussions in contrast to the amount of teacher talk in these discussions. Figure 7.1 illustrates that the quality of reasoning was consistently high and that it was highest when the teacher did not dominate discussions (Lee & Majors, 2000).

Figure 7.1 captures each of the first 10 days of instruction through modeling. It's findings are revealing. First, on the whole there is an inverse relationship between the quality of student reasoning and the level of talk by the teacher. In the first 2 days, students' reasoning is high and the teacher's involvement is high as well. It is expected that the teacher's direction would be high at the beginning, but generally we don't expect students to be as adept at the task being taught from the beginning of instruction. This level of reasoning from the beginning is testimony to their activation of very useful prior knowledge about the task, in this case interpreting cultural data sets from their everyday lives. The lower level of student reasoning on days 3 and 4 occurred when the cultural data sets were an old R & B song, "People Make the World Go Round" (Stylistics, 1990), and an African American spiritual. This suggests to me that cultural data sets must be directly relevant to students' experiences. "People Make the World Go Round" is not a song they would have heard, as it came out decades before they were born. I had assumed that since the genre was R & B they would relate to it. This was not the case. They also did not respond to the spiritual as a source of symbolism, although later in the discussions of *Beloved*, their knowledge of

Figure 7.1. Quality of Reasoning in Modeling Discussions

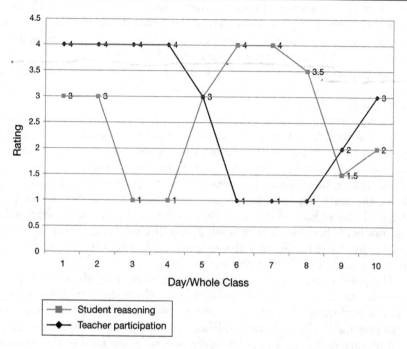

the Bible was often invoked as a really powerful source of prior knowledge for interpreting tropes and actions in that novel. This suggests that careful attention must be paid to the cultural data sets selected. I have found it useful to involve students in the selection of such cultural data sets. Cultural data sets must have two crucial features. First, making sense of them must require problem-solving processes analogous to the school-based task to be taught. Second, students must be very familiar with them already.

A second observation from Figure 7.1 is that learning has a curve. Students have good days and not-so-good days, but our interest is in the overall trend. This trend is a positive one. We did the same analysis of instruction with *Beloved* and found a similar pattern of high levels of reasoning as the consistent pattern and an inverse relationship between high levels of reasoning and dominance of talk by the teacher. These patterns in both the modeling phase and the canonical phase of the unit suggest that a culture of inquiry and engagement was established in these classrooms and that culture emerged from the very beginning of instruction. Figure 7.2 describes patterns of student reasoning and teacher participation during this canonical phase of instruction (Lee & Majors, 2000).

Figure 7.2. Quality of Reasoning During Canonical Literature Phase of Instruction (*Beloved*)

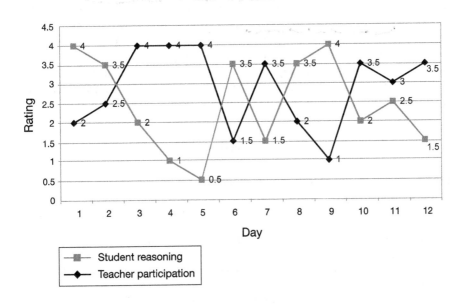

CONCLUSION

I argued earlier that these students faced multiple developmental challenges: the normative challenges of adolescence in American society as well as the challenges that result from racism and poverty. I further argued that an important feature in designing learning environments was how to make such environments into spaces where students felt safe to take intellectual risks. Part of that willingness has to do with understanding the nature and rules of the game we ask students to play and with understanding how to play that game. Beginning instruction with cultural data sets and organizing the talk of instruction in such a way as to invite community-based discourses as a meaningful medium of communication together helped students to stretch intellectually, to make hypotheses when they were unclear, to engage in heated debate, and to clarify uncertainty by others. They were being asked to play a game about which they already knew something. The game was authentic because they valued it outside of school. The lively days of heated debate drew out a genie that in most of their other classrooms had been hidden from public view.

In this work I have tried to accomplish the following: debunk the long-held tradition of viewing the community-based experiences of low-income African American students and their primary language of communication—African American English—as deficits that schools must overcome; demonstrate what high expectations can yield when coupled with instruction that makes the inner workings of a discipline evident and public and connected to students' lives; and contribute to the well-established literature on culturally responsive pedagogy a framework that is both culturally responsive yet firmly rooted in the knowledge of academic disciplines. It is this connection with the discipline that helps teachers and curriculum designers think more critically about the nature of the subject matter we teach and through such understandings make more generative connections to students' lives.

REFERENCES

Bennett, L. (1964). *Before the Mayflower: A history of the Negro in America, 1619–1964.* Johnson.

Cazden, C. (2000). *Classroom discourse: The language of teaching and learning* (2nd ed.). Heinemann.

Common Sense. (1994). I Used to Love H.E.R. On *Resurrection* [CD]. Relativity Records.

Dash, J. (Writer/Director). (1991). *Daughters of the dust* [motion picture]. Kino International.

Dash, J. (Director). (1997). *Sax cantor riff* [television series segment]. In *Subway stories: Tales from the underground.* HBO.

Dostoevsky, F. (1984). *Crime and Punishment* (C. Garnett, Trans.). Bantam. (Original work published 1866)

Fisher, M. T. (2003). Open mics and open minds: Spoken word poetry in African diaspora participatory literacy communities. *Harvard Educational Review, 73*(3), 362–389.

Fisher, M. T. (2004). "The song is unfinished": The new literate and the literary and their institutions. *Written Communication, 21*(3), 290–312.

Flavell, J. H. (1981). *The development of comprehension monitoring and knowledge about communication.* University of Chicago Press.

Fugees. (1996). The mask. On *The score* [Record]. Ruffhouse.

Goodwin, M. (1990). *He-said she-said: Talk as social organization.* Indiana University Press.

Hunter, M. (2005). *Race, gender, and the politics of skin tone.* Routledge.

Jean, W. (1998). Gunpowder. On *Gunpowder* [CD]. Sony.

Lee, C. D., & Majors, Y. J. (2000, April). *Cultural modeling's response to Rogoff's challenge: Understanding apprenticeship, guided participation and participatory appropriation in a culturally responsive, subject matter specific context.* Paper presented at the annual meeting of the American Educational Research Association, New Orleans, Louisiana.

Mehan, H. (1979). *Learning lessons.* Harvard University Press.

Mercado, C. I., & Moll, L. (1997). The study of funds of knowledge: Collaborative research in Latino homes. *CENTRO, Journal of the Center for Puerto Rican Studies, 9*(1), 27–42.

Morgan, M. (2002). *Language, discourse and power in African American culture.* Cambridge University Press.

Morrison, T. (1987). *Beloved.* Knopf.

O'Connor, M. C., & Michaels, S. (1993). Aligning academic task and participation status through revoicing: Analysis of a classroom discourse strategy. *Anthropology and Education Quarterly, 24*(4), 318–335.

Rabinowitz, P. (1987). *Before reading: Narrative conventions and the politics of interpretation.* Cornell University Press.

Saxe, G. (1991). *Culture and cognitive development: Studies in mathematical understanding.* Erlbaum.

Sophocles. (1977). *The Oedipus Cycle: Oedipus Rex, Oedipus at Colonus, Antigone* (D. Fitts & R. Fitzgerald, Trans.). Harcourt, Brace, Jovanovich.

Stylistics (Musical Group). (1990). People make the world go round. On *The best of the Stylistics* [CD]. Amherst.

TLC. (2004). Waterfalls. On *Now and forever: The hits* [CD]. Arista.

Vygotsky, L. (1978). *Mind in society: The development of higher psychological processes.* Harvard University Press.

Wells, G. (1995). Language and the inquiry-oriented curriculum. *Curriculum Inquiry, 25,* 233–269.

Whitehead, A. N. (1929). *The aims of education.* MacMillan.

Wideman, J. E. (1998). *Damballah.* Mariner Books.

CURRICULUM REFORM

HISTORY, ETHNIC STUDIES, AND ENGLISH LANGUAGE LEARNERS

CHAPTER 8

Teaching What Really Happened

History as a Weapon

James W. Loewen

A great nation does not hide its history. It faces its flaws and corrects them.

—President George W. Bush[1]

The first edition of *Teaching What Really Happened* won wide acceptance in schools of education across the United States. Many school districts also drew it to the attention of their teachers in social studies and U.S. and world history. To my disappointment, however, leaders in some other districts continue to believe that they should shield students from learning the truth about what the United States has done in the world.

Opposition to teaching the truth does not appear to be geographically determined. In 2013, I gave a workshop for teachers in far northwestern Wisconsin and Duluth, Minnesota. Talking with teachers from adjacent districts, I learned that one had helped to bring me and sent as many teachers as could make it to hear me. Another made clear to its faculty that they would be in trouble if they did anything but teach straight from the textbook; teachers from that district had to find out about the workshop on their own, pay their own way, and conceal their attendance.

In districts of this unfortunate second type, learning history and social studies[2] can hinder rather than help build students' understanding of how the world works. Indeed, my best-seller *Lies My Teacher Told Me* opens with the claim that American history as taught in grades 4 through 12 is in crisis and typically makes us stupider.

Of course, it's easy to make such a bold statement. At some point since 1980 just about *every* field in education has been declared "in crisis."[3] The reception of *Lies My Teacher Told Me*, however, implies that many readers, including many teachers of American history in grades 4 through 12, agree with my assessment. In 2018, *Lies* passed a million and a half copies sold and was selling at a higher rate than ever, even though it first came out in

1995.[4] Teachers have been special fans, leading to overflow workshops at venues like the National Council for the Social Studies and the National Association for Multicultural Education. So maybe I'm right. Maybe history and social studies *are* in crisis.

Certainly we can do better.

Since 1995 I have traveled the country, giving workshops for school districts and teacher groups on how to teach history and social studies better. Some of the ideas I present in these workshops come from K–12 teachers I have met over the years. Others derive from my own teaching experience and from my years of thinking about what Americans get wrong about the past. This chapter collects the best shticks from those workshops for the benefit of teachers and future teachers I will never meet.

Teachers who already teach beyond and occasionally against their U.S. history textbooks will find that this chapter will help them explain their approach to other teachers who still teach traditionally. For those who have not yet dared to break away from the security of just teaching the textbook, this chapter will provide specific ways to do so—ways that have worked for other teachers. It may also help them explain their new approach to principals and more traditional parents.

Before plunging into *how* to teach history better, however, we need to spend a few pages considering *why*. We begin with a cautionary tale from Mississippi, showing how history was used there as a weapon to mislead students and keep them ignorant about the past. Moving north to Vermont, I show that ignorance about the past is hardly limited to Mississippi. Mississippi merely exemplified the problem in exaggerated form, as Mississippi embodied many national problems in exaggerated form in the late 1960s and the 1970s. We then progress to dissect the usual reasons that teachers and textbooks give to persuade students that history is worth knowing. I suggest other more important reasons why history is important, both to the individual and society.

A LESSON FROM MISSISSIPPI

I first realized how history distorts our understanding of society in the middle of my first year of full-time teaching, at Tougaloo College in Mississippi. I had started teaching at Tougaloo, a predominantly black institution, in the fall of 1968, after finishing my doctorate in sociology at Harvard University. That first year, in addition to my sociology courses, I was assigned to teach a section of the Freshman Social Science Seminar. The history department had designed this seminar to replace the old "Western Civ" course—History of Western Civilization—then required by most colleges in America, including most black colleges. The FSSS introduced students to sociology, anthropology, political science, economics, and so on, in the context of African

American history—appropriate enough, 99% of our students being African Americans.

African American history uses the same chronology as American history, of course, so the second semester began right after the Civil War, with Reconstruction. I had a new group of students that first day of the spring semester in January 1969, and I didn't want to do all the talking on the first day of class. So I asked my seminar, "What was Reconstruction? What images come to your mind about that era?"

The result was one of those life-changing "Aha!" experiences—or, more accurately, an "Oh, no!" experience. Sixteen of my seventeen students told me, "Reconstruction was that time, right after the Civil War, when African Americans took over the governing of the Southern states, including Mississippi, but they were too soon out of slavery, so they messed up, and reigned corruptly, and whites had to take back control of the state governments."

I sat stunned. So many major misconceptions of facts glared from that statement that it was hard to know where to begin a rebuttal. African Americans never took over the Southern states. All Southern states had white governors and all but one had white legislative majorities throughout Reconstruction. Moreover, the Reconstruction governments did not "mess up." Mississippi in particular enjoyed better and less corrupt government during Reconstruction than at any point later in the century. Across the South, governments during Reconstruction passed the best state constitutions the Southern states have ever had, including their current ones. They started public school systems for both races. Mississippi had never had a statewide system for whites before the Civil War, only scattered schools in the larger towns, and of course it had been a felony to teach blacks, even free blacks, to read and write during slavery times. The Reconstruction governments tried out various other ideas, some of which proved quite popular. Therefore, "whites" did not take back control of the state governments. Rather, *some* whites—Democrats, the party of overt white supremacy throughout the nineteenth century—ended this springtime of freedom before full democracy could blossom. Spearheaded by the Ku Klux Klan, they used terrorism and fraud to wrest control from the biracial Republican coalitions that had governed during Reconstruction.

How could my students believe such false history? I determined to find out. I visited high schools, sat in on history classes, and read the textbooks students were assigned. Tougaloo was a good college—perhaps the best in the state. My students had learned what they had been taught. Bear in mind, they had been attending all-black high schools with all-black teaching staffs—massive school desegregation would not take place in Mississippi until January 1970, a year later. In school after school, I saw black teachers teaching black students white-biased pseudo-history because they were just following the book—and the textbooks were written from a white supremacist viewpoint.

The year-long Mississippi History course was the worst offender. It was required of all 5th- and 9th-graders, in public and private schools, owing to a state law passed after the 1954 U.S. Supreme Court decision in *Brown v. Board of Education*, intended to desegregate the public schools. This Mississippi statute was part of a package of obstructionist measures designed to thwart the Court and maintain "our Southern way of life," which every Mississippian knew meant segregation and white supremacy. The one textbook approved for the 9th-grade course, *Mississippi: Yesterday and Today* by John K. Bettersworth, said exactly what my students had learned. Other than "messing up" during Reconstruction, this book omitted African Americans whenever they did anything notable. Among its 60 images of people, for instance, just two included African Americans.[5]

I knew John Bettersworth. In my junior year in college, I attended Mississippi State University, where he taught history. He knew better. Indeed, when he reviewed several books on Reconstruction in the *New York Times Book Review*, he made clear that he knew that the interracial Republican coalition that governed Mississippi during Reconstruction had done a good job under difficult circumstances. But in his 9th-grade textbook, Bettersworth wrote what he imagined the Mississippi State Textbook Board wanted to read. He knew full well that historians did not (and still do not) review high school textbooks, so his professional reputation would not be sullied by his unprofessional conduct.[6]

Dr. Bettersworth could not have believed that his textbook was an innocent way to make a few thousand dollars without hurting anyone. At Mississippi State, he encountered the graduates of Mississippi high schools by the hundreds, and he knew how racist some of them could be—partly because they believed the BS (Bad Sociology) about African Americans in his textbook.

Perhaps as a passive form of resistance against their racist textbooks, many Mississippi teachers—white as well as black—spent hours of class time making students memorize the names of the state's 82 counties, their county seats, and the date each was organized as a county. Or, perhaps more likely, they did this because it had been done to them. Regardless, these 250 twigs of information were useless and soon forgotten.[7] Meanwhile, students learned nothing about the past from this book that would help them deal with the wrenching changes Mississippi was going through in the 1960s and '70s.

Black students were particularly disadvantaged. What must it do to them, I wondered that January afternoon, to believe that the one time their group stood center-stage in the American past, they "messed up"? It couldn't be good for them. If it had happened, of course, that would be another matter. In that case, it would have to be faced: Why did "we" screw up? What must we learn from it? But nothing of the sort had taken place. It was, again, Bad Sociology.

For more than a year, I tried to interest historians in Mississippi in writing a more accurate textbook of state history. Finally, despairing of getting anyone else to do so, I put together a group of students and faculty from Tougaloo and also from Millsaps College, the nearby white school, got a grant, and we wrote it. The result, *Mississippi: Conflict and Change*, won the Lillian Smith Award for best Southern nonfiction the year it came out. Nevertheless, the Mississippi State Textbook Board rejected it as unsuitable. In most subjects, the board selected three to five textbooks. In Mississippi history, they chose just one. Only two were available, which might be characterized "ours" and "theirs." By a two-to-five vote, the board rejected ours, accepting only theirs. Two blacks and five whites sat on the board.

Our book was not biased toward African Americans. Six of its eight authors were white, as were 80% of the historical characters who made it into our index. An index 20% nonwhite looks pretty black, however, to people who are used to textbooks wherein just 2% of the people referred to are nonwhite. Moreover, in contrast to the white supremacist fabrications offered in "their book," our book showed how Mississippi's social structure shaped the lives of its citizens. So, after exhausting our administrative remedies, we—coeditor Charles Sallis and I, accompanied by three school systems that wanted to use our book—eventually sued the textbook board in federal court. The case, *Loewen et al. v. Turnipseed et al.*, came to trial in 1980, Judge Orma Smith presiding. Smith was an 83-year-old white Mississippian who believed in the 1st amendment—students' right to controversial information—and was bringing himself to believe in the 14th amendment—blacks' right to equal treatment.[8]

For a week we presented experts from around the state and around the nation who testified that by any reasonable criteria, including those put forth by the state itself, our book was better than their book. Among other topics, they found *Conflict and Change* more accurate in its treatment of prehistory and archaeology, Native Americans, slavery, Reconstruction, Mississippi literature, the civil rights era, and the recent past.

Then came the state's turn. The trial's dramatic moment came when the Deputy Attorney General of Mississippi asked John Turnipseed, one of the board members who had rejected our book, why he had done so. Turnipseed asked the court to turn to page 178, on which was a photograph of a lynching. "Now you know, some 9th-graders are pretty big," he noted, "especially black male 9th-graders. And we worried, or at least *I* worried, that teachers—especially white lady teachers—would be unable to control their classes with material like this in the book."

As lynching photos go, ours was actually mild, if such an adjective can be applied to these horrific scenes. About two dozen white people posed for the camera behind the body of an African American man, silhouetted in a fire that was burning him. The victim's features could not be discerned, and no grisly details—such as whites hacking off body parts as souvenirs—were

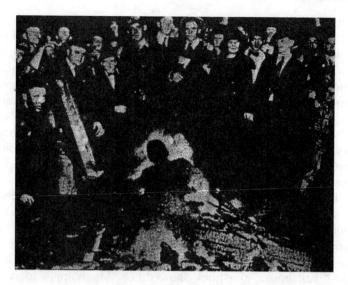

This is the lynching photo to which Turnipseed objected. A lynching is a public murder, done with considerable support from the community. Often, as here, the mob posed for the camera. They showed no fear of being identified because they knew no white jury would convict them.

I found this photo in *Black America*, by economist Scott Nearing, published in 1929. Nearing identified it only as a Mississippi lynching. Mississippi had more lynchings than any other state, but as our poorest state, it had few cameras, so photos of lynchings were rare. It turned out that Nearing had misidentified this photo. White residents of Nebraska burned this African American, Will Brown, during the Omaha race riot of 1919, after first shooting him, then hanging him. Per black capita, lynchings may have been as common in the North as in the South. Photos of Northern lynchings were often mislabeled Southern, making lynchings seem "merely" a regional problem.

shown or described. Nevertheless, our book was going to cause a race riot in the classroom.

We had pretested our book—along with Bettersworth's—in an over-whelmingly white classroom and an overwhelmingly black classroom. Both had preferred ours by huge margins. So we had material to counter this argument when our turn came for rebuttal. We never had to use it, however, because at that point Judge Smith took over the questioning.

"But that happened, didn't it?" he asked. "Didn't Mississippi have more lynchings than any other state?"

"Well, yes," Turnipseed admitted. "But that all happened so long ago. Why dwell on it now?"

"Well, it *is* a *history* book!" the judge retorted. And we nudged each other, realizing we were going to win this case. Eventually, in a decision the

American Library Association ranks as one of its "notable First Amendment court cases," the judge ordered Mississippi to adopt our book for the standard 6-year period and supply it to any school system, public or private, that requested it, like any other adopted book.[9]

Although we won the lawsuit, that experience proved to me that history can be a *weapon*, and it had been used against my students. This chapter helps teachers arm students with critical reading and thinking skills—historiography, for example—so they will not be defenseless. Indeed, they can even learn to do history themselves.

A LESSON FROM VERMONT

After 8 years, I moved to the University of Vermont. Again, I found myself teaching 1st-year undergraduates, this time in huge classes in Introductory Sociology. I enjoyed these freshman classes, not least because they opened a wonderful window on the world of high school. The view was mighty discouraging at times. My UVM students—as the University of Vermont is known—showed me that teaching and learning "BS history" in high school was and is a national problem. These students were also ignorant of even the basic facts of our past, as were my Mississippi students, despite the hours spent in most high schools memorizing them.

In 1989, their ignorance astounded me in a course I taught intended for advanced undergraduates in education, history, and sociology. On the first day of class I gave my students a quiz. It contained some comical items (some posted at my website, sundown.tougaloo.edu/quiz.php), but also perfectly straightforward questions like this one: "The War in Vietnam was fought between _____ and _____." To my astonishment, 22% of my students replied "North and South Korea!"

Now, please don't infer that something special—and specially wrong—has eroded history education in Vermont. The University of Vermont is a national institution; only 40% of its students come from within the state. Moreover, repeated national studies show that high school students learn history exceptionally badly. In 2003, for instance, the National Assessment of Educational Progress granted "advanced" status in U.S. history to only 1% of high school seniors. College graduates did little better. In 2000, the American Council of Trustees and Alumni commissioned the Center for Survey Research at the University of Connecticut to administer a 34-item "high school level American history test" to 556 seniors at 55 top colleges and universities. "Nearly 80% . . . received a D or F," according to a summary. More than a third didn't know that the Constitution established the three-way division of power in the U.S. government; 99%, on the other hand, could identify Beavis and Butt-Head as adolescent television cartoon characters.[10] NAEP scores in geography were similarly dismal, with only

25% scoring "proficient" in 2014. College courses failed to fill in the gaps in students' knowledge, partly because many college students never take a history course, it having been so boring in high school.[11]

University of Vermont students were particularly bad, however, in learning and applying the basic concepts of sociology. Indeed, they were so bad at it that I coined a new term for the syndrome that they exhibited: soclexia. This learning disorder makes it very difficult for its victims to grasp the basic idea of sociology. It may be genetic; certainly it strikes certain racial and economic groups more than others. Children from white (and Asian American) upper-class and upper-middle-class families are especially vulnerable.[12]

What is the basic idea of sociology? It is this: *Social structure pushes people around, influences their careers, and even affects how they think.* I was unprepared for the level of soclexia I experienced in Vermont. My Tougaloo students readily understood that social structure pushed people around. Not one of their parents was an architect, for example, because no school in the Deep South in their parents' generation both taught architecture and admitted African Americans. So my Tougaloo students knew how social structure might influence careers. Then, too, neighbors of theirs— white children—had been their friends when they were 4 and 5 years old, but by the time they were 14 and 15 a barrier had gone up between them. My black undergraduates could see that this racial bias was hardly innate; rather, it showed that social structure affects how people think. Hence they were open to the sociological perspective.

My UVM students, in contrast, were very different. To be sure, they could memorize. If I asked them on a quiz, "What is the basic idea of sociology?" they would reply, "Social structure pushes people around, influences their careers, even affects how they think." But when I asked them to apply that idea to their own lives or to the next topic we dealt with in introductory sociology, most were clueless.

To understand their soclexia, it helps to know that during the years I taught there (1975–1996), UVM usually ranked number 1 as the most expensive state university in America, both in-state and out of state. Hence, it drew extraordinarily rich students. In 1996, the last year I collected data (and no one else ever did), the median family income for out-of-state students at the University of Vermont (and most students came from out of state) was $123,500 (about $196,000 in 2018 dollars). In that year, the national median family income was $42,300 (about $67,000 in 2018 dollars). Only 5.5% of all families made $123,500 or more. Yet half of all out-of-state families at the University of Vermont came from this elite income group. The mean family income of UVM students was higher still.[13]

Despite being so rich, my students believed that they—not their parents' social positions—were responsible for their own success—which consisted mostly of their having been admitted to the University of Vermont. *They* pushed social structure around, most felt, and if some people were poor, that was their own damn fault—they simply hadn't pushed social structure around *enough*. Most of my students had no understanding that for children of their social class background, gaining admission to college was not an outstanding personal accomplishment but merely meeting expectations—going with the flow.

I tried to show them that their understanding of the social world was itself a product of social structure—indeed, was entirely predictable from their membership in the upper-middle and lower-upper classes. In short, their view that social structure made no difference was the ideology "appropriate" to their position in social structure. It is precisely these classes that hold the idea that class makes no difference.

Their class position was not the sole cause of their soclexia. Their high school education contributed as well. Not their high school coursework in sociology—few high schools offer sociology, even as an elective. But there is one course that everyone takes and that purports to be about our society—American history. Unfortunately, American history as presented in high school textbooks (and by teachers who rely on them) not only leaves out social class entirely, it also avoids any analysis of what causes what in our society, past or present. Thus, American history is a key breeding ground of soclexia.

Indeed, in my experience, the more history students have taken in high school, the *less* able they are to think sociologically. Some college history professors agree. A friend who taught the U.S. history survey at Vermont nicknamed its two semesters "Iconoclasm I and II," because he had to break the icons—the false images of the past that students carried with them from their high school history courses—to make room for more accurate information. He actually preferred students from other countries, who knew no American history at all or, as is often the case, knew it more accurately and more analytically than do American high school graduates.

In no other discipline do college professors prefer students with *less* preparation! On the contrary, the math department is delighted when high school graduates have taken a fifth year of math. After giving them a test to ensure they have retained what they learned, the department places such students in advanced instead of introductory calculus. Shakespeare professors are similarly happy to teach students who have already read *Lear* in high school, along with the standard *Romeo and Juliet*. While they may not place such a person in "Advanced Shakespeare" and may teach *Lear* differently, nevertheless, the student has read the play and thought about it and will be a pleasure to teach.

Not so in history.

I responded to my students' ignorance of history just as I had in Mississippi: I visited nearby high schools to watch teachers in history classrooms and studied the textbooks they used. I found that most of them relied far too much on these textbooks. This was not a local Vermont problem. Research shows that students spend more class time with their textbooks in history— reading the books in class, discussing them, answering the 60 questions at the end of each chapter—than in any other subject in the curriculum. This finding staggered me. I had thought the winner (or rather, loser) would be something very different—perhaps geometry. After all, students can hardly interview their parents about geometry. They can hardly use the web, or the library, the census, and so on, to learn about geometry. But all these resources, and many more besides, are perfectly relevant to the study of history.

When I studied the textbooks that so dominated these courses, my concern deepened. Although American history is full of gripping and important stories, these books were dull. Their basic storyline was that the United States started out great and has been getting greater ever since! Only without the exclamation point. They failed to let voices from the past speak; instead, they told everything themselves, in a boring monotone.

Few of the teachers I watched supplemented the textbooks, despite their soporific impact. In many cases, I came to learn, teachers didn't go beyond the book because they didn't know how. Eighteen percent of teachers in social studies and history did not major in history, social studies education, any social science, or any other relevant field.[14] Such woefully underprepared teachers use textbooks as crutches. I do not mean to slur all history teachers—not at all. Many teach history because they love it and think it is important. Unfortunately, some teachers who would love to go beyond the textbook with their students feel they cannot because their students have to take "standardized" multiple-choice tests at the end of the year based on the factoids with which textbooks abound.

As a result of this textbook-centric approach, many high school students come to hate history. In survey after national survey, when they list their favorite subject, history always comes in last. Students consider it "irrelevant," "borr-r-ring." When they can, they avoid it. Not every class, not every district, of course. I hope yours is an exception. But across the nation, history/social studies does not fare well. As they are typically taught, I believe students are right to dislike them.

Students from out-groups hate history with a special passion and do especially poorly in it. But even affluent young white males are bored by most American history courses in high school.

WHY HISTORY IS IMPORTANT TO STUDENTS

Yet history is crucial. It should be taught in high school, partly because five-sixths of all Americans never take a course in American history after they leave high school. What our citizens learn there forms the core of what they know of our past.

The first thing that students do *not* learn about history is why studying it is important. Teachers must go beyond the old saw by the philosopher George Santayana, "Those who cannot remember the past are condemned to repeat it."[15] This cliché won't do. Indeed, it is a mystification. The phrase itself is wrong, implying that knowing about the past somehow automatically makes us smarter. Consider the equal and opposite saying by the philosopher Georg Hegel, "People and governments have never learned anything from history."[16] Moreover, Santayana's saying sweeps conflict under the rug. My Tougaloo students—and their white counterparts at Ole Miss—were not repeating Mississippi's history of white supremacy because they could not remember the past. They were repeating it because they *did* remember the past—as it had been mispresented to them in school. To put this another way, who wrote the history students are asked to recall, and who did not—and for what purpose—can make a world of difference to how it influences the present.

There are much better reasons for learning about history. Once we come to some agreement—not necessarily total—as to why the field is important, that agreement can inform how we should go about teaching it. I submit that the course is gravely important because its purpose is to help students prepare to do their job *as Americans*. Students may grow up to be school bus drivers, computer programmers, or CEOs, but what is their job as Americans? Surely it is to bring into being the America of the future.

What does that task entail? Some vision of a good society is required: a society that allows and encourages its members to be all they can be.[17] A society enough in harmony with the planet that it can maintain itself over the long run. A society enough at peace with other countries that it does not live in fear of attack. Students might go beyond these basics, perhaps to some vision of the "beloved community." Their job as Americans—and ours—then consists of figuring out what policies help us move toward that community. What should the United States do about global warming? What should our policy be toward gay marriage? Regarding the next issue—the debate that is sure to engulf us next year, whatever it may be—what position should we take, and what concrete steps to implement it?

Every issue, every suggestion, every element of the America of the future entails an assertion of causation. "We must do X to achieve goal Y." Of course, history is full of causation—and arguments about causation.

Even when an event seems to be new, the causes of the acts and feelings are deeply embedded in the past. Thus, to understand an event—an election, an act of terror, a policy decision about the environment, whatever—we must start in the past.

Unfortunately, high school textbooks in American history present the past as one damn thing after another. Few of the facts are memorable because they are not shown as related. Therefore, most high school graduates have no inkling of causation in history. Consequently, they cannot use the past to illuminate the present—cannot think coherently about social life.

Why are textbooks compendiums of fact rather than arguments about causation? I don't think it's due to an upper-class conspiracy to keep us stupid, although it might be. One problem is precisely that there *are* arguments about causation. There are far fewer arguments about facts. So let's just stick with the facts. Another problem is that causation continues to the present, and arguments about the present are by definition controversial. Moreover, as the second edition of *Lies My Teacher Told Me* shows, high school history textbooks often aren't really written by the people whose names are on their title pages, especially after their first editions. The gnomes in the bowels of the publishing companies who write them aren't hired to interpret the past or sort out causation in the past and don't have the credentials for that task.

For all these reasons, textbooks downplay what causes what. Nevertheless, learning what causes what is crucial for our job as Americans.

So is critical thinking. Again, history textbooks—and courses centered on "learning" history textbooks—downplay critical thinking. Almost never does a textbook suggest more than one possible answer and invite students to assess evidence for each. Instead, they tell the right answers, over and over, in their sleep-inducing godlike monotone. It is sometimes the case that no one knows the right answer, yet history textbooks present one anyway!

A crucial ingredient of critical thinking is historiography. Earlier, talking about Mississippi, we noted that who wrote history, who did not, and for what purpose can make all the difference. That assertion comes from historiography—the study of the writing of history—and every high school graduate should know both the term and how to "do" it.

Perhaps the most basic reason students need to take history/social studies is this: history is power. That I saw firsthand in Mississippi. History can be a weapon. Students who do *not* know their own history or how to think critically about historical assertions will be ignorant and helpless before someone who does claim to know it. Students need to be able to fight back. This line of thought is a strong motivator, especially for "have-not" students,[18] but all students enjoy "wielding" history.

There are still other reasons to learn history. The past supplies models for our behavior, for example. From the sagas of Lewis and Clark, Laura Ingalls Wilder, Helen Keller, Rachel Carson, and a thousand others, students can draw inspiration, courage, and sometimes still-relevant causes. We're not talking hero worship here, however, and all of the individuals named above have their imperfections. Present them whole. Instead of suggesting heroes as models, suggest heroic actions. Typically people perform heroically at a key moment, not so heroically at other moments. Students need to do accurate history, coupled with historiography, to sort out in which ways their role models are worth following. Recognizing both the good and not-so-good element within historical individuals can also make it easier to accept that societies too contain the good and not so good.[19]

History can (and should) also make us less ethnocentric. Ethnocentrism is the belief that one's own culture is the best and that other societies and cultures should be ranked highly only to the degree that they resemble ours. Every successful society manifests ethnocentrism. Swedes, for example, think their nation is the best, and with reason: Sweden has a slightly higher standard of living than the United States, and on at least one survey of happiness Swedes scored happier than the American average. But Swedes can never convince themselves that theirs is the dominant culture, dominant military, or dominant economy. Americans can—and without even being ethnocentric. After all, our GNP is the largest, Americans spend more on our military than all other nations combined, and for years athletes in countries around the world have high-fived each other after a really good dive, or dunk, or bobsled run. They didn't learn that from their home culture, or from Sweden, but from us, the dominant culture on the planet.[20] It is but a small step to conclude that ours is the *best* country on the planet. Hence, the United States leads the world in ethnocentrism.

Unfortunately, ethnocentrism is, among other things, a form of ignorance. An ethnocentric person finds it hard to learn from another culture, already knowing it to be inferior. Ethnocentrism also has a Siamese twin: arrogance; the combination has repeatedly hampered U.S. foreign policy.

History *can* make us less ethnocentric, but as usually taught in middle and high school, it has the opposite effect. That's because our textbooks are shot through with the ideology called "American exceptionalism." In 2007, Wikipedia offered a fine definition:

> the perception that the United States differs qualitatively from other developed nations, because of its unique origins, national credo, historical evolution, or distinctive political and religious institutions.[21]

Wikipedia went on to note that superiority, not just difference, is almost always implied, although not necessarily.

Of course, every national story is unique. Consider Portugal: No other nation "discovered" half the globe, as Portugal's tourism board puts it. Or Namibia: No other nation in the 20th century had three-fourths of its largest ethnic group (the Hereros) wiped out by a foreign power (Germany). But by American exceptionalism, authors of U.S. history textbooks mean not just unique, but uniquely wonderful. Consider the first paragraph of *A History of the United States* by Daniel Boorstin and Brooks Mather Kelley:

> American history is the story of a magic transformation. How did people from everywhere join the American family? How did men and women from a tired

. Old World, where people thought they knew what to expect, become wide-eyed explorers of a New World?[22]

Surely that passage is meant to impart that the United States is truly special—and in a positive way. Presumably Boorstin and Kelley want students to be wide-eyed themselves as they learn more about the "magic transformation" that is American history.

I suggest that teachers want students to be clear-eyed, not wide-eyed, as they learn American history. American exceptionalism promotes ethnocentrism. Still worse, it fosters bad history. To get across the claim that Americans have always been exceptionally good, authors leave out the bad parts. Woodrow Wilson involved us in a secret war against Russia, for example. Let's leave that out. Americans committed war crimes as a matter of policy in our war against the Philippines. Let's suppress that. Ultimately, writing a past sanitized of wrongdoing means developing a book or a course that is both unbelievable and boring. Making our past seem ever-creditable comes at the expense of making it seem never credible.

Some people, including some school administrators, think lying to schoolchildren is in the nation's best interest. If we "dwell on" the bad things that we have done in the past, they imagine, then children will grow up to hate the United States, and we shall fall apart as a nation. Surely our national past is not so bad that teachers must protect students from it. It is not really worse than, say, Russia's, or South Africa's, or Germany's—and we want those nations to discuss their pasts honestly. "We do not need a bodyguard of lies," points out historian Paul Gagnon. "We can afford to present ourselves in the totality of our acts."[23] Textbook authors seem not to share Gagnon's confidence. But papering over everything bad in our past does not work anyway. It does not convince students that the United States has done no wrong; it only persuades them that American history is not a course worth taking seriously.

We need to distinguish between patriotism and nationalism. Defining "the duty of a true patriot," Frederick Douglass wrote: "He is a lover of his country who rebukes and does not excuse its sins."[24] A nationalist, in contrast, does not admit that the country has any sins and rebukes those who say it does. Surely nationalism, properly understood, is not patriotic.

The worst problem with this excuse for bad history is that people suggest we omit or sugarcoat topics not because they are unimportant, but precisely because they are important, even controversial, in the present. Therefore cutting them out by definition removes things that matter today, hence making history courses boring, which demoralizes both students and teachers.

Those who make this argument for bad history do not themselves want to be lied to. I've never met anyone who suggests that they should not know the truth about something in the past. True, some leftists may not want schools "to dwell" on how communist nations almost invariably wind up as dictatorships. Some rightists may not want schools "to dwell" on how the United States almost invariably winds up supporting dictatorships. But everyone wants to be in on the decision as to what to leave out. People want to be the liars, not the dupes.

Other adults think we should lie to schoolchildren because doing so is in the children's best interest. "Childhood should be a happy time," goes this line of thought. Let's not trouble children's tender little minds with any tough stuff. A father of a Massachusetts high school student told an audience I had just addressed that his daughter had come home in tears after a week-long unit on the Holocaust. He was not happy. "Why can't they let kids be kids?" he asked. As a single father who had custody of my daughter during her high school years, I empathized with him. "No father wants to see his daughter in tears," I replied. "But I'm not sure it's a bad thing to cry after a unit on the Holocaust. I'm almost in tears myself, just talking with you about it." Then I asked him how old his daughter was now. "In her thirties," was his reply. "Have you talked with her about this event since it happened?" He admitted he had not. "I suggest you might want to have that conversation," I said. "I bet first that she will remember the unit, and she won't remember very many other units from her high school social studies and history courses. I also suspect she won't regret having had it." The father agreed that might be the case.

There is such a thing as age-appropriate education. I would not teach the Holocaust to 2nd-graders. But if high school students cannot handle it because it is too intense, then we are in a sorry state. Where else might they discuss it? In college? Some students—many students in some districts—never graduate from high school. Of high school grads, fewer than two-thirds go on to college, and most of those never take a history course, having found the subject boring in high school. If students don't think about tough subjects like the Holocaust in high school, when will they? If they don't learn how to think about tough subjects now, when will they?

Thus far we have noted four reasons why history is an important course:

- History helps students be better citizens by helping them understand what causes what in society.
- History helps students become critical thinkers. Doing historiography (and learning that word) is part of that process.
- History helps students muster countervailing power against those who would persuade them of false ideologies. This is the "history as weapon" point.
- History helps students become less ethnocentric.

All four relate to history's effects upon students, which make sense, since this chapter is part of a book for teachers. But history—what we say about the past—also has effects upon our society as a whole.

WHY HISTORY IS IMPORTANT TO SOCIETY

There is a reciprocal relationship between justice in the present and honesty about the past. When the United States has achieved justice in the present regarding some past act, then Americans can face it and talk about it more openly, because we have made it right. It has become a success story. Conversely, when we find a topic that our textbooks hide or distort, probably that signifies a continuing injustice in the present. Telling the truth about the past can help us make it right from here on.

This insight hit me between the eyes as I compared American history textbooks of the 1960s and 1990s in their handling of the incarceration of Japanese Americans during World War II. In 1961, Thomas Bailey's *The American Pageant*, for example, made no mention of the internment. Five years later, it got a paragraph, telling that "this brutal precaution turned out to be unnecessary," for their loyalty "proved to be admirable." The paragraph ends, "Partial financial adjustment after the war did something to recompense these uprooted citizens. . . ."

In 1988, Congress passed the Civil Liberties Act, apologizing for the "grave injustice" and paying $20,000 to each survivor of the camps. This amount hardly sufficed to recompense more than 3years of life and labor lost behind barbed wire, as well as the loss of homes and businesses, but it was more than a token. Around that time, textbooks expanded their coverage of the incident. By 2006, *Pageant* had more than doubled its paragraph, added an ironic photograph of two Japanese Americans in Boy Scout uniforms posting a notice that read "To Aliens of Enemy Nationalities," and included a boxed quote from a young Japanese American woman that described her angry reaction to the order. It also devoted the next two pages to the Japanese as "Makers of America," providing a summary of the group's entire history in the United States, including a photograph of deportees getting into a truck and another of Manzanar Camp, with lengthy captions. The last sentence in the main text treats our 1988 apology and payment of $20,000.[25]

Because textbooks began to increase their treatment of the incarceration before 1988, historian Mark Selden suggests they may have helped to cause the 1988 apology and reparations payment. I suspect the textbooks merely reflected the change in the spirit of the times. But either way, there seems to have been an interrelationship between truth about the incarceration and justice toward its victims.

Evidence shows that our society is ready to look at many past atrocities without flinching. In 2000, for example, the exhibit of lynching photos, *Without Sanctuary*, broke all attendance records at the New York Historical Society.[26] To be sure, lynchings are over. Americans don't do that anymore.[27] So the lack of lynchings has become a success story and the topic is thus easier to face. Nevertheless, many visitors to the museum were surprised to

On June 15, 1920, a mob took Elias Clayton, Elmer Jackson, and Isaac McGhie, three black circus workers, from the Duluth, Minnesota, jail and lynched them.

learn that lynchings were not the work of a few hooded men late at night. The open daytime photos showing a white community proud to be photographed in the act startled them. Most Americans have not seen such images. Not one high school textbook on American history includes a lynching photo. Presented here is an example of the lynching photographs that are available but never included in U.S. history textbooks. Surely publishers' caution is mistaken. After all, in 2003 Duluth faced this event, dedicating a memorial to the victims after decades of silence.

Images like the Duluth mob can help students understand that racism in the United States has not typically been the province of the few, but of the many; not just the South, but also the North. Today, too, the discrimination facing African Americans (and to a degree, other groups, such as Native Americans and Mexican Americans) does not come from a handful of extremist outcasts late at night. Leaving out lynchings, sundown towns,[28] and other acts of collective discrimination impoverishes students and hurts their ability to understand the present, not just the past.

History is important—even crucial. Helping students understand what happened in the past empowers them to use history as a weapon to argue for better policies in the present. Our society needs engaged citizens, including students. I've found that learning new things about our American past is exciting, for me as well as for students and other teachers. So will you.

FOCUSED BIBLIOGRAPHY

The following five books (choose either book by Percoco) are key preparation for any social studies or U.S. history teacher.

Either James A. Percoco's *A Passion for the Past* (1998, Heinemann) or *Divided We Stand* (2001, Heinemann) supplies a daunting list of innovations for history classes, from visiting cemeteries to getting students talking about controversial historic photographs. It's daunting because Percoco lays out so *many* ideas; but if a teacher chooses just two or three and makes them work, his book will have done its job.

In *Beyond the Textbook*, David Kobrin (1996, Heinemann) suggests only a handful of innovations but explores each in depth, showing pitfalls to avoid.

Note Bill Bigelow's how-to accounts of several innovative classroom exercises in Wayne Au, Bill Bigelow, and Stan Karp, eds., *Rethinking Our Classrooms* (2007, Rethinking Schools, Milwaukee).

After the Fact, by James Davidson and Mark Lytle (1992, McGraw-Hill), written by two college professors and intended for college history majors, covers about 20 topics, providing examples of how to treat a topic at some length.

Please do read Loewen, *Lies My Teacher Told Me* (2018, New Press).

NOTES

1. President George W. Bush at the dedication of the National Museum of African American History & Culture, September 24, 2016.

2. I don't fully grasp the distinction between history and social studies. According to the National Council for the Social Studies, "Social studies is the integrated study of the social sciences and humanities to promote civic competence" (National Council for the Social Studies 1972 statement, reprinted in "Curriculum Standards for Social Studies: I. Introduction," socialstudies.org/standards/introduction). Seems vague, but otherwise, who can argue with it? To be competent, historians, too, must use the insights and methods of the social sciences. They must know how to construct a table, read the census, and employ theoretical ideas like social structure or cognitive dissonance. Moreover, when competently taught, history provides marvelous preparation for "civic competence."

In some districts, social studies is taught in middle school, history in high school. Some college professors routinely put down social studies as more concerned with building students' self-image than imparting knowledge. At a conference for K–12 teachers organized by the National Council for History Education, I listened to a famous history professor extol history and denounce social studies. He may not have known that more than half of his audience actually taught "social studies" and were interested in teaching it better, which was why they were attending his lecture. All he did was make them feel bad. He did not help them teach better. I shall use "history" and "social studies" interchangeably.

3. The National Commission on Excellence in Education came out with the most influential jeremiad of all, *A Nation At Risk*, in 1983 (1983, GPO).

4. Later in 2007, a second edition came out, completely revised in light of six new U.S. history textbooks published between 2000 and 2007. It also contained a new chapter analyzing what textbooks do and do not say about 9/11 and Iraq.

5. John K. Bettersworth, *Mississippi: Yesterday and Today* (1964, Steck Vaughn). These were two "Old South" images: a drawing of a white mistress reading from the Bible to a group of slaves and a painting by a white artist showing cotton pickers. In addition, an illustration of boys on the deck of a steamboat may include a black boy dancing a jig; since he is just 3/8" tall, we cannot be sure. Robert B. Moore, *Two History Texts: A Study in Contrast* (1974, Center for Interracial Books, New York), compared his book and ours systematically.

6. John Bettersworth, "After the War Was Won," NY *Times Book Review*, July 25, 1971.

7. There are about 250 items because some counties have more than one county seat.

8. Actually, nothing in our book was new to historians. It was controversial only in the context of Mississippi's educational climate of the time.

9. *Loewen et al. v. Turnipseed et al.*, 488 F. Supp. 1138.

10. Between about 2004 and 2007 an uptick occurred, with slightly fewer students falling below "basic" on the American history test of the National Assessment of Educational Progress, for example. Can we credit the No Child Left Behind Act? The widespread use of *Lies My Teacher Told Me* in teacher education programs? Improvements in textbooks? (The 2007 edition of *Lies* argues that textbooks have not materially improved.) Increased viewing of the History Channel?

11. Caren Benjamin, "College Seniors Flunk History Test," *Chicago Sun-Times*, June 28, 2000; National Assessment of Educational Progress (NAEP) results discussed in Richard Rothstein, "We Are Not Ready to Assess History Performance," *Journal of American History*, March 2004, 1389.

12. In workshops, I deliver these lines deadpan, and audiences crack up, so I hope readers grasp that I'm trying to be comical. I don't really believe for a moment that soclexia is genetic. But then, neither is the difficulty poor and minority children have when they try to learn history from the usual textbook approach.

13. Mean incomes are always pulled up by very rich families; median is therefore a better measure. Data from U.S. Census Bureau, "Current Population Survey, 2005 Annual Social and Economic Supplement." pubdb3.census.gov/macro/032005/hhinc/new06_000.htm

14. Richard M. Ingersoll (2019), "Measuring Out-of-Field Teaching." In L. Hobbs & G. Törner (Eds.), *Examining the Phenomenon of "Teaching Out-of-field."* Springer. https://doi.org/10.1007/978-981-13-3366-8_2

15. George Santayana, *Life of Reason* (1905, Scribner's), 284.

16. G. W. F. Hegel, "Introduction," *Philosophy of History*, widely quoted, e.g., EpistemeLinks, August 2008. epistemelinks.com/Main/Quotations.aspx?PhilCode=Hege

17. Nothing wrong with a good cliché now and then!

18. Unfortunately, textbook authors are too timid to use it. "History as power" implies that some people are not amicable, that they may lie or cover up, and that ideas matter and are worth battling over. Santayana's maxim sounds so much nicer.

19. The lives of some potential role models were distorted or removed from view altogether during the "Nadir of race relations."

20. Specifically, from African American culture.

21. Wikipedia, "American exceptionalism," June 2007. en.wikipedia.org/wiki/American_exceptionalism

22. Daniel Boorstin and Brooks Mather Kelley, *A History of the United States* (2005, Pearson/Prentice Hall), xix.

23. Paul Gagnon, *Democracy's Untold Story* (1987, American Federation of Teachers, Washington, DC), 19.

24. Frederick Douglass, "Love of God, Love of Man, Love of Country." Talk, September 24, 1847, Syracuse, New York (*Douglass Papers, Vol. I*, 2, 103).

25. Thomas A. Bailey, *The American Pageant* (1961, Boston), summarized by Mark Selden in "Confronting World War II: The Atomic Bombing and the Internment of Japanese-Americans in U.S. History Textbooks," in Andrew Horvat and Gebhard Hielscher, eds., *Sharing the Burden of the Past: Legacies of War in Europe, America, and Asia* (2003, Asia Foundation and F. E. Stiftung, Tokyo); Bailey, *Pageant* (1966, Little, Brown), 881; David M. Kennedy, Lizabeth Cohen, and Bailey, *Pageant* (2006, Houghton Mifflin), 822–825.

26. Kathleen Hulser, New York Historical Society, talk at Organization of American Historians, April 2002.

27. What of the dragging death of James Byrd Jr. in Jasper, Texas, in 1998? That was horrific, to be sure, and a hate crime, but not a lynching. Byrd was killed after midnight on a deserted road, and when the community found out, the perpetrators were arrested, tried, convicted, and punished.

28. Sundown towns are communities that for decades were all-white on purpose (and some still exist). See Loewen, *Sundown Towns* (2005, New Press).

CHAPTER 9

What the Research Says About Ethnic Studies

Christine E. Sleeter and Miguel Zavala

Chicano, Nahuatl, Cubano, that's all me. I didn't grow with my biological father, who's Cuban. I grew up with my mom more than anything, single mother. . . . My mom, Mexican from Jalisco, ancestrally Nahuatl roots. . . . My own experience and so many of my peers around me is like, "Yeah we have to reconnect, because if not it's just erased." Within us, at least. That's part of why I connect to ethnic studies so much, because it's literally doing that within education.

—R. Tolteka Cuauhtin, December 23, 2018

Tolteka Cuauhtin, an ethnic studies teacher in Los Angeles, speaks to the need for an education that is rehumanizing, one that enables reclaiming identity and ancestral knowledge. His own elementary and secondary education did not provide these things; he sought them out, eventually by becoming an ethnic studies teacher. Cuauhtin's words point toward a potentially powerful positive impact of ethnic studies on students.

Conversely, we sometimes hear that students should learn the common curriculum that includes everyone before they focus on ethnic studies. This claim perceives the common curriculum as widely inclusive and as building cross-group understanding; some who make this claim perceive ethnic studies as divisive. For example, former Arizona state superintendent John Huppenthal vigorously opposed ethnic studies on the basis that, in his view, "framing historical events in racial terms 'to create a sense of solidarity' promotes groupthink and victimhood. It has a very toxic effect, and we think it's just not tolerable in an educational setting" (cited in Cesar, 2011).

What kind of impact on students does the research actually substantiate? This question was put to Christine by the National Education Association in 2010. Her research review addressing that question resulted in the publication *The Academic and Social Value of Ethnic Studies* (Sleeter, 2011). In this chapter, we update and expand on that review.

For this research review, we sought published studies and reviews of research that systematically document the impact of ethnic studies (including Afrocentric education, Mexican American studies, and so forth) on U.S. students, pre-K through higher education. We analyzed everything we could find, regardless of whether results supported ethnic studies or not. (As you will see, very few studies did not find a positive impact on students.) For this chapter, we did not seek studies of ethnic studies teachers' development, or case studies of ethnic studies teaching and learning processes that did not also report outcome data. Rather, we focused on studies reporting data of the impact of ethnic studies on students.

This chapter is organized into two main sections that emerged from the nature of the research. The first section examines the academic and personal impact of ethnic studies on students of color. The second examines the impact of ethnic studies on the racial attitudes and racial understandings of diverse student groups that include White students.

ACADEMIC AND PERSONAL IMPACT ON STUDENTS OF COLOR

Ideally, the ethnic studies projects that have been researched would exemplify all seven hallmarks of ethnic studies discussed in Chapter 1 of our book. In practice, that is not the case. Ethnic studies is a developing field, an unfinished project. Some curriculum projects in this review exemplified all or most of the hallmarks, most often the creation of curriculum from perspectives of specific marginalized and/or colonized groups. After that, there is wide variation.

Researching the impact of ethnic studies on students poses a challenge in that the purposes of ethnic studies—eliminating racism, decolonizing students' minds, sustaining minoritized cultures—are expansive. How does one operationalize them for research? So researchers have landed on more measurable outcomes, such as achievement on tests (standardized or otherwise), retention rates, graduation rates, and scales for academic self-concept, academic engagement, and ethnic identity.

We organized this section of the chapter into four parts that differ on the basis of which hallmarks of ethnic studies the projects emphasized and which student outcomes (academic achievement or personal outcomes) the studies assessed. We begin with identity and sense of self, since other student outcomes, especially achievement, flow from students' understanding of themselves as capable and centered in who they are.

Ethnic Studies and Student Identity/Sense of Self

Students' sense of identity, particularly their ability to claim their ethnic identity and link it with an academic identity, is crucial. If students have been taught implicitly that people like themselves are incapable and unimportant, doing well in school has little meaning. Conversely, we know from research in social psychology that having a strong sense of ethnic identity and high racial awareness is linked with young people's mental health and achievement. Feeling secure in who one is and whom one is connected to provides the basis for doing other things.

For example, Chavous and colleagues (2003) found that Black high school students most likely to graduate and go on to college expressed high awareness of race and racism, and high regard for being Black, while those least likely to stay in school expressed low awareness of race and racism, and low personal regard for being Black. Altschul, Oyserman, and Bybee (2008) found that Latinx 8th-graders (ranging from recent to second- and third-generation immigrants) earning higher grades tended to have bicultural identities, while those earning lower grades identified either little or exclusively with their cultural origin. These kinds of findings by social psychologists underlie several projects designed to strengthen students' ethnic identity.

Several studies have focused mainly on the impact of ethnic studies on student ethnic identity and sense of self, foregrounding the importance of curriculum for reclaiming identity. Studies of six curriculum projects that range from small after-school programs to the whole-school curriculum are summarized in Table 9.1.

Lewis, Sullivan, and Bybee (2006) and Lewis et al. (2012) reported experimental studies of a 1-semester African American emancipatory class for urban middle school students. Project EXCEL, which met three times per week, taught African and African American history and culture and African rituals and practices. It was designed to build communalism, student leadership and activism, and school–community partnerships. It included considerable attention to racism, oppression, discrimination, White privilege, Black empowerment, and self-reliance. In each study, the sample consisted of about 60 students, half in Project EXCEL and half in a life studies class. In Lewis, Sullivan, and Bybee's (2006) study, youth in the experimental curriculum scored higher than those in the control group on communal orientation, school connectedness, motivation to achieve, and overall social change involvement. But in the Lewis et al. (2012) study, there was a decrease in experimental students' ethnic identity, which was this second study's main outcome. The authors suggest perhaps too much emphasis was placed on racism and oppression, leading students to distance themselves psychologically from membership in a victimized group.

Table 9.1. Ethnic Studies Curriculum and Student Identity/Sense of Self

Author(s), date	Ethnic studies curriculum perspective	Research design	Level	Outcomes
Lewis, Sullivan, & Bybee, 2006	Project EXCEL, an African-centered, 1-semester class	Pre–post control group	8th grade	Communalism, achievement motivation
Lewis et al., 2012	Project EXCEL, an African-centered, 1-semester class	Pre–post control group	8th grade	Ethnic identity
Thomas et al., 2008	African American after-school program	Pre–post no control group	High school	Ethnic identity, sense of empowerment
Belgrave et al., 2000	Afrocentric extracurricular program	Pre–post control group	Ages 10–12	Ethnic identity, self-concept
Wiggan & Watson-Vandiver, 2017	Multicultural and African-centered school	Case study	High school	Academic achievement, critical thinking, identity
Halagao, 2004, 2010	*Pinoy Teach*: Filipino studies class	Interviews	Higher education	Critical thinking, identity, empowerment
Vasquez, 2005	Chicano literature course	Interviews	Higher education	Ethnic identity

Two additional similar studies produced positive results. Thomas, Davidson, and McAdoo (2008) studied the impact of a school-based program for African American high school girls. The goals and nature of this 10-week program were similar to those of Project EXCEL: to nurture Black identity and a collectivist orientation, and to develop racism awareness and liberatory action. The program taught African American history and contemporary culture, weaving in African cultural values, Freire's critical consciousness, and holistic learning. For the study, a control group of matched students not participating in the program was constructed. On various measures of ethnic identity, racism awareness, and liberatory action, participants scored higher than nonparticipants. Belgrave and colleagues (2000) studied the impact of a 4-month extracurricular program for middle school girls. Weekly meetings featured various activities such as a Rites of Separation Ceremony, an overnight retreat, and arts activities. These were all taught through an Afrocentric approach that included cultural practices and relationship building. Using various measures of racial identity and self-concept, the authors found a positive impact on students in the experimental group as compared with the control group.

Wiggan and Watson-Vandiver (2017) conducted a case study of a high-performing school that served African American students and featured a curriculum centered on critical multiculturalism, anti-racism, and African-centered perspectives. Similar to Ginwright's (2000) study, this was a qualitative case study of a school attempting to link the curriculum with student outcomes. Data sources included interviews with teachers and students and observations in school. Results of the interviews confirmed that students valued the African-centered curriculum that linked them with their ancestors and instilled cultural empowerment in them. The authors concluded that this kind of education produced "organic intellectuals" (p. 16) who were able to critically examine the world around them as well as achieve academically.

Halagao (2004, 2010) examined the impact of *Pinoy Teach* on Filipino American college students. *Pinoy Teach* is a curriculum she co-developed that focuses on Philippine and Filipino American history and culture, using a problem-posing pedagogy that encourages students to think critically through multiple perspectives on history. It offers a different perspective about history than students learned before, and some of it is uncomfortable; the program helps students grapple with and think their way through diverse and conflicting perspectives, and then consider what to do with their new knowledge. As part of the learning process, the college students mentor and teach what they are learning to younger students. Through a series of interviews, Halagao (2004) examined the curriculum's impact on six Filipino American college students at the end of the course. She found that since none of them had learned about their own ethnic history in school, they described *Pinoy Teach* as "filling in the blanks." Students also described collisions between their prior knowledge of Philippine history, learned mainly from their parents, and that in the curriculum, which critiqued Spanish and then U.S. colonization. The students expressed interest in learning about their own history in relationship to that of other groups. They moved from seeing other Filipinos through learned stereotypes to building a shared sense of community, and they developed a sense of confidence and empowerment to stand up to oppression and to work for their own communities. Several years later, Halagao (2010) reported a follow-up survey of 35 students who had participated in the program about 10 years earlier; 30 were Filipino American and 5 were Euro-American. Students reported that what remained with them was a "deeper love and appreciation of ethnic history, culture, identity, and community" (p. 505). The curriculum, through its process of decolonization, had helped them to develop a sense of empowerment and self-efficacy that persisted, as well as a life commitment to diversity and multiculturalism. They also developed ongoing activism in their work as teachers, in other professions, and/or through civic engagement where they lived.

Vasquez's (2005) case study of the responses of 18 college students to a Chicano literature course closely parallels Halagao's finding. All of the literary selections were authored by Chicana/os and dealt with topics such as immigration, migrant labor, poverty, and Catholicism. Eleven of the 18 students were Latinx. The Latinx students all said they identified with the texts and that the texts filled in blanks in their understandings of their families' biographies. They reported developing a sense of community based on recognition of similar experiences and hardships. Realizing that there is an abundance of Chicano literature prompted feelings of ethnic and personal affirmation, confidence, empowerment, and finally occupying the place of "insider" in an academic institution. For one student, recognition that there is a strong Latin American culture strengthened his identification as American. The non-Latinxs found shared human issues in the texts to identify with; they had to wrestle with recognition of differences while also seeing cross-group human similarities, and because they lacked the authority of shared experiences with the authors and characters, they could not direct where discussions went.

In sum, all but one of the studies in this section found a positive link between ethnic studies programs that feature a curriculum designed and taught from the perspective of a historically marginalized group, and students' ethnic identity development and sense of empowerment. Criticality was a central feature of all of the curricula, and descriptions of all of the projects featured culturally mediated, or culturally responsive, pedagogy as central.

Ethnic Studies Curriculum and Student Achievement

Research investigating the academic impact of ethnic studies curriculum builds on earlier case studies showing increased engagement of children and youth when people of their own racial ethnic group are in the curriculum. For example, Copenhaver (2001) worked with and recorded African American elementary schoolchildren as they read and discussed *Malcolm X: A Fire*. She found that the children brought considerably more knowledge of the life of Malcolm X than their teachers (including her) were aware they had, and in groups composed of only African Americans they drew readily on their shared knowledge of African American media, civil rights leaders, and everyday racial issues to follow the plot, make connections, and interpret the story. In other words, the students became "smarter" in the classroom. Case studies such as these capture what teachers notice about student intellectual engagement when teaching ethnic studies.

But there are tensions between ethnic studies and academic achievement as measured by standardized tests, mirroring larger tensions that revolve around who has the power to define what schooling is for. While ethnic studies should challenge students academically, standardized tests arise from a paradigm that rank-orders students based on their mastery of a traditional curriculum, and then blames students of color for their lower average performance. Tests also ignore outcomes that students' communities may value, such as cultural identity and respectful engagement with the community (McCarty & Lee, 2014). Beaulieu (2006), for example, points out that education for Native students should "serve the interests of specific tribal communities. That interest is first defined in terms of maintaining social and cultural continuity with the past while adapting to change" (p. 53). However, as Cabrera and colleagues (2014) argue, because standardized tests are part of the reality students must confront, and act as gatekeepers to further opportunities, test results are useful, even if they are not (nor should they be) the only way of assessing impact on students.

Fourteen studies investigated the academic impact of 11 ethnic studies programs or classes. Table 9.2 lists these studies in relationship to the curriculum project studied, the grade level of students, the research study design, and the nature of outcomes for which data were gathered. As the table shows, most of these curriculum projects were intentionally designed through knowledge frameworks of peoples who have been marginalized by racism and/or colonization. All of them sought to engage students intellectually by connecting them with knowledge that originates from peoples with whom they are connected. We organized our discussion of these studies in relationship to the cultural group being served.

Dee and Penner (2017) evaluated the impact of San Francisco Unified School District's 9th-grade ethnic studies program, which serves a racially and ethnically diverse population. The curriculum is organized around six concepts that unpack the working of institutional racism. The program was piloted in five high schools, and then 4 years later extended to all 19 high schools in the district. Using a regression discontinuity design, Dee and Penner (2017) evaluated the program's impact on five cohorts of 9th-grade students in three pilot high schools, using data on student GPA, attendance, and credits earned toward graduation. After controlling for several variables (such as students' entering GPA and measures of teacher effectiveness), their "results indicate that assignment to this course increased 9th-grade student attendance by 21 percentage points, GPA by 1.4 grade points, and credits earned by 23" (p. 217).

The impact of Mexican American Studies (MAS) in Tucson has been studied both by program participants (Cammarota & Romero, 2009) and by external researchers (Cabrera et al., 2014). Cabrera and colleagues compared graduation rates and achievement scores (using AIMS—the state's achievement tests) of 11th- and 12th-grade students who did, and did not, enroll in MAS courses, constructing a matched comparison group. They found that although students in MAS courses entered, on the average, with

Table 9.2. Ethnic Studies Curriculum and Student Achievement

Author(s), date	Ethnic studies curriculum perspective	Level	Research design	Outcomes
Dee & Penner, 2017	San Francisco Unified School District's 9th-grade course focusing on critical consciousness, self-love, and action	9th grade	Quasi-experimental	Grade point average (GPA), attendance, credits toward graduation
Cabrera et al., 2014	Tucson's Mexican American Studies program developed through Chicano and Indigenous epistemologies	High school	Quasi-experimental	Standardized skill tests, graduation rates
Cammarota & Romero, 2009	Tucson's Mexican American Studies Social Justice Education Project focusing on Chicano intellectual knowledge	High school	Pre–post no control group, interviews	Test scores, graduation rates, sense of empowerment
Kisker et al., 2012	Math in a Cultural Context, developed in collaboration with Yup'ik elders	2nd grade	Pre–post control group	Math achievement
Lipka et al., 2005	Math in a Cultural Context, developed in collaboration with Yup'ik elders	6th grade	Pre–post control group	Math achievement
McCarty & Lee, 2014	Native American Community Academy, developed with community collaboration	Middle, high school	Qualitative; pre–post no control group	Basic skills achievement

Author(s), date	Ethnic studies curriculum perspective	Level	Research design	Outcomes
McCarty, 1993	Rough Rock English-Navajo Language Arts program	Elementary	Qualitative	Reading scores
Matthews & Smith, 1994	Culturally relevant science content consisting of biographies of American Indian scientists	4th–8th grades	Pre–post control group	Science achievement, attitudes toward science and Native Americans
Green-Gibson & Collett, 2014	African American cultural infusion	3rd–6th grades	Causal-comparative	School Adequate Yearly Progress rating
Duncan, 2012	Afrocentric U.S. history course	8th grade	Quasi-experimental	Academic achievement, student self-efficacy
Rickford, 2001	Culturally relevant texts	Middle school	Post-interviews, no control group	Comprehension, higher-order thinking
Tyson, 2002	Multicultural literature in social studies, using Banks's transformative and social action curriculum levels	Middle school	Interviews, classroom observation	Use of text, knowledge of social issues
Ginwright, 2000, 2004	Afrocentric culture infused through curriculum and school as a whole	High school	Qualitative case study	Academic achievement, academic participation

lower 9th- and 10th-grade GPA and achievement test scores than control students, by 12th grade they attained "significantly higher AIMS passing and graduation rates than their non-MAS peers" (p. 1106). Because this finding seems counterintuitive, they tested it with a variety of statistical modeling and sampling strategies, all of which reached the same conclusion: MAS improved the achievement of mainly Mexican American students significantly more than the traditional curriculum, and the more courses students took, the stronger the impact on their achievement.

Several studies have examined the academic impact of different programs that aim to decolonize Indigenous education. Math in a Cultural Context (MCC) grew from collaboration among Alaska Yup'ik Native elders, teachers, and math educators to develop an elementary-level curriculum supplement for 2nd through 7th grades that connects Yup'ik culture and knowledge with the National Council of Teachers of Mathematics standards (www.uaf.edu/mcc/). The curriculum includes 10 modules. Its pedagogy supports traditional ways of communicating and learning, such as collaborative learning and cognitive apprenticeship. Lipka and colleagues (2005) compared 160 6th-grade Yup'ik students' math achievement after using the module "Building a Fish Rack: Investigations into Proof, Properties, Perimeter, and Area" with 98 similar students in classrooms that did not use MCC. They found that students in classrooms using the MCC curriculum made more progress toward the state mathematics standards than comparison students.

Kisker and colleagues (2012) conducted an experimental study in which 50 schools that enrolled large proportions of Native students were randomly assigned to either experimental or control conditions. The authors tested the impact of two modules on 2nd-graders' mathematics achievement. Since the schools had not used the curriculum previously, teachers in the experimental schools were trained to use it, and researchers recorded them on video. In the absence of a state achievement math test for 2nd grade, the researchers constructed pre- and posttests to closely resemble the math tests for later grades. They found the impact of the MCC curriculum "positive, statistically significant, and moderate to large in terms of effect sizes" (p. 100), with a positive impact on both Alaska Native and mixed-ethnic student groups. They also found that in the following semester students retained what they had learned.

McCarty and Lee (2014) report a case study of the Native American Community Academy (NACA) that serves middle and high school students in Albuquerque. About 95% of the students identify as Native American, representing about 60 Native nations. The school, founded in 2006, collaborates with Native communities to construct the program's curriculum and pedagogy. NACA teaches three Native languages (Navajo, Lakota, and Tiwa), along with protocols for using them. The curriculum, following a model of culturally sustaining education, integrates Native perspectives through English reading and writing, social studies, math, and science; teachers create respectful family-type relationships with students in the classroom. The overall vision of the school is decolonization by strengthening students' cultural identities and cultural knowledge, and by grounding them as Indian within Native community contexts. McCarty and Lee (2014) report that student achievement, even using dominant-society standards, has improved: Test scores of 8th-graders in 2011–2012 increased over the previous year by 21% in math, 20% in reading, and 9% in writing. Because of the school's ongoing success in closing achievement gaps between Native and non-Native students, there is now a network of NACA-inspired schools that draw on its model.

Earlier, McCarty (1993) had worked with and studied the Rough Rock English–Navajo Language Arts Program, designed to develop biliteracy skills of K–6 students, the majority of whom spoke Navajo as their primary language. Because a written Navajo literacy curriculum did not exist, the teachers developed one that was in Navajo and relevant to the lives of the children, such as the thematic unit Wind, "an ever-present force at Rough Rock" (McCarty, 1993, p. 184). McCarty reports that after 4 years in the program, the students' achievement on locally developed measures of comprehending spoken English increased from 51% to 91%, and their scores on standardized reading tests rose steadily after the second year. Those who participated in the program for 3–5 years made the greatest gains.

Matthews and Smith (1994) used experimental research (pretest–posttest control group design) to study the impact of Native American science materials on Native students' attitudes toward science, attitudes toward Native people, and understanding of science concepts. The study investigated 4th- through 8th-graders in nine schools. The 10-week intervention included science content as well as biographies of 12 Native Americans using science in their daily lives (such as a silversmith or a water quality technician). The control group experienced just the science content. The experimental group made greater gains in achievement than the control group and developed more positive attitudes toward science and toward Native Americans.

Several studies have examined the academic impact of some version of African American curriculum on Black students. Green-Gibson and Collett (2014) utilized a causal-comparative research design to compare the achievement of students in grades 3–6 in two predominantly African American schools in Chicago, using 2009 Adequate Yearly Progress (AYP) reports as the main measure of achievement. The researchers used school documents to determine how culture was infused throughout the schools. One school used an African-centered approach to curriculum in all classrooms and infused African culture throughout the school; the other did not. The researchers found "a significant lower performance in third, fourth, fifth, and sixth grade students' AYP results in the school that does not infuse African culture . . . , as compared to students who attend the school that infuses African culture" (p. 35).

In a brief article, Duncan (2012) reported a quasi-experimental study of the impact of an Afrocentric U.S. history curriculum on the self-efficacy, connection to the curriculum, and academic achievement of 217 8th-grade students, most of whom were African American, using New York State social studies test data. She found a significant positive impact in all three areas.

Two qualitative case studies investigated the impact of culturally relevant literature on African American middle school students. In Rickford's

(2001) study of 25 low-achieving students, culturally relevant texts (African American folktales and contemporary narratives) were coupled with emphasis on higher-order thinking. She found that the texts engaged the students, who could identify with themes such as struggle, perseverance, and family tensions, as well as with features in the texts such as African American vernacular. In assessing their comprehension, she found that students excelled on the higher-order questions, but missed many lower-order questions. She concluded that familiarity with situations and people in stories increased students' motivation, and that even though they missed many lower-order questions, students were able to analyze and interpret the stories well. Framed through Banks's (1999) transformation and social action levels of curriculum, Tyson's (2002) case study examined the use, in a social studies class, of adolescent novels about social issues. Of the five novels, three were African American, one was multiethnic, and one was set in Japan; all featured characters addressing social issues such as working with neighbors to transform a vacant lot into a community garden. Tyson documented students' developing understanding of the complexities of social action, as well as their ability to use text to derive meaning; most of the students demonstrated growth in both areas over the semester.

In contrast to the rest of the research reviewed in this section, one study did not find a positive impact. Ginwright (2000, 2004) documented an initiative to transform a low-achieving urban high school that served mainly Black youth from low-income families. To formulate a plan, school district leaders consulted with several prominent African American scholars whose work focused on Afrocentric curriculum and pedagogy, who subsequently persuaded the district leaders to base reform in "African precepts, axioms, philosophy" (2004, p. 80) and to structure the curriculum around themes in African knowledge. Over the 5 years of the reform, academic indicators (enrollment, GPA, dropout rate, suspension rate, numbers of graduates, and higher education enrollment numbers) did not improve and in some areas worsened. Ginwright argued that the reform plan pitted two conceptions of Blackness against each other: that of middle-class Black reformers who connected African and African American knowledge systems with origins in Egypt, and low-income urban Black youth whose central concerns revolved around needs such as housing, employment, and health care, and whose identity was formed through urban youth cultural forms (such as hip-hop) and local experiences with racism and poverty. Ginwright argues that cultural identity is important, but that we need to attend to intersections between race, culture, and class. Because the Afrocentric reform plan ignored students' class-based needs and identity forms, students rejected it. Ginwright's study calls into question the pervasive tendency to conceptualize culture in terms of racial origins, without considering the everyday culture young people experience in environments shaped by the intersection between race and class.

In sum, 12 of the 14 studies in this section found a positive impact on students' academic learning, as well as other student outcomes some studies attended to. While all 11 projects emphasized ethnic studies curriculum content designed and taught through perspectives of peoples marginalized by race and/or colonialism, most also were taught well. For example, the San Francisco Unified School District ethnic studies program includes teacher professional development as an important feature. As Beckham and Concordia (2019) explain, "We remain committed to the belief that anyone who honestly engages in developing themselves as a teacher of ethnic studies can become skilled at it" (p. 325) and that students will benefit as a result. In other words, ethnic studies curriculum matters greatly; pedagogy matters as well.

Ethnic Studies Curriculum Infused Into Asset-Based Pedagogies

Thirteen studies investigated the academic impact of six projects that infused ethnic studies curriculum into asset-based pedagogies, connecting the hallmark of curriculum as counternarrative with that of culturally responsive pedagogy and cultural mediation. Table 9.3 lists these studies. López (2018) defines asset-based pedagogies as providing "a bridge that connects the dominant school culture to students' home and heritage culture, thus promoting academic achievement for historically marginalized students" (p. 9). Similarly, Lee (1995) posits that knowledge of language use "for the African American adolescent is often tacit," constituting a learning asset. But, "because the knowledge is tacit and has been applied only to community oral interactions, its applicability to other related problems of interpretation is limited" (p. 612). By infusing knowledge that is culturally familiar or culturally relevant to students, teachers who take a sociocultural approach to teaching and learning connect students' knowledge, including tacit knowledge, with new and unfamiliar academic knowledge.

While most research reviewed in this chapter assesses the impact of a particular program or set of practices, a body of work by López (2016, 2017, 2018; Sharif Matthews & López, 2018) seeks teaching practices that matter most to Latinx student achievement. Her studies use multiple regression analysis, path analysis, and/or hierarchical linear modeling to identify teacher-related factors that contribute to the achievement of Latinx students in elementary schools. The teacher-related factors include academic expectations, critical awareness (knowledge of historical and sociocultural oppression and how schools perpetuate racial power imbalances), cultural knowledge (knowledge of students' household funds of knowledge), cultural content integration (ability to integrate culturally relevant content into the curriculum), and beliefs about/use of Spanish language in instruction. Together, these dimensions constitute asset-based pedagogy.

López's research has involved Latinx students in grades 3–5. In a study of 568 Latinx students and their teachers, she found that "students with teachers who have high levels of both expectancy and critical awareness perform approximately ½ SD higher in student reading achievement over the course of one academic year" (2017, p. 13). In an earlier study of 244

Table 9.3. Ethnic Studies Curriculum Infused Into Asset-Based Pedagogies

Author(s), date	Program or focus of study	Level	Research design	Outcomes
López, 2016, 2017, 2018; Sharif Matthews & López, 2018	Asset-based pedagogy: academic expectations, critical awareness, cultural knowledge, cultural content integration, beliefs about/use of Spanish language in instruction	Grades 3–5	Correlation	Reading achievement, math achievement, ethnic identity, achievement identity
Lee, 1995, 2001, 2006, 2007	Cultural Modeling	High school	Pre–post control group	Literary analysis skills
Krater et al., 1994; Krater & Zeni, 1995	African American literature infused	Middle, high school	Pre–post no control group	Writing skills (various tests used over time)
Adjapong & Emdin, 2015	Hip-hop in science classroom	Middle school	Various qualitative	Understanding, enjoyment of science
Stone & Stewart, 2016	Critical Hip Hop Rhetoric Pedagogy	Higher education	Qualitative	Successful course completion
Hall & Martin, 2013	Critical Hip-Hop pedagogy	Higher education	Qualitative	Engagement, retention

Latinx students and their teachers, she found that "teachers' reported CRT [culturally responsive teaching] behaviors in terms of language and cultural knowledge (formative assessment) were both significantly and positively related to students' reading outcomes. For teachers reporting the highest level of each of the aforementioned dimensions, students' reading scores were associated with approximately 1 SD higher reading outcomes" (2016, pp. 27–28). In a study of 368 students and their teachers, Sharif Matthews and López (2018) found that teacher expectations alone were not enough; rather, student achievement in math was mediated by teachers' honoring of students' heritage language and integrating cultural content into the curriculum. In other words, the teachers who used asset-based pedagogy most consistently produced students with the highest average reading achievement.

Cultural Modeling (Lee, 1995, 2001, 2006, 2007) connects the language-reasoning skills of African American English speakers with the English curriculum. Lee (2006) explains that African American life affords young people a wealth of cultural scripts and contexts that can be used in the classroom to develop literary analysis strategies that students can then apply to unfamiliar texts. Speakers of African American English routinely interpret symbolism in rap and hip-hop, but do not necessarily apply it to the analysis of literature in school. Pedagogy that enables students to use their cultural frames of reference engages them immediately in much higher levels of cognition than is usually the case in a traditional classroom. Cultural Modeling moves from analysis of specific language data sets that students are familiar with and that draw on elements of Black cultural life, such as Black media or the Black church, to more general strategies of literary analysis and application to canonical literary works. Lee's research assessed the impact of Cultural Modeling, using tests in which students write an analysis of a short story they have not seen before. For example, in a quasi-experimental study in two low-achieving African American urban high schools, four English classes were taught using Cultural Modeling and two were taught traditionally. The experimental students' gain from pretest to posttest was more than twice that of the control group students (Lee, 1995). Lee's qualitative research documents that when Cultural Modeling is used, students gradually learn to direct discussions interpreting and analyzing texts (Lee, 2001, 2006), although traditional English achievement tests often do not capture this learning process (Lee, 2007).

In the Webster Groves Writing Project (Krater, Zeni, & Cason, 1994), 14 middle and high school English teachers worked to improve writing achievement of their African American students; the project was then extended to all students (Black and White) performing below grade level. The project developed several principles based on what was working. One important principle was use of various literary works by African American authors. Over time the teachers realized they needed to "acknowledge [students'] culture—not just by incorporating their cultural heroes into the curriculum, but by weaving the threads of their culture into the tapestry of our classroom" (Krater & Zeni, 1995, p. 35). Acknowledging students' culture meant recognizing teachers' own implicit biases. A significant bias was toward students' dialect, a problem only when teachers focused on correcting grammar rather than on helping students communicate ideas. As students' ability to communicate ideas developed, they became more intentional about their own use of grammar. Over the years of the project's existence, participating students made greater gains in writing than nonparticipating students on the local writing assessment, and then later on the state writing test (Gay, 2018).

Three studies examined the use of hip-hop pedagogy: one in science (Adjapong & Emdin, 2015) and two in historically Black university (HBU) English classes (Hall & Martin, 2013; Stone & Stewart, 2016). Adjapong and Emdin define hip-hop pedagogy "as a way of authentically and practically incorporating the creative elements of Hip-Hop into teaching, and inviting students to have a connection with the content while meeting them on their cultural turf by teaching to, and through their realities and experiences" (p. 67). Adjapong and Emdin investigated use of co-teaching and call-response (two elements of hip-hop pedagogy) in 6th-grade science in an urban school. Using qualitative research methods, the authors found that hip-hop pedagogy engaged the students. Call-response memorization deepened their science content knowledge, as did co-teaching what they were learning to their peers. Stone and Stewart (2016) studied Critical Hip-Hop Rhetoric Pedagogy in a writing course designed to increase the academic success of first-generation, 1st-year students in an HBU. Among students who attended class regularly, the authors found a decrease in the number failing to complete the course, particularly its required assessments. Hall and Martin (2013) used interviews with students to explore the impact of three courses taught by an HBU English professor. They found that the use of hip-hop pedagogy increased student engagement and willingness to participate; it also helped them connect with historical material being taught.

In sum, all of these studies found a positive relationship between the achievement (or achievement-oriented behaviors) of minoritized students, and teachers connecting academics with students' home and community culture through a combination of curriculum content students could relate to and culturally mediated/culturally responsive pedagogy. Conceptually, we do not see a huge difference between the approaches to curriculum and pedagogy in this set of studies compared with the previous set, except in the emphasis given to content versus culturally mediated pedagogy. What is significant is that all studies but one (Ginwright, 2000, 2004) demonstrated a positive impact on the academic learning of minoritized students.

Culturally Responsive Teaching, Cultural Mediation, and Student Achievement

Much of the pedagogy used in ethnic studies embodies learning principles articulated by sociocultural theory. A major contribution of sociocultural approaches, the concept of cultural mediation, describes ways in which cultural tools and artifacts "mediate" learning. Within this framework meaningful learning is optimal when teaching strategies make use of and enrich the sociocultural context in which learning takes place. With an emphasis on learning as contextual social practice and a clear conceptualization of the formative role that cultural tools and resources play in learning (Cole, 1998; Rogoff, 2003), sociocultural theory points to the richness and complexity of cultural mediation that draws upon such aspects as discourse patterns, interactional routines, text structures, language-rich interactions, meta-communication, modeling, and so on. Culturally responsive teaching, therefore, is not a formulaic pedagogy defined by and limited to specific scaffolds.

Table 9.4. Culturally Responsive Teaching, Cultural Mediation, and Student Achievement

Author(s), date	Program or approach	Level	Research design	Outcomes
Au & Carroll, 1997	Kamehameha Elementary Education Program: literacy adapted to Hawaiian participation structures	Elementary	Classroom observation, writing portfolio audit	Writing skill achievement
Tharp & Gallimore, 1988	Kamehameha Elementary Education Program	Elementary	Posttest control group	Reading achievement
Hilberg, Tharp, & DeGeest, 2000	Five Standards for Effective Pedagogy	8th grade	Pretest–posttest control group	Math achievement
Doherty et al., 2003	Five Standards for Effective Pedagogy	Elementary	Correlation	Reading achievement
Doherty & Hilberg, 2007	Five Standards for Effective Pedagogy	Elementary	Nonequivalent pretest—posttest control group	Reading achievement
Bailey & Boykin, 2001	Academic task variation (verve)	Grades 3–4	Correlation	Academic task performance, motivation

While culturally responsive teaching leverages the cultural resources that students bring to classroom settings—and thus conceptualizes students' cultural backgrounds as assets rather than deficits—sociocultural theory emphasizes the context-specific and nuanced ways in which cultural tools and resources are transformed into purposeful learning. Here we review six studies of three projects, summarized in Table 9.4.

The Kamehameha Elementary Education Program (KEEP), designed to improve literacy achievement of Native Hawaiian students, grew from research on communication and participation structures in Native Hawaiian families and community settings (Au, 1980). Elementary teachers were trained to organize literacy instruction in ways that capitalized on Native Hawaiian culture and interaction patterns, such as using "talk story." Over time, the project added additional features, like student ownership over literacy and a constructivist approach to teaching. Much of the research on the program's impact appears in unpublished technical reports, but there are some published studies. Au and Carroll (1997) reported a study of the program's impact on writing in classrooms of 26 experienced and skilled teachers. After the first year, using program-developed writing assessment, they found that students moved from 60% below grade level and 40% at grade level, to 32% below and 68% above grade level. Tharp and Gallimore (1988) compared the reading achievement in KEEP classrooms with achievement in traditional classrooms. They found huge and consistent achievement differences. For example, while the average reading achievement of 1st-graders was above the 50th percentile in KEEP classrooms, it hovered around the 37th percentile in traditional classrooms. Students in KEEP classrooms were also more academically engaged, and their teachers gave them far more positive academic feedback and less negative behavioral feedback than students in traditional classrooms.

The Five Standards for Effective Pedagogy, built on the KEEP model, grew from research on sociocultural pedagogical practices that improve student academic achievement in elementary classrooms serving culturally and linguistically diverse students. The standards include: (1) facilitating learning through "joint productive activity," or conversations with students about their work; (2) developing language and literacy across the curriculum; (3) connecting new information with what students already know from home and community contexts; (4) promoting complex thinking; and (5) teaching through dialogue. Research studies (many of which are in technical reports rather than journal articles) find improved student achievement when teachers use these standards.

In a small experimental study involving two classes of 8th-grade Native American students, Hilberg, Tharp, and DeGeest (2000) found that the experimental group, taught by a teacher using collaborative pedagogy to create meaningful products in an environment of content-rich dialogue, enjoyed mathematics more and achieved at a higher level than students taught through traditional pedagogy, although the achievement results were not statistically significant. Doherty and colleagues (2003) studied the relationship between 15 elementary teachers' use of the standards and reading achievement gains (measured on the Stanford Achievement Test) of mainly low-socioeconomic Latinx students, many of whom were designated English language learners. They found that the more teachers used the five standards, the greater the gains. Further, "students of teachers who had transformed both their pedagogy and classroom organization had significantly greater overall achievement gains in comprehension, reading, spelling, and vocabulary than students of teachers who had not similarly transformed their teaching" (p. 18). Similarly, in a carefully designed nonequivalent pretest–posttest control group study involving two elementary schools (one experimental, the other control), Doherty and Hilberg (2007) found that as teachers' use of the five standards increased, the reading achievement of their predominantly low-income Latinx students increased, although gains were small. Students in classrooms in which teachers used the five standards along with supportive classroom organization made the greatest achievement gains; gains were most pronounced for low-English-proficient students.

Following a different chain of inquiry, Bailey and Boykin (2001), in an effort to identify classroom practices that appeal to African American students, studied the relationship between academic task variation and student academic learning. Academic task variation refers to the variety of stimulation children are afforded in instructional activities. The authors wanted to address the boredom African American children often experience in school compared with the stimulation ("verve," in Boykin's terminology) they are used to in their homes and communities. Using an experimental research design in which children participated in a task of either low or high variability, they found that the children's academic performance was much higher when they were taught in a manner using high task variability.

In sum, all six of these studies find that conceptualizing teaching as cultural mediation, shaping teaching processes around students' cultural learning processes, engages students and leads to higher achievement. While the three projects did not take up the matter of whose culture shapes the curriculum itself, we included these studies because they highlight ways in which cultural artifacts, such as discourse patterns, collaborative and joint meaning-making, and task variation, mediate rich learning experiences that draw from a sociocultural environment that stretches from school to home and community settings. Including studies that emphasize sociocultural contexts in a review of the impact of ethnic studies broadens our understanding of how cultural resources function as purposeful and effective tools for learning, pointing to cultural mediation and learning processes that often can be overlooked.

ETHNIC STUDIES FOR DIVERSE GROUPS
THAT INCLUDE WHITE STUDENTS

What does it mean to include White students in ethnic studies, and what do White students gain? Some fear that ethnic studies foments racial antagonism. While White students are not the center of ethnic studies curricula, it is important to consider how White students experience such curricula. Here, we review research on the impact of ethnic studies designed for diverse groups that include White students. Most of that research has investigated its impact on students' racial attitudes and knowledge about race. We organized this section by general age level of students, since that follows how the research usually is framed.

Early Childhood Level

At the early childhood level (age 8 and younger), Aboud and colleagues' research review is very helpful (Aboud et al., 2012). The authors reviewed 32 experimental studies located in various countries (e.g., Ireland, South Africa, and the United States); 14 reported the impact of cross-group contact, and 18, the impact of instruction. Studies of cross-group contact tended to use peer relations as the main outcome, while studies of instruction tended to look at changes in attitudes. Overall, the authors found that 60% of the effects were positive, only 10% were negative, and the rest showed no statistically significant change. Sixty-seven percent of the outcomes for majority-group children were positive; most of the outcomes for minority-group children were not statistically significant one way or the other. Studies found instruction about racial diversity to have a more positive impact than direct contact with children who differed from themselves, although both generally produced a positive impact. The authors identified three types of instructional interventions: stories in which children identify with a character of their own racial or ethnic group who has friends from another group, stories exclusively about members of a different racial or ethnic group, and anti-bias instruction that focuses on how one might respond to prejudice and exclusion. Least effective were stories or lessons that featured another racial or ethnic group.

Studies by Aboud and Fenwick (1999) and by Bigler and colleagues (Bigler, 1999; Bigler, Brown, & Markell, 2001; Hughes, Bigler, & Levy, 2007) elaborate on the nature of instruction that has an impact on attitudes, especially among White children. This research supports the research noted above regarding most and least impactful interventions. Simply infusing representation of racially and ethnically diverse people into the curriculum has only a marginal impact on students' attitudes. Bigler (1999) explained that since racial attitudes are acquired actively rather than passively, curricula that simply depict or label groups or group members (e.g., pointing out a person's race, ethnicity, or gender) may draw students' attention to group markers and differences, inviting stereotyping without engaging students in questioning their own thinking. What is more effective is to focus explicitly on stereotyping and bias, present strong counter-stereotypic models, and engage students in thinking about multiple features of individuals (e.g., race and occupation), within-group differences, and cross-group similarities.

For example, Hughes and colleagues (2007) documented the impact on African American and White elementary children of a few short lessons that included information about Black and White historical figures and (in the treatment condition) about racism. They found that lessons teaching about racism, and about successful challenges to it, improved racial attitudes among White children, allowing them to see how racism affects everybody and offering them a vision for addressing it. The authors posited that children's value for fairness accounts for much of the positive impact. Lessons about racism had less impact on the African American children (probably because they duplicated what they already knew), but the information about historical figures improved their regard for African Americans.

Using a pretest–posttest design, Aboud and Fenwick (1999) investigated two curricular inventions designed to help elementary children talk about race. They found that talk that reduces prejudice, especially among high-prejudiced children, directs attention toward individual qualities rather than group membership only, offers positive information about a group, and directly addresses a listener's concerns. Such talk is more effective than general talk about race that does none of these.

What this research on young children reveals is that positive racial attitudes can be developed best by directly confronting children's actual questions and assumptions about race, racism, and differences they see among people. It is also helpful to draw young children's attention to the complexity of individuals, as well as to examples of people like themselves who challenge racial discrimination. Interracial contact is not unhelpful, but by itself may not improve attitudes. The kind of teaching that impacts students' racial attitudes at the early childhood level is what provides a basis for ethnic studies at the elementary and secondary levels.

Elementary and Secondary Levels

Surprisingly little research has occurred for the elementary and secondary levels. Okoye-Johnson's (2011) review is useful, although the reviewed studies were not as strong methodologically as those reviewed by Aboud and colleagues (2012). Okoye-Johnson conducted a statistical meta-analysis of 30 studies that compared the impact of a traditional curriculum, versus a multicultural curriculum or extracurricular intervention, on racial attitudes of pre-K–12 students. The 21 studies of the impact of a multicultural curriculum that was part of the regular instructional program reported an effect size of 0.645, meaning that exposure to it "brought about more positive changes in students' racial attitudes than did exposure to traditional instruction" (p. 1263). Studies of the impact of extracurricular cross-cultural interventions (outside the regular instructional program) reported a much smaller positive effect size (0.08), suggesting that multicultural curriculum that is part of the school's regular programming has a considerably more powerful positive impact on students' racial attitudes than extracurricular cultural programming or no direct attention to multiculturalism, race, or ethnicity.

Two additional studies investigated the impact of curriculum on student attitudes at the high school level. Klepper (2014) studied the impact of his own social studies course about Islam and Muslims on the attitudes of 64 female students in a Catholic high school. He designed the course to provide historic and cultural background and to engage students in writing projects that asked them to think critically about their own assumptions about issues such as jihad and Muslim women. He found that by the end of the semester, students' thinking was more nuanced and for the most part their attitudes were more positive.

San Pedro (2018) described how a White high school student changed during a semester-long course in Native American literature. He points out that by centering Indigenous perspectives and decentering the Whiteness that traditional schooling reinforces and renders invisible to White students, the course radically disrupted the White student's point of view. Initially she felt she needed to defend her race, which she turned to social media to do. But through the teacher's gentle affirmation of all the students' questions and sense-making, gentle prodding of students' thinking, and use of Humanizing Through Storying (San Pedro & Kinloch, 2017), the White student came to reconceptualize her identity and knowledge in a way that took "into consideration the lives, knowledges, and perspectives of others" (San Pedro, 2018, p. 1224).

Higher Education

Much of the extensive higher education research examines development of democracy outcomes among students. Gurin and colleagues (2003) defined these as including "commitment to promoting racial understanding, perspective taking, sense of commonality in values with students from different racial/ethnic backgrounds, agreement that diversity and democracy can be congenial, involvement in political affairs and community service during college as well as commitment to civic affairs after college" (p. 25). Research examines the impact of various diversity experiences, with a focus on course-taking and interracial interaction. For the most part, the courses in these studies are required diversity courses, lists of which include ethnic studies, women's studies, and general diversity courses.

The overwhelming and most consistent finding is that in most studies such courses have a positive impact on students (Denson, 2009; Gurin et al., 2002; Lopez, 2004; Martin, 2010). Engberg's (2004) review of 73 studies of the impact of a diversity course, a diversity workshop, a peer-facilitated invention, or a service intervention found that 52 of the studies reported positive gains, 14 reported mixed gains, and only 7 reported no change. Although most studies had methodological weaknesses (such as use of convenience samples and limitations stemming from wording of some of the survey questions), there was still a consistent pattern of finding a positive impact of diversity coursework on reducing students' biases.

The impact of such courses is considerably stronger when they include cross-group interaction (Antonio et al., 2004; Bowman, 2010a; Chang,

2002; Denson, 2009; Gurin et al., 2002; Lopez, 2004), or, as Nagda, Kim, and Truelove (2004) put it, "enlightenment and encounter." Because of the importance of cross-group interaction, some research focuses specifically on its nature. Gurin and Nagda (2006) found that participation in structured intergroup dialogues

> fosters active thinking about causes of social behavior and knowledge of institutional and other structural features of society that produce and maintain group-based inequalities, . . . increases perception of both commonalities and differences between and within groups and helps students to normalize conflict and build skills to work with conflicts, . . . [and] enhances interest in political issues and develops a sense of citizenship through college and community activities. (p. 22)

Required diversity courses generally have a greater positive impact on White students' racial attitudes than on those of students of color (Bowman, 2010b; Denson, 2009; Engberg, 2004; Lopez, 2004), probably because exposure to a systematic analysis of power is newer to White students than to students of color, and because while most students of color have engaged in cross-racial interaction previously, a large proportion of White students have not.

A growing body of research examines the impact of ethnic studies, Critical Whiteness studies, or other diversity courses on White students. Several studies use the Psychosocial Costs of Racism to Whites Scale (Spanierman & Heppner, 2004), which examines three kinds of impact: (1) White empathic reactions toward racism, (2) White guilt, and (3) White fear of others. For example, Paone, Malott, and Barr (2015) found that a Whiteness studies course produced significant positive changes among 121 White students, although there were some nuances such as increased levels of White guilt and no overall changes in levels of empathy. In a survey study of 270 White students, Todd, Spanierman, and Poteat (2011) found that empathy, guilt, and fear changed differently through coursework and were moderated by color-blind attitudes students brought. While guilt tended to rise with exposure to information about racism, guilt often prompted White students to engage in more learning; the authors noted that too little guidance is available for helping White students deal with guilt. Students who brought a high level of racial awareness didn't experience a rise in racial fear, while those who ascribed to color-blindness initially did so. Neville and colleagues (2014), in a 4-year longitudinal study of 845 White undergraduate students, found that participation in university diversity experiences, such as courses and having close friendships with Black peers, reduced the likelihood of their saying they were "color-blind," and that the more diversity courses White students took, the greater their racial awareness. Overall, the research finds that diversity courses help White students, but not in linear or uniform ways.

For many students—particularly White students—the first diversity course is emotionally challenging (Hogan & Mallott, 2005). In a large survey study of students in 19 colleges and universities, Bowman (2010b) examined the impact of taking one or more diversity courses on students' well-being and comfort with and appreciation of differences. He found that many students who took a single diversity course experienced a reduced sense of well-being due to having to grapple with issues they had not been exposed to before. However, students who took more than one diversity course experienced significant gains, with gains being greatest for White male students from economically privileged backgrounds (who had the farthest to go).

CONCLUSION

We have framed ethnic studies as an antiracist, decolonial project that seeks to rehumanize education for students of color, center subjugated knowledge narratives and ancestral knowledge, and build solidarity across racial and ethnic differences for the purpose of working toward social justice. This vision goes beyond the nuts and bolts visible in most ethnic studies projects, but it is a vision consistent with most of them. The research on the impact of ethnic studies on students, while limited in terms of research outcomes and (in many cases) the ethnic studies hallmarks of the projects themselves, lends strong support to the positive value of ethnic studies for all students— students of color as well as White students.

As noted throughout the chapter, almost all researched projects gave serious attention to offering curriculum grounded in perspectives of specific racially marginalized groups. While some undoubtedly did this better and in more depth than others, attending to the perspective of curricular knowledge is what makes curriculum an ethnic studies curriculum. Attention to culturally responsive pedagogy and cultural mediation was also a common feature of project descriptions. Some projects, such as KEEP (Au & Carroll, 1997), focused on doing this well, and some, such as the Mexican American Studies Social Justice Education Project (Cammarota & Romero, 2009), developed their own frameworks for what such pedagogy looks like. We suspect that the consistently positive impact of ethnic studies projects results from an interaction between what is being taught and how students are being engaged as learners.

The other five hallmarks received less direct and consistent attention in the program descriptions. Attention to criticality, while visible to some extent in most project descriptions, varied. For example, while Halagao (2004) explained that the critical perspective in *Pinoy Teach* was difficult initially for some students, Math in a Cultural Context (Lipka et al., 2005), which connects math with Yup'ik everyday culture, did not appear to employ criticality. Does every ethnic studies project need to do so? Probably not, although teachers of ethnic studies should consider whether this makes sense in any given project.

Helping students reclaim cultural identities was central to some projects, such as Project EXCEL (Lewis et al., 2006) and *Pinoy Teach* (Halagao, 2004). Ethnic identity and achievement identity were conceptually linked in several projects, such as López's (2017) studies of Latinx student achievement and the Mexican American Studies Social Justice Education Project (Cammarota & Romero, 2009). But reclaiming cultural or ethnic identities was not directly mentioned in several other projects.

Much less visible in the descriptions was attention to intersectionality and multiplicity, students as intellectuals, and community engagement. Consideration of students' social class backgrounds and student gender identity occasionally surfaced, such as in Ginwright's (2000) critique of an Afrocentric school reform; we suspect this area merits more attention. Ethnic studies arose in part to make education more responsive to historically marginalized communities; while several project descriptions briefly mentioned community engagement, the only one we know that included direct community engagement was Tucson's Mexican American Studies Social Justice Education Project (Cammarota & Romero, 2009). Finally, while a central part of rehumanizing education for students of color is to treat them as intellectuals, few project descriptions specifically addressed this as a core feature.

REFERENCES

Aboud, F. E., & Fenwick, V. (1999). Exploring and evaluating school-based interventions to reduce prejudice. *Journal of Social Issues, 55*(4), 767–786.

Aboud, F. E., Tredoux, C., Tropp, L. R., Brown, C. S., Niens, U., Noor, N. M., & Una Global Evaluation Group. (2012). Interventions to reduce prejudice and enhance inclusion and respect for ethnic differences in early childhood: A systematic review. *Developmental Review, 32*, 307–336.

Adjapong, E. S., & Emdin, C. (2015). Rethinking pedagogy in urban spaces: Implementing hip-hop pedagogy in the urban science classroom. *Journal of Urban Learning, Teaching, and Research, 11*, 66–77.

Altschul, I., Oyserman, D., & Bybee, D. (2008). Racial-ethnic self-schemas and segmented assimilation: Identity and the academic achievement of Hispanic youth. *Social Psychology Quarterly, 71*(3), 302–320.

Antonio, A. L., Chang, M. J., Hakuta, K., Kenny, D. A., Levin, S., & Milem, J. F. (2004). Effects of racial diversity on complex thinking in college students. *Psychological Science, 15*(8), 507–510.

Au, K. H. (1980). Participation structures in a reading lesson with Hawaiian children: Analysis of a culturally appropriate instructional event. *Anthropology & Education Quarterly, 11*(2), 91–115.

Au, K. H., & Carroll, J. H. (1997). Improving literacy achievement through a constructivist approach: The KEEP demonstration classroom project. *The Elementary School Journal, 97*(3), 203–221.

Bailey, C. T., & Boykin, A. W. (2001). The role of task variability and home contextual factors in the academic performance and task motivation of African American elementary school children. *Journal of Negro Education, 70* (1–2), 84–95.

Banks, J. A. (1999). *An introduction to multicultural education* (2nd ed.). Allyn & Bacon.

Beaulieu, D. (2006). A survey and assessment of culturally based education programs for Native American students in the United States. *Journal of American Indian Education, 45*(2), 5–61.

Beckham, K., & Concordia, A. (2019). We don't want to just study the world, we want to change it. In R. T. Cuauhtin, M. Zavala, C. Sleeter, & W. Au (Eds.), *Rethinking ethnic studies* (pp. 319–327). Rethinking Schools.

Belgrave, F. Z., Chase-Vaughn, G., Gray, F., Addison, J. D., & Cherry, V. R. (2000). The effectiveness of a culture- and gender-specific intervention for increasing resiliency among African American preadolescent females. *Journal of Black Psychology, 26*(2), 133–147.

Bigler, R. S. (1999). The use of multicultural curricula and materials to counter racism in children. *Journal of Social Issues, 55*(4), 687–705.

Bigler, R. S., Brown, C. S., & Markell, M. (2001). When groups are not created equal: Effects of group status on the formation of intergroup attitudes in children. *Child Development, 72,* 1151–1162.

Bowman, N. A. (2010a). College diversity experiences and cognitive development: A meta-analysis. *Review of Educational Research, 80*(1), 4–33.

Bowman, N. A. (2010b). Disequilibrium and resolution: The non-linear effects of diversity courses on well-being and orientations towards diversity. *The Review of Higher Education, 33*(4), 543–568.

Cabrera, N. L., Milam, J. F., Jaquette, O., & Marx, R. W. (2014). Missing the (student achievement) forest for all the (political) trees: Empiricism and the Mexican American student controversy in Tucson. *American Educational Research Journal, 51*(6), 1084–1118.

Cammarota, J., & Romero, A. (2009). The social justice education project: A critically compassionate intellectualism for Chicana/o students. In W. Ayers, T. Quinn, & D. Stovall (Eds.), *Handbook of social justice in education* (pp. 465–476). Routledge.

Cesar, S. (2011, November 20). Arizona educators clash over Mexican American studies. *LA Times.* https://www.latimes.com/archives/la-xpm-2011-nov-20-la-na-ethnic-studies-20111120-story.html

Chang, M. J. (2002). The impact of an undergraduate diversity course requirement on students' racial views and attitudes. *The Journal of General Education, 51*(1), 21–42.

Chavous, T., Bernat, D. H., Schmeelk-Cone, K., Caldwell, C. H., Kohn-Wood, L., & Zimmerman, M. A. (2003). Racial identity and academic attainment among African American adolescents. *Child Development, 74*(4), 1076–1090.

Cole, M. (1998). *Cultural psychology: A once and future discipline.* Harvard University Press.

Copenhaver, J. (2001). Listening to their voices connect literary and cultural understandings: Responses to small group read-alouds of *Malcolm X: A fire. New Advocate, 14*(4), 343–359.

Dee, T., & Penner, E. (2017). The causal effects of cultural relevance: Evidence from an ethnic studies curriculum. *American Educational Research Journal, 54*(1), 127–166.

Denson, N. (2009). Do curricular and co-curricular activities influence racial bias? A meta-analysis. *Review of Educational Research, 79*(2), 805–838.

Doherty, R. W., & Hilberg, R. S. (2007). Standards for effective pedagogy, classroom organization, English proficiency, and student achievement. *The Journal of Educational Research, 101*(1), 23–34.

Doherty, R. W., Hilberg, R. S., Pinal, A., & Tharp, R. G. (2003). Five standards and student achievement. *NABE Journal of Research and Practice, 1*(1), 1–24.

Duncan, W. (2012). The effects of Africentric United States history curriculum on Black student achievement. *Contemporary Issues in Education Research, 5*(2), 91–96.

Engberg, M. E. (2004). Improving intergroup relations in higher education: A critical examination of the influence of educational interventions on racial bias. *Review of Educational Research, 74*(4), 473–524.

Gay, G. (2018). *Culturally responsive teaching: Theory, research, and practice* (3rd ed.). Teachers College Press.

Ginwright, S. A. (2000). Identity for sale: The limits of racial reform in urban schools. *The Urban Review, 32*(1), 87–104.

Ginwright, S. (2004). *Black in school: Afrocentric reform, urban youth, and the promise of hip-hop culture.* Teachers College Press.

Green-Gibson, A., & Collett, A. (2014). A comparison of African & mainstream culture on African American students in public elementary schools. *Multicultural Education, 21*(2), 33–37.

Gurin, P. Y., Dey, E. L., Gurin, G., & Hurtado, S. (2003). How does racial/ethnic diversity promote education? *The Western Journal of Black Studies, 27*(1), 20–29.

Gurin, P. Y., Dey, E. L., Hurtado, S., & Gurin, G. (2002). Diversity and higher education: Theory and impact on educational outcomes. *Harvard Educational Review, 72*(3), 330–367.

Gurin, P., & Nagda, B. R. A. (2006). Getting to the what, how, and why of diversity on campus. *Educational Researcher, 35*(1), 20–24.

Halagao, P. E. (2004). Holding up the mirror: The complexity of seeing your ethnic self in history. *Theory and Research in Social Education, 32*(4), 459–483.

Halagao, P. E. (2010). Liberating Filipino Americans through decolonizing curriculum. *Race Ethnicity & Education, 13*(4), 495–512.

Hall, T., & Martin, B. (2013). Engagement of African American college students through the use of hip-hop pedagogy. *International Journal of Pedagogies and Learning, 8*(2), 93–105.

Hilberg, R. S., Tharp, R. G., & DeGeest, L. (2000). The efficacy of CREDE standards-based instruction on American Indian mathematics classes. *Excellence & Equity in Education, 33*(2), 32–40.

Hogan, D. E., & Mallott, M. (2005). Changing racial prejudice through diversity education. *Journal of College Student Development, 46*(2), 115–125.

Hughes, J. M., Bigler, R. S., & Levy, S. R. (2007). Consequences of learning about historical racism among European American and African American children. *Child Development, 78*, 1689–1705.

Kisker, E. E., Lipka, J., Adams, B. L., Rickard, A., Andrew-Ihrke, D., Yanez, E. E., & Millard, A. (2012). The potential of a culturally based supplemental mathematics curriculum to improve the mathematics performance of Alaska Native and other students. *Journal for Research in Mathematics Education, 43*(1), 75–113.

Klepper, A. (2014). High school students' attitudes toward Islam and Muslims: Can a social studies course make a difference? *The Social Studies, 105*, 113–123.

Krater, J., & Zeni, J. (1995). Seeing students, seeing culture, seeing ourselves. *Voices from the Middle, 3*(3), 32–38.

Krater, J., Zeni, J., & Cason, N. D. (1994). *Mirror images: Teaching writing in Black and White*. Heinemann.

Lee, C. D. (1995). A culturally based cognitive apprenticeship: Teaching African American high school students skills in literary interpretation. *Reading Research Quarterly, 30*(4), 608–630.

Lee, C. D. (2001). Is October Brown Chinese? A cultural modeling activity system for underachieving students. *American Educational Research Journal, 38*(1), 97–142.

Lee, C. D. (2006). "Every good-bye ain't gone": Analyzing the cultural underpinnings of classroom talk. *International Journal of Qualitative Studies in Education, 19*(3), 305–327.

Lee, C. D. (2007). *Culture, literacy, and learning: Taking bloom in the midst of the whirlwind*. Teachers College Press.

Lewis, K. M., Andrews, E., Gaska, K., Sullivan, C., Bybee, D., & Ellick, K. L. (2012). Experimentally evaluating the impact of a school-based African-centered emancipatory intervention on the ethnic identity of African American adolescents. *Journal of Black Psychology, 38*(3), 259–289.

Lewis, K. M., Sullivan, C. M., & Bybee, D. (2006). An experimental evaluation of a school-based emancipatory intervention to promote African American well-being and youth leadership. *Journal of Black Psychology, 32*(1), 3–28.

Lipka, J., Hogan, M. P., Webster, J. P., Yanez, E., Adams, B., Clark, S., & Lacy, D. (2005). Math in a cultural context: Two case studies of a successful culturally-based math project. *Anthropology & Education Quarterly, 36*(4), 367–385.

López, F. A. (2016). Culturally responsive pedagogies in Arizona and Latino students' achievement. *Teachers College Record, 118*(5), 1–42.

López, F. A. (2017). Altering the trajectory of the self-fulfilling prophecy: Asset-based pedagogy and classroom dynamics. *Journal of Teacher Education, 68*(2), 193–212.

López, F. A. (2018). *Asset pedagogies in Latino youth identity and achievement*. Routledge.

Lopez, G. E. (2004). Interethnic contact, curriculum, and attitudes in the first year of college. *Journal of Social Issues, 40*(1), 75–94.

Martin, K. J. (2010). Student attitudes and the teaching and learning of race, culture and politics. *Teaching and Teacher Education, 26*(3), 530–539.

Matthews, C. E., & Smith, W. S. (1994). Native American related materials in elementary science instruction. *Journal of Research in Science Teaching, 31*(4), 363–380.

McCarty, T. L. (1993). Language, literacy, and the image of the child in American Indian classrooms. *Language Arts, 70*(3), 182–192.

McCarty, T. L., & Lee, T. S. (2014). Critical culturally sustaining/revitalizing pedagogy and Indigenous education sovereignty. *Harvard Educational Review, 84*(1), 101–124.

Nagda, B. A., Kim, C. W., & Truelove, Y. (2004). Learning about difference, learning with others, learning to transgress. *Journal of Social Issues, 60*(1), 195–214.

Neville, H. A., Poteat, V. P., Lewis, J. A., & Spanierman, L. B. (2014). Changes in White college students' color-blind racial ideology over 4 years: Do diversity experiences make a difference? *Journal of Counseling Psychology, 61*(2), 179–190.

Okoye-Johnson, O. (2011). Does multicultural education improve students' racial attitudes? Implications for closing the achievement gap. *Journal of Black Studies, 42*(8), 1252–1274.

Paone, T. R., Malott, K. M., & Barr, J. J. (2015). Assessing the impact of a race-based course on counseling students: A quantitative study. *Journal of Multicultural Counseling and Development, 43*, 206–220.

Rickford, A. (2001). The effect of cultural congruence and higher order questioning on the reading enjoyment and comprehension of ethnic minority students. *Journal of Education for Students Placed at Risk, 6*(4), 357–387.

Rogoff, B. (2003). *The cultural nature of human development*. Oxford University Press.

San Pedro, T. (2018). Abby as ally: An argument for culturally disruptive pedagogy. *American Educational Research Journal, 55*(6), 1193–1232.

San Pedro, T., & Kinloch, V. (2017). Toward projects in humanization: Research on co-creating and sustaining dialogic relationships. *American Educational Research Journal, 54*(1), 373–394.

Sharif Matthews, J., & López, F. (2018). Speaking their language: The role of cultural content integration and heritage language for academic achievement among Latino children. *Contemporary Educational Psychology, 57*, 72–86.

Sleeter, C. E. (2011). *The academic and social value of ethnic studies: A research review*. National Education Association.

Spanierman, L. B., & Heppner, M. J. (2004). Psychosocial costs of racism to Whites scale (PCRW): Construction and initial validation. *Journal of Counseling Psychology, 51*(2), 249–262.

Stone, B. J., & Stewart, S. (2016). HBCUs and writing programs: Critical hip hop language pedagogy and first-year student success. *Composition Studies, 44*(2), 183–186.

Tharp, R. G., & Gallimore, R. (1988). *Rousing minds to life: Teaching, learning, and schooling in social context*. Cambridge University Press.

Thomas, O., Davidson, W., & McAdoo, H. (2008). An evaluation study of the Young Empowered Sisters (YES!) Program: Promoting cultural assets among African American adolescent girls through a culturally relevant school-based intervention. *Journal of Black Psychology, 34*(3), 281–308.

Todd, N. R., Spanierman, L. B., & Poteat, V. P. (2011). Longitudinal examination of the psychosocial costs of racism to Whites across the college experience. *Journal of Counseling Psychology, 58*(4), 508–521.

Tyson, C. A. (2002). "Get up off that thing": African American middle school students respond to literature to develop a framework for understanding social action. *Theory and Research in Social Education, 30*(1), 42–65.

Vasquez, J. M. (2005). Ethnic identity and Chicano literature: How ethnicity affects reading and reading affects ethnic consciousness. *Ethnic and Racial Studies, 28*(5), 903–924.

Wiggan, G., & Watson-Vandiver, M. J. (2017). Pedagogy of empowerment: Student perspectives on critical multicultural education at a high-performing African American school. *Race Ethnicity and Education, 22*(6), 767–787.

CHAPTER 10

Realistic Expectations

English Language Learners and the Acquisition of "Academic" English

Guadalupe Valdés

Educating children in a language they neither speak nor understand is an enormous challenge. The dimensions of the challenge have become most clearly obvious under the No Child Left Behind Act of 2001 (NCLB) because of its role in the movement for accountability in public education. The main federal law affecting K–12 education, NCLB has led to an increased focus on the achievement gap between language-minority children and -majority children (e.g., Capps et al., 2005; Fry, 2007; Hakimzadeh & Cohn, 2007; Short & Fitzsimmons, 2007). In the case of ELLs, many questions exist about the role of language in school performance and about appropriate interventions for developing the types of English-language proficiency that children need in order to succeed in school. These questions include: How long does it take to learn a second language? What is the role of instruction in the language acquisition process? What kinds of instruction are successful in the acquisition of which aspects of language? Are there ways to accelerate the acquisition of English? The hope is that answers to these questions will allow practitioners to develop and document a set of practices that are based on a clear understanding of the process of second language acquisition and that can be implemented widely across the country.

Unfortunately, language is extraordinarily complex. There are no easy or quickly generalizable answers to the above questions, and disagreement persists on many of the fundamental issues in the fields of both second language acquisition and second language pedagogy. There is also little agreement about the assessment of English language proficiency and about the aspects of language that can be measured in assessing children's growth in the acquisition of a second language. What is evident is that if we are to make progress in educating children who do not speak English in this country, educators, researchers, and policymakers need to be provided with information to help them understand the complexities of the process of second language acquisition, the many unanswered questions surrounding the ultimate attainment of second languages, and the conditions essential for acquisition to take place.

In this chapter, then, I present an overview of the field of second language acquisition and make a deliberate attempt to capture the dilemmas and the debates currently taking place in this field. I also provide information about existing and continuing disagreements on various types of second language instruction that have engaged the second-language teaching profession as well as a brief overview of research conducted on the effectiveness of various approaches. I call attention to the fact that evidence on second language acquisition in children in both tutored and naturalistic environments is limited and emphasize the need for an increasing number of longitudinal studies with both children and adults that will allow us to understand the process of second language acquisition over time. In the final section of the chapter, I discuss key issues surrounding the development of English by immigrant children and the challenges of assessing both language development and content knowledge in ELLs on high-stakes, standardized assessments. I also touch on the debate surrounding the acquisition of what is referred to as "academic English" or "academic language" and on the ways that various different definitions have influenced conceptualizations about both instruction and assessment. I conclude with a brief discussion of the ways in which our qualitative, small-scale study of language development in K–3 children might contribute to our deeper understanding of the acquisition of English in children and of the social and cultural nature of this process. As Baker (2007) and Durán (2008) suggest, such work is needed if we are to better map curriculum goals and students' growth in the acquisition of a second language and if we are to accumulate evidence of growth that is sensitive to students' backgrounds and to the unique contexts in which children learn.

THE FIELD OF SECOND LANGUAGE ACQUISITION

The field of second language acquisition (SLA) studies the learning or acquisition of a language other than a native language, which is referred to as a *second language* or by the shorthand term *L2*. A first or native language (*L1*) is used with a child by parents or other interlocutors in infancy and/ or in very early childhood for primary socialization; an L2 is not. Still a relatively young field of inquiry, SLA has employed theories and methodologies drawn from the disciplines of linguistics, psycholinguistics, social psychology, neurolinguistics, and sociolinguistics in order to understand the process of second language acquisition in instructional and noninstructional (naturalistic) settings. As Bardovi-Harlig and Dörnyei (2006) point out, SLA itself is an umbrella term that covers a range of research approaches and perspectives. It is, moreover, a field in which there are many debates and disagreements about the theoretical foundations underlying the field, about the methodologies used to study the process of second language acquisition/learning, and about the goals and ultimate outcomes of the process itself.

From the perspective of educational researchers and practitioners who are concerned about the practices that can support children's acquisition of English in order to succeed in school, the field of SLA offers limited clear guidance. Policymakers want to mandate the implementation of effective practices for accelerating children's acquisition of English, and teachers want to understand how best to teach English language learners. Faculty members working in the area of teacher preparation often look to SLA research hoping that it might provide future teachers with knowledge about ELLs and about the process of second language acquisition. It is sometimes the case that they present SLA findings in their classes in order to support particular views about appropriate pedagogies and learning goals that they believe will work effectively for new teachers in their classrooms. Ellis (2005b), however, suggests that, given controversies in the field, it might be unwise to attempt to formulate a set of general principles of instructed language acquisition and suggests that Hatch's (1978) warning, "apply with caution," is as pertinent today as it was some 30 years ago. He concludes that:

> If SLA is to offer teachers guidance there is a need to bite the bullet and provide advice, so long as this advice does not masquerade as prescriptions or proscriptions (and there is always a danger that advice will be so construed) and so long as it is tentative, in the form of what Stenhouse (1975) called "provisional specifications." (Ellis, 2005b, p. 210)

In the case of immigrant-background children who acquire the societal language in school contexts and who must use this language in order to learn academic content (mathematics, social studies, language arts, science), the question of what needs to be acquired by children and what needs to be taught by teachers is possibly much more complex and more urgent. Certainly, immigrant children who need to learn English in order to be educated in that language must acquire the linguistic system. But, as Van Patten (2003) argues, second language acquisition is a slow and time-consuming process. What this means is that young learners, if they are to achieve in school, will need to use English while they are still learning it—before they have had time to acquire the full linguistic system. If they are to understand instruction, to learn how to read and write, and to display what they have learned about academic content, they must use an "interlanguage," that is, a learner's variety of English that is not yet grammatically accurate or consistently fluent. In American schools, ELLs cannot be made to wait to use the language until they speak and write like native speakers. They must learn through and with flawed English, and teachers must become skilled at supporting their subject matter learning during the time that they are acquiring English and using "defective" language for many classroom assignments and activities. They must keep in mind, moreover, that nativelike ultimate attainment is characteristic of only a small number of L2 learners of all ages and of all languages.

SLA: The Development of the Field

A number of recent works have attempted to offer a brief history of the field of second language acquisition, including Block (2003), Johnson (2004), and Sharwood Smith (1994). While not identical, all three works divide the development of the field into periods and stages, including the behaviorist period, the creative construction period (focusing on the role of the learner and encompassing the studies of interlanguages), and a current period focused more on producing basic research in the disciplines of linguistics, psychology, and cognitive science than on informing the practice of language teaching.

The groundwork for the field of SLA was first established during and after World War II, at a time of increased interest by the defense community in the use of foreign languages in counterintelligence. Drawing from structural linguistics and behaviorism, early work on the learning of second or foreign languages focused on the influence of the first language on the *target language* (TL)—the language to be acquired—and developed a set of classroom practices known as audio-lingualism that were widely adopted by language teachers. Language was seen as a set of first language habits that would directly interfere with the establishment of a new set of habits to be acquired in the process of learning a second language. Much attention, therefore, was given to the development of *contrastive analysis* (CA) in which researchers contrasted learners' native languages with the particular target language that learners hoped to acquire. By carrying out such analyses, they hoped to anticipate the L2 structures most likely to cause difficulties for learners and to develop language teaching curricula to attend to those aspects of a target language in which the structures of the learners' L1 and L2 most differed.

The second period of the field of SLA, according to Sharwood Smith (1994), is one in which the learner was seen as an autonomous creator of linguistic systems. This period rejected the perspectives of contrastive analysis, noting that learners did not exhibit predicted difficulties nor did the similarities between their L1 and the target language result in positive transfer. By the 1960s and 1970s, moreover, theories of language had shifted, and psychology had moved from behaviorism to the information-processing model of cognition. Conscious of the limits of contrastive analysis and convinced that similar errors in particular grammatical structures could be found in learners speaking very different native languages, a number of researchers carried out work in what is known as *error analysis*, that is, the systematic study of learners' errors in order to describe the *interlanguages*—the intermediate stages in learners' development (Corder, 1967, 1981; Selinker, 1972) or approximative systems (Nemser, 1971) exhibited by L2 learners. Block (2003) maintains that, given changing views of language, errors came to be seen not as undesirable habits but as evidence of a developing competence at a particular stage of development, which is systematic and coherent. Error analysis had many implications for language teaching. Corder (1981), for example, argued that learners have a built-in syllabus and that, therefore, they will only learn those structures according to an internally programmed order. He thus conjectured that the direct teaching of structures in an order dictated by, for example, traditional views of language instruction would be unsuccessful at altering the systematicity of the developing system.

As pointed out by Johnson (2004), the field of SLA was strongly influenced by the work of Chomsky (1965, 1980, 1981) on first language acquisition and by his views on grammatical competence, that is, of a native speaker's implicit (unconscious) knowledge of the formal properties of his or her L1 grammar. For Chomsky, *grammatical competence* is the implicit knowledge of syntax that all native speakers acquire as the result of a genetically programmed *universal grammar* (UG) as well as a result of input (i.e., the available language data of variable quality that normally surrounds children). Given the poverty of the stimulus (the often questionable systematic exposure to well-formed, audible language) and at the same time the striking uniformity of the grammars of native speakers, Chomsky posited that children are able to acquire an L1 only because they are born with an innate language mechanism that is independent of other cognitive mechanisms. The innate system needs only be triggered by the language of the environment and does not depend on the social aspect of language use.

Chomsky's theory of first language acquisition has influenced the field of SLA, and researchers have strongly debated whether L2 learners have or do not have access to UG. Unfortunately, results of studies attempting to answer that question have not resolved the issue. Some researchers (e.g., Bley-Vroman, 1989) argue that L1 and L2 acquisition processes are fundamentally different and that adult L2 learners do not have access to UG, thus accounting for their less-than-perfect ultimate attainment. Other researchers (e.g., Flynn, 1987) believe that L2 learners do indeed have full access to UG, while others (White, 1989) believe that UG is available to learners only through the language they have already acquired. As Johnson (2004) points out, unresolved though the issue of UG access in L2 learners may be, the impact of Chomsky's theories have been profound on the field of L2 acquisition.

According to Block (2003), the second stage of the field of SLA drew directly from work on L1 acquisition and led to a series of morpheme acquisition studies exemplified by the work of Dulay and Burt (1973, 1974) who argued that L1 interference errors were much less frequent than natural developmental errors across learners of English from various language backgrounds. According to these researchers, children learning English produced errors similar to those of native English speakers acquiring the same morphemes. These early morpheme studies, although now questioned seriously from methodological and other perspectives, nevertheless raised important questions about the primary role of L1 transfer in the process of L2 acquisition. Block (2003) places Krashen's work (he credits Krashen with developing the first wide-ranging theory of SLA) within this particular period of the development of the field and points out that Krashen drew directly on the morpheme studies in his five interrelated hypotheses.

Krashen's work had extensive influence on language teachers and particularly on bilingual education teachers in this country. Summarizing briefly, Krashen (1985) proposed there was a natural order for morpheme acquisition that was fixed and predictable and independent of the order that rules might be taught in a formal context. He further argued that acquisition (a subconscious and incidental process) was different from learning (a conscious and intentional process). The first process, he maintained, led to tacit or implicit learning and the second to explicit linguistic knowledge. For Krashen, according to his input hypothesis, language is acquired from comprehensible input, language that is at the developmental level of the learner or just slightly beyond it. Moreover, according to his affective filter hypothesis, learners, because of motivation, anxiety, or stress, can put up an affective filter that blocks the internalization of comprehensible input surrounding them and thus the acquisition of an L2. Finally, the monitor hypothesis predicted that in order for learners to monitor the accuracy of their production, they require sufficient time to use their explicitly learned rules to correct and rephrase their utterances.

Criticisms of Krashen's position have been many and have focused on the fact that his hypotheses cannot be subjected to empirical testing (McLaughlin, 1987), on aspects of his theory such as the noninterface position between acquisition and learning, the exact definition of comprehensible input, and its failure to distinguish between child and adult second-language learners. Johnson (2004) points out that Krashen did not distinguish between the understanding of a message and simple exposure to comprehensible input. She further argues that while input became far more important in Krashen's theory than it was in L1 acquisition theory, Krashen confused the social and the cognitive and failed to distinguish between one-way and two-way interaction.

It is important to stress, however, that, in spite of the criticism that his hypotheses generated, Krashen's influence on the field of second language acquisition was extensive. It drew attention to the importance of input, to the possibly limited role of grammar instruction in second-language teaching, and to the difference between implicit and explicit learning. Moreover, as Block (2003) maintains, Krashen's theories drew on the three epistemological databases of SLA: the experiential, the observational, and the empirical. Krashen was a learner of languages, a former ESL teacher, and a language researcher, and his perspectives were those of the original applied linguists who worked in the early period of second-language learning and acquisition. Although some have been dismissive of his work, in part because of the broad acceptance of his theories by language teachers, it is important to recall that, as Lightbown (1984) concluded, Krashen brought attention to the complexity of SLA and drew from the fields of linguistics, psychology, and sociolinguistics at a time when no one else had proposed a broad encompassing theory of L2 learning. Importantly for those of us concerned about English language learners and the pedagogies and practices that might impede or enhance their acquisition of the target language, Krashen—especially in his work with Terrell (Krashen & Terrell, 1983)—sought to contribute both to basic theories of SLA as well as to the application of these theories to the teaching of language in classrooms. In many ways, moreover, his ideas have directly influenced ongoing examinations of a number of key issues including the nature of input, the distinction between explicit and implicit learning, and the role of instruction in second language acquisition. Gass and Mackey (2007) for example, emphasize that the current SLA approach known as the interaction hypothesis (Gass, 1997) subsumes Krashen's (1985) input hypothesis, adding to it the dimensions of interaction and output (Swain, 1993, 1995, 2000, 2005).

Recent Research and SLA Theory

The third period of SLA has been characterized by Sharwood Smith (1994) as one in which much less interest has been placed in the application of SLA theory to second-language teaching but an increasing interest placed in basic research including the contributions of SLA theory to other theoretical disciplines. As Doughty and Long (2003) point out in their introduction to the *Handbook on Second Language Acquisition*, "A good deal of what might be termed 'basic research' goes on in SLA without regard for its potential applications or social utility" (p. 6). SLA researchers, for example, have engaged in testing very different theories of acquisition, including nativism, functionalism, emergentism, and connectionism; and they have sought to contribute to cognitive psychology by studying implicit and explicit learning, incidental and intentional learning, automaticity, attention, memory, and individual differences. They have also contributed to the understanding of topics in linguistics by studying variation, language processing, cross-linguistic influences, fossilization, and the relationship of second language acquisition processes to the processes of pidginization and creolization. Finally, SLA researchers have sought to contribute to knowledge in neuroscience by focusing on how and where the brain stores linguistic knowledge, which areas are involved in the L2 acquisition process, how maturation affects L2 acquisition, and the differences in ultimate attainment between children and adults.

Two relatively recent handbooks of SLA (Doughty & Long, 2003; Ritchie & Bhatia, 1996) both include the following topics: universal grammar and second language acquisition; maturational constraints, universal grammar, and SLA; crosslinguistic influence (language transfer); information processing in L2 acquisition (implicit and explicit learning, incidental and intentional learning, attention, memory automaticity, variation, stabilization, and fossilization), and the role of the environment in SLA (including the social context as well as input and interaction).

According to Zuengler and Miller (2006), in the last 15 years the field of SLA has been divided into two parallel worlds, the positions of which have been characterized as incommensurable. One group of researchers (cognitivists) see the acquisition of an L2 as an individual cognitive process that takes place in the mind of the individual learner, while another group of researchers (sociointeractionists) see language acquisition primarily as a social process that takes place in interactions between learners and speakers of the target language. The cognitive view has been dominant in the field, and work in this tradition is often referred to as "mainstream SLA." Researchers working within this tradition take the position that SLA's area of interest is the internal mental processes of what they term second language acquisition, which exclusively involves the development of the internal linguistic system of learners. According to Larsen-Freeman (2007), who provides a concise view of the two existing views of SLA, cognitivist SLA researchers view language as a mental construct and learning as change in a mental state. They are interested in "the aggregation of and increasing complexity and control of linguistic structures by learners," and they measure progress by "where along the route toward target language proficiency the learner is as indicated by the learner's linguistic performance" (p. 780). Representative of this perspective are what Johnson (2004) categorizes as information-process approaches to SLA, such as Krashen's (1985) input hypothesis; Swain's comprehensible output theory (1985, 1993, 1995), Gass and Selinker's (2001) model of SLA acquisition, Van Patten's (1996) input-processing model, and Long's (1983, 1996) interaction hypothesis. According to Block, the input-interaction-output model (Gass, 1997), which subsumes the views of Krashen, Swain, and Long, is "the most tangible result of over thirty years of increasingly more intensive research into how individuals learn second languages" (Block, 2003, p. 30).

By comparison, socially oriented theorists argue that the cognitivist orientation views learners from a deficit perspective and focuses on learners' limitations and their failure to become identical to native speakers. These researchers criticize mainstream SLA for taking the position that what is to be acquired is "a stable a-priori system that is used only for the transfer of information from one person's mind to the other" (Mori, 2007, p. 850). Lafford characterizes this same perspective as "decontextualized minds learning grammatical rules" (Lafford, 2007, p. 742). Critics of mainstream SLA point out that views about approximative systems, interlanguages, and non-nativelike ultimate attainment rests on the acceptance of a single native-speaker norm as the goal and the measure of the acquisition of a language other than the first.

The socially oriented position considers that SLA, rather than focusing exclusively on the developing linguistic systems of learners, should be concerned with understanding how speakers of one language become *users* (speakers, writers, readers) of a second language. Such perspectives include Vygotskian sociocultural theory (Frawley & Lantolf, 1985; Lantolf, 2000, 2006; Lantolf & Appel, 1994; Lantolf & Frawley, 1983; Lantolf & Thorne, 2006); language socialization perspectives (Duff, 1995, 2002; Harklau, 1994; Ochs, 1988, 1991; Schieffelin & Ochs, 1986; Watson-Gegeo, 2004); notions of learning communities and communities of practice (Lave & Wenger, 1991, Toohey, 1999); Bakhtinian perspectives on dialogism (Toohey, 2000); ecological perspectives on language acquisition (Kramsch, 2002; van Lier, 2002, 2004); and critical theory (Canagarajah, 1993, 1999, 2005; Norton, 1995, 1997, 2000; Pennycook, 1990, 1999, 2001). For these researchers, the goal of second-language learners is not to become like native speakers of the language but to use the language to function competently in a variety of contexts for a range of purposes. Moreover, since it is estimated that only 5% of L2 learners achieve nativelike competence (Han & Odlin, 2006), and yet most of these learners go on to use the language in their everyday lives for a number of purposes both inside and outside of L2-speaking countries, it seems unwise to perpetually brand individuals who use a less-than-perfect second language in their everyday lives as mere learners. Cook (2002) argues for the term *L2 users*, rather than *L2 learners*, for individuals who "exploit whatever linguistic resources they have for real-life purposes" (p. 2).

The fundamental difference between cognitivist and social views of second language acquisition involves their contrasting views about exactly what must be acquired in the process of learning a language other than the first. Cognitively oriented researchers are focused on understanding how speakers of one language internalize the linguistic system of another language. They want to know, for example, how learners develop an implicit grammar of a second language, how they process input (the language that they hear and read), what the developing linguistic system looks like at different stages, what kinds of errors learners make with different structures at different points of acquisition, and whether direct instruction on grammatical structures can change the pace of acquisition of those structures. Socially oriented researchers, by comparison, are concerned with the ways that second-language learners learn "how to mean," that is, with the ways in which learners, by interacting with speakers of the L2, are able to develop and use evolving/imperfect linguistic, sociolinguistic, textual, and pragmatic systems to carry out numerous communicative actions. Zuengler and Miller (2006) conclude, moreover, that the debate between the two perspectives involves conflicting ontologies (basic questions about the nature of reality) and reflects an irreconcilable debate on the role of positivism and relativism in theory construction. They are not optimistic about the possibility of integrating the social and the cognitive. For Larsen-Freeman (2007), however, there is hope. She proposes chaos/complexity theory (C/CT) as a possible perspective "that is large enough to accommodate two competing points of view" (p. 33). She believes that C/CT supports a social view of language but does not exclude the individual psychological perspective of the cognitivist SLA perspectives.

As is the case for many areas of inquiry, the field of SLA has undergone a number of shifting emphases over the many years it has been in existence. Klein (1998), however, argues that there is no one SLA theory in sight because the field wants "to discover the principles according to which people who have already mastered one language acquire another" (p. 529), and many acquisitional phenomena (e.g., vocabulary learning, pronunciation, syntax, and interactive behavior) must be accounted for. From Klein's perspective, SLA has, at best, "reliably and generally explained some few specific phenomena, for example certain selected syntactical or morphological constructions, and even these explanations are arguable" (p. 329).

For teachers, what this review of the second language acquisition field (SLA) is intended to suggest is that language acquisition is complicated and that researchers focused on understanding the process disagree not only about what is to be acquired but also about how the process takes place. Unfortunately, within the language teaching profession few agree on what to teach and how. As Kelly (1976) indicated, in the 25 centuries during which educators have been concerned about the teaching of second languages, "theories have been put forward about every aspect of language teaching, the matter of the course, the methods of transmission, and the media of teaching" (p. 2). In the section that follows I offer a brief overview of current concerns in the field and conclude with a summary of shifting perspectives over a longer period.

SLA and Second Language Pedagogy

As I pointed out above, the field of SLA has been primarily concerned not with practice but with the development of theories that can contribute to the understanding of the human language faculty. As a result, agreement is uncommon on whether and to what degree there should be a relationship between SLA and language pedagogy, and concern continues regarding the perceived lack of relevance of SLA to classroom teaching (Crookes, 1997).

Lightbown, in two articles published 15 years apart (1985, 2000), maintains that while SLA theories might still be one component of teachers' knowledge base, these theories cannot be the principal source of information that guides teachers in their everyday practices. She recalls suggesting in 1985 that "the proper role for SLA research in teacher education was to help in setting realistic expectations for what language teachers and learners could accomplish in a second or foreign language classroom. SLA research on order of acquisition, crosslinguistic transfer effects, and age factors could potentially explain why some things were so difficult, in spite of effort and good will on the part of both teachers and learners" (Lightbown, 2000, p. 431).

Despite concerns by major figures in the SLA field about the relationship between second language pedagogy and SLA, second language and foreign language teachers, and in many states content teachers, are currently required to take courses in the field of second language acquisition. Not surprisingly, as Van Patten (2003) comments, teachers approach these courses asking for answers to concrete teaching questions. They want to know, for example, how best to teach grammar, how vocabulary is to be presented, how errors are to be corrected, and how to deal with *long-term ELLs* (students not officially redesignated as fluent English speakers by state mandated criteria after many years of residence and study in this country). Some teachers come to these courses with clear ideas about teaching and learning languages and often assume that there are known facts about the process of acquisition. Lightbown (2000), for example, comments that over the years teachers in her classes have had strong opinions about what "everybody knew" about learning languages. In the 1950s and 1960s, "everybody knew" that second languages were learned through reading and translating literary texts. In the late 1960s, "everybody knew" they were learned through imitation, repetition, drill, and overlearned dialogues. By the 1970s, the period of communicative language teaching (CLT), prospective teachers and everybody else "knew" that exposure to comprehensible input and group interaction was essential. Interest in focusing on language forms was minimal. Lightbown points out that some of these changes were indeed informed to some degree by SLA research, but she points out that these changes were due to factors other than research findings and included specific movements in language pedagogy itself (e.g., views about learners' needs, trends such as the British national-functional syllabus movement, and the rejection of structure-based approaches).

The questions asked by teachers of second or foreign languages who focus only on the teaching of the L2 language in classrooms are in many ways different from those asked by bilingual teachers and content teachers who must teach both content and English in their classes. Their questions, moreover, often reflect current concerns that directly affect both teachers and learners in the present policy context. For example, the impact of the NCLB legislation and the focus on both subject matter and L2 testing for ELLs has had a clear impact on what "everybody knows" must be "taught" in order for ELLs to achieve in school. Faculty members working with teachers of ELLs in content classrooms, for example, might expect answers to questions such as the following:

1. What are the best ways of making instruction in specific discipline areas comprehensible to beginning ELLs?
2. What are the best ways of teaching vocabulary to ELLs?
3. What are the best ways of teaching the language of specific disciplines to ELLs?

On the other hand, teachers who are also concerned about students' ability to do well on state-mandated tests of English language development (CELDT, ACCESS, ELDA, LAB-R) and about the interaction between subject matter tests and the development of children's English language proficiency might expect answers to questions such as the following:

1. What is the role of instruction in developing children's second language?
2. What kinds of instruction are successful in the acquisition of which aspects of language?
3. What evidence is there that systematic and explicit ELD instruction for learners—especially young children—makes a difference?
4. Do learners have a built-in syllabus and can it be altered by instruction?
5. What is the best way to deal with students' interlanguages (their imperfect and developing learner varieties)?
6. Should teachers be concerned about fossilization?
7. Can accuracy be accelerated by instruction?
8. What is the impact of corrective feedback on the development of accuracy in the L2?
9. What is the role of "practice" in L2 acquisition?
10. What is the impact of "junky" data (the flawed language of peers) on language learners?
11. What is the role of input and exposure to the target language in language acquisition?
12. How long does the process of L2 acquisition take? Is there a point at which L2 acquisition can be said to be complete?

Finally, both groups might want suggestions about specific methods to be used in "teaching" language.

Approaches to Language Teaching in the Classroom

In a detailed and extensive literature review prepared for the New Zealand Ministry of Education (Auckland Regional Office), Ellis (2005b) presents a number of perspectives on several of the above questions. He begins by discussing the three approaches to language teaching that he identifies as representative of classroom instruction: the oral situational approach, the notional functional approach, and the task-based approach. He identifies the learning theories that underlie each of these pedagogies and argues that both the oral situational and the notional functional approaches are under-girded by skill-learning theory and built around a present-practice-produce (PPP), accuracy-oriented methodology. From his perspective, task-based approaches that have interactional authenticity, by comparison, give primacy to fluency over accuracy without denying that learners have to attend to language form.

Ellis (2005b) then reviews classroom-based research on language teaching and learning and makes a distinction between two main theoretical perspectives that have informed instruction: the computational model (associated with concepts such as input processing, input, intake, interlanguage development, and the learner's built-in syllabus) and the sociocultural theory of mind perspective (associated with social interaction, collaboration, zone of proximal development, and scaffolding). He divides curriculum into two broad types of curriculum—direct and indirect intervention—and reviews research related to both types of intervention. Drawing from the work of Norris and Ortega (2000) in terms of the direct teaching of grammar, Ellis (2005b) concludes that "learners can benefit from instruction on specific grammatical features if their goal is to perform well on discrete-point tests like the TOEFL" (p. 10). He points out there is little or no evidence, however, that grammar instruction results in the development of learner's ability to use these features spontaneously in oral communication. He concludes, moreover, that grammar instruction cannot circumvent the learners' natural route of acquisition. Contrary to what is now the position of ELD development programs in some parts of the country where "systematic and explicit" instruction in English is being advocated for elementary school children, Ellis's review of the research literature leads him to conclude that the results of explicit teaching are evident only when learners' knowledge was examined through "experimentally elicited responses rather than in communicative use" (p. 14), and that explicit approaches researchers reported on were implemented in narrow and restricted ways. He thus argues that "caution needs to be exercised in concluding that explicit instruction is more effective than implicit" (p. 14).

A close reading of Norris and Ortega (2000) makes evident the difficulty of using the terms *explicit* and *implicit* instruction casually. In their synthesis of the effectiveness of L2 instruction, Norris and Ortega reviewed findings from 77 experimental and quasi-experimental studies published between 1980 and 1998, which they categorized as instruction (1) involving focus-on-form or focus-on-forms, (2) using explicit or implicit approaches, and (3) measuring responses through metalinguistic judgments, selected responses, constrained constructed responses, or free constructed responses. Studies were characterized as *focusing on form* (FonF) if there was an integration of form and meaning, if learning was unobtrusive and documented students' mental processes, if forms were selected by taking into account learners' needs, and if interlanguage constraints were considered. Studies were categorized as *focused on forms* (FonFS) when none of the above strategies could be identified and learner attention was somehow focused on particular structures. Instructional treatments were considered *explicit* if rule explanation was a part of the instruction or "if learners were asked to attend to particular form and to try to arrive at a metalinguistic generalization on their own" (p. 437). Norris and Ortega report that in all the studies reviewed, learner proficiency levels were either noted minimally or noted inconsistently. Only 1 of the 77 studies was conducted with elementary school learners, 10 were conducted with junior high school students, 5 with high school learners, and 51 with college students. A total of 11 studies were conducted with adults outside of a college context. Instructional treatments ranged from a low of under 1 hour to a maximum of 7 hours.

In reporting their conclusions about what appeared to be superior results of explicit instruction that focused on forms, the authors remind their readers that

> measurement of change induced by instruction is typically carried out on instruments that seem to favor more explicit memory-based performance. Thus, in the current domain, over 90% of the dependent variables required the application of L2 rules in highly focused and discrete ways, while only around 10% of the dependent variables required relatively free productive use of the L2. Thus, it is likely that effect sizes observed within any given study may be directly associated with the type of response required from learners on outcome measures, and associated interpretations of study findings should be tempered by the realization that a different test type would likely have produced different results. (pp. 483, 486–487)

Ellis (2005a, 2005b) presents a much more abbreviated summary of indirect interventions. He characterizes them as having been conducted both from the perspective of the information-processing or computational model of L2 acquisition and from the sociocultural perspective. Work on task-based approaches to implicit instruction within the computational model of L2 learning has examined issues such as off- or online planning (Crookes, 1989; Wendel, 1997). Research within the sociointeractional model, by comparison, has examined scaffolding, collaborative dialogue, and task engagement. In both cases, Ellis maintains that work on implicit, task-based pedagogies conducted as part of both models of L2 acquisition has tended to focus more on language use rather than on the acquisition of the linguistic system.

Shifting Perspectives in the Language Teaching Profession

According to Kelly (1976), the language teaching profession can be said to have had its beginning 25 centuries ago. The profession has been rooted in traditions associated with the teaching of Latin and other classical languages structured around translation and the methodologies of grammar. Over time, the modern-language teaching (as opposed to the classical-language teaching) profession has engaged in a continuing search of pedagogies and practices appropriate for developing students' ability to comprehend and/ or to produce a language other than the first. Ideas from the study of logic, grammar, rhetoric, philosophy, and later from linguistics and psychology, have deeply influenced the teaching of languages. Comparing the linear development of sciences with the cyclical development found in art, Kelly argues that all teachers, including language teachers, "unwittingly rediscover old techniques":

> Whereas artists are willing to seek inspiration from the past, teachers, being cursed with the assumption that their discoveries are necessarily an improvement on what went on before, are reluctant to learn from history. Thus it is that they unwittingly rediscover old techniques by widely different methods of research. (p. 396)

This same discovery and rediscovery of ideas informing language teaching in the United States is well captured in the recent retrospective summaries of articles published since 1916 in the *Modern Language Journal*, a journal specializing in language learning and teaching. According to Mitchell and Vidal (2001), articles published over this 94-year period make evident that language instruction has been influenced by a set of dichotomous views (e.g., the importance of fluency versus accuracy, the need to teach integrated skills versus separate skills) as well as by various theoretical positions (e.g., contrastive analysis, behaviorism, structural linguistics, and generative linguistics). Among the major mainstream methods listed by Mitchell and Vidal are (1) the Grammar Translation Method, used in the teaching of Greek and Latin, (2) the Direct Method, which taught language by the direct association of words with actions and objects, (3) the Reading Method, which argued for reading as the principal skill to be acquired by college foreign language learners, and (4) the Audiolingual Method, which derived from the Army Specialized Training Program (ASTP) and involved

memorization and pattern drill. This program was implemented during
World War II to meet the nation's need for military personnel who could
"identify, decode, translate, and interpret strategic messages" (Mitchell &
Vidal, 2001, p. 29). The Audiolingual Method first appeared in the late
1940s and became dominant in the 1960s and 1970s. Focusing primarily
on oral language, its theory of language learning was behaviorist. Stimulus,
response, and reinforcement were important. The syllabus was organized
around key phonological, morphological, and syntactic elements. Contrastive analysis was used for selection of elements, and grammar was taught in-
ductively. Dialogues and drills were used extensively as students responded
to stimuli, memorized, repeated, and imitated. Teachers were seen as models of language, conducting drills, teaching dialogues, and directing choral
responses. The Audiolingual Method was abandoned largely as a result of
shifting views about language based on the work of Chomsky (1957, 1959),
which argued that language is not merely a process of habit formation, but
rather a process of creative construction.

Since the 1970s, members of the second-language teaching profession
have moved to the implementation of what have been called "communicative teaching methods." These varied methods view language as communication and consider the goal of language study as the acquisition of
functional competence in actual communicative interactions using both the
written and the oral mode. Moreover, they assume that activities involving communication and meaningful tasks will promote learning. Syllabi for
communicative courses vary, but generally include lessons on structures and
functions and task-based activities. Instructors expect students to play the
role of negotiators, contributors, and actors, while instructors are expected
to facilitate the communication process, act as participants in communication, and serve as analysts of the communicative needs of students. The
dilemma for these educators is how to design teaching programs that can
result in both functional competence in face-to-face communication as well
as in the accurate use of the written language in both receptive and productive modes.

In sum, profound changes have occurred in the thinking of researchers and practitioners involved in second-language teaching over time. However, in spite of strong efforts by professional associations to change the
focus and emphasis of language teaching, the day-to-day practice of classroom instruction draws primarily from "traditions of practice." The audiolingual and contrastive analysis theories identified as central to students'
second-language learning are still present in language teaching materials used
currently. The materials continue to present the same set of linguistic items.

New theories about the stages and order of acquisition of structures in
a second language conducted by SLA researchers (e.g., that the order of acquisition of particular structures may not be amenable to direct instruction)
have had little impact in most classrooms.

Many ESL teachers and programs continue to focus primarily on the teaching of grammatical structures using grammar-based syllabi. As long as the focus is accuracy, and as long as teachers continue to believe that the direct teaching of grammatical rules can increase accuracy, grammatical syllabi and grammatical approaches will continue to dominate the practice of language teaching. Other teachers describe themselves as "eclectic" and report combining grammar and translation with communicative language teaching. Given the very different theories of language and language learning that underlie these two methods, it is highly possible that teachers are not fully aware of the contradictory positions of the two approaches. Conversely, it may be that ESL teachers and regular teachers engaged in English language development (ELD) are less concerned about the incompatibility of underlying theories than they are about students' passing the types of language proficiency assessments that are required of them.

KEY LIMITATIONS OF EXISTING RESEARCH ON SLA

For those concerned about the acquisition of a societal language by children and about understanding developmental sequences and progressions that can inform instruction, there are two key limitations in existing research in SLA that must be attended to by all researchers. The first limitation is the result of a very small number of existing longitudinal studies of language learners in both instructed and naturalistic settings. The second limitation is that surprisingly few studies have been carried out on the process of SLA in children in comparison to the large numbers of studies conducted on adult learners.

Longitudinal Studies of Second Language Acquisition

It is important to emphasize that SLA, from both the cognitivist and socio-interactional perspectives, has had very little to say about a process of L2 acquisition as it takes place through and over time. Reviewing the longitudinal SLA research literature and concluding that discussions about longitudinal research are rare, Ortega and Iberri-Shea (2005) argue that time is central in SLA and that many questions in second language acquisition are "questions of time and timing" (p. 37). SLA researchers, therefore, must be necessarily concerned about questions that focus on "at what age" and "for how long." Time, moreover, is central in policy and instructional decisions about early or late exit from programs, about optional instructional time devoted to language development in classrooms, about articulation between levels (e.g., high school and college), and more recently about the earliest time in the L2 acquisition process that children can be required to take large-scale assessments on subject matter knowledge in their second language.

Ortega and Iberri-Shea note a tendency for SLA researchers to implicitly posit longitudinal claims for cross-sectional studies carried out from a variety of perspectives. As was the case in the review of experimental and quasi-experimental studies discussed above (Norris & Ortega, 2000), the majority of the 38 longitudinal studies examined by Ortega and Iberri-Shea (2005) focused on the college-level population of L2 learners. Different epistemological perspectives were represented by the selected studies, including descriptive-quantitative examinations of linguistic features as well as qualitative interpretive studies of sociointeractional dimensions of language use. Four categories were used for grouping studies included in the review: (1) descriptive-quantitative longitudinal studies of L2 development, (2) longitudinal research on L2 program outcomes, (3) longitudinal investigations of L2 instructional effectiveness, and (4) recent qualitative longitudinal SLA research. Ortega and Iberri-Shea conclude their discussion with suggestions for future directions and raise important questions about the optimal length of observation in longitudinal studies, the choice between biological time and institutional time as units of analysis, the challenges of multiwave data collection, the need to use statistical analyses specifically available for use with longitudinal data, and the importance of thick descriptions in ethnographic longitudinal studies. The authors conclude by advocating for "the diversity and accumulation of recent and future longitudinal research" that they hope "will help chart the development of advanced L2 capacities and help us understand the appropriate timing, duration, and content of optimal educational practices for L2 learning across educational settings and multilingual contexts" (p. 43).

Focus on Children in the Study of Second Language Acquisition

Contrary to what might be expected given the large number of children around the world who must acquire a second language in order to obtain access to education, the field of second language acquisition has focused primarily on adults. Philp, Oliver, and Mackey (2008) consider the lack of focus especially noteworthy because research carried out with children informs many of today's leading approaches to the study of SLA. It is important to point out, however, that the study of second language acquisition in children has been complicated by questions about categorizations and definitions—particularly views about simultaneous versus sequential or successive bilingualism. For most researchers, children raised from infancy with two languages are referred to as child bilinguals and are considered to have acquired two first languages simultaneously. McLaughlin (1978), for example, includes in this category children who have been regularly exposed to two languages before the age of three. De Houwer (1995) and Deuchar and Quay (2000), however, consider that children engage in the process of bilingual acquisition only when they are exposed to two languages within the first month of birth. De Houwer considers children exposed to two languages after the first month of birth and up to the age of 2 as involved in a different process, which she refers to as "bilingual second language acquisition." Most researchers currently distinguish child SLA from bilingual acquisition, setting the lower boundary between the ages of 2 and 4. Schwartz (2003), for example, points out that in bilingual acquisition contexts, the grammars of two languages are being worked out simultaneously or sequentially, while in L2 acquisition context, the child acquires a new language after acquiring an almost complete grammar of a first language.

Interpreting existing research on child SLA has presented some challenges. Bialystok (2001) argues that this is the case because there are problems in defining a point at which a child has "almost" completely acquired the L1 grammar and when the acquisition of L2 can be said to begin, as well as which children can or should be included in the category of child bilingual. Paradis (2007), for example, argues that the term *child bilingual* has unfortunately been used as synonymous with "child L2 learner" and further points out:

> Second language (L2) acquisition in children has been seldom studied as a subfield with its own issues and questions separate from adult L2 acquisition on the one hand, or bilingualism and educational outcomes on the other. Consequently, we know little about second language acquisition (SLA) issues, such as individual differences, as they pertain to child as opposed to adult learners, and we know less about the developing oral language proficiency of L2 children than we know about their literacy development. (p. 387)

In the introduction to a recent volume—intriguingly titled *Second Language Acquisition and the Younger Learner: Child's Play?*—Philp, Oliver, and Mackey (2008) remind readers of the current problematic views about children's L2 acquisition as "child's play" and point out that much more work is needed in the area of child SLA, including the different periods of child SLA, the uniqueness of the child learner, ultimate attainment in children, and the processes and mechanisms of L2 acquisition in children. They strongly argue for longitudinal studies, for richly detailed descriptions of "the many and various factors which interact to impact a given child's L2 development" (p. 13), and for close attention to the study of pedagogy and child L2 learning.

Philp et al. (2008) also call attention to the fact that since the 1960s much interest in child SLA has focused on whether or not there is a critical or sensitive period for second language acquisition and whether or not there are age-related effects that, as Hyltenstam and Abrahamsson (2003) state, offer an advantage to children in terms of both rate of acquisition and ultimate attainment of a second language. As opposed to what is generally believed by the public about the natural superiority of children as L2 learners, disagreement is rampant among researchers about age and L2 acquisition. Most researchers agree that—in general—children are more successful language learners than adults, but debate persists about the explanation for these effects and about the degree to which most child learners attain nativelike proficiency in all subcomponents of language. Bialystok and Hakuta (1994), in reviewing existing research, conclude that older learners are faster in terms of rate of acquisition of morphology and syntax, and younger learners are better in terms of final level of attainment of accent-free, nativelike proficiency. They also point out, however, that explanations for differences in attainment (including social and experiential factors as well as biological explanations such as the critical period hypothesis or the sensitive period hypothesis) are limited in explanatory power. Hyltenstam and Abrahamsson (2003) report that research has found "non-native features in the ultimate attainment of even some very young starters" (p. 545). They conclude their extensive review of the literature on maturational constraints in SLA by stating that "both adults, in rare cases, and children, in most cases, seem to reach nativelike proficiency in a second language" (p. 578). However, they also note that "much of the data discussed in the literature on maturational constraints and specifically on the CPH has not been analyzed in sufficient detail to make possible any claims about whether the subjects are nativelike in all respects" (p. 571). They suggest, therefore, that rather than nativelike, many of the learners—including young children—described in existing studies should be referred to as "near-native." Because maturation has a strong influence on L2 acquisition, they view nativelike proficiency as unattainable and suggest that what is remarkable is that learners—both adults and children—can compensate for subtle differences between even near-native and native-like proficiency in their everyday use of language that are seen as highly problematic by linguists in their research laboratories.

SLA work focusing on children can generally be grouped into several categories: (1) research focused primarily on the acquisition of the linguistic system (Philp & Duchesne, 2008; Unsworth, 2005); (2) research concentrating on the acquisition of linguistic and participatory competence (Achiba, 2003; Toohey, 2000; Wong Fillmore, 1976); and (3) an extensive body of work that has investigated the relationship between second language acquisition and school achievement (August & Hakuta, 1997; and more recently by Genesee et al., 2006).

While the purpose of some research focusing on the acquisition of the linguistic system has been to compare the L2 acquisition processes of adults and children including, for example, responses to feedback, negotiation of meaning in task-based interactions (e.g., Leeman, 2003; Oliver, 1998, 2000; Unsworth, 2005), other research has studied children on their own terms. As compared to research on adult SLA, which all too often takes place in intact language-as-a-subject classrooms, about which few details are given by researchers, and in laboratory settings, most studies of child SLA have tended to provide information about the context and the circumstances surrounding the acquisition experience. The collection edited by Philp et al. (2008) brings together good examples of current research on child SLA informed by broader SLA perspectives and includes work on the effect of age on two Russian sisters acquiring L2 German morphology (Dimroth, 2008); the impact of social goals and participation in the L2 development of a 6-year-old in a 1st-grade classroom (Philp & Duchesne, 2008); language-learning affordances in a Swedish immersion classroom (Cekaite, 2008); the negotiation of meaning and reading comprehension (Van den Branden, 2008); the acquisition of the pronouns *his* and *her* (White, 2008); and learning how to explain and describe in an L2 within a family context (Mitchell & Lee, 2008).

Given the dearth of research on second language acquisition in children in both instructed and in naturalistic settings, it is extraordinarily difficult for program designers and instructors to find ways of building meaningfully on research conducted on second-language teaching and learning in general. If they do so, it is imperative that they take into account the fact that existing knowledge on instructed second language acquisition is drawn from work done primarily on adult learners. We know little at this time about the direct teaching of language to children and about the ways that such teaching can accelerate young learners' performance on standardized measures of both content area knowledge *and* progress in acquiring English. In the section that follows, I discuss the challenges related to the assessment of English language learners in the current policy context and in the light of our limited knowledge about second language acquisition in children.

SECOND LANGUAGE ACQUISITION, ASSESSMENT, AND IMMIGRANT CHILDREN IN SCHOOLS

As compared to the basic research perspective of SLA research, work on the study of second language acquisition as it relates to school achievement for minority children is being carried out under much more pressing real-world circumstances and in a political context in which popular debates often inform policy decisions about the appropriate education for such children. As U.S. citizens have become increasingly concerned about "new" arrivals and about the ways that they can be integrated into American society, much attention has been given both by the public and by educators to the ways that educational institutions can successfully prepare large numbers of immigrant children to contribute to America's continued progress. Language itself has taken on a central role in discussions surrounding the education of immigrant students as heated debates take place in the national media about the number of both authorized and unauthorized immigrants in this country, about the security of our borders, and about the challenge of assimilating groups of individuals who appear not be learning English (Huntington, 2004). In many parts of the country, concern about the deep changes in American society coupled with misconceptions about the supposed effortlessness of L2 acquisition by children has led to educational policies based on the assumption that a second language can be acquired by young children in a single year. These misconceptions are supported by recollections of successful adults of immigrant origin and the supposed relative ease with which they acquired English in a single year, a single summer, or even a few weeks.

To date, research focusing on the challenges of educating L2 learners in English language classrooms in the United States has focused on a number of different issues and questions having to do with the learning of English in school settings, the relationship between L1 and L2 proficiencies combined with a variety of other factors (e.g., age, length of residence, parent education, SES, previous education in an L1, language of instruction), and educational achievement measured and defined in a variety of ways. The work of August and Hakuta (1997) and Genesee et al. (2006) synthesizes the research literature on the education of K–12 English language learners that was published primarily in the last 20 years.

Since the passage of NCLB, educators in every state in the country have given increasing attention to English language learners. In a National Council of La Raza's (NCLR) Issue Brief, Lazarin (2006) explains that the No Child Left Behind Act holds schools accountable for improving academic achievement among all groups, including ELL students, and ensures that information is gathered and reported on their academic outcomes. ELLs can no longer be excluded from state accountability systems, and current law includes requirements to close the achievement gap specifically for English language learners. As might be expected, much controversy has surrounded the implementation of NCLB requirements, and efforts have been made to change or modify them significantly. Lazarin provides an overview of the manner in which local, state, and federal decisionmakers have implemented these provisions and presents policy recommendations informing the future of the law as it relates to English language learners. Summarizing briefly, Lazarin outlines the promise of closing the achievement gap and bringing all students to 100% proficiency in core academic subjects by the year 2014. As a result, states have been asked to set yearly benchmarks for all students as well as for certain subgroups including ELLs. As summarized by Abedi (2007), within the context of NCLB, ELLs are defined as students who are between the ages of 3 and 21, who are enrolled or preparing to enroll in an elementary or secondary school, who were not born in the United States or whose native language is not English, who are Native Americans, Alaskan natives, or native residents of outlying areas, or from environments where a language other than English has had a significant impact on students' levels of English proficiency, who are migratory and from environments where English is not the dominant language, and/or who have difficulties in speaking, reading, and writing the English language to the degree that these limitations may deny students opportunities to achieve in school or to participate fully in society. English language learners are one of the several disadvantaged populations on which NCLB specifically focuses. States are required to identify and implement educational programs and curricula for language instruction based on scientific research on teaching limited English proficient children and to help limited English proficient children meet the same challenging state academic achievement standards as all other children are expected to meet (NCLB, 2001). By 2007–2008, states were required to administer reading/language arts and math assessments on an annual basis that were aligned to state academic content standards. Additionally, the tests designed to measure children's performance were required to be valid, reliable, and of adequate technical quality.

Valid and reliable assessment, therefore, is a critical component of accountability and of the continuous improvement processes in schools and districts. Moreover, the assessment of ELLs used in schools today must address both content area knowledge and progress in learning English. Unfortunately as a number of recent discussions of assessment and ELLs have made clear (Abedi, 2004, 2007, 2008; Durán, 2008; Kopriva, 2008; Lazarin, 2006; Parker, Louie, & O'Dwyer, 2009; Solorzano, 2008), questions persist about the validity and reliability of currently used instruments and measurement procedures used across the country, and many are uneasy about the types of testing accommodations (e.g., extra time, small-group administration, use of dictionaries) currently being provided for ELL students in recognition of the fact that tests currently being used were not developed for use with this population of students and may therefore be invalid and inappropriate for assessing ELL's academic competence (Durán, 2008; Lazarin, 2006; Rivera et al., 2000; Solorzano, 2008). Additionally, the unnecessary linguistic complexity of test items has also raised a number of questions. Work conducted by Haladyna and Downing (2004) and by Solano-Flores and Trumbull (2003) revealed that this unnecessary complexity leads ELL students to misinterpret and misunderstand test questions and is an additional source of measurement error.

English language proficiency (ELP) assessments used in the classification of English language learners have also been found to be problematic. Abedi (2008), for example, examines the impact of existing assessments on the ways in which the various definitions of English language proficiency have been used in creating ELL classifications. Differentiating between pre- and post-NCLB assessments, he notes that pre-NCLB language proficiency assessments exhibited discrepancies in theoretical bases and differed in their approaches to defining language proficiency, types of tasks to be included in specific item content, and grade-level ranges and specific time limits. He claims, moreover, that they may not have measured the types of language proficiency needed to be successful in mainstream classrooms. Citing Del Vecchio and Guerrero (1995), Abedi also comments on the wide disparities in these ELP assessments with respect to purpose, administration, items, test design, theoretical foundation, and validity. From Abedi's (2004, 2008), Kopriva's (2008), Lazarin's (2006), and Solorzano's (2008) perspectives, problems also exist with post-NCLB language proficiency assessments. Abedi underscores the fact that while, in theory, these assessments are supposed to be aligned with ELP content standards, the term ELP has not been defined in the literature. The various state consortia that developed new ELP instruments used or created different ELP standards as well as different standard-setting approaches, which may have introduced inconsistencies of various types in the definition of the proficiency levels in the different modalities (listening, speaking, reading, and writing). Abedi (2007) is particularly concerned about dimensionality issues, that is, the degree to which the overall composite of the four subscales is used by some states while other states use a weighted composite proficiency score, using subscores in the different modalities and giving more weight, for example, to reading and writing than to speaking and listening. He argues that researchers must ask whether the four domains should be considered as four separate subscales/dimensions or if they should be considered as a single latent trait that encompasses all four domains. He argues that if an overall proficiency test score is based on the total test of all four modalities, there should be evidence that the four modalities are highly correlated. Abedi further maintains that the issue of dimensionality needs to be addressed before deciding whether to use subscale or total scores.

Like Abedi (2008), a number of researchers currently focusing on NCLB and the resulting classification of English language learners at the state level, including Solorzano (2008) and Durán (2008), point out the challenges involved in classifying ELLs for the purposes of reporting adequate yearly progress (AYP). They mention problems of definition as well as differences in identification and redesignation procedures across the states. Abedi (2008), in particular, raises questions about the use of standardized achievement tests in conjunction with scores from language proficiency tests to reclassify ELL students in 76% of the states surveyed. Noting the lack of appropriateness of many standardized achievement tests for assessing the content knowledge of the students, Abedi is particularly concerned about the various cutoff scores set by different states, ranging from the 33rd percentile to the 40th percentile, with some states using reading/language arts and/or math. From his own research on the validity of the ELL classification based on data from several randomized field studies, Abedi concludes that "standardized achievement tests may not be a valid criterion for assessing ELL students for classification purposes as a single criterion or even when combined with other criteria" (p. 24).

In sum, a cursory examination of the efforts carried out to date by individual states and state consortia to assess English language proficiency and to measure ELL students' subject matter knowledge suggests that our current understanding of the best methods for assessing L2 acquisition and growth continues to be limited. We have much to learn not only about assessing language growth and development uniformly but also about the ways in which language limitations interact with the measurement of content area knowledge in standardized assessments.

THE CONCEPT OF ACADEMIC LANGUAGE

We want to emphasize that in all the materials we have reviewed that discuss post-NCLB assessment practices, including both ELP and content-based assessments, a strong concern was expressed about the concept of academic language, and much attention was given to discussing, defining, and examining the characteristics of the language needed by students to succeed in school. Francis and Rivera (2007), for example, indicate that this concern has its roots in the interpretation of NCLB that requires a fair assessment and evaluation of the degree to which children develop oral language and reading and writing skills in English. Abedi (2007) cites the goals of NCLB Title III as committed to ensuring that limited English proficient students develop high levels of "*academic competence* in English, and meet the same challenging state *academic* achievement standards that all children are expected to meet" (p. 126, emphasis added). Both Francis and Rivera (2007) and Durán (2008) note that under Title III states are required to conceptually align their English development standards and ELP assessments with subject matter standards in reading, mathematics, and science. This is interpreted as requiring them to expand their ELD standards and ELP assessment blueprints so that they include "academic language" relevant to subject matter learning in these three areas. In theory, this goal will require schools to attend to the academic language learning needs of EL students as well as to their attainment of subject matter knowledge.

Unfortunately, however, as Francis and Rivera (2007) emphasize, there is not an agreed-upon definition of academic language. They cite the work of Cummins (1981), Solomon and Rhodes (1995), Scarcella (2003), and Bailey and Butler (2007) and call attention to different definitions of and perspectives on *academic language*, including the fact that it is contrasted with conversational language, that it is thought to be context reduced, that it is a register of language used in professional books, and that it is characterized by linguistic features that are associated with academic disciplines.

From the perspective of a second language acquisition field, the current tendency to contrast *academic language* with *conversational language* adds one more set of dichotomies (e.g., learning versus acquisition, context-reduced versus context-embedded language) that Snow (1987) has characterized as capturing a single underlying opposition. While to some degree useful, dichotomous views of language often simplify complex realities that matter in important ways to both students and their teachers. The concept of academic language has penetrated into educational thinking because of its links to assessment without a very deep or broad agreement about its meaning and without an understanding of children's progress over time in the acquisition of various ways of speaking in a second language. Unfortunately, we know very little about the acquisition of linguistic repertoires (various ways of speaking or using language for different purposes) by either adults or children. The term *academic language* and its assumed opposites—*oral, conversational,* or *ordinary language*—are being used by well-meaning practitioners, researchers, and test developers with a variety of meanings. More important, however, the use of these terms often incorporates views about the characteristics of the language to be attained by second-language learners at various stages of development based on very little empirical evidence. Advanced proficiency, for example, is often assumed to be characterized by accurate or nativelike features in spite of a body of research evidence that has raised many doubts about nativelike ultimate attainment in all second-language learners (Cook, 2002; Firth & Wagner, 2007; Han & Odlin, 2006).

SCHOOLS, IMMIGRANT CHILDREN, AND SECOND LANGUAGE ACQUISITION

We are concerned in this chapter with contributing to the understanding of the progress made by children in acquiring a second language in a linguistically isolated school in which they had very few opportunities to interact with fluent English speakers other than in a many-to-one ratio. In carrying out an intervention in which children regularly worked one-on-one with ordinary speakers of English, we hoped to increase our knowledge about the ways that a second language is used in interaction while it is being acquired and about changes in the participatory/interactional competence of children in an L2 as they engaged in various activities with trusted adults over time. We wanted to understand how youngsters moved or did not move from limited to fuller participation in interactions, how they interpreted cues about ways of speaking and behaving with members of the broader English-speaking society, and whether and to what degree they appropriated the utterances of their interlocutors. While not our main goal, we also expected to provide some evidence of the ways in which children's linguistic system changed over time.

In reviewing the literature on both second language acquisition and second language pedagogy, I have suggested that we have limited knowledge about second language acquisition in children and that we have very modest evidence about the role of instruction in the second language acquisition process for children. As states move forward to draft NCLB-influenced policies and practices that support ELL children's second language development and subject matter knowledge, we believe it is essential for policymakers, researchers, and practitioners to have realistic expectations about the kinds of attainment possible for children under different kinds of circumstances. If we are to assess the development of English language proficiency and provide support for such development, we must not penalize children for not making the kinds of progress that may only be the product of the imagination of monolingual policymakers or well-meaning, standards-setting panels and not supported by research on children's L2 development in real-life settings. Academic language—especially when defined as nativelike oral and written production—may not be attainable under the best of circumstances as quickly or as completely as might be desired by those who hope to accelerate the acquisition of English in immigrant-origin children.

REFERENCES

Abedi, J. (2004). The No Child Left Behind Act and English language learners: Assessment and accountability issues. *Educational Researcher, 33*, 4–14.

Abedi, J. (2007). *English language proficiency assessment in the nation*. Davis: University of California.

Abedi, J. (2008). Classification system for English language learners: Issues and recommendations. *Educational measurement: Issues and practice, 27*(3), 17–31.

Achiba, M. (2003). *Learning to request in a second language: A study of child interlanguage pragmatics*. Multilingual Matters.

August, D., & Hakuta, K. (Eds.). (1997). *Improving schooling for language-minority children: A research agenda*. National Academy Press.

Bailey, A. L. & Butler, F. A. (2007). A conceptual framework of academic English language for broad application to education. In A Bailey (Ed.), *The language demands of school: Putting English to the test*. Yale University Press.

Baker, E. L. (2007). 2007 presidential address—the end(s) of testing. *Educational Researcher, 36*(6), 309–317.

Bardovi-Harlig, K., & Dörnyei, Z. (2006). Introduction to the special issue on themes in SLA research. In K. Bardovi-Harlig & Z. Dornyei (Eds.), *Themes in SLA Research, AILA Review* [Special issue], *19*, 1–2.

Bialystok, E. (2001). *Bilingualism in development: Language, literacy, and cognition*. Cambridge University Press.

Bialystok, E., & Hakuta, K. (1994). *In other words: The psychology and science of second language acquisition*. Basic Books.

Bley-Vroman, R. (1989). What is the logical problem of foreign language learning? In S. Gass & J. Shacter (Eds.), *Linguistic perspectives on second language acquisition* (pp. 41–68). Cambridge University Press.

Block, D. (2003). *The social turn in second language acquisition.* Edinburgh University Press.

Canagarajah, A. S. (1993). Critical ethnography of a Sri Lankan classroom: Ambiguities in student opposition. *TESOL Quarterly, 27*(4), 601–626.

Canagarajah, A. S. (1999). *Resisting linguistic imperialism in English teaching.* Oxford University Press.

Canagarajah, S. (2005). Critical pedagogy in L2 learning and teaching. In E. Hinkel (Ed.), *Handbook of research in second language teaching and learning* (pp. 931–949). Erlbaum.

Capps, R., Fix, M. E., Murray, J., Ost, J., Passel, J. S., & Herwantoro, S. (2005). *The new demography of America's schools: Immigration and the No Child Left Behind Act.* Urban Institute.

Cekaite, A. (2008) Developing conversational skills in a second language: Language learning affordances in a multiparty classroom setting. In J. Philp, R. Oliver, & A. Mackey (Eds.), *Second language acquisition and the younger learner: Child's play?* (pp. 105–129). John Benjamins.

Chomsky, N. (1957). *Syntactic structures.* Mouton.

Chomsky, N. (1959). Review of "verbal behavior" by B.F. Skinner. *Language, 35,* 26–58.

Chomsky, N. (1965). *Aspects of the theory of syntax.* MIT Press.

Chomsky, N. (1980). *Rules and representations.* Columbia University Press.

Chomsky, N. (1981). Principles and parameter in syntactic theory. In N. Hornstein & D. Lightfoot (Eds.), *Explanation in linguistics: The logical problem of language acquisition* (pp. 32–75). Longman.

Cook, V. (2002). *Portraits of the L2 user.* Multilingual Matters.

Corder, S. P. (1967). The significance of learners' errors. *International Review of Applied Linguistics, 5,* 161–170.

Corder, S. P. (1981). *Error analysis and interlanguage.* Oxford University Press.

Crookes, G. (1989). Planning and interlanguage variability. *Studies in Second Language Acquisition, 11,* 367–383.

Crookes, G. (1997). SLA and language pedagogy: A socioeducational perspective. *Studies in Second Language Acquisition, 19*(1), 93–116.

Cummins, J. (1981). The role of primary language development in promoting educational success for language minority students. In California State Department of Education (Ed.), *Schooling and language minority students: A theoretical framework* (pp. 3–49). National Dissemination and Assessment Center.

De Houwer, A. 1995. Bilingual language acquisition. In P. Fletcher & B. MacWhinney (Eds.), *The handbook of child language* (pp. 219–250). Blackwell.

Del Vecchio, A., & Guerrero, M. (Eds.). (1995). *Handbook of English language proficiency tests.* Evaluation Assistance Center-Western Region.

Deuchar, M., and Quay, S. (2000). *Bilingual acquisition: Theoretical implications of a case study.* Oxford University Press.

Dimroth, C. (2008). Perspectives on second language acquisition at different ages. In J. Philp, R. Oliver & A. Mackey (Eds.), *Second language acquisition and the younger learner: Child's play?* (pp. 53–79). John Benjamins.

Doughty, C., & Long, M. H. (Eds.) (2003). *The handbook of second language acquisition.* Blackwell.

Duff, P. A. (1995). An ethnography of communication in immersion classrooms in Hungary. *TESOL Quarterly, 29*(3), 505–537.

Duff, P. A. (2002). The discursive co-construction of knowledge, identity, and difference: An ethnography of communication in the high school mainstream. *Applied Linguistics, 23*(3), 289–322.

Dulay, H., & Burt, M. (1973). Should we teach children syntax? *Language Learning, 23*(2), 245–258.

Dulay, H., & Burt, M. (1974). Natural sequences in child second language acquisition. *Language Learning, 24*(1), 37–53.

Durán, R. P. (2008). Assessing English-language learners' achievement. *Review of Research in Education, 32,* 292–327.

Ellis, R. (1997). SLA and language pedagogy: An educational perspective. *Studies in Second Language Acquisition, 19*(1), 69–92.

Ellis, R. (2005a). Instructed language learning and task-based teaching. In E. Hinkel (Ed.), *Handbook of research in second language teaching and learning* (pp. 713–728). Lawrence Erlbaum.

Ellis, R. (2005b). *Instructed second language acquisition: A literature review.* Research Division, Ministry of Education, Wellington, New Zealand.

Firth, A., & Wagner, J. (2007). Second/foreign language learning as a social accomplishment: Elaborations on a reconceptualized SLA. *Modern Language Journal (Focus Issue), 91,* 800–819.

Flynn, S. (1987). *A parameter-setting model of L2 acquisition: Experimental studies in anaphora.* Reidel.

Francis, D., and Rivera, M. (2007). Principles underlying English language proficiency tests and academic accountability for ELLs. In J. Abedi (Ed.), *English language proficiency assessment in the nation: Current status and future practice* (pp. 13–32). University of California.

Frawley, W., & Lantolf, J. P. (1985). Second language discourse: A Vygotskyan perspective. *Applied Linguistics, 6*(1), 19–44.

Fry, R. (2007). *How far behind in math and reading are English language learners?* Pew Hispanic Center.

Gass, S. M. (1997). *Input, interaction, and the second language learner.* Erlbaum.

Gass, S. M., & Mackey, A. (2007). Input, interaction, and output in second language acquisition. In B. Van Patten & J. Williams (Eds.), *Theories in second language acquisition: An introduction* (pp. 175–199). Erlbaum.

Gass, S. M., & Selinker, L. (2001). *Second language acquisition: An introductory course.* Erlbaum.

Genesee, F., Lindholm-Leary, K., Saunders, W., & Christian, D. (2006). *Educating English language learners: A synthesis of research evidence.* Cambridge University Press.

Hakimzadeh, S., & Cohn, D. (2007). *English usage among Hispanics in the United States.* Pew Hispanic Center.

Haladyna, T. M., & Downing, S. M. (2004). Construct-irrelevant variance in high-stakes testing. *Educational Measurement: Issues and Practice, 23*(1), 17–27.

Han, Z., & Odlin, T. (2006). Introduction. In Z. Han & T. Odlin (Eds.), *Studies of fossilization in second language acquisition* (pp. 1–20). Multilingual Matters.

Harklau, L. (1994). ESL versus mainstream classes: Contrasting L2 learning environments. *TESOL Quarterly, 28,* 241–272.

Hatch, E. (1978). Applied with caution. *Studies in Second Language Acquisition, 2,* 123–143.

Huntington, S. P. (2004). *Who are we? The challenges to America's national identity.* Simon & Schuster.

Hyltenstam, K. & Abrahamsson, N. (2003). Maturational constraints on SLA. In C. Doughty & M. Lang (Eds.), *The handbook of second language acquisition* (pp. 539–588). Blackwell.

Johnson, M. (2004). *A philosophy of second language acquisition.* Yale University Press.

Kelly, L. G. (1976). *Twenty-five centuries of language teaching.* Newbury House Publishers.

Klein, W. (1998). The contribution of second languge acquisition research. *Language and Learning, 48*(4), 527–550.

Kopriva, R. J. (2008). *Improving testing for English language learners.* Routledge.

Kramsch, C. (Ed.). (2002). *Language acquisition and language socialization: Ecological perspectives.* London: Continuum.

Krashen, S. (1985). *The input hypothesis: Issues and implications.* Longman.

Krashen, S., & Terrell, T. D. (1983). *The natural approach: Language acquisition in the classroom.* Oxford University Press.

Lafford, B. A. (2007). Second language acquisition reconceptualized? The impact of Firth and Wagner (1997). *Modern Language Journal, 91 (Focus Issue),* 735–756.

Lantolf, J. P. (Ed.). (2000). *Sociocultural theory and second language learning.* Oxford University Press.

Lantolf, J. P. (2006). Sociocultural theory and L2. *Studies in Second Language Acquisition, 28,* 67–109.

Lantolf, J. P., & Appel, G. (1994). Theoretical framework: An introduction to Vygotskian approaches to second language research. In J. P. Lantolf & G. Appel (Eds.), *Vygotskian approaches to second language research* (pp. 1–32). Ablex.

Lantolf, J. P., & Frawley, W. (1983). *Second language performance and Vygotskyian psycholinguistics: Implications for L2 instruction.* Paper presented at the Eleventh Linguistic Association of Canada and the United States (LACUS) Forum, Laval University, Québec.

Lantolf, J. P., & Thorne, S. L. (Eds.). (2006). *Sociocultural theory and the genesis of second language development.* Oxford University Press.

Larsen-Freeman, D. (2002). Language acquisition and language use from a chaos/complexity theory perspective. In C. Kramsch (Ed.), *Language acquisition and language socialization* (pp. 33–46). Continuum.

Larsen-Freeman, D. (2007). Reflecting on the cognitive-social debate in second language acquisition. *Modern Language Journal, 91(Focus Issue),* 773–787.

Lave, J., & Wenger, E. (1991). *Situated learning: Legitimate peripheral participation.* Cambridge University Press.

Lazarin, M., (2006). *Improving assessment and accountability for English language learners in the No Child Left Behind Act* (Issue Brief No. 16). National Council of La Raza.

Leeman, J. (2003). Feedback in L 2 learning: Responding to errors during practice. In R. M. DeKeyser (Ed.), *Practice in a second language* (pp. 111–137). Cambridge University Press.

Lightbown, P. (1984). The relationship between theory and method in second language acquisition research. In A. Davies, C. Criper, & A. Howatt (Eds.), *Interlanguage* (pp. 241–252). Edinburgh University Press.

Lightbown, P. M. (1985). Great expectations: Second-language acquisition research and classroom teaching. *Applied Linguistics, 6*(2), 173–189.

Lightbown, P. M. (2000). Anniversary article: Classroom SLA research and second language teaching. *Applied Linguistics, 21*(4), 431–462.

Long, M. H. (1983). Native speaker/non-native speaker conversation and the negotiation of comprehensible input. *Applied Linguistics, 4*(2), 126–141.

Long, M. H. (1996). The role of the linguistic environment in second language acquisition. In W. C. Ritchie & T. K. Bhatia (Eds.), *Handbook of second language acquisition* (pp. 413–468). Academia Press.

McLaughlin, B. (1978). *Second-language acquisition in childhood.* Erlbaum.

McLaughlin, B. (1987). *Theories of second language acquisition.* Edward Arnold.

Mitchell, C. B., & Vidal, K. E. (2001). Weighing in the ways of the flow: 20th-century language instruction. *The Modern Language Journal, 85*(1), 26–38.

Mitchell, R., & Lee, C. N. (2008). Learning a second language in the family. In J. Philp, R. Oliver & A. Mackey (Eds.), *Second language acquisition and the younger learner: Child's play?* (pp. 255–277). John Benjamins.

Mori, J. (2007). Border crossings? Exploring the intersection of second language acquisition, conversation analysis, and foreign language pedagogy. *Modern Language Journal, 91(Focus Issue)*, 849–862.

Nemser, W. (1971). Approximate systems of foreign language learners. *International Review of Applied Linguistics in Language Teaching, 9*(2), 115–124.

No Child Left Behind Act of 2001, 20 U.S.C. § 6319 (2008).

Norris, J. M., & Ortega, L. (2000). Effectiveness of L2 instruction: A research synthesis and quantitative meta-analysis. *Language Learning, 50(3)*, 417–528.

Norton, B. (1995). Social identity, investment, and language learning. *TESOL Quarterly, 29*(1), 9–31.

Norton, B. (1997). Language, identity, and the ownership of English. *TESOL Quarterly, 30*(2), 409–429.

Norton, B. (2000). *Identity and language learning: Gender, ethnicity, and educational change.* Longman.

Ochs, E. (1988). *Culture and language development: Language acquisition and language socialization in a Samoan village.* Cambridge University Press.

Ochs, E. (1991). Socialization through language and interaction: A theoretical introduction. *Issues in Applied Linguistics, 2*(2), 143–147.

Oliver, R. (1998). Negotiation of meaning in child interactions. *Modern Language Journal, 82*, 372–386.

Oliver, R. (2000, February). Age difference in negotiation and feedback in classroom and pair work. *Language Learning, 50*, 119–151.

Ortega, L., & Iberri-Shea, G. (2005). Longitudinal research in second language acquisition: Recent trends and future directions. *Annual Review of Applied Linguistics, 25*, 26–45.

Paradis, J. (2007). Second language acquisition in childhood. In E. Hoff & M. Shatz (Eds.), *Blackwell handbook of language development* (pp. 387–405). Blackwell.

Parker, C., Louie, J., & O'Dwyer, L. (2009). *New measures of English language proficiency and their relationship to performance on large-scale content assessments* (Issues and Answers Report, REL 2009-No. 066). U.S. Department of Education, Institute of Educational Sciences, National Center for Education Evaluation and Regional Assistance, Regional Educational Laboratory Northeast and Islands.

Pennycook, A. (1990). Towards a critical applied linguistics for the 1990s. *Issues in Applied Linguistics, 1*(1), 8–28.

Pennycook, A. (1999). *English and the discourses of colonialism.* Routledge.

Pennycook, A. (2001). *Critical applied linguistics: A critical introduction.* Erlbaum.

Philp, J., & Duchesne, S. (2008). When the gate opens: The interaction between social and linguistic goals in child language development. In J. Philp, R. Oliver & A. Mackey (Eds.), *Second language acquisition and the younger learner: Child's play?* (pp. 83–103). John Benjamins.

Philp, J., Oliver, R., & Mackey, A. (Eds.). (2008). *Second language acquisition and the younger learner: Child's play?* John Benjamins.

Ritchie, W. C., & Bhatia, T. K. (Eds.) (1996). *Handbook of second language acquisition.* Academia Press.

Rivera, C., Stansfield, C. W., Scialdone, L., & Sharkey, M. (2000). *An analysis of state policies for the inclusion and accommodation of English language learners in state assessment programs during 1998–1999.* George Washington University, Center for Equity and Excellence in Education.

Scarcella, R. (2003). *Academic English: A conceptual framework* (Technical Report No. 2003-1). Linguistic Minority Research Institute.

Schieffelin, B. B., & Ochs, E. (1986). *Language socialization across cultures.* Cambridge University Press.

Schwartz, B. (2003). Child L2 acquisition: Paving the way. In B. Beachley, A. Brown, & F. Conlin (Eds.), *Proceedings of the 27th BUCLD* (pp. 26–50). Cascadilla Press.

Selinker, L. (1972). Interlanguage. *International Review of Applied Linguistics in Language Teaching, 10*(3), 209–231.

Sharwood Smith, M. (1994). *Second language learning: Theoretical foundations.* Longman.

Short, D. J., & Fitzsimmons, S. (2007). *Double the work: Challenges and solutions to acquiring language and academic literacy for adolescent English language learners.* Alliance for Excellent Education.

Snow, C. (1987). Beyond conversation: Second language learners acquisition of description and explanation. In J. P. Lantolf & A. Labarca (Eds.), *Research and second language learning: Focus on the classroom* (pp. 3–16). Ablex.

Solano-Flores, G., & Trumbull, E. (2003). Examining language in context: The need for new research and practice paradigms in the testing of English-language learners. *Educational Researcher, 32,* 3–13.

Solomon, J., & Rhodes, N. (1995). *Conceptualizing academic language* (Research Report No. 15). National Center for Research on Education, Diversity, and Excellence.

Solorzano, R. (2008). High stakes testing: Issues, implications, and remedies for English language learners. *Review of Educational Research, 78*(2), 260–329.

Stenhouse, L. (1975). *An introduction to curriculum research and development.* Heinemann.

Swain, M. (1985). Communicative competence: Some roles of comprehensible input and comprehensible output in its development. In S. Gass and C. Madden (Eds.), *Input in second language acquisition.* Newbury House.

Swain, M. (1993). The output hypothesis: Just speaking and writing aren't enough. *Canadian Modern Language Review, 50*(1), 158–164.

Swain, M. (1995). Three functions of output in second language learning. In G. Cook & B. Seidlhofer (Eds.), *Principle and practice in applied linguistics: Studies in honour of H. G. Widdowson* (pp. 125–144). Oxford University Press.

Swain, M. (2000). The output hypothesis and beyond: Mediating acquisition through collaborative dialogue. In J. P. Lantolf (Ed.), *Sociocultural theory and second language learning* (pp. 97–114). Oxford University Press.

Swain, M. (2005). The output hypothesis: Theory and research. In E. Hinkel (Ed.), *Handbook of research in second language teaching and learning* (pp. 471–483). Lawrence Erlbaum Associates.

Toohey, K. (1999). The author responds to comments on Kellen Toohey's "Breaking them up, taking them away": ESL students in Grade 1. *TESOL Quarterly*, *33*(1), 132–136.

Toohey, K. (2000). *Learning English at school: Identity, social relations, and classroom practice*. Multilingual Matters.

Unsworth, S. (2005). *Child L2, Adult L2, Child L1: Differences and similarities: A study on the acquisition of direct object scrambling in Dutch*. Unpublished dissertation. Utrecht University.

Van den Branden, K. (2008). Negotiation of meaning in the classroom: Does it enhance reading comprehension? In J. Philp, R. Oliver & A. Mackey (Eds.), *Second language acquisition and the younger learner: Child's play?* (pp. 149–169). John Benjamins.

van Lier, L. (2002). An ecological-semiotic perspective on language and linguistics. In C. Kramsch (Ed.), *Language acquisition and language socialization: Ecological perspectives* (pp. 140–164). Continuum.

van Lier, L. (2004). *The ecology and semiotics of language learning: A sociocultural perspective*. Kluwer Academic.

Van Patten, B. (1996). *Input processing and grammar instruction: Theory and research*. Ablex.

Van Patten, B. (2003). *From input to output: A teacher's guide to second language acquisition*. McGraw-Hill.

Watson-Gegeo, K. A. (2004). Mind, language, and epistemology: Toward a language socialization paradigm for SLA. *Modern Language Journal*, *88*(3), 331–350.

Wendel, J. (1997). *Planning and second language production*. Unpublished doctoral dissertation. Temple University.

White, J. (2008). Speeding up acquisition of his and her: Explicit L1/L2 contrasts help. In J. Philp, R. Oliver & A. Mackey (Eds.), *Second language acquisition and the younger learner: Child's play?* (pp. 193–228). John Benjamins.

White, L. (1989). *Universal grammar and second language acquisition*. John Benjamins.

Wong Fillmore, L. (1976). *The second time around: Cognitive and social strategies in second language acquisition* [Unpublished doctoral dissertation]. Stanford University.

Zuengler, J., & Miller, E. R. (2006). Cognitive and sociocultural perspectives: Two parallel SLA worlds. *TESOL Quarterly*, *40*(1), 35–58.

PART V

SCHOOL REFORM

CHAPTER 11

The Role of Schools in Reducing Racial Inequality

Pedro Noguera and Esa Syeed

Amid the rising immigrant backlash and xenophobia stoked over the last decade, several states have taken steps to further marginalize and criminalize undocumented students. Despite the tenuous victory of the Deferred Action for Childhood Arrivals (DACA) during the Obama administration, states like Georgia have passed laws that have essentially barred undocumented students from applying to or receiving aid to attend top public universities (Lee, 2017). Undaunted, educators and other allies in the state came together to establish an alternative and underground school for undocumented students. Aptly named Freedom University, the volunteer-based school was founded in 2011 and aims to create a safe space to cultivate education for liberation according to its executive director, Dr. Laura Emiko Soltis (2015).

That this act of educational resistance took place in Georgia is no coincidence. When Black children of previous generations were effectively barred from public schools in the South, civil rights groups established freedom schools to provide spaces for learning and empowerment. Drawing on the history of freedom schools and support from veteran activists, Soltis situates Freedom University as a contemporary version of those vital educational institutions of years past. The emergence of the school and the interracial and cross-generational connections it has fostered offer a critical rejoinder to achievement gap conversations. Freedom University students, who believed their ambition and academic success would lead to higher education success, intimately understand how institutionalized racism can stunt student potential. "By contextualizing educational segregation alongside economic injustice and voter suppression," Soltis (2015) explained, "students were able to recognize the prolonged historical injustice that separate and unequal education was, and continues to be, part of a racial project that structures economic and political powerlessness among people of color in the South" (p. 34). The shared legacy of these schools, Soltis wrote, reflects oppressed people's undying "freedom dreams." We are reminded that now, as before, schools continue to serve as a key battleground in the fight for racial justice.

In this chapter we revisit the issue of how race influences and shapes schooling experiences in urban areas. We analyze several theories and approaches used to study the role of race in reproducing and maintaining educational inequality. As we discuss and critique the different ways in which these approaches may be useful or fall short in capturing the realities of race in urban settings, we also call attention to how such analyses can be helpful in efforts to pursue racial equity and justice. Where the previous version of this chapter focused primarily on problems with the ways in which race and culture are often used to explain the persistence of racial inequality in academic achievement, in this revised chapter we provide an updated and thorough examination of several other ways in which race influences educational policy and practice, as well as the experiences of children in racially isolated schools.

STRUCTURAL RACISM AND THE PERSISTENCE OF RACIAL DISPARITIES

Since the enactment of No Child Left Behind (NCLB) in 2001, a variety of education measures have been used to document racial disparities in student academic outcomes—aka the so-called racial achievement gap. Most of the existing literature on this topic has focused on outcome measures such as test scores or graduation rates, which are typically used to describe and analyze the persistence of racial disparities in education. Although such analyses are certainly relevant to any conversation about race and achievement, in this chapter we shift our focus by examining the ways in which structural racism shapes the context of educational experiences and academic outcomes for many low-income students of color.

The term "structural racism" has been used by social scientists to analyze the ways in which the U.S. political economy, and certain public policies and institutional practices, continue to have a discriminatory impact on racial minorities in the post–civil rights period (Bonilla-Silva, 1997; Massey & Denton, 1998; Wilson, 2012). Scholars who have studied structural racism point out that in contrast to the explicit and legalized forms of racism widespread during the pre–civil rights era, the structural racism of the present is often disguised by economic patterns and social policies that appear to be race-neutral and nondiscriminatory but have an adverse impact on people of color. Structural racism draws attention to the ways in which race and class have historically been embedded in the structure of American society, and the ways in which they continue to be manifest in everyday life (Bonilla-Silva, 1997).

Unlike interpersonal racism, which remains pervasive, structural racism is not necessarily premised on the actions, motivations, or beliefs of individuals. Sociologist Eduardo Bonilla-Silva describes structural racism as a form of "racism without racists" (Bonilla-Silva, 2017, p. 4). Although individual racists may play a role in perpetuating racism and racial disparities, structural racism calls our attention to the operation of systems such as the market (particularly financial and housing markets), the political process, and the machinations of institutions such as banks, schools, the criminal justice system, and the health care system, which all work to reinforce the marginalization of historically oppressed racial minorities. Although these systems may operate without explicit racial objectives, racial minorities (especially Blacks, Native Americans, and Latinxs) frequently become disproportionate victims of certain public policies because of how they have historically been situated and treated by the larger society. Most importantly, regardless of whether or not the individuals running the courts or the schools are members of racial minority groups, they are almost always unable to bring about sustained improvement to those who have been historically subjugated, oppressed, and discriminated against unless they are able to make changes to the structure (Forman, 2017). Structural racism is useful as an analytical framework for studying social problems such as those evident in education because it makes it possible to connect the presence of racial disparities to the history of racial oppression in American society, and to the ways in which social institutions such as schools operate in the minoritized communities they are supposed to serve.

Americans typically suffer from an inability to acknowledge the presence of social structure—class hierarchies, the labor market, the geography of opportunity, and so on—and for this reason, many have trouble making sense of the racial dynamics connected to social problems such as homelessness, crime, slum conditions, or school failure. In the popular imagination, bad schools and bad neighborhoods are caused by bad people, criminals, and corrupt politicians who control ghettos and marginalized communities. The assumption that the schools and neighborhoods are bad because bad people attend and reside in them is often implicit. Our tendency is to locate the problem (e.g., crime, drug use, and teen pregnancy) within an individual or their culture (Patterson & Fosse, 2015) rather than to recognize the structural forces that produce ghettos and failing schools throughout the United States. Our inability to recognize the structure often makes it difficult to advocate for policies to significantly alter the conditions that contribute to the problems experienced by the most disadvantaged schools and communities.

Several scholars have pointed to structural racism as the primary factor contributing to the prevalence of racial disparities in key areas that impact one's quality of life and well-being in the United States, including access to housing (Korver-Glenn, 2018), healthy food (Barker et al., 2012), health care and life expectancy (Gee & Ford, 2011), infant mortality (Wallace et al., 2017), and even clean air (Shonkoff et al., 2011). Not surprisingly, structural racism also contributes to pervasive disparities in educational opportunities and outcomes (Ladson-Billings & Tate, 1995). However, most policies designed to reduce the so-called achievement gap ignore the role of structural inequities and racism.

Moreover, when the achievement gap is discussed by researchers and policymakers, there tends to be an overemphasis on the outcomes and what should be done to ameliorate them, rather than a focus on how to increase and improve the opportunities available to students. This prevents us from taking seriously the tremendous disparities in inputs and opportunities that have a bearing on how disparities in achievement become manifest and persist over time. In *Creating the Opportunity to Learn* (2011), Boykin and Noguera developed a framework that is useful in understanding how schools, communities, and society in general shape conditions that play a major role in determining whether students will achieve. Boykin and Noguera call our attention to the conditions surrounding schools and classrooms that either promote or hinder teaching and learning, to shift our lens away from the tendency to locate the problem in the students or their teachers (who are also presumed to be bad).

Similarly, the Opportunity to Learn agenda launched by the Schott Foundation has utilized measures in such areas as the quality of facilities, teacher quality, course offerings, and extracurricular activities to ascertain how opportunities are provided to students at different schools. The Education Trust and the Learning Policy Institute have also drawn attention to the ways in which students of color are systematically denied access to advanced courses or qualified teachers (Cardichon et al., 2020; Patrick, Socol, & Morgan, 2020). By focusing attention on access and whether specific educational opportunities are available, we are compelled to recognize the systemic barriers and institutional racism that normalize these inequities and keep them firmly in place. In order to find solutions to racial disparities in student achievement, it is essential to understand that racial inequality and injustice are rooted in America's history of racial oppression, and continue to be a central feature of the social, political, and economic structure of the United States today.

A DAY IN THE LIFE: RACIAL DISPARITIES IN LIVED EXPERIENCE

To explore the ways in which race remains relevant, we take stock of the wide-ranging ways in which it contributes to the daily, lived experiences of urban students. Not long ago, a wave of viral videos presented the hazards of being Black in otherwise mundane settings: waiting for a meeting at a Starbucks, picking up garbage in front of your own apartment building, or barbequing in the park. These cases have drawn attention because of the obvious ways in which Black people are scrutinized, policed, and monitored even when engaged in ordinary activities. Similarly, many cases illustrate the ways in which race plays a role in the granular, everyday experiences of students of color. Ultimately, whether or not the individuals who summon the police or the police themselves are racist is of less importance than the fact that such targeting behaviors are pervasive and apparently continue to be endemic to American society, long after the adoption of civil rights laws.

A closer examination of the experiences of students of color in urban areas reveals that the disparities start before they even enter school, and are reinforced every day. Education policies that appear to be race-neutral often have a disparate impact on individuals and communities that have historically been discriminated against. Although the Obama administration and its allies would almost certainly object to charges that the reform policies it carried out were discriminatory, when analyzed through the lens of structural racism the adverse impact that such policies had on communities of color is undeniable. For example, in New York City where school choice has made school boundaries far less relevant, a recent study showed that Black students carry the greatest travel burdens (Blagg et al., 2018).

In her ethnography of Chicago, Shedd (2015) captures the daily odyssey of young people navigating challenging terrain to just get to school. She notes that as students of color cross boundaries demarcated by race, class, and physical boundaries, at times coming into contact with police, they often become aware of the differences among "the people with whom they interact, their experiences, and their perceptions of themselves and the world" (p. 38). Moreover, the neighborhoods they navigate are more susceptible to chronic and environmentally induced illnesses like asthma and obesity (Oberg et al., 2016). Similarly, digital tools developed by Akom and his colleagues at San Francisco State University reveal the abundance of liquor stores, check-cashing outlets, pawnshops, and beauty parlors, but few if any banks, museums, or stores that offer nutritious food options in communities of color (Akom et al., 2016). The prevalence of structural racism normalizes these differences in conditions and opportunities and renders them acceptable simply because it is impossible to prove overt racial malice or intent on the part of decisionmakers.

Walking into school, what type of building can students who reside in racially marginalized communities expect? Just like the overpolicing they often experience in their neighborhoods, urban school students are also more likely to attend schools with metal detectors and staffed by armed school resource officers (Kupchik, 2010). Sociologist Victor Rios (2011) views the high emphasis on security at the expense of support as evidence of what he calls the "youth control complex." Like the pervasive and powerful military industrial complex, the youth control complex is a costly system designed to monitor and control young people of color. The goal of the youth control complex is not to ensure their safety and well-being, but to control their movements, keep them under surveillance, and when deemed necessary, arrest and incarcerate them (Rios, 2011).

Beyond the fixation with security that has turned many urban schools into facilities that bear a strong resemblance to prisons, a host of other factors can make urban schools dangerous to the well-being of the children meant to learn within them. During a recent and bitterly cold winter when temperatures dipped below freezing, many Baltimore city schools were without heat as a blizzard approached. The issue set off a political storm of its own, as teachers and parents fought to close schools until the heat was switched on (Madden, 2018). The unseemly conditions of another city high school where we conducted a study became evident when a student proudly shared her science project with a team of visiting researchers. The student explained that she had tested different types of bait to see which would be the most effective at catching mice within the school building. To her surprise, and likely the chagrin of school administrators, within a fairly short period of time she had captured a relatively large sample of mice to work with. In recent years, many urban school districts have initiated multibillion-dollar construction and modernization projects to address the dire state of school facilities. However, too often when significant investments in infrastructure are made, they are often not directed at the communities with the greatest needs that struggle to keep up with shorter-term maintenance issues (Filardo, 2016).

Lack of attention to conditions within schools is evident in many cities throughout the United States. In his book *Spectacular Things Happen Along the Way*, Brian Schultz, a former teacher in Chicago, describes how a harmless civic activity aimed at getting his students involved in their school and community ended up becoming a major political conflict and an embarrassment for public officials (Schultz, 2018). When given the opportunity to name conditions in their schools and neighborhoods that they wanted to change, students not only generated a long list that included broken windows, rodents, lack of ventilation, and so on but they also pushed Schultz to allow them to present their concerns at a meeting of the Chicago School Board and, later, at a press conference. Embarrassed by the public airing of the students' concerns, district and city officials promised to address them expeditiously. To their dismay, the officials soon found that the students would not be appeased by their promises, and continued to draw attention to the state of their school for a full year until corrective actions were taken (Schultz, 2018).

Beyond the condition of facilities, there are questions regarding the types of educators and staff whom students interact with once in school. Structural racism calls our attention to issues with hiring practices. Despite several studies showing that teachers of color can have a positive impact on academic outcomes for an increasingly diverse student population (Cherng & Halpin, 2016; Egalite, Kisida, & Winters, 2015), a 2016 report by the U.S. Department of Education found that teachers of color make up just 18% of the workforce. In California, the state with the largest and most diverse public school population in the country, the shortage of teachers of color in many school districts is only just beginning to receive attention. The state has the largest percentage gap between students of color, at 73%, and teachers of color, at 29% (Boser, 2014). Studies on the reasons behind the shortage of teachers of color shed light on the broken educator pipeline that should be producing a more diverse teacher force. These factors include gross inequities in higher educational attainment by race, inhibiting credential requirements, and poor rates of teacher retention (Putman et al., 2016). Although most school district and state officials publicly state their desire to hire more teachers of color, the unwillingness of policymakers to address the structural obstacles in their hiring practices has made it extremely difficult to increase the diversity of the teacher workforce.

By focusing on structural racism and the way it shapes the educational experiences of students, our attention is directed to the opportunities—or lack thereof—that are provided. Test scores may be relevant to whether students in a particular school or district are being well served, but if we only examine test scores and fail to examine conditions within schools, we may draw the wrong conclusions. By directing our attention to the learning opportunities available to students, we can see that racial disparities in education are correlated with other racial disparities in health, income, and wealth, and closely tied to inequities in opportunities.

In response to these disparities, some districts are taking practical steps to change the way they think about student needs, opportunities, and outcomes. In Los Angeles, for instance, the school district has developed a Student Equity Needs Index that uses measures like incidences of asthma or gun violence to determine which schools should be allocated greater resources. In the following sections, we deconstruct different paradigms for understanding the role of race in academic achievement.

CHANGING PARADIGMS OF RACE

A plethora of publications and studies have examined the relationship between race and education. A perusal of this body of work could lead one to readily conclude that it is not for a lack of attention that race continues to carry paramount importance in shaping educational outcomes and experiences. However, as a phenomenon that permeates a wide array of disciplines—genetics, sociology, geography, psychology, to name a few—race remains a difficult concept to operationalize because its meaning and the categories used to define and identify groups shift over time.

Below we survey a few dominant paradigms of how race is often viewed and understood in the field of education, with a particular emphasis on its role in perpetuating inequality. In our discussion we bring up aspects of race not always apparent or pronounced, and which often go undetected. The advent, and ongoing legacy, of the Trump administration shifted our attention to the ways in which outright and blatant expressions of racism shape political discourse, particularly as some political leaders continue to breathe new life into White supremacist ideologies. Despite the need to meet these brazen challenges head on, we try not to lose sight of the long, complex history and enduring impact of race on educational inequality. After all, the poor conditions present in many urban schools throughout the country were present before the election of Donald Trump and the resurgence of neo-Nazis. Why such conditions endure even when liberals espousing good intentions hold power is a central issue that we tackle directly. In each of the following sections we discuss how an approach to education that we characterize broadly as antiracist can be instrumental in overcoming challenges associated with each paradigm.

Before delving into particular paradigms, a few notes on how we approach race here are important to share. Although they persist, we will not address perspectives on race that draw on biology and genetics to explain traits such as intelligence or performance on standardized tests. We recognize that such views did not simply fade into obscurity after the publication of *The Bell Curve* (Herrnstein & Murray, 1994) with its claims of a racialized natural distribution of intelligence. We also recognize that some analysts (though rarely actual geneticists) continue to pursue these questions and explore the relationship between intelligence and race. Moreover, we recognize that biologically based definitions of race continue to be embraced by some individuals in American society (Morning, 2011). We addressed this topic directly in the first edition of *City Schools* and in a subsequent publication, *Creating the Opportunity to Learn* (Boykin & Noguera, 2011). For this reason, we will not rehash that debate here.

Instead, we draw on recent developments in the deployment of intersectionality as a framework that is useful for understanding the formation of racial categories and other expressions of identity (e.g., gender, class, and sexuality). Over the years, debates over the nature of inequality in the United States have often attempted to substitute class for race. We have even heard colleagues go so far as to suggest that class has become the "new race." Intersectionality as developed by scholars such as Patricia Hill Collins and Kimberle Crenshaw, and further applied to educational contexts (Tefera et al., 2018), has dispelled the need to see these as competing categories. Increasingly, researchers have embraced intersectionality as a tool for analysis because it offers a more holistic way in which to understand educational issues.

However, embracing an intersectional analysis does not mean that we seek to diminish the importance or salience of race as a category of analysis. Following the example set by many feminist scholars of color, we recognize that particular injustices impact specific populations. Within the larger undocumented youth movement, for instance, undocumented Black students have struggled to be seen and recognized. Despite the fact that race is often minimized as an important factor in everyday life or hidden in the glare of postracialism (Bonilla-Silva, 2017), we choose to keep race central to our analysis of urban education because it continues to have a profound impact on the character of schools and the experience of students in America today.

Shaping Student Character: Linking Race and Behavior

In spite of the choppy waves of reform that continually crash on the schoolhouse door, an important idea has remained constant. Ironclad beliefs about mobility in American society have bolstered the near universal notion that working hard in school leads to future economic success. The notion that individual success and social mobility are tied to merit, grit, or natural ability continues to be an alluring myth. Despite substantial evidence that American society has become more unequal (Putnam, 2015), and that factors such as family income and parent education continue to profoundly shape mobility patterns (Chetty et al., 2014), the idea that American society is a place where hard work and talent are rewarded reinforces the enduring appeal of the American Dream.

No matter one's race or socioeconomic status, the notion of individual success or failure in school continues to be an alluring myth. Macleod's *Ain't No Makin' It* (2009), a classic ethnography on working-class, urban youth, revealed that Black youth were even more likely than their White peers to cling to the American Dream and to blame themselves when they came up short in their educational achievements and career goals. On the flipside, in his study of an elite boarding school, Khan (2011) observed that even the most privileged White students come to see their success as the fruit of their own labors.

When such personal narratives are widely embraced, they can have very real consequences for public policy. Ongoing attempts to roll back race-conscious education policies such as affirmative action and busing have long found support among self-proclaimed advocates of meritocracy who maintain that race ceases to be a barrier to opportunity (McWhorter, 2000; Steele, 1990). Similarly, calls for all students to graduate from high school "college and career ready" are rooted in the notion that adequate academic preparation is all one needs to partake in the bounty of the American economy. Thus, while beliefs about the prevalence or desirability of meritocracy (Au, 2013), and the importance of grit (Duckworth, 2016) and hard work to student success may not appear to be steeped in overt racialized sensibilities, they do have direct bearing on how we think schools should be reformed and how efforts to mold student behavior should be directed. The not-so-subtle takeaway for a nation facing a persistent racial achievement gap is that students of color, especially Blacks, Latinxs, and Native Americans, are in need of substantial character alteration if they are to experience success and share in the elusive American Dream.

Typically rooted in a behavioral paradigm, we have witnessed a resurgent interest in student character as a driver for school improvement. In recent years, grit and growth mindset have been regarded as essential to promote higher academic achievement. Paul Tough's (2012) widely read book *How Children Succeed* centered on the thesis that noncognitive traits are the most important in supporting academic and lifelong achievement. The turn toward social-emotional dimensions of learning in some ways comes as a respite from the overwhelming demands of testing. It is also hard to argue against the fact that traits such as optimism, perseverance, impulse control, and deferred gratification may impact one's various life outcomes in school or work. But whether or not one is in possession of certain attributes does not provide a complete story of all the factors that influence educational outcomes.

What we have seen is that when the development of character traits is understood in color-evasive terms and divorced from a critical reading of the social and economic constraints that shape the lives of children in impoverished urban communities, practices intended to cultivate those attributes actually do very little to foster success and development within urban schools. For example, a number of nonprofits and philanthropic organizations have embraced adult mentoring of inner-city youth as a means to promote youth development and as a solution to the so-called achievement gap. Despite that mentoring does little to address the structural obstacles that shape the character of urban communities (e.g., environmental degradation, unemployment, and the inadequacy of public institutions and services), mentoring is often embraced both because it conforms to the notion that shaping character will change behavior and because it is cheaper and easier to pursue than structural change. Character matters, but a substantial body of research in the social sciences reveals that context matters even more in shaping the lives of children.

The Social-Emotional Turn: A Renewed Focus on Student Character. In the wake of failed efforts to integrate schools post-*Brown*, policymakers and reformers turned their attention inward to changes they hoped were possible to achieve even within underresourced, racially segregated schools. In addition to ramping up standardization and accountability systems, the 1980s and 1990s saw a renewed interest in character education. Echoing the vision of moral education represented in the famed McGuffey readers of the previous century, a new wave of scholars and educators found promise in reinvigorating character education (Sojourner, 2012; Watz, 2011). Character education would become lodged in the national consciousness as a result of its embrace by some high-level supporters. President Clinton himself notoriously referenced character education in his 1996 State of the Union address. In the speech, he exhorted schools "to teach good values and good citizenship," going so far as to encourage them to require students to wear school uniforms "if it means that teenagers will stop killing each other over designer jackets " (Clinton, 1996).

The sensational reference and racial dog-whistling reflected in Clinton's address was also adopted by President Obama, who once exhorted "brothers" to "pull up their pants" on MTV, though he rejected attempts to legislate against sagging pants (Harris, 2008). Prior to being charged with sexual assault, comedian Bill Cosby also became a promoter of character and a scolder of Black parents whom he accused of failing to provide the moral guidance their children needed. Although to many educators, parents, and students, such exhortations to elevate character and adopt "responsible" behavior traits were taken as a form of distasteful victim-blaming aimed at communities of color, when espoused by powerful elites, the call to focus on character resonated and was widely embraced.

The more recent return of student character on the reform agenda reflects its successful rebranding. Moving away from overly patronizing terms like "character education," social-emotional or noncognitive learning are now the preferred phrasing. Educators and some think tanks and foundations have seized on the popular idea that a student's disposition toward learning is malleable and therefore can be altered in ways that promote academic achievement and good behavior. When teachers grasp what psychologist Carol Dweck (2008) termed a "growth mindset," they see in their students the potential for improvement. Although Dweck has maintained that the most important shift in mindset must occur in educators and the way in which they perceive students, some educators and reformers have co-opted the concept of growth mindset under the "no excuses" banner, claiming they are rejecting the "soft bigotry of low expectations" by pushing their students to excel.

The swing back toward social-emotional learning is not exactly fleeting. In fact, it has become enshrined in federal policy. As No Child Left Behind was morphed into the Every Student Succeeds Act (ESSA) in 2016, policymakers added a provision that required school districts to be evaluated on additional measures of student learning that go beyond test scores. As a result, while it has long been a part of teacher training curricula and the source of much conversation within schools, social-emotional learning is no longer a tangential issue.

We are not opposed to the focus on social and emotional learning. In fact, one of us (Noguera) served on a national commission created by the Aspen Institute to promote the idea that schools must respond to the social and emotional needs of children and to encourage states and school districts to embrace it in policy. If a focus on the social and emotional needs of children compels policymakers to address hunger, lack of health care, and the prevalence of trauma among poor children, it could bring additional resources to schools that serve the most disadvantaged children. This would be a positive shift in direction. However, several researchers have found in early analyses of the changes brought about by ESSA that districts are still not receiving adequate support to respond to the social and emotional needs of children (Melnick, Cook-Harvey, & Darling-Hammond, 2017). Additionally, some scholars have raised the concern that ESSA may perpetuate a focus on individual students' capacities while ignoring the social-emotional competencies of educators and the need for resources that have the power to shape overall school climate and the ability of schools to respond to student needs (Gregory & Fergus, 2017).

It is important to note that the renewed focus on student character belies an educational landscape that is often lacking in basic social-emotional supports for students of color in many schools. KIPP, the national charter network, was an early adopter of character education initiatives. However, KIPP's attempts at character building occur in the context of a school network that has historically relied on harsh forms of punitive discipline tied to high rates of suspension and attrition among students of color at some schools, as well as feelings of unfairness attributed to "no excuses" policies and practices (Golann & Torres, 2018; Marsh & Noguera, 2017). Similarly, research using a nationally representative dataset found that schools with higher proportions of non-White/non-Asian students have significantly less access to school counselors (Gagnon & Mattingly, 2016). Although often utilized to administer testing and to support the college application process, when their caseloads are not too high, counselors can also play an important role in addressing the social and emotional needs of students. However, urban schools are typically provided limited access to counselors. Only 4.2% of urban districts met or exceeded the recommended student/counselor ratio of 250:1, their bloated median ratio reaching 499:1 (Gagnon & Mattingly, 2016). Even as states respond to new provisions under the ESSA to include social-emotional learning outcomes, just as they have scrambled to raise test scores in response to previous legislation, the necessary supports and climate needed to increase the likelihood of their students' success are left wanting.

Holistic Approaches: Reorienting Social-Emotional Learning. We are not making an argument against the importance and value of social and emotional learning in school. Anyone who has worked in schools knows how important resilience and hard work can be for students who face obstacles in their educational journeys. We can all point to inspiring young people who push through and defy the odds stacked against them. Nancy Barile (2015), a nationally board-certified teacher, knows these kinds of students well and wrote about her experiences:

> I witness grit in my classroom and students every day. I see it in the Bosnian refugee turned AP student and track star. I see it in the undocumented immigrant who lands a Posse scholarship. And I see it in the homeless student who

graduates while working full time and helping raise his younger handicapped brother. (p. 8)

However, she also reflected on other students who, despite their best efforts, simply cannot reverse the immense pressures that cause them to fall short of their goals. "Will students who don't triumph over poverty be blamed for lacking grit?" she plaintively wonders. In the end, while these character-building efforts may appear more pragmatic in developing behaviors that can support student success without having to drastically alter the machinery of schooling, they tend to minimize the significance of structural obstacles that are rooted in the persistence of race and class boundaries.

For this reason, even as we push for more contextual and sociologically informed ideas that acknowledge the enduring realities of structural racism and class suppression, we must not neglect the social conditions that are common in impoverished urban communities, such as interpersonal violence, substance abuse, and human trafficking that often crush aspirations and stymie the efforts of even the most hard-working individuals. Trauma and toxic stress are increasingly common among children of color in such communities (Raver & Blair, 2016). If our efforts to counter the effects of institutionalized racism do not include strategies aimed at mitigating the very real psychological and emotional effects of these conditions, it is unlikely that schools in such communities or the students they serve will thrive.

Various forms of familial or environmental stress, starting in early childhood, can lead to chronic or lasting trauma in students. It should come as no surprise that marginalized groups, such as court-involved or foster youth, experience higher rates of trauma (Crosby et al., 2019). Simply belonging to a racially marginalized group can also present its own traumas, rooted in both a history of oppression and navigating systemic racism on a day-to-day basis (Comas-Díaz, Hall, & Neville, 2019; Sotero, 2006). Scholars even find that students of color may experience forms of "racial battle fatigue" that may have enduring physiological consequences (Smith, Allen, & Danley, 2007). The notion that experiencing racism in their daily lives can produce physical pain and emotional duress is thus not metaphorical.

In response to these various pressures, some school districts are developing trauma-informed social-emotional curricula and programming. Programs like Healthy Environments and Response to Trauma in Schools (HEARTS), created as a collaboration between the University of California–San Francisco and local school districts, represent a more holistic approach to social-emotional learning. The model centers on capacity building in schools—training educators and administrators to better understand and address student trauma. In addition to training educators to respond to student trauma, the HEARTS program promotes staff wellness and resilience in schools where they are likely to experience vicarious or secondhand trauma and burnout. The program incorporates elements of restorative justice, designed as an alternative to zero-tolerance discipline policies that aim to cultivate healthier school climates and make it possible for schools to demonstrate concern for students' holistic experiences. Similar programs have introduced mindfulness and yoga classes into urban schools that are proving to help students engage their emotions and cope with stress (Gould et al., 2012).

Such initiatives do not compensate for the effects of structural racism, but they can, to some degree, mitigate them. Many school-based trauma-informed programs are directed with explicit concerns for racial justice and equity. Whereas traditional interventions seek to rehabilitate young people of color, they often do little to uncover and heal the sometimes hidden wounds created by racial trauma (Hardy, 2013). For example, in the wake of police shootings, the National Child Traumatic Stress Network (2017) has sought to center treatment for racial trauma in the way educators support students. The organization encourages educators to cultivate safe environments where authentic engagement on racial justice issues through emotional validation, circle dialogues, and leadership development. Trauma-informed programs that address racial injustice are built on an orientation toward students' social and emotional well-being that goes over and above the demands of testing outcomes or behavior management to create a whole school support system. Instead of gritting their teeth and steeling themselves to the challenges they will face, such programs support the well-being of urban students by teaching practices that encourage self-care, such as yoga and meditation, which are typically reserved for their more privileged counterparts. Insisting on this type of approach to students' well-being in a society that is often dismissive of their trauma reminds us of Audre Lorde's oft-cited pronouncement: "Caring for myself is not self-indulgence, it is self-preservation, and that is an act of political warfare."

As researchers or educators, we must also be prepared to think critically about how the behaviors or traumas of urban students are represented and addressed. As Eve Tuck (2009) notes, while research is often driven by an interest in exposing damage done to communities, it is critical that we do not allow it to wholly define them. The line between pity and pathology becomes blurred when marginalized peoples are seen as embodying their problems. Although the crucible of racism in America has clearly left scars, it has also shattered commonly held assumptions about the nature of the subjugation experienced by historically oppressed peoples. If those peoples and the communities where they reside are to organize for social justice, their potential for agency and resistance must be recognized and acknowledged. Tuck notes that instead of damage, our focus must turn toward communal desires and aspirations. Social-emotional learning that is trauma-informed and community-oriented and that engages racial injustice in concrete and practical ways can help ensure we do not slide into the shallows of deficit thinking. Even as great as the pain may be, we must never lose sight of the possibilities for action and change.

Cultural Paradigms: Rewriting a Troubling Legacy

When Tom Torlino first sat for his portrait at the Carlisle Indian Industrial School in 1882, the Diné (Navajo) student looked to the camera with a steely gaze. His long, flowing hair fell over large hoop earrings and reached past his shoulders onto the patterned garments he wore. He was part of a generation of indigenous students who—often forcibly—attended boarding schools meant to impart the cultural values of White settler society.

In another portrait dated just three years later, Tom is wearing a dark suit with his hair cut in a neat part. Suspiciously, his skin appears significantly lighter. The shocking before-and-after photos are part of an entire archive of similar images from the time that represent the kind of forced assimilation that was integral to the genocide experienced by indigenous people in the United States (Lomawaima, 2018). By stripping them of their language and their culture, indigenous peoples could also become alienated from their traditions and heritage.

The experiences of indigenous students in boarding schools reflect just how powerful a force culture is in the institution of schooling. Schools are the spaces in which grand ideas and everyday customs are transmitted to future generations. Given that some schools generate relatively little evidence that they are capable of preparing their students academically, some scholars even suggest that the primary function of schools is simply to reinforce norms or beliefs that are embedded in the dominant culture (Bowles & Gintis, 1976). By conjuring this troubling legacy, we come to see the abiding role of culture and how the "civilizing" impulse within schools and the mandate to assimilate those who are culturally and linguistically different continues to be operative in the present. Indeed, for many of the nonindigenous first-generation and immigrant students we teach, this history of indigenous schooling resonates deeply and painfully.

However, what is missing from this grim account are the ways in which students, families, and educators have managed to resist being overwhelmed by schools seeking to impart the dominant culture. While the stunning before-and-after photos appear to convey a story of loss, Tom Torlino's actual life trajectory points to alternative possibilities. His family recalled that when Tom returned home from Carlisle, he remained comfortable in traditional clothing, continued his career as a medicine man, and used his English skills to be an intermediary between the federal government and Diné leaders (Lomawaima, 2018). As we discuss later in the chapter, schools can play a vital role in sustaining or revitalizing culture, and have done so in the same indigenous communities that were once oppressed by these institutions.

Since its founding, American society periodically descends into vexing culture wars between traditionalists and those calling for change (Hartman, 2015). Schools often serve as a proxy site for these debates because they play an inordinate role in determining what the country's enduring values and beliefs are or should be. Debates over the acknowledgment of Ebonics as a distinct language, over whether or not the pledge of allegiance should be mandated, the degree to which multiculturalism and ethnic studies are embraced in the curriculum, and whether or not the religious holidays and customs of non-Christians should be permitted have all ignited controversy in public education over the years. We are once again in the throes of culture wars brought about in part by the expression of racist and xenophobic rhetoric at the highest political levels. As the country experiences a resurgence in such debates, it becomes even more important to be clear about the contemporary meaning and significance of race in American society. In this section, we focus first on the problematic ways in which culture has been understood in education and its connection to race. Rather than dismiss culture altogether, we seek to find a place for it in educational discourse and practice.

The Hyper Visibility of Culture and the Danger of Essentialism. At the most fundamental level, scholars who specialize in studying culture understand it as shared systems of meaning that may be represented in language, symbols, customs, and norms. Despite increasingly nuanced and critical ways of understanding how culture operates, popular conceptions of culture continue to treat it as static, immutable, and monolithic, particularly when referencing particular racial groups. In fact, culture often becomes essentialized in ways that are similar to the study of biological traits (Bonilla-Silva, 2017). In other words, cultural traits are often seen as hardwired to particular racial groups, and certain traits—industriousness, frugality, business acumen, and so on—are presumed to be shared by members of cultural groups (Chua & Rubenfeld, 2015). In the field of education, when biological ascriptions fail in their utility as explanations for differences in patterns of achievement, cultural explanations may easily replace them. Unlike biology, the use of culture as an explanation for differences between groups continues to be widely embraced, even though such arguments generally bear a striking resemblance to the racist ideologies of the past.

Unlike structural racism, cultural explanations of inequality in educational outcomes and performance continue to be widely held. To some degree, this is because they seem to be less overtly racist. Whereas biological explanations of differences in achievement are associated with the racist views of Nazis and proponents of eugenics, cultural explanations are more nuanced, and the most popular have been espoused by scholars of color (McWhorter, 2000; Ogbu, 2004). How hard students work, how much their families prioritize education, how respectful they are, whether they have the compunction to defer gratification, and which subjects they are presumed to excel at have all been subject to cultural logics.

At a scholarly level, the shadow of John Ogbu's work looms large. The Nigerian American anthropologist, along with some of his colleagues, left a lasting imprint on scholarship in the field of education based on the theory that Black students failed in school due to their embrace of an "oppositional identity" that led them to view academic achievement as a form of "acting White" (Fordham & Ogbu, 1986; Ogbu, 2004). His dissertation served as the basis for several subsequent studies that launched thousands of articles, books, and op-eds pushing for and against cultural explanations and their role in producing inequality in educational outcomes. Ogbu argued that so-called "voluntary minorities" (e.g., Asians and Africans) performed better than "non-voluntary minorities" (e.g., African Americans, Puerto Ricans, Chicanos, and Native Americans) because they were willing to accommodate the dominant culture and conform to the behavioral expectations of schools (Ogbu, 2004). Ogbu's theory of race and school performance had a profound impact on the field of education because it seemed to explain the achievement gap and the longstanding relationship between race and school performance. Although Ogbu never analyzed the educational experience of White students or Black students who did well in school, and he completely ignored the role of class and parent education on student achievement patterns, for over 20 years his theory was extremely influential because it seemed to offer a compelling explanation for why disparities in achievement based on race persisted over time.

Scholars have long voiced critiques of Ogbu's thesis, arguing that culture cannot and should not be seen as a primary or independent factor for explaining inequality. Culture is neither static nor monolithic. Individuals from the same culture, like individuals from the same family, often exhibit significant differences in achievement, attainment, and aspirations. One of the most succinct rejoinders to the cultural thesis so closely associated with Ogbu's legacy can be found in the pages of Ta-Nehisi Coates's (2009) memoir, *The Beautiful Struggle*: "No matter what the professional talkers tell you, I never met a black boy who wanted to fail" (p. 180).

In order to refute cultural explanations of educational performance, we must examine why they are so appealing and enduring. Because they paint groups with broad strokes and rely on gross generalizations, cultural explanations are generally prone to reinforcing stereotypes and glossing over the variations that exist within groups. For example, the broad depiction of Asian Americans as a high-achieving model minority blots out the experiences of Southeast Asians who often experience higher rates of discipline and marginalization in American schools (Nguyen et al., 2019). As refugee communities fleeing political violence, the experiences of Cambodians, Vietnamese, and other groups who have had to make a home in a new and often hostile land are considerably different from that of other Asian groups. For this reason, a local Cambodian community group in Long Beach, Khmer Girls in Action, has worked to bring attention to the particular challenges facing these students. In a survey administered to Cambodian students, the group found that the vast majority of youth reported that their parents expected them to attend college. Despite having similar aspirations to other Asian ethnic groups, 41% of Cambodian students left high school without a diploma (Khmer Girls in Action, 2011). Clearly, the obstacles facing Khmer students are not because they are insufficiently Asian. Although culture is certainly relevant to understanding their identities and perhaps their experiences in school, a focus strictly on their culture is unlikely to yield insights into how to support their education and development. The report produced by Khmer Girls in Action calls for more resources to be directed at these students, such as counseling for trauma and language resources to assist those who are not proficient in English.

The tendency to rely on cultural explanations of student performance often results in stereotypes of students based on race going unchallenged. Cultural explanations also tend to reinforce racial hierarchies and provide a rationalization for the existence and persistence of racial disparities in academic performance. Moreover, because cultural attributes are often wielded for political reasons, they do not have to be supported by data or even make logical sense. Comedian Hari Kondabolu often points out the ridiculousness and contradictory nature of such cultural ascriptions, such as in this popular bit:

> People say, "Mexicans are lazy," and, "Mexicans take all the jobs." How the hell do those two things work together exactly? "Well, some Mexicans are lazy and some Mexicans take all of the jobs." Like all human beings? If your argument is that Mexicans are just like all human beings, then you're just not a very good racist. (quoted in Ghitelman, 2014, n.p.)

As educators, we must be keenly aware of how culture may be deployed to these ends. To the degree that we accept broad generalizations about the relationship between culture and academic performance, we are not only more likely to accept stereotypes about groups but also less likely to be aware of how culture may be deployed as a resource by the same groups to support academic success.

For example, in a study of an urban high school serving a large Black student population as well as a more recent immigrant population from East Asia, cultural labels came to inform how the school was organized (Garver & Noguera, 2014). Succumbing to common stereotypes, school staff came to see Asian immigrant students as motivated and respectful while Black students were written off as apathetic toward learning and poorly behaved. These racial stereotypes informed the school's organization and resulted in a separate academy being created to serve the immigrant students on a separate floor of the building. The separate newcomer academy and perceived preferential treatment was viewed by Black students and the broader school community as deeply unfair. Tensions boiled over at the school when a violent incident between Black and Asian students erupted. In response, the school emphasized the need for changes in school safety, deploying dozens of security officers to the school. However, school officials neglected to address the fact that many Black students had been victimized as well, by individuals who also happened to be Black. Confusion about race prevented the school district from responding effectively to the incident and prevented the school from addressing the underlying racial biases and divisive school climate that led to resentment between groups. In the absence of a critical perspective on race and culture, and well-grounded research on race relations, schools may unwittingly draw on stereotypes about racial/ethnic groups and miss the need to ground their response to student needs in a concrete analysis of their experiences at school.

Creating a Place for Culture: Toward Culturally Responsive and Sustaining Pedagogy. In the social sciences, some have claimed that culture is making a comeback in the study of inequality after years of being swept under the proverbial rug (Cohen, 2010; Patterson & Fosse, 2015). In fact, it could be argued that cultural explanations for differences between racial groups never truly disappeared. The question for us is not *whether* culture has a role to play in the educational achievement for students of color, but rather *how* it can further equity and justice. Based on the examples and research cited above, there are a few questions educators should consider when drawing connections between culture and schooling: What are my own cultural values and beliefs, and how might they influence the way I perceive students? Whose culture is centered in my curriculum and throughout our school? Conversely, which cultures are marginalized or perceived negatively, and how might cultural ascriptions erase or marginalize students? How might cultural beliefs shape practices or student orientations toward learning in my school? Although there are many levels at which culture can operate, it is also important to recognize the ways in which culture can also be used to foster equity through pedagogy and community engagement.

In some school settings and for some researchers, the relationship between pedagogy and culture has evolved in meaningful ways. Moving beyond the tokenism of multiculturalism of previous decades, some educational researchers have begun focusing on how cultural knowledge can be used to help students code-switch and provide them with skills to navigate institutions and the workplace where the dominant culture prevails. Although learning to code-switch is often interpreted as deferring to the dominant culture, when students are provided with an affirmative grounding in their own language and culture, learning to code-switch or effectively navigate multiple cultures can also be empowering. In this light, when learning to code-switch is not premised on the debasement of a student's primary culture, it can be as empowering as acquiring the ability to speak multiple languages. Rather than simply switching off a student's native culture, code-switching can be deployed by students as a means to avoid being stereotyped, limited, and victimized. When students have access to the "codes of power" (Delpit, 2006), they are better able to handle interactions with employers, educators, and police officers. When seen in this light, code-switching is not a form of forced assimilation. Rather, it can serve as a means to empower students to cope with and resist racism, and to recognize which codes are needed or most helpful in various settings.

A number of schools have also begun adopting strategies broadly described as "culturally responsive" in their approach to teaching. Though the term encompasses many things, it implicitly focuses on the "otherness" and potential alienation that often exists between teachers and students when cultural differences are present and the culture of students is perceived as inferior. Providing educators with the tools to unlearn their biases and to establish meaningful and supportive relationships with their students is critical to educational efficacy (Hammond, 2014). More recently, scholars have called for the development of pedagogical frameworks that go beyond simply responding to culture and instead finding ways to critically engage culturally sustaining practices that address systemic inequalities (Paris & Alim, 2014).

The recent burgeoning of ethnic studies in K–12 contexts has opened up new possibilities for developing curricula and pedagogical strategies that make it possible to promote cultural sustainability. In some districts, ethnic studies is making it possible for cultural practices and resources that are rooted in the experiences of students and their families to find their way into the curriculum and classrooms. Unlike the boarding schools that once sought to extinguish the language, culture, and heritage of indigenous students, scores of schools and programs have recently been established to sustain and strengthen their linguistic and cultural identities. The Native American Community Academy in Albuquerque and Puente de Hózhó in Flagstaff each promote culturally revitalizing educational practice by teaching indigenous languages and building community with parents (McCarty & Lee, 2014). An important aspect of culturally sustaining curricula is that they are most meaningful when taught by those who authentically reflect the experiences of those being educated. As discussed elsewhere in this chapter, teacher diversity remains a critical issue because you can't teach what you don't know (Howard, 2016).

In order to foster culturally responsive educational environments, schools must also contend with their complex relationships with the communities they serve. Even when schools attempt to promote parent and family engagement, underlying cultural disconnects play out in strained communication and relationships. One study, for example, reveals that Black and Latinx students were more likely to receive the feared call home from their teachers regarding disruptive behavior than their White peers, and Asian parents were less likely to be contacted even when students struggled. Teachers were also less likely to reach out to share the accomplishments of students of color (Cherng, 2016). Even when schools do reach out, they are likely to adopt a deficit-oriented perspective that may assume parents of color are apathetic toward their children's education.

An important corrective to deficit thinking is found in the cultural wealth model first introduced by Yosso (2005) that proves helpful in mapping out the various strengths and resources that communities of color can bring to bear on their schooling experiences. Yosso encourages educators to recognize the various forms of capital that can be nurtured through the cultural wealth that students possess. These include aspirational capital (the hopes and dreams of communities), navigational capital (the way communities address obstacles), social capital (the way communities are empowered through networks and organizing), as well as linguistic, familial, and resistant capital. By acknowledging these types of resources, educators are not only more likely to treat the culture of their students as a resource rather than a deficit but also more likely to use it to empower their students as learners (Cummins, 2001).

These insights are particularly useful when schools attempt to connect with their surrounding communities. Teaching for Change, a social justice education organization in Washington, DC, addresses these issues by directly confronting race in their parent-organizing work (Syeed, 2018). Whereas White and middle-class parent groups often seek to professionalize parent roles that focus on functions like fundraising (Posey-Maddox, 2013), the group's signature Tellin' Stories parent engagement program is founded on the importance of building strong relationships with parents based on their interests. Story sharing, community walks, and cultivating a bilingual environment are all cultural components of the parent organizing model the group employs. Most importantly, these initiatives do not shy away from issues of race. Rather, they explicitly challenge the assumptions that educators may hold toward minority parents, and create a context where relationships premised on respect and empathy can be nurtured. Organizations like Teaching for Change seek to create the conditions where school culture and leadership reflect the community's diversity and where the culture of children can be treated as a resource to support learning. Although institutional changes may be needed to effectively engage parents, such as hiring or training staff, underlying cultural beliefs, biases, and assumptions must also be addressed.

Social Construction Paradigms: Racial Hierarchies at Work

Recently, the ongoing battle over affirmative action policies in higher education opened up a new chapter. Backed by the Pacific Legal Foundation, a conservative legal organization, some Asian Americans have alleged discrimination and have sued Harvard University to challenge race-conscious admission policies designed to admit underrepresented groups. The group behind the high-profile lawsuit was founded by a White conservative strategist, and its efforts won the support of the Trump administration's Justice Department. Similar challenges occurred in New York City in response to efforts by the Department of Education to change its admissions policies at its premier exam schools. Although some within the Asian American community actively supported these lawsuits, others, such as attorney Jason Wu, attempted to communicate the need to understand context in the Asian American defense of affirmative action. Writing about the unfairness of the current approach to admissions at NY exam schools, which rely on a single test to determine which students to admit, Wu (2019) recalled his own days as a student:

> I wish my 17-year-old self at Brooklyn Tech had known enough to make these points to classmates, some of whom I heard express negative and misguided assumptions that their "spot" at an elite college had been "taken" by a less deserving black or Latinx student. But back then, I and others assumed testing and admissions systems were fair and objective—an illusion that persists in regard to admission to the specialized high schools today. Yet we now know such assumptions are unwarranted, ignoring as they do the historical context of racism and racial privilege, which plays out in different ways among different racial groups. (n.p.)

The recent flare-up over affirmative action underscores the importance of seeing race as a social and political construction (Omi & Winant, 2015). Once one recognizes that throughout history racial categories have been fluid rather than static and rooted in innate biological differences, the political use of racial categories becomes clear. While today, Asian Americans are often valorized as a model minority to discredit race-conscious admissions, in the not too distant past they were viewed as a threat, untrustworthy and unassimilable (Kawai, 2005). As the only ethnic group to be legally barred from entering the United States, some Asian Americans recognize that the tactics deployed by the Pacific Legal Foundation come from a well-worn playbook of pitting subordinate groups against each other to maintain racial hierarchies (Kim, 1999).

Omi and Winant (2015) brought the notion of the social construction of race to the fore, drawing on history to demonstrate how changing social and political realities lead to the formation and alteration of these categories. The process of racialization is apparent enough in the context of Black and Latinx students, but can also be understood in the way the model minority construct is used to bestow an honorary White status on some Asians and even white Latinxs who assimilate and conform. Since 9/11, Muslims, whose ethnic diversity complicates traditional racial categories (Ali, 2013), have increasingly been regarded as "other," and in the ongoing political context their targeting by politicians and hate groups serves as yet another reminder that the process of racial formation and racial subjugation is ongoing. In this section we explore how the formation of such racial categories perpetuates racial inequality by restricting access to resources and opportunities for students of color.

Walking the Line: Racial Categories and Stratification. Over a century ago, W. E. B. Du Bois (1903) famously asserted that "the problem of the Twentieth Century is the problem of the color-line." In its simplicity, the phrase remains a powerful metaphor. Lines—whether physical, legal, or imagined—demarcate boundaries, clearly designating those within and outside them. Even as the color line snakes its way into the present, shifting and changing shape, it nevertheless remains a fundamental marker of opportunity and exclusion in American society. The drawing of these lines takes place both at the microlevel of interactions and through the operations of institutions. What emerges through these processes is the reification of racial groups and their subsequent stratification in educational contexts.

The social construction of race becomes all the more real when students are sorted and grouped within and among schools. These sorting processes, whether implicit or explicit, have the same result: racial stratification. A useful case to explore racial stratification in student sorting processes at micro- and macrolevels is in special education designation. The Individuals with Disabilities Education Act heralded a new era for special education when it became law in 1990, signaling serious support and investment in serving students with special needs. Even as changes were made to the law in the following decades, troubling racial and gender trends began to appear. Students of color, and in some cases males, have been found to be at heightened risk for being designated for special education (Sullivan & Bal, 2013; Voulgarides, Fergus, & King Thorius, 2017). From the outside, such designations might seem race neutral—a clinical process carried out by professionals to address the learning needs of students who are struggling academically. To others, the disproportionate placement of Black students generally and Black males particularly in special education are reflections of genetic variations in race and ability. However, research on this phenomenon reveals that there is clearly more to the story. In a comprehensive study of racial disproportionality in special education, Edward Fergus (2016) showed that institutional practices have created the conditions that lead to these outcomes. Some of these include curriculum and teacher quality, overcrowded classes, and poor compliance with IDEA's loose guidelines, which allow states to focus on compliance with a "least restrictive environment" provision of the law but do not ensure that when students with Individualized Educational Plans are placed in traditional classrooms their teachers are trained to meet their needs (Albrecht et al., 2012). In her study of IDEA compliance, Voulgarides (2018) finds that while there are several structural factors that explain this phenomenon, there are also situated interactions between teachers and students that we must more closely examine. Through ethnographic observations of special education leaders in three school districts, Voulgarides illustrates how their unexamined racial biases lead to Black and Latinx students disproportionately being designated as students with special needs.

Toward Antiracist Policy and Practice. The cementing of racial categories through institutional practices compels us to acknowledge that race-conscious education policy is needed. Good intentions are simply not enough. Although there may not be a conspiracy to suspend or place students of color in special education, it doesn't matter. The results of the decisions made by educators across the country, some of whom may be well meaning, is what we must critically examine. Further, if education policy is to take racial inequality seriously, it will need to go beyond simply identifying the problem. When No Child Left Behind was enacted into law, for instance, racial subgroups were highlighted to ensure that a light was shone on gaping disparities. Despite bringing attention to their plight, NCLB did little to suggest what should be done to address the problem or to provide schools serving students with greater needs with adequate support and resources. Antiracist policy must not only lay bare the problem of racial disparities in education but also expose the ways in which structural racism contributes to these patterns and point to strategies to ameliorate them. Antiracist policy must be used to develop a bolder vision that actually seeks to accord greater opportunity to those marginalized by systemic inequality.

One way that all school districts must contend with antiracist policy is in how students are assigned to attend public schools. As desegregation era orders have largely lapsed, local school districts may consider such factors as racial distribution, distance, or school choice in determining how to assign students to schools. As a result of the immense pushback they often generate from White parents, attempts to racially integrate schools have often fallen by the wayside (Hannah-Jones, 2019). But far from the scenes of violent desegregation efforts in the South, the nation's most lively cosmopolitan center remains one of the most racially segregated. New York state has the most racially segregated schools in the nation, thanks in large part to the massive and heavily segregated school district of New York City (Kuscera & Orfield, 2014). Coming to terms with the state of their schools, parents, educators, and city officials have been trying to devise schemes to integrate their schools in neighborhoods across the city. However, pushback from affluent White parents has been fierce, and as evidenced by a widely circulated video of White middle-class parents angrily bashing recommendations that would reserve seats at their schools for traditionally lower-performing students, it will not easily be overcome. Despite the opposition, Brooklyn's District 15, a diverse and gentrifying community, has become a focal point for the city's effort to promote voluntary integration. Through a community-based process, a desegregation plan has emerged that recommends sweeping changes, including the removal of school admissions screening criteria like test scores or attendance. The district's willingness to recognize that seemingly race-neutral admissions practices have prevented Black and Latinx students from gaining entrance to sought-after schools may be the beginning of advancing access to educational opportunity (New York City Department of Education, 2018).

In comparison to other cities that have recently made changes to school enrollment patterns, such as Washington, DC, New York City stands out as keenly focused on putting race at the center of their policy reforms. In our observations of DC's revision of its school boundaries and student assignment policies, community meetings have reflected a deep ambivalence toward conversations about race, that is, when it was even discussed. District 15's desegregation plan directly addresses elements of racial justice and reducing inequality. The plan calls for setting aside a certain percentage of seats at sought-after schools for homeless students, English language learners, and low-income students—groups that are disproportionately non-White. The broad vision of the plan also goes beyond changing admissions policies to focus on inclusion efforts as well, committing to culturally responsive curricula like ethnic studies and training educators in antiracist teaching methods. The district's process of desegregation attends to teaching and learning in ways that will hopefully respond to the changing face of the student body. Despite District 15's relatively comprehensive approach, change remains uneven in other parts of the city. There are a great many questions about the city's overall plan, and measurable outcomes will take some time to emerge. Although requiring considerable political will, New York's leaders are to be applauded for recognizing that the introduction of antiracist education policy also fundamentally requires standing against the status quo that would presume we have arrived at a postracial meritocracy.

Critical Paradigms: Deconstructing Domination, Creating New Possibilities

Rising above the bodegas, sneaker shops, and fast-food restaurants on Flatbush Avenue in Brooklyn, the towering entrance of the Erasmus High School complex conjures a Gothic building suited for an Ivy League campus. The school's storied history results from its early founding as one of the first secondary schools in America. As the borough's population grew in the early 20th century, the school began to serve immigrants and their families. In subsequent years, the school would boast several notable personalities among its students, including Barbra Streisand, Neil Diamond, and Bobby Fischer (Cullen, 2003). Today, the campus has been divided into several schools, and the overwhelming majority of students are Black. When admiring the structure, something becomes clear: The school was not built for the students it now serves. The realization carries both literal and metaphorical implications. Upon further reflection, we are drawn to a more fundamental and unsettling question about how public education can be designed in ways that center students of color who have long faced various forms of marginalization in their lives. Critical perspectives on public education demand answers about whose behavior, culture, or definitions are normalized or centered in school, thereby uncovering power dynamics that may otherwise go unnoticed. Given the near universal experience of schooling and its normalization, these questions are especially vital.

In many respects, schooling experiences are so mundane, so commonplace, that what we observe seems inevitable, almost natural. Building on the work of earlier critical theorists, Kumashiro (2004) notes that the "common sense" of schooling has allowed us to accept or even find comfort in the current—and often oppressive—educational status quo. In schools, educational common sense overlaps with racial common sense about teaching, learning, and educational opportunity. Which students are seen as having potential or are a lost cause, and thereby which schools are worthy of attention and investment, for example, are shaped by the ingrained common sense of race and education. If we take a moment to critically unpack the common sense of schooling, we find not only the foundations of institutionalized racism, but also the shortcomings of public education itself. Early in the 20th century, urban schools became subjected to corporate bureaucratic models that sought to rationalize education and prepare students for the demands of industrialization (Tyack, 1974). Of course, non-White students were not fully included in this vision, as their schools typically served to assimilate, contain, and sort them into positions defined by dominant society. Students today are the inheritors of a system that falls short of its central promise of equality. As Pope (2001) demonstrates in her profiles of diverse students "doing school," young people caught in an overly competitive and alienating education system may grow to be frazzled, disingenuous, and adversarial.

As Gloria Ladson-Billings (1998) reminds us, however, a critical perspective is not only about dissecting dominant racial assumptions shaping a host of schooling realities but also requires that we develop radical alternatives. A critical perspective, then, neither longs for the "good old days" of public education nor fully embraces new reforms that seek to disrupt the education system. Invoking a healthy skepticism more than a paralyzing cynicism, the critical paradigm is also inherently hopeful. If current schooling conditions have grown out of particular interests that perpetuate racial hierarchies, then a new set of arrangements based on justice could also be established. Although the critical perspective has a rich intellectual legacy and wide applications, be they in the fields of law, policy analysis, geography, curriculum studies, or a host of other education-related fields, we think it is most important to emphasize its penchant for reflection. Writing about transformational social change, Paulo Freire (2014) emphasized that all transformative action must be accompanied by reflection. He united these two essential elements of change with the notion of praxis. In short, Freire believed action without reflection was mindless, and reflection without action was impotence. He wrote,

> Let me emphasize that my defense of the praxis implies no dichotomy by which this praxis could be divided into a prior stage of reflection and a subsequent stage of action. Action and reflection occur simultaneously. A critical analysis of reality may, however, reveal that a particular form of action is impossible or inappropriate *at the present time.* Those who through reflection perceive the infeasibility or inappropriateness of one or another form of action (which should accordingly be postponed or substituted) cannot thereby be accused of inaction. Critical reflection is also action. (p. 128)

Thus, in his view, action married to reflection becomes more informed, deliberate, and intentional in its pursuit of justice. Unfortunately, the pace and focus of education reform often leaves little room for such reflection. Policy too often is crafted for short-term political gains or subject to the whims of particular personalities. Decisive leaders are often applauded for taking drastic steps, but the communal work of critical reflection—be it through research, analysis, or discussion—must also become a priority. In the pursuit of immediate results amid seemingly eternal crisis, the space for critical reflection is rarely available. Even some of the most outspoken education activists have had to come to terms with their own beliefs and stances over the years. Randi Weingarten (2015), the tenacious president of the American Federation of Teachers, reflected on her—and by extension, the union's—changing stance on zero-tolerance school discipline:

> These policies were promoted by people, including me, who had hoped they would standardize discipline procedures and free students from the disruptions of misbehaving peers; it was analogous to the broken windows theory of policing. We were wrong. Data have shown both that these policies have failed to make schools safer and that their discriminatory application violates the 1964 Civil Rights Act. The facts are stark: over the past two decades, zero-tolerance policies have disproportionately affected students of color—particularly African American and Latino boys—as well as students with disabilities and lesbian, gay, bisexual, and transgender youth. (p. 1)

Weingarten's statement indicates the importance of contending with dominant ideologies, implementation contexts, and intersectional impacts in the development of educational policy. We also realize what is at stake when we seek decisive action absent critical reflection. Educators, for their part, are often encouraged to develop critical reflective practices that promote antiracist pedagogy and inclusive classroom environments (Howard, 2003; Paris & Alim, 2014). Similar reflective practices may be of use in decisionmaking circles where critical dimensions of policy are either woefully unexamined, minimized, or simply dismissed. We do not argue that simply adopting a critical perspective will always steer educational leaders to making all the right decisions. But, increasing reflective capacity with an eye toward racial inequality is paramount in determining a path toward equity. In the remainder of this section, we look at other ways in which critical perspectives can be particularly illuminating in understanding teacher preparation.

Deconstructing Domination: The Role of Whiteness. In addition to centering the experiences of students of color, critical frameworks also emphasize the need to examine the role of privilege and the ways in which dominant groups maintain their power. At a time when organized White supremacist groups are empowered and emboldened by their tacit alliance with the Trump agenda, it may be easy to lose sight of more latent forms of Whiteness that seem benign because they are so deeply embedded in the hegemonic frameworks that operate in society. Conceived in myriad ways, Whiteness may be understood as an ideology that supports a system of White dominance (Picower, 2009). Scholars have highlighted how Whiteness has operated on numerous fronts, such as in the efforts to reverse desegregation efforts, the exclusion of parents of color from gentrifying schools, and the marginalization of Latinx students in bilingual education (Flores, 2016; Freidus, 2016; Rosiek & Kinslow, 2016).

Teacher education has been a particular target of Whiteness studies since the profession has historically escaped racial critique. Sleeter (2017) reviews various ways in which Whiteness has preserved and maintained a White-dominated teaching force: the use of supposedly race-neutral licensure and credential requirements that disproportionately inhibit and limit opportunities for teachers of color, poor quality of diversity-oriented curricula in teacher education programs, and the dismissal of non-White teacher education students' experiences among their predominately White cohorts.

Although the racial makeup of the teacher workforce may be staggering in light of a diverse student population, the numbers alone do not account for how Whiteness may pervade daily schooling experiences. For example, teachers of color are often subject to hostile racial climates where microaggressions may make them feel unqualified or invisible in comparison to their colleagues (Kohli, 2018). Juan Carrillo (2010) poignantly and painfully captures the experiences of Christina, one of his former students, who went on to teach in a predominately working-class Latinx school that matched her own background. In spite of the connections to her students and her commitment to critical pedagogy, the pain of alienating testing practices and disrespect from administrators she faced was too great as she prepared a tearful goodbye to the classroom. Christina's story, unfortunately, is not a novel one. Black and Latinx teachers have lower retention rates and are more likely to leave the profession than their White peers (U.S. Department of Education, 2016).

Whiteness normalizes the experiences and concerns of White people. Pushing back on critical conversations on race, Whiteness attempts to mystify systems of inequality and disrupt such conversations by utilizing tools rooted in their emotions, beliefs, or behaviors (Picower, 2009). Although student teachers are increasingly exposed to coursework on diversity through foundations or other courses in their training, studies show some White future teachers remain ambivalent to race at best, and resistant at worst (Matias, 2016; Picower, 2009; Sleeter, 2017). A powerful tool in cementing the normalization of Whiteness comes in the form of expressions of White fragility. DiAngelo (2018) describes how society has allowed for Whites to live in zones of racial comfort. When even a little racial stress disturbs this equilibrium—such as when a White student is challenged by a student of color over an expression of racial bias—White fragility often kicks in and a series of defensive moves are made.

Such reactions are readily observable in school settings. In a professional development seminar we attended in an urban school district, facilitators asked teachers to discuss the importance of having teachers who reflected students' racial backgrounds. A large contingent of teachers of color said they felt strongly that educators in the building should reflect the largely Black and Latinx student population. In the course of the discussion, one White teacher broke down in tears because they felt as though their role, good intentions, and passion were being diminished because of their race. The session's focus was disrupted, and meaningful discussion on the topic of diversity in the teaching profession was vacated to make room for the teacher's emotional reaction. Even in this example taken from a single interaction, the powerful place of Whiteness overtook an attempt to center the concerns of non-Whites. Research demonstrates that teacher education programs often cater to the emotional needs of White students over others (Matias, 2016). In creating a pipeline for teachers of color, the work of centering their experiences is still largely a work in progress.

Seeking Possibilities: Teaching for Racial Justice. Of all the paradigms discussed, the critical paradigm most radically shifts what we may imagine is possible in schools. However, it must be accompanied by practical recommendations on what can be done to address the needs of schools and children. Critical analysis is essential for it forces us to see the connections between the history of racial oppression and the ways in which the political and economic structure of society have shaped the current realities in urban schools. However, we must do more than critique. Taking nothing for granted, we can recognize the insidious ways in which race comes to perpetuate various forms of inequality. But with such incisive critique we must also make room to imagine creative possibilities for change.

At a fundamental level, teachers of color are subverting White-centered educator spaces in many schools by amplifying their own voices, by advocating on behalf of underserved and poorly served children, and by challenging the narratives that are used to marginalize them and their families through courageous leadership and *testimonios*. Critical paradigms embrace narratives as a way to validate the lived experiences of people of color, but also to critique the dominant social order, thereby opening the door to alternative possibilities (Stovall, 2005).

Milner and Howard (2013) demonstrate how counternarratives can defy commonly held assumptions in teacher preparation. For example, they point out how alternative certification programs such as Teach for America have historically focused on recruiting the so-called best and the brightest to underserved schools. Such criteria place value on elite education or subject matter knowledge, but do not recognize the importance of cultural capital or building relationships with students or communities. Similarly, groups such as Philadelphia's Fellowship of Black Male Educators are attempting to break through narratives of Black male educators who are often pigeonholed into roles as disciplinarians or diversity gurus, while their roles as intellectual leaders and subject matter experts often go unrecognized. William Hayes, one of the group's board members, said, "Putting a black man in the front of a classroom does a lot to shift the narrative about how young children perceive black men in this country" (Hanford, 2017, n.p.).

One key insight we draw from research on antiracist education is that schools or individual teachers cannot do the work on their own. When attempting to train teachers to reflect on race more critically, the help of outside organizations or groups can become particularly important. Milner (2008) describes how teacher preparation may borrow lessons from social movements and break away from traditional institutions in order to build a base of teachers committed to racial justice. Community-based or union-affiliated groups across the country are showing that such partnerships can bring new levels of understanding on issues related to race and class to teachers so that they can function as allies to the children and communities they serve.

For example, the New York Collective of Radical Educators (NYCoRE), Educolor, and Philadelphia's Caucus of Working Educators are helping to make racial justice essential to the profession. In Seattle, a union-affiliated group successfully organized a Black Lives Matter at School Day in 2016 with a series of events that highlighted anti-Black racism. Leaders of the group reflected that their accomplishment was possible because they were able to take advantage of the political space created by the broader social movement (Au & Hagopian, 2017). Following Seattle's grassroots work, other teacher groups in other cities adapted a Black Lives Matter at School Week that translated the movement into a series of educational activities centering on racial justice issues. Far from the lonely work of isolated educators, these examples demonstrate how decentering Whiteness and advocating for racial justice in the teaching profession will require broader collaborative and community-based support.

Finally, at Ball State University in Indiana, student-teachers are paired with a community mentor in the historic Black community. Over the course of the semester the community mentor educates the student-teacher about the history and culture of the community, and the needs of its children. When student-teachers in this program were asked what was hardest about the experience, several reported that leaving would be hardest because of the strong bonds formed. One student-teacher explained it like this: "I'm White and from rural Indiana. I haven't had much contact with Black people before. There's no way that I could teach at a school serving Black children in Gary or Indianapolis without an experience like this." Programs like this demonstrate how White teachers who choose to serve in communities of color can learn to operate as genuine antiracist allies.

WITHOUT HONORS: RACE AND THE MECHANISMS OF TRACKING

Dr. Martin Luther King Jr. once remarked that it was "appalling" that the most segregated hour in America was on Sunday morning, as churchgoers generally attended separate services. A similar comment could be made about many schools today. More often than not, our students learn in heavily segregated classrooms, and in particular those in AP or honors classes. In this final section, we build on the various paradigms discussed above in examining the case of AP and honors enrollment to better grasp the complex racial dynamics at play in schools and how students are granted access to these important educational opportunities.

AP and honors courses are considered an important stepping stone in college readiness and provide rigorous coursework for students to experience before they graduate. Students of color, namely Black, Latinx, and Native students, who are deemed AP-ready participate significantly less in those courses than their peers (College Board, 2014). What explains this predicament? Research shows that even within relatively diverse schools, formal and informal mechanisms of racialized tracking often sort students into higher- or lower-performing groups, effectively denying many students of color access to these courses. One reason lies in what Ochoa (2013) terms "academic profiling." The concept refers to the way in which educators may sort or guide students toward schooling trajectories that appear to match their racial background and supposed ability level. Sorting students into ability groups can also lead to students internalizing racist messages. In her ethnographic observations of tracking within schools, Tyson (2011) observed the racialized language used in discourse about achievement. In addition to being labeled "advanced" or "gifted," Tyson finds that AP and honors classes are often referred to as "White classes" by Black students. This characterization, she finds, has little to do with their own aspirations or rejection of rigorous coursework. Rather, the school becomes organized in such a way that it marginalizes them from those spaces; they know that such classes are simply not intended for them.

Similarly, we have observed students in various schools who are socialized to understand official terminology of their standardized testing results. Through pullouts and focused tutoring that group them according to their testing results, they come to identify themselves with their performance bracket ("I'm below basic" or "I'm a 2"). In one observation of a special education class, a 4th-grader told his teacher who was trying to get him to read a book: "I can't read that. Haven't you seen my IEP?" As a result, deficits are not exhibited by students of color who reject rigorous courses, but are thrusted on to them by a system that perpetuates and maintains racial inequality. For this reason, in order to advance racial equity in schools, educators must be willing to take on the systems and beliefs that perpetuate and maintain racial inequality.

The 2018 documentary series *America to Me* captured a year in a diverse high school in a Chicago-area town. The film displayed the hand-wringing of the predominately White teaching staff over equity concerns with their largely segregated honors and AP classes. In an interview about the documentary, acclaimed director Steve James shared that AP teachers at Oak Park River Forest High School did not want his crew to follow Black students into their classrooms over their fears that viewers would see their overwhelmingly White peers (Adams, 2018). A self-proclaimed liberal town, the series recounts how local residents largely welcomed diversifying neighborhoods and student body generations ago. However, as the Black population of Oak Park grew, White parents advocated for a tracking system in the school that would allow for a form of White flight, leaving Black students in general education courses. As some White parents and staff say in the film, they think detracking is good in theory, but that it could come at a cost to their own children. Meanwhile, Black parents also understand that unless teachers truly embrace teaching their children, detracking is unlikely to alter academic outcomes (Rubin & Noguera, 2004). A critical perspective allows us to peek below the liberal veneer of schools like Oak Park (or Berkeley High School, as described in *City Schools*, 2003) to see the less overt forms of stratification that have managed to situate diverse students within a racialized hierarchy of opportunity within the very same school.

CONCLUSION

In this chapter we have laid out the constellation of forces that ensure race continues to be the foundation for educational inequality in urban schools and in America generally. A similar constellation of forces will be needed to replace that foundation with one rooted in racial justice. Unfortunately, it is not work that follows a simple formula or sequence of steps. Rather, it is a battle that must be waged along many fronts, one strengthened by locating and honoring its many intersections. Color-evasive policy must be replaced by antiracist policy. A focus on student behavior that emphasizes individual character instead of student wellness and does not contend with race or trauma will not have the desired impacts. Referencing culture in terms of student or family deficits must be replaced by commitments to sustaining culture and creating school environments where diverse students can thrive. Educational practices or policies that do not critically examine their relation to the interests of the dominant society will be incapable of presenting alternatives that break from the status quo. Finally, as we find our place within these varied struggles, we cannot allow ourselves to be isolated. The same color line that has for so long excluded, dismissed, and disenfranchised our communities is also one that must draw us together to work for change.

REFERENCES

Adams, S. (2018, October 30). Steve James on how Oak Park has reacted to *America to Me*. *Slate*. Retrieved from slate.com/culture/2018/10/steve-james-interview-america-to-me-starz-documentary-series.html

Akom, A., Shah, A., Nakai, A., & Cruz, T. (2016). Youth participatory action research (YPAR) 2.0: How technological innovation and digital organizing sparked a food revolution in East Oakland. *International Journal of Qualitative Studies in Education, 29*(10), 1287–1307.

Albrecht, S. F., Skiba, R. J., Losen, D. J., Chung, C.-G., & Middelberg, L. (2012). Federal policy on disproportionality in special education: Is it moving us forward? *Journal of Disability Policy Studies, 23*(1), 14–25.

Ali, A. (2013). A threat enfleshed: Muslim college students situate their identities amidst portrayals of Muslim violence and terror. *International Journal of Qualitative Studies in Education, 27*(10), 1243–1261.

Au, W. (2013). Hiding behind high-stakes testing: Meritocracy, objectivity and inequality in U.S. education. *The International Education Journal: Comparative Perspectives, 12*(2), 7–19.

Au, W., & Hagopian, J. (2017). How one elementary school sparked a citywide movement to make Black students' lives matter. *Rethinking Schools, 32*(1). Retrieved from www.rethinkingschools.org/articles/how-one-elementary-school-sparked-a-citywide-movement-to-make-black-students-lives-matter

Bailey, A. L. & Butler, F. A. (2007). A conceptual framework of academic English language for broad application to education. In A Bailey (Ed.), *The language demands of school: Putting English to the test*. Yale University Press.

Barile, N. (2015). Is "getting gritty" the answer? *Educational Horizons, 93*(2), 8–9.

Barker, C., Francois, A., Goodman, R., & Hussain, E. (2012). Unshared bounty: How structural racism contributes to the creation and persistence of food deserts. https://digitalcommons.nyls.edu/racial_justice_project/3/

Blagg, K., Chingos, M., Corcoran, S., Cordes, S., Cowen, J., Denice, P., Gross, B., . . . et al. (2018). *The road to school: How far students travel to school in the choice-rich cities of Denver, Detroit, New Orleans, New York City, and Washington, DC*. Urban Institute, Washington DC.

Bonilla-Silva, E. (1997). Rethinking racism: Toward a structural interpretation. *American Sociological Review, 62*(3), 465–480.

Bonilla-Silva, E. (2017). *Racism without racists: Color-blind racism and the persistence of racial injustice in the United States* (15th ed.). Rowman & Littlefield.

Boser, U. (2014). *Teacher diversity revisited: A new state-by-state analysis*. Center for American Progress.

Bowles, S., & Gintis, H. (1976). *Schooling in capitalist America: Educational reform and the contradictions of economic life*. Basic Books.

Boykin, A. W., & Noguera, P. (2011). *Creating the opportunity to learn: Moving from research to practice to close the achievement gap*. ASCD.

Cardichon, J., Darling-Hammond, L., Yang, M., Scott, C., Shields, P. M., & Burns, D. (2020). *Inequitable opportunity to learn: Student access to certified and experienced teachers*. Learning Policy Institute.

Carrillo, J. (2010). Teaching that breaks your heart: Reflections on the soul wounds of a first-year Latina teacher. *Harvard Educational Review, 80*(1), 74–81.

Cherng, H. Y. (2016). Is all classroom conduct equal? Teacher contact with parents of racial/ethnic minority and immigrant adolescents. *Teachers College Record, 118*(11), 1–36.

Cherng, H. Y., & Halpin, P. (2016). The importance of minority teachers: Student perceptions of minority versus White teachers. *Educational Researcher, 45*(7), 407–420.

Chetty, R., Hendren, N., Kline, P., & Saez, E. (2014). Where is the land of opportunity? The geography of intergenerational mobility in the United States. *The Quarterly Journal of Economics, 129*(4), 1553–1623.

Chua, A., & Rubenfeld, J. (2015). *The triple package: How three unlikely traits explain the rise and fall of cultural groups in America*. Penguin Books.

Clinton, W. (1996). State of the Union address. Retrieved from clintonwhitehouse2.archives.gov/WH/New/other/sotu.html

Coates, T. N. (2009). *The beautiful struggle: A memoir*. Spiegel & Grau.

Cohen, P. (2010, October 17). "Culture of poverty" makes a comeback. *New York Times*.

College Board. (2014). *The 10th annual AP report to the nation*. College Board.

Comas-Díaz, L., Hall, G. N., & Neville, H. A. (2019). Racial trauma: Theory, research, and healing: Introduction to the special issue. *American Psychologist, 74*(1), 1–5. Retrieved from dx.doi.org/10.1037/amp0000442

Cook, V. (2002). *Portraits of the L2 user*. Multilingual Matters.

Crosby, S. D., Day, A., Baroni, B. A., & Somers, C. (2019). Examining trauma-informed teaching and the trauma symptomatology of court-involved girls. *The Urban Review, 51*(4), 582–598.

Cullen, J. H. (2003). *Barbara McClintlock: Geneticist.* Chelsea House.

Cummins, J. (2001). Empowering minority students: A framework for intervention. *Harvard Educational Review, 71*(4), 649–676.

Delpit, L. (2006). *Other people's children: Cultural conflict in the classroom.* New Press.

DiAngelo, R. (2018). *White fragility: Why it's so hard for white people to talk about racism.* Beacon Press.

Du Bois, W. E. B. (1903). *The souls of Black folk: Essays and sketches.* A. C. McClurg.

Duckworth, A. (2016). *Grit: The power of passion and perseverance.* Scribner.

Dweck, C. (2008). *Mindset: The new psychology of success.* Ballantine.

The Education Consortium for Research and Evaluation. (2014). *Community and family engagement in DC public education: Officials' reports and stakeholders' perceptions.* George Washington University Press.

Egalite, A. J., Kisida, B., & Winters, M. A. (2015). Representation in the classroom: The effect of own-race teachers on student achievement. *Economics of Education Review, 45,* 44–52.

Fergus, E. (2016). *Solving disproportionality and achieving equity: A leader's guide to using data to change hearts and minds.* Corwin Press.

Filardo, M. (2016). *State of our schools: America's K–12 facilities.* 21st Century School Fund.

Firth, A., & Wagner, J. (2007). Second/foreign language learning as a social accomplishment: Elaborations on a reconceptualized SLA. *Modern Language Journal (Focus Issue), 91,* 800–819.

Flores, N. (2016). A tale of two visions: Hegemonic Whiteness and bilingual education. *Educational Policy, 30*(1), 13–38. Retrieved from doi.org/10.1177/0895904815616482

Fordham, S., & Ogbu, J. (1986). Black students' school success: Coping with the "burden of 'acting White.'" *Urban Review, 18,* 176–206.

Forman, J. (2017). *Locking up our own: Crime and punishment in Black America.* Farrar, Straus and Giroux.

Freidus, A. (2016). "A great school benefits us all": Advantaged parents and the gentrification of an urban public school. *Urban Education.* https://doi.org/10.1177/0042085916636656

Freire, P. (2014). *Pedagogy of the oppressed: 30th anniversary edition.* Bloomsbury Academic.

Gagnon, D., & Mattingly, M. (2016). *Most U.S. school districts have low access to school counselors.* National Issue Brief #108. Carsey Research, University of New Hampshire.

Garver, R., & Noguera, P. (2014). Supported and unsafe: The impact of educational structures for immigrant students on school safety. *Youth Violence and Juvenile Justice, 13*(4), 323–344.

Gee, G. C., & Ford, C. L. (2011). Structural racism and health inequities: Old issues, new directions. *Du Bois Review: Social Science Research on Race, 8*(1), 115–132.

Ghitelman, S. (2014). Hari Kondabolu walks in a bar. Retrieved from https://www.bklynr.com/hari-kondabolu-walks-into-a-bar/

Golann, J., & Torres, A. C. (2018). Do no-excuses disciplinary practices promote success? *Journal of Urban Affairs.* doi:10.1080/07352166.2018.1427506

Gould, L. F., Dariotis, J. K., Mendelson, T., & Greenberg, M. T. (2012). A school-based mindfulness intervention for urban youth: Exploring moderators of intervention effects. *Journal of Community Psychology, 40*, 968–982. doi:10.1002/jcop.21505

Gregory, A., & Fergus, E. (2017). Social and emotional learning and equity in school discipline. *The Future of Children, 27*(1), 117–136.

Hammond, Z. (2014). *Culturally responsive teaching and the brain: Promoting authentic engagement and rigor among culturally and linguistically diverse students.* Corwin Press.

Han, Z., & Odlin, T. (2006). Introduction. In Z. Han & T. Odlin (Eds.), *Studies of fossilization in second language acquisition* (pp. 1–20). Multilingual Matters.

Hanford, E. (2017). A fellowship of the few: Black male teachers in America's classrooms are in short supply. *APM Reports.* Retrieved from www.apmreports.org/story/2017/08/28/black-male-teachers-fellowship

Hannah-Jones, N. (2019, July 12). It was never about busing. *New York Times.* Retrieved from www.nytimes.com/2019/07/12/opinion/sunday/it-was-never-about-busing.html

Hardy, K. V. (2013). Healing the hidden wounds of racial trauma. *Reclaiming Children and Youth, 22*(1), 24–28.

Harris, C. (2008, November 3). Barack Obama weighs in on sagging-pants ordinances: "Brothers should pull up their pants." *MTV News.* Retrieved from www.mtv.com/news/1598462/barack-obama-weighs-in-on-sagging-pants-ordinances-brothers-should-pull-up-their-pants

Hartman, A. (2015). *A war for the soul of America: A history of the culture wars.* University of Chicago Press.

Howard, G. (2016). *We can't teach what we don't know: White teachers, multicultural schools.* (3rd ed.). Teachers College Press.

Howard, T. C. (2003). Culturally relevant pedagogy: Ingredients for critical teacher reflection. *Theory into Practice, 42*(3), 195–202.

Kawai, Y. (2005). Stereotyping Asian Americans: The dialectic of the model minority and the yellow peril. *The Howard Journal of Communications, 16*(2), 109–130.

Khan, S. (2011). *Privilege: The making of an adolescent elite at St. Paul's School.* Princeton University Press.

Khmer Girls in Action. (2011). *Step into Long Beach: Exposing how Cambodian American youth are under resourced, over policed and fighting back for their wellness.* Khmer Girls in Action.

Kim, C. J. (1999). The racial triangulation of Asian Americans. *Politics and Society, 27*, 105–138.

Kohli, R. (2018). Behind school doors: The impact of hostile racial climates on urban teachers of color. *Urban Education, 53*(3), 307, 333. Retrieved from doi.org/10.1177/0042085916636653

Korver-Glenn, E. (2018). Compounding inequalities: How racial stereotypes and discrimination accumulate across the stages of housing exchange. *American Sociological Review, 83*(4), 627–656.

Kuscera, J., & Orfield, G. (2014). *New York state's extreme school segregation inequality: Inaction and a damaged future.* Civil Rights Project, University of California–Los Angeles.

Kumashiro, K. (2004). *Against common sense: Teaching and learning toward social justice.* Routledge.

Kupchik, A. (2010). *Homeroom security: School discipline in an age of fear.* New York University Press.

Ladson-Billings, G. (1998). Just what is critical race theory and what's it doing in a nice field like education? *International Journal of Qualitative Studies in Education, 11*(1), 7–24.

Ladson-Billings, G., & Tate, W., IV. (1995). Toward a critical race theory of education. *Teachers College Record, 97*(1), 47–68.

Lee, J. (2017). *Georgia's higher education goals hurt by undocumented student policies.* Georgia Budget and Policy Institute. Retrieved from gbpi.org/2017/georgias-higher-education-goals-hurt-by-undocumented-student-policies

Lomawaima, K. T. (2018). Indian boarding schools, before and after: A personal introduction. *Journal of American Indian Education, 57*(1), 11–21.

Macleod, J. (2009). *Ain't no makin' it: Aspirations and attainment in a low-income neighborhood.* Westview Press.

Madden, M. (2018, January 18). Baltimore schools' heating crisis a "day of reckoning" for the city and state. *NPR.* Retrieved from www.npr.org/2018/01/18/578731411/baltimore-schools-heating-crisis-a-day-of-reckoning-for-the-city-and-state

Marsh, L. T. S., & Noguera, P. A. (2017). Beyond stigma and stereotypes: An ethnographic study on the effects of school-imposed labeling on Black males in an urban charter school. *The Urban Review, 50,* 447–477.

Massey, D., & Denton, N. (1998). *American apartheid: Segregation and the making of the underclass.* Harvard University Press.

Matias, C. (2016). "Why do you make me hate myself?" Re-teaching Whiteness, abuse, and love in urban teacher education. *Teaching Education, 27*(2), 194–211.

McCarty, T., & Lee, T. (2014). Critical culturally sustaining/revitalizing pedagogy and indigenous education sovereignty. *Harvard Educational Review, 84*(1), 101–124.

McWhorter, J. (2000). *Losing the race: Self-sabotage in Black America.* Free Press.

Melnick, H., Cook-Harvey, C. M., & Darling-Hammond, L. (2017). *Encouraging social and emotional learning in the context of new accountability.* Learning Policy Institute.

Milner, H. R. (2008). Critical race theory and interest convergence as analytic tools in teacher education policies and practices. *Journal of Teacher Education, 59*(4), 332–346.

Milner, H. R., & Howard, T. (2013). Counter-narrative as method: Race, policy and research for teacher education. *Race Ethnicity and Education, 16*(4), 536–561.

Morning, A. (2011). *The nature of race: How scientists think and teach about human difference.* University of California Press.

National Child Traumatic Stress Network, Justice Consortium, Schools Committee, and Culture Consortium. (2017). *Addressing race and trauma in the classroom: A resource for educators.* National Center for Child Traumatic Stress.

New York City Department of Education. (2018). *D15 diversity plan: Final report.* New York City Department of Education.

Nguyen, B. M. D., Noguera, P., Adkins, N., & Teranishi, R. T. (2019). Ethnic discipline gap: Unseen dimensions of racial disproportionality in school discipline. *American Educational Research Journal, 56*(5), 1973–2003.

Oberg, C. N., Colianni, S., & King-Schultz, L. (2016). Child health disparities in the 21st century. *Current problems in pediatric and adolescent health care, 46*(9), 291–312.

Ochoa, G. (2013). *Academic profiling: Latinos, Asian Americans, and the achievement gap.* University of Minnesota Press.

Ogbu, J. U. (2004). Collective identity and the burden of "acting White" in Black history, community, and education. *The Urban Review, 36,* 1–35.

Omi, M., & Winant, H. (2015). *Racial formation in the United States* (3rd ed.). Routledge.

Paris, D., & Alim, S. (2014). What are we seeking to sustain through culturally sustaining pedagogy? A loving critique forward. *Harvard Educational Review, 84*(1), 85–100.

Patrick, K., Socol, A., & Morgan, I. (2020). *Inequities in advanced coursework: What's driving them and what leaders can do.* Education Trust.

Patterson, O., & Fosse, E. (2015). *The cultural matrix: Understanding Black youth.* Harvard University Press.

Picower, B. (2009): The unexamined Whiteness of teaching: How White teachers maintain and enact dominant racial ideologies. *Race Ethnicity and Education, 12*(2), 197–215.

Pope, D. (2001). *Doing school: How we are creating a generation of stressed out, materialistic, and miseducated students.* Yale University Press.

Posey-Maddox, L. (2013). Professionalizing the PTO: Race, class, and shifting norms of parental engagement in a city public school. *American Journal of Education, 119*(2), 235–260.

Putman, H., Hansen, M., Walsh, K., & Quintero, D. (2016). *High hopes and harsh realities: The real challenges to building a diverse workforce.* Brookings Institute.

Putnam, R. (2015). *Our kids: The American dream in crisis.* Simon & Schuster.

Raver, C., & Blair, C. (2016). Neuroscientific insights: Attention, working memory, and inhibitory control. *Future of Children, 26*(2), 95–118.

Rios, V. (2011). *Punished: Policing the lives of Black and Latino boys.* New York University Press.

Rosiek, J., & Kinslow, K. (2016). *Resegregation as curriculum: The meaning of the new racial segregation in U.S. Public Schools.* Routledge.

Rubin, B. C., & Noguera, P. A. (2004). Tracking detracking: Sorting through the dilemmas and possibilities of detracking in practice. *Equity & Excellence in Education, 37*(1), 92–101.

Scarcella, R. (2003). *Academic English: A conceptual framework* (Technical Report No. 2003-1). Santa Barbara, CA: Linguistic Minority Research Institute.

Schultz, B. (2018). *Spectacular things happen along the way: Lessons from an urban classroom* (10th ed.). Teachers College Press.

Shedd, C. (2015). *Unequal city: Race, schools, and perceptions of injustice.* Russell Sage Foundation.

Shonkoff, S. B., Morello-Frosch, R., Pastor, M., & Sadd, J. (2011). The climate gap: Environmental health and equity implications of climate change and mitigation policies in California—a review of the literature. *Climatic Change, 109*(1), 485–503.

Sleeter, C. E. (2017). Critical race theory and the whiteness of teacher education. *Urban Education, 52*(2), 155–169.

Smith, W. A., Allen, W. R., & Danley, L. L. (2007). "Assume the position . . . you fit the description": Campus racial climate and the psychoeducational experiences and racial battle fatigue among African American male college students. *American Behavioral Scientist, 51*(4), 551–578.

Sojourner, R. J. (2012). *The rebirth and retooling of character education in America* (pp. 2–16). CEP and McGraw-Hill Research Foundation.

Solomon, J., & Rhodes, N. (1995). *Conceptualizing academic language* (Research Report No. 15). National Center for Research on Education, Diversity and Excellence.

Soltis, L. (2015). From freedom schools to Freedom University: Liberatory education, interracial and intergenerational dialogue, and the undocumented student movement in the US South. *Souls, 17*(1–2), 20–53.

Sotero, M. (2006). A conceptual model of historical trauma: Implications for public health practice and research. *Journal of Health Disparities Research and Practice, 1*(1), 93–108.

Steele, S. (1990). *The content of our character: A new vision of race in America.* St. Martin's Press.

Stovall, D. (2005). Critical race theory as educational protest: Power and praxis. *Counterpoints, 237*, 197–211.

Sullivan, A. L., & Bal, A. (2013). Disproportionality in special education: Effects of individual and school variables on disability risk. *Exceptional Children, 79*(4), 475–494.

Syeed, E. (2018). There goes the PTA: Building parent identity, relationships, and power in gentrifying schools. *Equity & Excellence in Education, 51*(3–4), 284–300.

Tefera, A., Powers, J., & Fischman, G. (2018). Intersectionality in education: A conceptual aspiration and research imperative. *Review of Research in Education, 42*, vii–xvii.

Tough, P. (2012). *How children succeed: Grit, curiosity, and the hidden power of character.* Houghton Mifflin Harcourt.

Tuck, E. (2009). Suspending damages: A letter to communities. *Harvard Educational Review, 79*(5), 409–427.

Tyack, D. (1974). *The one best system: A history of American urban education.* Harvard University Press.

Tyson, K. (2011). *Integration interrupted: Tracking, Black students, and acting White after Brown.* Oxford University Press.

U.S. Department of Education. (2016). *The state of racial diversity in the educator workforce.* Retrieved from www2.ed.gov/rschstat/eval/highered/racial-diversity/state-racial-diversityworkforce.pdf

Voulgarides, C. K. (2018). *Does compliance matter in special education? IDEA and the hidden inequities of practice.* Teachers College Press.

Voulgarides, C., Fergus, E., & King Thorius, K. A. (2017). Pursuing equity: Disproportionality in special education and the reframing of technical solutions to address systemic inequities. *Review of Research in Education, 41*(1), 61–87.

Wallace, M., Crear-Perry, J., Richardson, L., Tarver, M., & Theall, K. (2017). Separate and unequal: Structural racism and infant mortality in the US. *Health & Place, 45*, 140–144.

Watz, M. (2011). An historical analysis of character education. *Journal of Inquiry and Action in Education, 4*(2), 34–53.

Weingarten, R. (2015). Moving past punishment toward support. *American Educator, 39*(1), 1.

Wilson, W. (2012). *The truly disadvantaged: The inner city, the underclass, and public policy* (2nd ed.). University of Chicago Press.

Wu, J. (2019, March 20). I'm an Asian American graduate of Brooklyn Tech. Please don't use me as a wedge in your education lawsuit. *Chalkbeat.* Retrieved from chalkbeat.org/posts/ny/2019/03/20/im-an-asian-american-graduate-of-brooklyn-tech-please-dont-use-me-as-a-wedge-in-your-education-lawsuit

Yosso, T. (2005). Whose culture has capital? A critical race theory discussion of community cultural wealth. *Race Ethnicity and Education, 8*(1), pp. 69–91.

CHAPTER 12

Embracing a Structural View of Poverty and Education

Ditching Deficit Ideology and Quitting Grit

Paul C. Gorski

Take a moment to reflect on this question: Why on average do students experiencing poverty not do as well in school as their wealthier peers? Why, despite all the educator workshops on the mindsets of poverty, the brains of low-income youth, grit, and growth mindset do educational outcome disparities persist across socioeconomic status? What comes to mind first? Make a mental note of it.

POVERTY ATTRIBUTION AND THE IMPORTANCE OF IDEOLOGY

Conversations about the "achievement gap" usually are thick with references to parent involvement. These conversations tend to revolve around bemoaning this fact: Parents from families experiencing poverty are less likely than their wealthier peers to participate in family involvement opportunities that require them to visit their children's schools (Noel et al., 2013). Although research has shown that the same parents may be just as likely to be engaged in their children's learning at home (Williams & Sánchez, 2012), their lower rate of at-school involvement is presumed to be one of the core causes, if not *the* core cause, of educational outcome disparities (Barton, 2004; Bridges, 2013). I often hear even from otherwise conscientious teachers how *those parents* are the problem.

There is no debate here. Parents from families experiencing poverty do not visit their children's schools for family involvement opportunities at the same rate as wealthier parents. It has been measured a hundred different ways. It is a fact.

A lot of people and entire organizations are working to change the disparity. The trouble is, many are trying to change it based on misunderstandings about why it exists. They are asking why *those parents* don't value education, why *those families* are unmotivated, why they lack grit, why their mindsets are out of whack. Usually these people and organizations are short on equity literacy. As a result, often they do more harm than good.

If we want to avoid the same fate, we need to ask a different set of questions. We need to know, first of all, that there is a different set of questions to ask. From a policy and practice intervention perspective, we might start by asking ourselves how we should interpret the family involvement disparity. How do our existing belief systems, our existing *ideologies*, influence what we define as the problem to be resolved? After all, how we interpret the disparity drives our understanding of the problem. Our understanding of the problem drives the solutions we are capable of imagining for responding to and redressing the problem. Our choices of solutions determine the extent to which the strategies and initiatives we adopt threaten the existence of inequity or threaten the possibility of equity (Gorski, 2016). It all tracks back to ideology.

This lands us in a tough spot in the education world, where many of us seem desperate for *five easy strategies for eliminating the achievement gap* and at times reluctant to dig into the ideological muck. Too many of us see practical strategies as *something I can use in my classroom*, but don't see deep understandings of equity issues the same way. Often I'm invited to schools or school districts in hopes that I will provide a list of practical solutions for outcome disparities without delving into the difficult ideological work—into the biases and prejudices and socializations that hamper our abilities to be a threat to inequities. It doesn't work. It can't work. It is impossible to develop meaningful strategies through misinterpretations of the problems we're trying to solve. No list of practical strategies will make us effective educators for students experiencing poverty if our view of them and their families is muddied by the ideological roots of inequity. There is no path to equity literacy without taking stock of our ideologies and, if necessary, shifting them toward views that will help us recognize, respond to, and redress inequities.

When asked why these disparities in on-site family involvement or test scores or other measures exist—why, indeed, poverty itself exists—people tend to attribute them along a continuum between two big ideological positions. On one end of the continuum are people, including educators and policymakers, who see those experiencing poverty as the agents of their own economic conditions. They adhere to a *deficit ideology* (Gorski, 2008; Sleeter, 2004), believing that poverty itself is a symptom of ethical, dispositional, and even spiritual deficiencies in the individuals and communities experiencing it.

This is the dominant view in the United States (Gans, 1996) and, in my experience working with educators in more than 20 countries spanning five continents, a common view among people everywhere who have not experienced poverty. Its adherents are likely to believe that in-school involvement disparities, like other disparities, reflect these deficiencies in people experiencing poverty. Studies suggest that even among educators, the deficit view is the dominant view (Mulvihill & Swaminathan, 2006; Prins & Schafft, 2009). Its remnants are everywhere in education. We can hear them every time a colleague says, or we catch ourselves thinking, despite decades of research demonstrating otherwise, that people experiencing poverty do not value education, lack role models, or need more grit.

On the other end of the continuum are people who tend to understand poverty and issues like the family involvement disparity as logical and unjust outcomes of economic injustice and inequity. Adherents to a *structural ideology*, they define gaps in in-school family involvement as interrelated with the inequities with which people experiencing poverty contend. So, by recognizing people experiencing poverty as targets, rather than causes, of these unjust conditions, they might understand lower rates of family involvement as a symptom of in-school and out-of-school conditions that limit economically marginalized parents' abilities to participate at the same rates as their wealthier peers. Acknowledgment of these conditions—families' lack of access to transportation, child care, and paid leave, or schools' tendencies to schedule opportunities for in-school involvement in ways that make little sense for people who often work evenings—is suppressed by the deficit view. The structural view brings them into the light.

To be clear, deficit and structural ideology are at the far ends of a long continuum of ideological positions. They are not a simple binary. Still, I generally can predict the extent to which a school's policies and initiatives related to poverty and educational disparities reflect a deficit or structural view by asking whoever's in charge a single question: *Why, on average, do parents from families experiencing poverty not attend opportunities for family involvement at their children's schools with the same frequency as their wealthier peers?* Based on the response to this question, I often know the effectiveness of the school's policies and initiatives that are meant, at least ostensibly, to eradicate educational disparities across socioeconomic status. This is why, in my view, any evaluation of a school's commitment to equity begins not with an accounting of this or that policy or initiative, but rather with an accounting of the ideological positions of the leadership and staff—the views that underlie the policies and practices those schools are likely to adopt.

It also is why if we want to attend to equity, we must attend to ideology. No set of curricular or pedagogical strategies can turn a classroom led by a teacher with a deficit view of families experiencing poverty into an equitable learning space for those families (Gorski, 2013; Robinson, 2007).

THE DANGERS OF DEFICIT IDEOLOGY

As described earlier, deficit ideology is rooted in the belief that poverty is the natural result of ethical, intellectual, spiritual, and other shortcomings in people who are experiencing it. Adherents to deficit ideology point to educational outcome disparities—differences in test scores or graduation rates, for example—as evidence of these shortcomings (Sleeter, 2004; Valencia, 2009). Low rates of in-school family involvement among parents experiencing poverty or higher relative rates of school absences among students experiencing poverty are interpreted, in their view, as evidence that people experiencing poverty do not value their children's education. People experiencing poverty are deemed the problem. Their attitudes, behaviors, cultures, and mindsets block their potential for success. Deficit ideology is a blame-the-victim mentality.

Sometimes these deficit ascriptions are explicit. Some of the most popular teacher development models related to poverty and education associate a variety of negative attributes with people experiencing poverty. They might paint people experiencing poverty as ineffective communicators, promiscuous, violent, criminally oriented, addiction-prone, and spiritually underdeveloped. Some state explicitly, against decades of research to the contrary, that people experiencing poverty don't value education the way their wealthier peers do (Payne, 2005). We especially should be suspicious of frameworks or approaches that suggest people experiencing poverty share a singular and predictable culture or mindset. As it turns out, economically marginalized people are just as diverse as any other group defined around a single identity. Unfortunately, reality is of little mitigating consequence against ideology. The power and the danger of deficit ideology is that it speaks to popular misperceptions and biases. *People in poverty are broken. Here's how to fix them.*

So we must build institutional change efforts first around ideological shifts. If we believe people experiencing poverty are inherently deficient, no amount of instructional strategies will adequately prepare us to see and respond to the conditions that *actually* underlie educational outcome disparities. As a teacher, can I believe a student's mindset is deficient, that she is lazy, unmotivated, and disinterested in school, *and also* build a positive, high-expectations relationship with her?

Just as importantly, what realities are masked by deficit ideology, and to what are we *not* responding when we respond through a deficit lens? Can we expect to erase outcome disparities most closely related to the barriers and challenges experienced by people experiencing poverty by ignoring those barriers and challenges? Of course not.

Returning to the example of family involvement, the natural inclination of the educator who ascribes to deficit ideology is to believe that parents experiencing poverty show up less often because they do not care, because they do not value education. The logical response to that interpretation is to try to convince people experiencing poverty to care. Across the United States, schools invest time and resources in initiatives designed to solve a problem that does not exist, not only wasting time and resources, but also risking further alienation of the most marginalized families. What we might fail to see are the barriers that make opportunities for family involvement less accessible to families experiencing poverty, so those barriers go unaddressed. Inequity persists.

MEET DEFICIT IDEOLOGY'S COUSIN, GRIT

As advocates for a more sophisticated examination of educational outcome disparities have challenged the deficit view more loudly (Dudley-Marling, 2015; Ullicci & Howard, 2015), an enticing but equally troublesome alternative has emerged. Growing out of the popularity of grit theory (Duckworth et al., 2007), the notion that certain personal attributes enable some people to overcome adversity that could overwhelm others is *grit ideology*. It differs from deficit ideology in one important way: Unlike people who adhere to deficit ideology, who ignore inequities and other barriers altogether and focus instead on mythical "cultures" or "mindsets" of the targets of those barriers, adherents of grit ideology acknowledge the barriers and inequities. However, rather than responding to or redressing those barriers, they want to bolster the grit of economically marginalized students (Gorski, 2016).

The most obvious problem with grit ideology is that of all the combinations of barriers that most impact the educational outcomes of students experiencing poverty—housing instability, food insecurity, inequitable access to high-quality schools, unjust school policies, and others—not a single one is associated even slightly with students' grittiness. As Alfie Kohn (2014) notes, adherents of the grit view are grasping for amoral solutions to inequities, which are moral problems. Anindya Kundu (2014), raising a voice of caution against the fascination with grit, explained how the grit view is a cousin to deficit ideology. "By overemphasizing grit," Kundu wrote, "we tend to attribute a student's underachievement to personality deficits like laziness. This reinforces the idea that individual effort determines outcomes" (p. 80). It also ignores that the most economically marginalized students, who show up for school *despite* the inequities and barriers they experience in and out of school, are already the grittiest students.

Like deficit ideology, grit ideology is no threat to educational outcome disparities. In the end, it represents another attempt to sidestep the core causes of those disparities, requiring students to overcome inequities they never should have to bear.

To be clear, the trouble with grit ideology is not necessarily the notion of grit itself. Perhaps it is worthwhile to consider attributes that bolster resilience in everyone: students, teachers, administrators. The trouble comes when we are so intent on finding a simple solution to complex inequities that we apply concepts like grit through a deficit lens in ways they never were intended to be applied. Suddenly we are talking about how to fix students experiencing poverty with grit and not talking about how to fix the conditions that deny students experiencing poverty the access and opportunity afforded their wealthier peers (or how to fix poverty itself). We reinvest in the old *everything is about hard work* bootstraps mentality that masks the barriers we ought to be destroying. Ariana Stokas (2015) nails it:

> [The need for grit] often arises as a way for the individual to cope with suffering and for society to justify social failure through instructing the individual that their condition—poverty, for instance—is related to an intrinsic deficit. It has the potential to indoctrinate the student, through individual metrics such as standardized tests, with the belief that failure is due to an intrinsic lack rather than to systemic inequality. (p. 522)

Replacing the necessary reckoning with systemic barriers with an initiative to cultivate grit is itself an example of deficit ideology and inequitable practice.

While we're exploring the trouble with grit, we might consider other concepts popularly adopted in the perpetual, impossible quest to find an equity panacea without confronting inequity. *Growth mindset* comes to mind. A growing body of research supports some aspects of growth mindset—the notion that if we deemphasize the role of intelligence and emphasize the role of effort in school achievement, students will see intelligence as more malleable than static. They then will believe they *can* grow and improve, and so they *will* grow and improve (Dweck, 2010). The problem is, no matter what mindset students adopt, they only have the access and opportunity provided for them. Their mindset, whatever it might be, is no solution to gross inequities in access to health care, well-funded schools, and engaging pedagogies (Yeager & Walton, 2011). Their mindsets are not the problem. We need a more transformative approach.

THE HOPE OF STRUCTURAL IDEOLOGY

Educators with a structural ideology understand that educational outcome disparities are the result of structural barriers, the logical if not purposeful implication of unfair distributions of opportunity and access in and out of school (Gorski, 2016; Stokas, 2015). This inequitable access tracks most closely to the symptoms of income and wealth inequality (Berliner, 2013)—to poverty and its implications. Outside schools, a lack of access to adequate financial resources might mean students experiencing poverty are coping with some combination of unstable housing, food insecurity, time poverty, and inadequate or inconsistent health care. They likely have less access than wealthier peers to Internet technology, books, tutoring, formal opportunities to engage with the arts, and other resources and experiences that bolster school achievement (Lineburg & Ratliff, 2015). Often students experiencing poverty are even cheated within their schools out of similar levels of access to experienced teachers, higher-order pedagogies, affirming school cultures, arts education, co-curricular programs, and other resources and opportunities their wealthier peers may take for granted (Battey, 2013; Dudley-Marling, 2015). The barriers and challenges are diverse, but they have this in common: They are wholly unrelated to the mindsets or grittiness of families experiencing poverty.

They have this in common, too: As long as they exist, educational outcome disparities will exist. There simply is no way to erase educational outcome disparities while sidestepping inequities. That's why, as Peter Cookson (2013) argues, "We need to reframe the debate from focusing on individuals and personalities and instead focus on restructuring a broken system" (p. 5). Stepping back a couple paces for a wider view, it even can be instructive to consider the possibility that the system is not broken at all. Perhaps it works exactly as it is designed to work, re-creating existing patterns of opportunity, privilege, and disadvantage. When we consider this view, we are forced to look more deeply at the structural roots of outcome inequalities and how those roots are implanted firmly in "commonsense" policy and "tradition" based practice. It requires serious reckoning.

What makes this reality difficult to manage from an educator point of view is that all these out-of-school inequities appear outside our spheres of influence (Gorski, 2012). In fact, neither teachers nor schools are equipped with the knowledge, resources, or time to resolve the scarcity of living-wage work or affordable housing—not in the immediate term, at least. This, in part, is what makes deficit and grit ideology so alluring: They allow us to define problems in ways that call for straightforward and practical solutions. *Teach families the value of education. Cultivate grit in students.* With a structural ideology, we recognize big structural conditions we cannot rectify so easily or practically.

The hope of structural ideology is that even if we cannot fully rectify those conditions, equity policy and practice should be *responsive* to them and not punish economically marginalized students for their implications. We can mitigate even the barriers we cannot eliminate. Returning again to the example of family involvement, rather than blaming parents experiencing poverty for lower at-school involvement rates, the educator with a structural ideology steps back and reflects with greater equity literacy. Do we organize opportunities for family involvement in ways that respond to the challenges economically marginalized families face, perhaps a lack of paid leave, difficulty securing transportation, the inability to afford child

care, and the necessity of working multiple jobs? Even if we cannot eliminate these barriers entirely, can we create policy and practice that do not
exacerbate them and might even mitigate them? Perhaps we cannot afford
to buy every family a car and ensure every family has living-wage work. But
we can adjust opportunities for family involvement by taking these barriers
into account: providing transportation, offering on-site child care, becoming
more flexible with scheduling, ensuring each person in the school is trained
to engage with parents respectfully. These moves are within our spheres of
influence.

   This is equity literacy: knowing that equity requires us to ask these
questions and having the will to ask them. Then, with our deeper understandings, equity literacy means shifting policies, practices, and initiatives to
be more equitable. A critical early step in this process is to ditch the deficit
ideology, quit the grit ideology, and cultivate in ourselves and one another
a structural ideology. This is an essential ideological base, positioning us to
be a threat to inequity in our spheres of influence.

AN EXERCISE IN STRUCTURAL FRAMING AND LANGUAGE

The concept *generational poverty* never sat right with me. For a long time
I couldn't quite put my finger on the problem. Then I thought about the
generations of people in my own family who had experienced poverty.
When people say *generational poverty*, the explicit intention is generally
to differentiate between families whose poverty has spanned generations
and families whose poverty is situational: a parent lost a job, a child had a
medical emergency not covered by health insurance, that sort of thing. It can
be an important distinction, but the distinction means something different
through a deficit lens from what it means through a structural lens. The
implicit suggestion of "generational poverty" always seemed to me to be
a deficit suggestion: the idea that poverty is the result of a set of cultures,
behaviors, and attitudes reproduced in families experiencing poverty and
passed down from generation to generation. If I interpret generational poverty in this way, I might be easily allured by initiatives designed to interrupt
the transference of these cultures, behaviors, and attitudes. If we look more
deeply, we see how in a more implicit way the idea that we interrupt poverty
by fixing the cultures, behaviors, and attitudes of families experiencing poverty before they can be passed to the next generation is a central (and awful)
deficit feature of the culture of poverty or mindset of poverty framework.
The language we use in this case lends itself to a deficit view: generational
poverty, culture of poverty, mindset of poverty. It frames poverty as a personal failure, not as a social condition attached to a long list of inequitable
systems and structures, including public education.

What if, instead of talking about generational poverty, we talked about *generational injustice*? How would it change the way we defined, understood, responded to, and redressed the problem? Suddenly we're not looking at poverty as a personal or cultural failure, focusing on how deficient mindsets are passed from generation to generation, but instead examining how policies, practices, and institutions marginalize generation after generation of some families and communities. We're examining structural conditions. We are making ourselves a threat to inequity.

In my teacher education courses I challenge students who talk about generational poverty to practice reconsidering their ideas using *generational injustice* instead. It's an exercise in noticing what happens to our interpretation, problem identification, and solution strategizing when we shift from a deficit view to a structural view.

In the same way, when I hear participants in one of my workshops talk about the *dropout problem*, I suggest an exercise: *Let's try having this conversation again using the concept of* pushouts *instead of* dropouts. If you think this is only semantics, try it with a group of your colleagues. How does looking at disparities in school completion as a *pushout* problem and not a *dropout* problem change the solutions we're capable of imagining?

Achievement gap, opportunity gap: same thing. Framing matters. This simple exercise can help us tone our equity literacy by consciously choosing a structural view and noticing how our understandings shift.

CONCLUSION

If we think of achievement gaps solely in terms of test score disparities, "dropout" rates, or other symptoms of economic injustice, and not as the *opportunity gaps* they actually are, we likely are embracing a deficit or grit view unconducive to equity. If we seek practical instructional strategies but fail to cultivate in ourselves the ideological shifts necessary to recognize and confront structural barriers (even if we cannot eliminate those inequities altogether), we become conveyors of deficit ideology. It is not easy. I have written about the challenges I face attempting to cultivate these shifts in teacher education students and in myself (Gorski, 2012). Despite the difficulties, this is the only way to position ourselves to be a threat to the existence of inequity. We root the deficit view out of ourselves and our spheres of influence.

Note: This chapter is derived in part from an article published in *Journal of Education for Teaching* (Gorski, 2016), 42(4), copyright the Taylor & Francis Group, Informa Group Plc, available online at tandfonline.com. doi: 10.1080/02607476.2016.1215546.

REFERENCES

Barton, P. E. (2004). Why does the gap persist? *Educational Leadership*, 62(3), 8–13.

Battey, D. (2013). "Good" mathematics teaching for students of color and those in poverty: The importance of relational interactions within instruction. *Educational Studies in Mathematics*, 82, 125–144.

Berliner, D. C. (2013). Effects of inequality and poverty vs. teachers and schooling on America's youth. *Teachers College Record*, 115, 1–26.

Bridges, L. (2013). *Make every student count: How collaboration among families, schools, and communities ensures student success*. Scholastic.

Cookson, P. W. (2013). *Class rules: Exposing inequality in American public schools*. Teachers College Press.

Duckworth, A. L., Peterson, C., Matthews, M. D., & Kelly, D. R. (2007). Grit: Perseverance and passion for long-term goals. *Journal of Personality and Social Psychology*, 92(6), 1087–1101.

Dudley-Marling, C. (2015). The resilience of deficit thinking. *Journal of Teaching and Learning*, 10(1), 1–11.

Dweck, C. S. (2010). Even geniuses work hard. *Educational Leadership*, 68(1), 16–20.

Gans, H. J. (1996). *The war against the poor*. Basic Books.

Gorski, P. (2008). The myth of the "culture of poverty." *Educational Leadership*, 65(7), 32–35.

Gorski, P. (2012). Perceiving the problem of poverty and schooling: Deconstructing the class stereotypes that mis-shape education policy and practice. *Equity & Excellence in Education*, 45(2), 302–319.

Gorski, P. (2013). Building a pedagogy of engagement for students in poverty. *Phi Delta Kappan*, 95(1), 48–52.

Gorski, P. (2016). Poverty and the ideological imperative: A call to unhook from deficit and grit ideology and to strive for structural ideology in teacher education. *Journal of Education for Teaching*, 42(4), 378–386.

Kohn, A. (2014). Grit? A skeptical look at the latest educational fad. *Educational Leadership*, 74, 104–108.

Kundu, A. (2014). Grit, overemphasized; Agency, overlooked. *Phi Delta Kappan*, 96, 80.

Lineburg, M. Y., & Ratliff, B. C. (2015). Teaching students in poverty in small and mid-sized urban school districts. *Advances in Educational Administration*, 22, 85–108.

Mulvihill, T. M., & Swaminathan, R. (2006). "I fight poverty. I work!" Examining discourses of poverty and their impact on pre-service teachers. *International Journal of Teaching and Learning in Higher Education*, 18(2), 97–111.

Noel, A., Stark, P., Redford, J., & Zukerberg, A. (2013). *Parent and family involvement in education, from the National Household Education Surveys Program of 2012*. U.S. Department of Education.

Payne, R. K. (2005). *A framework for understanding poverty. aha!* Process.

Prins, E., & Schafft, K. A. (2009). Individual and structural attributions for poverty and persistence in family literacy programs: The resurgence of the culture of poverty. *Teachers College Record*, 111(9), 2280–2310.

Robinson, J. G. (2007). Presence and persistence: Poverty ideology and inner-city teaching. *Urban Review, 39,* 541–565.

Sleeter, C. (2004). Context-conscious portraits and context-blind policy. *Anthropology and Education Quarterly, 35*(1), 132–136.

Stokas, A. G. (2015). A genealogy of grit: Education in the new gilded age. *Educational Theory, 65*(5), 513–528.

Ullicci, K., & Howard, T. (2015). Pathologizing the poor: Implications for preparing teachers to work in high-poverty schools. *Urban Education, 50*(2), 170–193.

Valencia, R. R. (2009). A response to Ruby Payne's claim that the deficit thinking model has no scholarly utility. *Teachers College Record.* https://files.eric.ed.gov/fulltext/EJ883756.pdf

Williams, T. T., & Sánchez, B. (2012). Parental involvement (and uninvolvement) at an inner-city high school. *Urban Education, 47,* 625–652.

Yeager, D. S., & Walton, G. M. (2011). Social-psychological interventions in education: They're not magic. *Review of Educational Research, 81*(2), 267–301.

CHAPTER 13

Organizing for Success

From Inequality to Quality

Linda Darling-Hammond

School should not be mass production. It needs to be loving and close. That is what kids need. You need love to learn.

—A student at Vanguard High School in New York City[1]

Small size means I can do a literature seminar with the bottom 20% of kids in the city. Kids who didn't read are reading books like *Jane Eyre* to write their essays. We can work with them during lunch. You find out who can't read, type, etc. These are the kids who would sit in the back of the room, be in the bathroom, and would deliberately get lost. I know dedicated teachers in big schools who teach 150 kids. They can't do this.

—A teacher at Vanguard High School in New York City

It is possible to develop more expert teachers on a wide scale, as many nations and some states and districts have done, but skillful teachers are only part of the puzzle. For teachers to be highly effective, they need to work in schools that are organized for success—schools that enable them to know and reach their students, teach to worthwhile learning goals, use productive tools and materials, and continually improve their practice.

In addition to ensuring that teachers have the knowledge and skills they need to teach a wide range of students, a growing number of urban schools have abandoned the factory-model assumptions of a century ago and have redesigned school structures to support more intensive learning for both students and teachers, with much stronger results. Many of these schools, serving low-income students of color and new immigrants, have demonstrated that they can graduate more than 80% of their students, most of whom would have failed to graduate from traditional schools, and can send more than 80% to college.[2]

326

These include several hundred new model high schools in New York City that are graduating students at twice the rate of the factory-model warehouses they replaced,[3] and a range of successful new public schools in cities such as Chicago, Oakland, Los Angeles, and San Diego that launched new schools initiatives in the 1990s. Some, like the New Tech High and High Tech High networks of schools launched in California, have organized their work around a project-based, technology-supported curriculum. Others, like the network of International High Schools started in New York City, use what they call an activity-based curriculum designed for English language learners to launch new immigrants on successful paths to college. Career academies around the country have teamed up with local industries to create a hands-on curriculum that prepares students for college and careers. Early College high schools, partnered with universities, are enabling students to take college courses while they are still in high school.

Community school models, like those operated by the Children's Aid Society in Chicago, New York, Portland, and elsewhere, combine high-quality K–12 schooling with vital services such as health care, preschool, and before- and after-school care. The Harlem Children's Zone, launched by Geoffrey Canada, takes this idea to scale in a community-wide initiative. Other elementary models, supported by organizations ranging from the Comer School Development Program to the Basic Schools Program and the Core Knowledge Foundation, have helped to create more coherent curricula and more effective support systems to enhance student learning.

Demonstrating the folly of the recurring curriculum wars, in which polarized advocates have battled over content versus skills and basics versus deep understanding, these schools illustrate how knowledge and skills can be taught well together. They are living proof that strong disciplinary (and interdisciplinary) learning is not at odds with the development of so-called 21st-century skills, such as problem solving, critical and creative thinking, the capacity for independent learning, reflection, and communication. Indeed, as Diane Ravitch has appropriately noted, aside from the uses of new technologies, most of these skills have been central to the definition of a well-educated person for centuries, although they are in higher demand in today's economy.[4]

So, for example, at a Core Knowledge School in Brooklyn, New York, developed around the ideas of E. D. Hirsch, students engage in project-based learning and performance assessments as they study a coherent sequential curriculum that treats English, history and geography, mathematics and science, the art of many civilizations, visual arts, and music. Both organized acquisition of central ideas and opportunities to develop thinking and performance skills are emphasized. As Ravitch described when visiting the school's annual Core Knowledge Fair:

The day's festivities began with the sixth-grade chorus singing Beethoven's "Ode to Joy," followed by Duke Ellington's classic "Take the A Train." . . . Two radiant sixth-grade children declaimed Maya Angelou's poem "On the Pulse of Morning," which she wrote for President Clinton's inauguration. A first-grade group of twenty played violins, bowing out *Twinkle, Twinkle, Little Star* by Mozart. Fifth graders reenacted the writing of the Declaration of Independence and hailed its significance in today's world; another group from the same grade declaimed on the historical injustices that had violated the spirit of Mr. Jefferson's great document. Third graders dramatized the tragedy of Julius Caesar, betrayed by his friends and the Roman mob. . . . The walls of the school overflow with student projects about ancient Greece, ancient Rome, American history, the principles of science, and African American achievements.[5]

Similarly, in the many successful urban schools I have seen and studied, students generally follow a common core curriculum that prepares them for college and for the kind of work they will need to do in a world where thinking and invention matter, and they are challenged to meet high standards embodied in graduation requirements requiring scientific investigations, historical and social science research papers, mathematical problems and models, essays and literary critiques, and oral defenses of their work—the kind of work these same students in most schools would be presumed unable to attempt, much less master.

Some of these are among the more successful charter schools that have been released from state and district regulatory constraints. Most are district-run schools created by innovative teachers and leaders who began to develop new designs as long ago as the 1970s and who mentored new school models into existence in the intervening years. Their strategies have often included creating smaller schools as well as advisory structures, "looping" that keeps groups of students with their teachers for 2 or more years, cooperative, project-based learning, and teaching teams that ensure that students are well known and teachers have opportunities to work together. Many of the successful urban high schools teach a college preparatory curriculum supported by performance assessments that enable students to apply their knowledge and that provide rich information for improving teaching and learning. And they ensure that targeted supports and services are available for students when they are needed. These schools also invariably create many opportunities for developing shared knowledge and commitments among teachers, administrators, parents, and community members.[6]

In this chapter, I discuss how successful urban schools serving low-income students have created conditions for high-quality student and teacher learning by redesigning the school organization, curriculum, instruction, and assessments so that they enable high standards with high supports.

where are we wi thin??

THE NEED FOR MAJOR REDESIGN

Today's expectation that schools will enable *all* students, rather than just a small minority, to learn challenging skills to high levels creates an entirely new mission for schools. Instead of merely "covering the curriculum" or "getting through the book," this new mission requires that schools substantially enrich the intellectual opportunities they offer while meeting the diverse needs of students who bring with them varying talents, interests, learning styles, cultures, predispositions, language backgrounds, family situations, and beliefs about themselves and about what school means for them. This demands not only more skillful teaching but contexts in which students can be well known, in which they experience a coherent curriculum that lets them learn essential concepts in ways that develop strong thinking skills.

Major changes in school organizations and the systems in which they sit are needed to accomplish this. Unfortunately, the bureaucratic school created at the turn of the 20th century was not organized to meet these needs for intellectual development or for individual responsiveness. Most of today's schools were designed when the goal of education was not to educate all students well but to batch process a great many efficiently, selecting and supporting only a few for "thinking work." Strategies for sorting and tracking students were developed to ration the scarce resources of expert teachers and rich curriculum, and to justify the standardization of teaching tasks and procedures.

Teaching work was designed to be routine, with little need for professional skill and judgment, and no built-in structures for developing these abilities. Instead of investing directly in teachers' knowledge, a bureaucracy was constructed to prescribe, manage, and control the work of teachers, deflecting funds from the classroom to a long hierarchy of managers and a bevy of personnel outside the classroom. Texts and tests were designed to support and monitor the transmission of facts and basic skills, with little demand for complex applications. Indeed, the rote learning needed for early 20th-century objectives still predominates in many of today's schools—especially those that serve the children of the poor—reinforced by top-down prescriptions for teaching practice, scripted curriculum packages, standardized tests that focus on low-cognitive-level skills, and continuing underinvestment in teacher knowledge.

A business world maxim holds that "every organization is perfectly structured to get the results that it gets." A corollary is that substantially different results require organizational redesign, not just incentives for staff to try harder within traditional constraints. This lesson was learned by U.S. businesses that saved themselves from extinction in the 1980s by realizing that they needed to restructure from the old bureaucratic, assembly line model to new quality management systems emphasizing problem-solving teams rather than prescriptive hierarchies. In education, however, most initiatives have focused on trying to make the educational system inherited from the early 1900s perform more efficiently, rather than fundamentally rethinking how schools are designed, how systems operate, how teaching and learning are pursued, and what goals for schooling are sought. As David Kearns, the CEO who helped restructure the Xerox Corporation, explained:

> Lockstep, myopic management is still the norm in American education today, just as it was in American business. . . . Our entire way of thinking needs to be replaced. Today's high-tech firm is lean: It has stripped away middle management. It is decentralized, relying on the know-how and professionalism of workers close to the problem. It is innovative in the deployment of personnel, no longer relying on limiting job classifications. It spends heavily on employee education and training. It invests heavily in research.[7]

The effort to create learning organizations in both the business and education sectors has sought to replace the bureaucratic forms of organization dominant throughout the 20th century with new organizational designs that are less rigid and more adaptive, more able to accommodate diversity, and more capable of continuous invention. Efforts to invent 21st-century organizations tend to

- Use incentives and structures that motivate through collaboration rather than coercion
- Build strong relationships and norms rather than relying solely on rules for governing behavior
- Encourage quality by structuring work around whole products or services rather than disconnected piecework (in the case of schools, organizing teams that can take responsibility for children's overall success, not just for stamping them with a lesson and moving them along the assembly line)
- Create information-rich environments that support widespread learning and self-assessment among workers, rather than relying primarily on hierarchical supervision of work routines

Such organizations aim to stimulate greater thoughtfulness and creativity, rather than focusing largely on enforcing compliance with predetermined procedures.[8] Their success, then, depends on the creation of new opportunities for teacher and school learning, new modes of accountability, and new kinds of incentives for continual improvement and problem solving.

Just as businesses that have survived major economic changes have had to restructure their work to obtain significantly better results, schools that have achieved much greater levels of success have restructured staffing patterns, reconceptualized the use of time, reallocated funds, and redesigned curriculum, teaching, and assessment. These changes have been made not only to afford more time for teacher learning and collaboration but also to create settings in which teachers can work much more productively with students toward more ambitious learning goals.

The kinds of changes needed are not a mystery. A number of studies have found that, all else being equal, schools have higher levels of achievement when they create smaller, more personalized units in which teachers plan and work together around shared groups of students and common curriculum.[9] In addition to many case studies of successful schools, research on 820 high schools in the National Education Longitudinal Study (NELS) found that schools that had restructured to personalize education and develop collaborative learning structures produced significantly higher achievement gains that were also more equitably distributed.[10] The schools' practices included

- Creating small units within schools
- Keeping students together over multiple years
- Forming teaching teams that share students and plan together
- Ensuring common planning time for teachers
- Involving staff in schoolwide problem solving
- Involving parents in their children's education
- Fostering cooperative learning

Researchers have discovered that in such "communitarian" schools, students are better known, and faculty develop a more collective perspective about the purposes and strategies for their work.[11]

Intellectual content also matters. For example, a study of more than 2,000 students in 23 restructured schools found higher achievement on intellectually challenging tasks for students who experienced what the researchers termed *authentic pedagogy*—that is, instruction, curriculum, and assessment that requires students to apply their learning in real-world contexts, consider alternatives, use knowledge as disciplinary experts do (e.g., engage in scientific inquiry, historical research, literary analysis, or the writing process), and communicate effectively to audiences beyond the individual teacher.[12] The NELS study noted above also found that students in schools with high levels of *authentic instruction*—instruction focused on active learning calling for higher-order thinking, extended writing, and products that resemble how knowledge is used in the world outside of school—experienced greater achievement gains.[13]

What do these kinds of schools look like and what do they do to create better outcomes for students, especially in high-need communities? In the next section, I describe the common strategies of many such schools, focusing especially on urban secondary schools because they are, in general, the most unsuccessful part of our educational system and the most toxic for low-income and minority students. The historic mission of high schools to select and sort, rather than support and develop, coupled with the inappropriateness of large warehouse settings for students who most need care and connections, leads to enormous temptations to allow or even encourage struggling students to drop out. To overcome these conditions, successful schools have had to return to first principles in designing settings that are more productively focused on teaching and learning.

DESIGNING SCHOOLS FOR TEACHING AND LEARNING

Eduardo Rodriguez had struggled in school all his life. As a special education student, he had managed to progress through to high school reading at only a 5th-grade level, and for a considerable time could not spell his last name. When he was in 10th grade, he attended a chaotic school that was unable to meet his needs: "He wasn't learning, he wasn't reading," his mother explained, adding that he was constantly teased and often drawn into the many fights that occurred. The last straw came when Eduardo was almost stabbed while trying to defend a student who was about to be attacked. His mother decided to pull him out of school that day. She felt at that time that "either they would have killed him in school, or he would have been in prison. They just did not expect anything of him."

Mrs. Rodriguez tried to enroll Eduardo in private school, but he could not pass the entrance requirements. When she found out about New Tech High School in Sacramento and went to visit in 2004, she was impressed with how courteous and articulate the students were. She enrolled her son at New Tech even though it was a 45-minute drive from her home. Mrs. Rodriguez warned the principal and the counselor that her son was unlikely to ask for help or talk to the teachers. However, Eduardo soon developed close relationships with his teachers and his counselor, whom he calls on a regular basis, including during holiday breaks. His mother reports that his reading level has risen six grade levels and is now nearly on par with his current grade level, that he creates products and writes enthusiastically, and has developed close friendships with other students. She voices her astonishment at the change:

> I'm so used to all the years since he was 5 years old, when nothing was expected of him. Here, he's a different person. . . . I never thought that would be possible. I would pay for my son to come here; it's amazing what he's learned. It is expected of him to perform. It's not, "We'll see if you can do it," but, "You can do it and you're going to do it." So he thinks like that now.[14]

At New Tech High School, Eduardo and his classmates use technology to complete complex projects in all of their classes, modeling the expectations of employees in a high-tech economy. Every classroom has a computer for each student, used in the course of each collaborative project, which represents a real-world problem drawing on skills in many domains. In a combined math and physics class, for example, small groups of students are working on the aftermath of a car crash. Students representing each driver and the driver's lawyers have to figure out what happened to cause the cars to crash, which driver was at fault, and how to prepare a defense of their client. Like other projects, this one calls upon their knowledge of physics and mathematics as they evaluate the physical crash and estimate the damage, as well as their skills in analysis, written and oral expression, personal presentation, collaboration, planning, and follow-through.

As a result of regular engagement with these kinds of projects, New Tech students stand out in their self-confidence and their ability to articulate the purpose of their work and its relevance. In addition, in 2007, when we studied the school, state data showed a graduation rate of 96%,[15] with 100% of the predominantly minority, low-income students going on to 2- or 4-year college—more than twice the rate of the state as a whole.[16] Students prepared for this during high school by completing, in addition to their high school courses, at least 12 college credits at the local community college and 40 community service hours, which helped build their independence and sense of responsibility.

In a study I conducted with colleagues at Stanford University and the Justice Matters Institute, New Tech High was one of five California high schools we examined in 2007 that graduated more than 85% of their primarily low-income students of color and sent 80 to 100% of their graduates to college. Two of these were new small schools recently started within school districts: Stanley E. Jordan Construction Tech Academy, a small school in what had become a complex of small schools within the former Kearney High School building in San Diego, and June Jordan School for Equity in San Francisco. Two were independent charters: Animo Leadership High School in Inglewood (Los Angeles) and Leadership High School in San Francisco. New Tech High was started as a dependent charter—part of the Sacramento district, staffed by regular district teachers belonging to the teachers union—but allowed autonomy in budget, curriculum, and hiring.

Despite their different governance arrangements, student populations, and locations, the schools have many design features in common, as I describe below. And, indeed, these schools are genealogical descendents of schools in other parts of the country launched more than a decade earlier, whose designs have since been emulated many times over. Colleagues and I identified very similar features in a set of distinctive new high schools, started in the 1990s in New York City, that also sent 80 to 100% of their predominantly low-income minority and recent immigrant students to college, having graduated them from high school at rates significantly above city averages.[17]

Several hundred new model schools have been created under the terms of six separate chancellors since Chancellor Joe Fernandez issued his first

Request for Proposals to innovators wanting to start new schools in 1989. Indeed, New York City's efforts to rethink schools on a large scale signal the invention of 21st-century school designs in a city that was the prototypic home of the factory model nearly a century ago. These successful school designs later seeded initiatives in Chicago, Milwaukee, Philadelphia, San Diego, Boston, and other major cities.

Launched by teachers and principals who had ideas about how schools could better support high-quality teaching and learning, often working in collaboration with community-based organizations, most of these schools are part of regular school districts, not charters or private schools. Many built on the early successes of models like Central Park East Elementary and Secondary Schools, started by school innovator Deborah Meier, who designed not only a set of schools that she created and ran personally but also 50 schools she helped others launch as part of the New York City Annenberg challenge and dozens more in a later Pilot Schools effort in Boston. These early schools, along with many others, including the Urban Academy, launched by Ann Cook and Herb Mack as a second-chance high school for students who had dropped out of other schools, and the International High School, created for new immigrant students by Eric Nadelstern, were protected from district regulations and political swings by the Alternative Schools Superintendency, a special division created inside the New York City schools during the early 1980s to tend and nurture nontraditional schools.

These "older" schools, which mentored a large group of 50 new schools in the early 1990s, providing both the designs and lead staff for many of them, had established track records of succeeding with students who typically would have failed in traditional New York high schools, regularly graduating 90% of their students and sending 90% or more to college.[18] The first of these birthing projects was the Coalition Campus Schools project, which closed down two of the city's more troubled large high schools— Julia Richman High School in Manhattan and James Monroe High School in the Bronx, each serving about 3,000 students—by not admitting new students while hothousing new schools at other sites. Later, some of the new schools moved into the original buildings with other small schools and social service agencies, while others occupied nearby sites serving students from the original catchment area.

In 1992, the city had 20 such neighborhood high schools, most of which exhibited high rates of academic failure. In that year, Julia Richman had a 4-year graduation rate of 36.9%, and Monroe graduated only 26.9%.[19] By 1998, when my colleagues and I studied the set of new small schools created to serve the students at Julia Richman, their 4-year graduation rate for a comparable population of students had climbed to 73%, and their college-going rate for these graduates was 91%, well above city averages despite the fact that they served a significantly larger number of low-income, minority, and limited English proficient students, special education students receiving resource room services, and students overage for their grade than the city as a whole. Continuing to support students who needed more time, the schools posted a 6-year graduation rate of 85% by 2000.[20]

The Coalition Campus schools project not only started a set of new schools but also transformed the Julia Richman campus—once a violent, graffiti-ridden building patrolled by police and vandalized daily—into a safe, vibrant community school complex. The new Julia Richman Education Complex (JREC) now comprises four high schools, including two of the Coalition Campus Schools (Vanguard and Manhattan International High Schools) and one of the parent schools (the Urban Academy), as well as a performing arts program (Talent Unlimited), a special education program serving autistic junior high school students, and the Ella Baker Elementary School. Also part of JREC are a day care coupled with a Teen Parenting Center, a health center offered by a neighborhood teaching hospital, and a professional development institute that collaborates with universities and the teachers union to provide seminars for teachers across the city. The other schools started by the project are housed in nearby buildings, collectively serving the student population that formerly attended Julia Richman.

This multigenerational approach brings adolescents into daily contact with children and babies, giving them opportunities to set a good example for the young ones, which they feel responsible for living up to. The high schools involve their students in reading to, tutoring, and taking care of the elementary and nursery school students as part of their community service and internships. While individual schools occupy their own floors of the building, schools share an auditorium, art and dance studios, a cafeteria, and the gymnasium where a joint set of JREC sports teams play. The airy, bustling building experiences almost no graffiti or vandalism; it houses a community, rather than a compound.

All but two of the so-called Coalition Campus schools adapted their designs from the model of Central Park East Secondary School (CPESS), a high school of 450 students founded by Deborah Meier in East Harlem in 1985. Teachers in most of the new schools—Vanguard, Landmark, Manhattan Village, and Coalition School for Social Change—decided to work in interdisciplinary grade-level teams responsible for groups of 40 to 80 students to whom they teach a college preparatory, core curriculum framed by a set of "habits of mind." The schools require students to weigh evidence, address multiple perspectives, make connections, speculate on alternatives, and assess the value of the ideas they have studied. In some of the schools, teachers "loop" with their students for 2 years. Class periods are generally 70 minutes or more in length, enabling intensive study and research. In the 11th and 12th grades, the schools developed variations on the portfolios developed at CPESS and the Urban Academy that engage students in performance assessments in each core subject area as a basis for graduation.

Another school—Manhattan International—was designed to serve new immigrant students and followed the model of its mentor school, International High School, which was started in 1985 in Queens, New York. With a population of 100% limited English proficient students, International's collaborative, activity-based instruction—now used in all International high schools in New York and California—supports students in learning English while they are engaged in academic study. Students who speak different native languages are placed in collaborative teams to complete teacher-developed performance tasks that require them to use English to communicate. Seventy-minute periods provide time for intensive project work that is evaluated through performance assessments and exhibitions. Teams of teachers in the core disciplines jointly plan for shared groups of about 75 students to whom they teach a thematic, interdisciplinary curriculum all day long. Teachers problem-solve around the curriculum and the needs of their students constantly. A counselor is also attached to each of these student groups to support everything from personal needs to college counseling. In some of the schools, the teams stay with a group of students for 2 years to promote accountability and student success.

And the schools are successful. Accepting only recent immigrant students who score in the bottom quartile on the English language proficiency test, in 2005, the Internationals network—then eight schools serving students speaking more than 100 different native languages in New York City—graduated 89% of the cohort of students who began in 1998 over the 7-year period tracked by New York City. This compared to only 31% for the same cohort of English language learners citywide. Of these, all were English proficient and 92% were college-bound by the time they graduated.[21]

The Julia Richman approach has since been the model used to replace most of the neighborhood "zoned" high schools in New York, with support from the Gates and Carnegie foundations, among many others, and leverage from subsequent chancellors. By 2009, there were more than 300 new small schools in New York City, begun over the previous 2 decades, and many dozens in other cities. Studies in Boston, Chicago, Philadelphia, and elsewhere have found similar design features for the most successful school models, especially in graduating low-income students of color and sending them to college.[22] These features, shared by elementary and secondary schools alike, include

1. Small size for the school or learning communities within the school
2. Structures that allow for personalization and strong relationships
3. Intellectually challenging and relevant instruction
4. Performance-based assessment
5. Highly competent teachers who collaborate in planning and problem solving

I discuss these features below, illustrating how they operate with examples from the five New York City high schools and five urban California high schools described earlier.[23]

Small School Units

In all of these schools, which typically serve from about 300 to 450 students (although several may be located within a larger building), teachers, students, and parents emphasize the importance of small size to the schools' success. Their comments focus on safety and being known, not surprising since one of the first indicators to improve when small urban schools are created is a sharp increase in safety and decrease in incidence rates when the adults know all of the students in the school well.[24] As a Landmark student commented,

> There is less violence compared to bigger schools. Everyone here knows one another. . . . Bigger schools are louder and crazier. No one will bother you here.

A Vanguard humanities teacher described "the family feeling," arguing:

> You are just not going to fall through the cracks here. You are an important individual. For the first time, [students] are seen as important individuals in the school system. I compare this with my experience in large schools with 35 students in a class, where kids regularly fall through the cracks.

And a parent at New Tech High observed:

> There's a lot more opportunity for the kids to be seen, be heard, and be noticed to participate in just about anything they want.

These experiences underscore evidence accumulated over several decades that suggests that, overall, smaller high schools are associated with greater safety, more positive student attitudes about school, higher levels of student participation and attendance, much lower dropout rates, and—depending on other design features described below—higher achievement.[25] Studies have found that a range of sizes may allow for these benefits, depending on the context and student population. However, schools above about 1,200 students in size are invariably found to be less effective for students, and those in the range of about 300 to 500 appear to be most effective for the lowest-income and traditionally lowest-achieving students. This is especially true when these schools are designed to offer close attachments to caring adults, a common curriculum, and personalized supports for learning.[26]

In analyses of school- and district-level achievement, small schools have been found to reduce the influence of poverty on school and district performance, "disrupting the usual negative relationship between socioeconomic status and student achievement."[27] One study found, for example, that the relationship between smaller school size and achievement is significant when at least 30% of students are low-income and grows ever stronger as the poverty rate increases.[28] At grade nine, the effect of a standard deviation increase in size (about 260 students) in the poorest communities was associated with a loss of just over 0.5 standard deviations in achievement, or about half a year of learning, while there was no effect in the wealthiest communities, where students may need fewer highly personalized supports to succeed.

These findings are particularly noteworthy given that so many failing urban schools still serve 2,000 or more students in organizations that spend enormous amounts of energy and dollars creating a prison-like environment focused on control rather than instruction. Metal detectors, security guards, truant officers, and scores of administrative staff are funded to manage students who are scheduled to see seven or eight different teachers a day (each of whom may see as many as 200 students a day) in 50-minute blocks of time where relationships are nearly impossible to forge. Even in suburban areas, violence such as the shootings at Columbine High School, where two students shot 15 others one day in 1999, and the many other middle and high school shootings that have occurred since then, are generally the result of students being poorly known and isolated from staff and peers, often in large, impersonal school settings.[29]

However, small size alone does not create better education; it merely creates conditions that can, if well used, foster greater attachment and more positive behavior. Any influence of school size on student achievement depends as well on other features of the environment that shape what students have the opportunity to learn—the quality of curriculum and teaching, as well as academic supports.[30]

Structures for Personalization

A key feature in these successful schools—perhaps most striking in contrast to the traditional urban high school—is their degree of personalization. The schools' efforts to ensure that students are well known include the construction of small learning communities; continuous, long-term relationships between adults and students; advisory systems that systematically organize counseling, academic supports, and family connections; and small class sizes and reduced pupil loads for teachers that allow them to care effectively for students.

Advisory Systems. In these high-performing schools, teachers have an advisory group of 15 to 25 students who meet with them several times a week and, in most cases, stay with them for 2 to 4 years. The advisor works closely with the student, the family, and with other teachers to ensure that the academic and personal supports needed for success are available. Advisors meet with parents or family members several times a year to review student work, call home if students are absent or have difficulties—and to celebrate successes—and are available to parents who need to discuss family and student problems and needs. As one teacher noted, "We look out after our advisees in all of their classes. Our conversations are informal, but it gets them back in the groove if they have fallen out."

Students do not have to fall through the cracks to get needed assistance. Support is proactive and built into the central organization of the school. For example, Landmark's advisory groups, which place 13 students with one adult for ongoing academic and personal support, meet five times per week. This teacher's explanation of how advisories work is typical: "We have daily conversations and know how they are doing. We contact parents. The advisor takes major responsibility. We may call in [the principal], but it doesn't get passed to the office to take care of kids' performance. It stays with us."

A community organizer who works closely with the staff at June Jordan School for Equity in San Francisco voiced the same commitment: "When kids are slipping, there's this expectation that teachers grab hold of them and will not let go." This expectation has been well tested. June Jordan was launched when a group of teachers and parents joined with community organizers to convince the school district to open a small school for low-income students of color who were failing at high rates. Located on the southeast side of San Francisco near the highest-poverty neighborhoods, the school provided the local community with its first college-going option, as the city's college prep–oriented high schools are on the other side of the city where affluent residents reside.

Most students, such as James Williams, enter the school many grade levels behind in their basic skills and with personal experience of the neighborhood's high levels of crime and homicide. The advisory system was critical to James's eventual success at June Jordan. Growing up in poverty and moving from one low-income neighborhood to the next, James faced the kind of challenges that lead many young Black men in similar circumstances to drop out of school. His mother was out of work for several years due to health challenges, and struggled to raise a family on her own, often leaving her son to care for his younger sister. James notes that, although he was raised "around drug use and alcoholism, I never got into gang violence or street life. I always knew that I wanted to go to college."

Although James's mother wanted him to attend a "nice high school and go to college," he could not get into any of the college prep high schools in San Francisco, so she enrolled him at June Jordan when it was initially founded. The school combines a college preparatory curriculum organized around social justice issues with highly personalized instruction and a strong advisory system. James notes that all of these supports were important to his success: "All throughout June Jordan I had close relationships with all my advisors. It made me give my trust to people more; there were so many people there to help me and make sure that I do well." With two other young children to care for, his mother could not easily attend parent conferences, so June Jordan teachers went to her home to meet with her, ensuring that a strong family connection would be built. James's advisor provided emotional, academic, and financial support to help him get through a rough patch when his family faced a number of hardships.

As a result of the school's constant support, as well as its emphasis on extensive writing and inquiry, James decided to attend the University of California at Santa Cruz, where he is now considering a major in literature or writing. When he first arrived at college, James reflected on how well he was prepared for this next chapter in his life:

> Today we had orientation about our core classes; they were telling us that we have just 10 weeks to do all these essays. I feel like I am very confident in writing. I enjoy it. June Jordan got me ready for a four-year college. They helped us become independent. We had a lot of help, and people had our backs at June Jordan, but they also made sure that we were able to take care of ourselves when we needed to.

James was not alone in this success. Among his colleagues in June Jordan's first graduating class in 2007, 95% were admitted to college, with 73% of them going to 4-year colleges at the University of California and California State campuses, as well as private colleges such as Clark Atlanta, Dartmouth, Smith, and Yale.

As suggested by research on communal school models,[31] we found that strong relationships between and among students and faculty were central to participants' views of what enabled them to succeed. Students often compared their school to a family and linked their achievement to their caring relationships with teachers. As the Vanguard student quoted at the chapter opening said,

> School should not be mass production. It needs to be loving and close. That is what kids need. You need love to learn.

Another, who was eligible for the most restrictive special education setting, said about his experience at Vanguard,

> I was bad all the way back from elementary and junior high school. I would have got lost in the system. I would not have made it. I would

have dropped out. I needed someone to be there to show they care about me for me to be motivated.

The principal at Animo-Inglewood described how the family relationship motivates students:

We build a really close family relationship between students, their families, and the staff in the school. Students work hard not to let the family down.

A senior at San Diego's Construction Tech Academy put it this way.

You're with [teachers] for much longer and you get to interact with your teachers a whole lot more and get to know them. . . . When you're learning from a friend, not just from some random person, it's a lot easier to learn.

Reduced Pupil Loads. In order to personalize instruction, these schools have redesigned staffing and scheduling to include more classroom-based staff teaching in longer blocks of time, thus enabling smaller class sizes and reduced pupil loads for teachers—typically as low as 40 or 50 for humanities teachers teaching English and history/social studies together—or as high as 80 to 100 for single-subject teachers. This is about half the pupil load of teachers in most urban schools, where teachers are likely to see 150 to 200 students each day. The reorganization of schedules allows teachers to teach fewer students for longer blocks of time (70 to 120 minutes), often in interdisciplinary configurations, which immediately reduces pupil load significantly. Students generally take fewer courses at a time, generally four rather than six or seven. The more streamlined set of offerings stands in contrast to the "shopping mall high school" approach[32] that has offered a dizzying array of courses and sections, rather than a focused, core curriculum.

The schools' allocation of resources to core instructional functions creates structures that allow teachers to care effectively for their students.[33] By knowing students well, teachers are more able to tailor instruction to students' strengths, needs, experiences, and developing interests. Both students and teachers describe how these structures enable teachers to support intellectually challenging work and to sustain a press for higher standards of performance. As a 22-year veteran of large schools who moved to Vanguard explained:

Small size means I can do a literature seminar with the bottom 20% of kids in the city. Kids who didn't read are reading books like *Jane Eyre* to write their essays. We can work with them during lunch. You find out who can't read, type, etc. These are the kids who would sit in the back of the room, be in the bathroom, and would deliberately get lost. I know dedicated teachers in big schools who teach 150 kids. They can't do this.

A student at Manhattan Village Academy reinforced this point:

> This school will get the worst student to do the work. Teachers are not like this at other high schools where they have [too many] kids. Troubled kids need attention and they can get it here. Kids can see other kids like them working.

An unanticipated benefit is that students can focus more effectively when they are taking a smaller number of classes. As a student at Landmark commented:

> I really like that it's only four classes that we take; in the old school you had to study a little on each subject and keep eight subjects in your head at once.

In this context, teachers can be committed to students' learning, not just to cranking through the assembly line each day. A student at Coalition School for Social Change (CSSC) expressed the sentiments of others when he said, "Because the school is small, teachers have more time to help us. They don't go crazy and we get to learn better." Another student at the same school observed, "The teachers here care for you and your work. They know your potential and keep pushing you to do your best." A student at Manhattan International explained, "If we have personal problems like depression we can talk to the teachers. . . . The teachers know us really well because we always work together, one on one." A Manhattan Village Academy student explained, "I was pregnant last year. The teachers were really behind me. I am still in school and I'm doing well in my classes. The teachers push you here. They want you to graduate."

Intellectually Challenging and Relevant Instruction

The structures described above help schools care more effectively for students. Equally important is how the schools facilitate intellectual development. Each of the schools has designed an ambitious, coherent instructional program that enables students to overcome barriers to access often associated with race, poverty, language, or initially low academic skill. In order to fill large skill gaps for students who have been previously underserved by the school system, schools must meet students where they are and enable them to make large strides.

Each school has addressed this by establishing high expectations, offering a common, untracked, college preparatory curriculum with a comprehensive set of academic supports, ensuring explicit teaching of intellectual and research skills in the context of rigorous coursework. The schools' efforts are consistent with research finding that schools offering a more common curriculum with a narrower range of academic courses tend to produce higher levels of achievement for all students, and greater equity in course-taking, graduation, and college-going.[34] This coursework includes both career-oriented and college preparatory learning, with a strong focus on applying knowledge in real-world settings through projects, community service, and internships.

Challenging and Engaging Curriculum. The schools' programs focus on preparing students for the demands of college. Teachers have worked out a coherent curriculum that teaches the core disciplinary concepts, sometimes in interdisciplinary ways, through carefully constructed and sequenced instructional units that add up across the grade levels. Most assignments require the production of analytic work—research papers and projects, demonstrations and discussions of problems, experiments and data collection organized to answer open-ended questions. Worksheets and fill-in-the-blank tasks are rare. Extensive reading and writing are expected in all academic courses. Many classes require large end-of-course projects that include extensive written documentation, often presented and defended orally.

Manhattan Village Academy's director, Mary Butz, described how reading, writing, and data collection skills are taught explicitly in the context of major projects:

> We demand a lot of work. In the 9th grade, students work on an autobiography that emphasizes writing skills. In the 10th grade there is an inter-cultural project where we teach them research skills. They must use three sources, respond to specific questions, and make comparisons.

As part of this work, students are taught research conventions such as compiling a bibliography, using multiple forms of documentation, and formats for report writing.

Teachers provide opportunities for ongoing revision of work in response to feedback from peers and outside experts as well as themselves, using a mastery approach to learning along with culturally relevant pedagogies to connect to students' needs and experiences. According to teachers and students, revision is a way of life. Faculty voice the belief that students learn by tackling substantial tasks and getting feedback against standards that guide their efforts to improve. Their beliefs are borne out by a large body of research showing very substantial gains in achievement for students who experience formative assessment and feedback with continuous opportunities to revise and improve their work.[35]

A 27-year veteran history teacher who had been at Vanguard for 5 years explained how this instruction is supported by the schools' flexible scheduling and small pupil loads:

> I can use in-depth approaches and assign college level research projects. For 2 months, each morning, we teach students research skills and essay skills so that they can do a minimum 20-page research paper in history. I give them internal motivation to come up against the challenge. They choose the topic. We develop their topic together. This gets them into the different sides of the topic. They are stimulated and internally motivated because it is something they want to learn. I take them to the Donnell Library. . . . They browse through different books, take notes, and order their thoughts in an outline. . . . Then, the kids have to listen to their teachers and peers criticizing their work. Then they have to rewrite. They have to cite references, show evidence, and prove their thesis.

The projects often combine library research with contemporary investigations in the community and studies of literature or the arts. A humanities teacher at CSSC described how a recent project made curricular connections among history, fiction, and contemporary life:

> Last year we did a study of Latin America with a focus on the Dominican Republic. We read Julia Alvarez's *In the Time of the Butterflies* to look at the extremes the dictatorship went to. We then went up to Washington Heights and interviewed senior citizens who had lived through this period. These interviews were powerful learning experiences for our students.

Although there are efforts to link the curriculum to students' own lives and interests, this does not limit the students' studies only to their immediate concerns. The assignments often blend classical studies with multicultural content. In our sampling of student portfolios, we found that students had studied works by Allende, Brecht, Ibsen, Chekhov, de Maupassant, Marquez, Arthur Miller, Toni Morrison, Poe, Sanchez, Shakespeare, R. L. Stevenson, Tolkien, and Richard Wright, among others. In social studies, students studied topics such as the U.S. Constitution, immigration, political prisoners, and Supreme Court cases. Some of the schools used curriculum such as the American Social History Project, which examines history from multiple perspectives. In science, students studied biology, chemistry, and physics as well as aerospace and the environment. The arts are both taught separately and integrated into other subject areas.

All of the schools also prepare students for higher education by making arrangements for students to enroll in courses at local colleges. These experiences enable students to learn about college demands firsthand. One student's account of his experience in a modern American history course at a college in the CUNY system reflects many others we heard:

> At first I was ready to quit because I felt I was not ready for it. But when I talked to my teachers, they gave me advice on study habits— how to manage time better, especially for doing homework for both my school and the college courses. I spent more time reading the books. If I didn't understand, teachers here would explain the material. They gave me other books. I took the mid-term and did O.K. It gave me insight on what college would really be like.

Explicit Teaching of Academic Skills. A key element of instruction in these schools is careful scaffolding for the learning of complex skills. In contrast to many high school curricula, which assume that students have already mastered skills of reading, writing, and research, the schools construct a curriculum that explicitly teaches students how to study, how to approach academic tasks, what criteria will be applied, and how to evaluate their own and others' work.

Sylvia Rabiner, founding principal of Landmark High School, described how skills instruction is built into Landmark's curriculum from the first day the students enter:

> When students enter Landmark in the 9th grade, they are immediately taught how a library works. They are taught how to do a research paper. They are introduced to the habits of mind and rubrics that will be used to assess their work as they progress from grade to grade and ultimately, their graduation portfolios. They are taught how to do exhibitions so that by the time they defend their portfolios, they have had several years' experience in oral presentations.

All of the schools offer structured supports for the teaching of reading and writing, either as part of courses in the 9th and 10th grades or as special classes for students who need support.

Flexible Supports. Access to challenging curriculum does not automatically translate into student success. The schools have sought to marry high standards with a variety of supports to help students negotiate the demands. As a group, the schools provide students—including those who enter high school below grade level, who are new English learners, or who are special education students—with integrated in-class and beyond-class supports. Almost all of the schools make time available before or after school so that students can obtain help. Some have peer tutoring programs and/or Saturday programs.

Because everyone is working together to help students meet standards, students typically perceive these additional learning opportunities as privileges, rather than punishments. For example, at New Tech, where Saturday school is one source of support, a parent explained:

> [Saturday school] was not punitive; it's help. [For] kids who aren't turning in assignments or kids who need to improve on their assignments, it's like a second chance. [My son] came a couple of times. The last time was because the semester was ending, and he knew that he had to do better on something. He didn't have to come; he said, "I need to go to Saturday school so I can do some assignment." It was the last Saturday before Christmas, and he chose to come because he knew he needed to improve.

Many schools provide additional skills classes focused on closing gaps in reading, math, or English language development alongside the untracked college preparatory classes in which all students are enrolled. English language learners and special education students are included in regular classes, often with additional classes or resource room supports to help them complete the same assignments other students receive.

Animo-Inglewood provides a good example of how a set of comprehensive supports can operate. The school's high expectations were modeled by the instructional leadership provided by the founding principal, Cristina de Jesus, who went on to lead professional development at Green Dot, the parent charter management organization that started Animo, and her successor, Annette Gonzalez. Both women are highly accomplished, National Board Certified teachers. Gonzalez, who came from the more affluent Santa Monica/Malibu school district, was determined to hold the same expectations and provide the same resources for her Animo students in Inglewood as she did for her former students in Santa Monica. She explained to them: "We have these really high expectations for you; we believe you're going to go to college; we know that you can do it. We're going to push you hard, hard, hard to get there, but we're going to support you every step of the way."

Struggling students are required to attend an afterschool support class taught by their teachers, and teachers talk with parents to help determine effective strategies for supporting each student. Other supports for student learning include office hours held by teachers; Homework Café, a free afterschool tutoring program staffed by local college students; and curriculum skills courses in SAT preparation and skill building.

The coupling of expectations with support is reflected in the way that Animo addresses algebra, among other gateway courses. All 9th-grade students are enrolled in an algebra course, regardless of placement scores or previous coursework. To ensure that all students can succeed, incoming 9th-graders are required to participate in a 5-week summer bridge program designed to build basic math skills and introduce higher-order math concepts. The lead math teacher in the Green Dot Network, who also serves as Animo's math department chair, was assigned to teach 9th-grade algebra. Algebra, like other classes, is taught on a block A/B schedule with 95-minute periods that allow teachers to teach concepts deeply and provide opportunities for student exploration of ideas. If students struggle when they are enrolled in algebra, they also take a curriculum skills math class, which meets three times a week and is taught by the same teacher.

As a consequence of these strategies, the proportion of Animo students scoring proficient on the state standards test in Algebra I in 2007, when we studied the school, far outstripped that for the state as a whole, and African American and Latino students at Animo were proficient at triple the rate of their peers elsewhere in the state.

Multiple Strategies for Active Learning. Psychologist Robert Glaser has argued that schools must shift from a selective mode—"characterized by minimal variation in the conditions for learning" in which "a narrow range of instructional options and a limited number of ways to succeed are available"—to an adaptive mode in which "the educational environment can provide for a range of opportunities for success. Modes of teaching are adjusted to individuals' backgrounds, talents, interests, and the nature of past performance."[36]

In all of these schools, teachers consciously use multiple instructional strategies to give students different entry points to the material under study. They engage in direct instruction through occasional class lectures and regular discussions as well as guided inquiry, small-group work, and coaching of independent research, projects, and experiments. Most classes involve students in a variety of learning strategies to tackle long-term projects as well as short-term tasks. At Vanguard a student remarked, "Teachers work around the differences in how kids learn to help you complete your projects." As another student put it, "You get to create 3D models, do research, and exhibitions. You do projects. You come up with your own topics and problems. You create the questions and answer them. You write theme, plot, and character essays. You do visuals. [The teachers] don't want it to be boring for you."

Well-managed small-group work is common. Although the group work we observed allowed students to take an active role in their own learning, the work was usually highly structured through activity guides that provided guidance for the tasks and deliberate teacher coaching that anticipated student needs. Teachers know the content they want students to master, have carefully selected texts and other materials, and have clear goals for student learning of both subject matter and specific skills. One of CSSC's humanities teachers described how the use of group work drawing on different learning and performance modes is structured to promote growing independence:

> We want students to do independent work and work in cooperative groups. We get them started and they work independently. Teachers circulate among the groups. . . . For example, in a recent project, students self-selected into groups, did research, close reading, individual writing assignments, and presentations. Each presenting group had to teach the class what they learned.

Real-World Connections. Curricula often incorporate real-life applications, which helps to sustain student interest and involvement in difficult tasks. A teacher at CSSC explained how a science class simulates the work done by environmental consulting firms:

> They identify a problem, make a plan for how to study it, do field work, and write up conclusions. Another class did a project with Central Park rangers, who are short-staffed, and identified tree samples for them. This is real-world, meaningful work.

A teacher at Manhattan Village Academy described how teachers link academic content to the students' lives:

> We try to relate historical issues to the present day and have them form an opinion. We connected Fourth Amendment rights to locker searches when a book bag was stolen. We discuss individual responsibility and what you want the government to take over. We discuss and debate to get them to develop their thoughts a step further.

Community Service and Internships. All of the schools place students in external learning experiences such as internships and community service activities that occur during the regular school day and are accompanied by seminars that help students process what they are learning about the world of work. Linked to students' interests, these may include placements in hospitals, medical research labs, nonprofit organizations, social service agencies, businesses, and schools. The experiences are part of the core program for all students, not a separate track. They are intended to help adolescents assume responsibility, learn how to engage the world outside of home and school, gain an understanding of how different kinds of organizations operate, and explore their interests.

Students reported that, even when they found they did not like the work or setting they had chosen, or when they experienced conflicts on the job, their internships made them feel more capable, responsible, and confident about solving problems and succeeding in the world beyond school. Many said the commitments they developed in these settings spurred them on in school and motivated them to persevere. As a 12th-grade student at San Diego's Construction Tech Academy (CTA) put it: "It makes it easier to come to school. . . . We learn from textbooks, and we go on to apply them to real-life projects that we're working on in class, and then you see how the textbook work is relevant."

While most of the schools use internships as part of their curriculum, Construction Tech Academy takes this concept further than most. The guiding vision behind the school is the desire to create authentic curriculum through "real-world immersion." CTA stakeholders believe that a focus on how knowledge is used in the world of work adds relevance to the curriculum, which in turn leads to increased student attendance, engagement, and retention, especially for those who often disconnect from school. CTA's focus on the construction trades—including architecture, construction, and engineering—prepares students for college, the destination for over 80%, and skilled trades, which the remaining students enter through apprenticeships after high school.

The school strives to emulate authentic work settings by having students work in heterogeneous teams on complex projects that require diverse skills and abilities. Professionals from the engineering, architecture, and construction fields collaborate with students on projects and review student work. All students take both a college preparatory sequence and a full complement of vocational courses. Teachers act as coaches to support student-based inquiry, projects, and collaborative group work, as well as provide one-on-one assistance.

The concept of "real-world" at CTA is grounded in two central assumptions. The first is that "expertise" is something that comes from a combination of study and "hands-on" application, rather than from books alone. As principal Glenn Hillegas explained: "Advanced Placement has a really high rigor to it, but a really low application. To me, the best education is when you take something of high rigor and you apply it. When kids *apply* knowledge, they gain a deeper understanding."

The second assumption is that students need to learn how to direct their own learning and to work in heterogeneous teams because that is how work in the "real world" happens. The best teachers at CTA act as coaches and guides, helping to support student-based inquiry with one-on-one assistance. The school also creates individual learning plans for each student, and sends home bimonthly reports tracking student's academic progress on "paydays."

"Real-world" applications occur as industry professionals come into the classroom to provide support to students and teachers as they work on projects and help review and evaluate project work once it is complete. For example, in 9th grade, students go to nearby Legoland when it is closed so they can see the "inner workings" of an amusement park and take an engineering tour. They then form small groups led by student foremen to design their own amusement parks, including two-dimensional plot plans and scale models of their parks. Students present their plans to industry professionals and receive a critique on their work.

Real-world application also occurs through the job shadows and internships that occur in the 11th and 12th grades. In their senior portfolios, seniors are required to prepare a resume, fill out an application for college, prepare a budget for college expenses, and interview a professional in a field of their interest. CTA also supports a range of field trips to help students think about the kinds of practical trade-offs that professionals make when designing or constructing buildings. For example, when students from the Architecture, Construction, and Engineering (ACE) afterschool club expressed interest in designing an airport for their spring project, a field trip was arranged so that they could go "behind the scenes" at San Diego airport to understand how airports really work. In the words of the principal, "Rigor and relevance are driven into the school from the outside. It's a different level of work for the kids."

Performance-Based Assessment

All of the schools engage students in completing complex projects and investigations of various kinds, and most of them require the completion of portfolios for graduation, which include high-quality work illustrating disciplinary inquiry in each of the major subject areas. These pieces of work are often exhibited before a jury of teachers, parents, students, and reviewers from outside the school. A sense of press is supported by these assessment systems, which set public expectations for performance. As a teacher at June Jordan explains:

> We have our portfolio system, which is really effective in making sure that all kids get pushed. There are requirements in order for them to graduate from the school. . . . If they don't get a passing score, they have to re-present. It's a really good way to make sure that students aren't just getting by.

A San Diego district official who attended the exhibitions at Construction Tech noted:

> Having industry [members] involved in the exhibition of student work has raised the rigor way beyond what these teachers could have done on their own. I believe that authenticity, having to stand up in front

of a group of professionals and defend your work, is so important. I remember the very first exhibition when a student wasn't prepared, and he admitted it, and the committee said, "Well, son, what is it going to take next time?" He was held accountable for why he didn't complete that work. He had to dig deep into his own heart to figure out why he didn't complete that work on time. That student became a very successful student here at Construction Tech, and he has graduated and moved on.

Students understand that this process deepens their learning. A student at Leadership High in San Francisco put it this way:

At other high schools, it's just "you passed." Kids can't tell what they got out of high school. Students here know what they've learned.

All of the New York schools we studied require students to complete a common set of seven or more performance tasks for graduation as part of their overall portfolio. These are mapped to each disciplinary area and involve research papers, including a social science investigation and a scientific experiment, a literary critique, an arts product or analysis, a mathematical model or project, and an analysis of one of the student's internship experiences. Often, students will have completed an autobiography and a graduation plan that looks ahead to their futures. Traditional tests are also sometimes included in the portfolio. The schools' portfolios vary in content and structure. However, all of the assessment systems include:

1. Written and constructed or performed products requiring in-depth study
2. Oral presentation by the candidate before a committee of teachers and a peer who assess the quality of the work and pose questions to test for understanding
3. Rubrics embodying the standards against which students' performances are judged
4. Rating scales to assess students' products and oral presentations

In order to graduate, each student's committee must pass on their entire set of portfolios. The rigor of the process and the varying levels of skills with which students enter mean that, in all of the schools, some students take more than 4 years to graduate. The schools' content and performance standards are mapped to New York State's curriculum standards and enabled the schools to receive a state waiver from the Regents examinations for all areas except English language arts.

The portfolios are not only evaluation instruments but also learning experiences that engage students in what Fred Newmann and colleagues call "authentic achievement."[37] The tasks require students to organize information, engage in disciplined inquiry and analysis, communicate orally and in writing, problem-solve, and make a cogent presentation before an audience. Students frequently remarked on how the portfolio experience deepened their understanding. These comments were common:

> You get to do most of the thinking when you work with your portfolio. You have to explain in detail how to do something or why something is important, so that someone who doesn't know it can understand it.

> When you take a test, you don't feel like you need to know it after it is done. The portfolio sticks in your brain better.

> You have to manage your time before, after, and during school to do the portfolio.

And as a new English language learner, noted:

> The portfolio makes you develop your writing. It makes more sense for us to have to do an oral presentation, to answer oral questions about our work to see how we learned English.

Our research team watched students defending their portfolios before committees of teachers and peers. The exhibitions we observed reflected a range from work that was rated as marginal, which students then revised, to work evaluated as distinguished. Even when the work was less developed and required multiple revisions, the schools enabled all of their students to produce these kinds of research papers and multipart projects, and in the process, to expand their skills and their ability to organize and persist at a complex undertaking.

At Vanguard, a special education student could not be distinguished from a regular education student as he presented his history portfolio on the role of Japan during World War II, displaying knowledge of the geography of the region and of the politics of Japanese imperialism. At Landmark, a student deconstructed his development as a writer and reader over the course of his 4 years at the school by referencing specific papers he wrote over the 4 years. Using a set of overheads with quotes and diagrams, he graphically compared and contrasted his current knowledge to his former ignorance, which the audience could see as his earlier and later papers were placed in parallel alignment. He made a similar presentation on the changes in his capacity to analyze literature and in his literary preferences. Without interruption, the student made a clear, tightly constructed argument on his development as a reader and writer for 40 minutes.

In all cases, the committees questioned the presenters, scored the presentations according to a common rubric and presented their evaluations to the students. The conversations about the work probed the students' reasoning, asked for evidence supporting key ideas, and referenced the schools' habits of mind (e.g., drawing connections to other ideas, using evidence, understanding perspectives, presenting clearly and with appropriate use of conventions). The process was personally supportive, but often substantively critical. Some students found that either their paper or their presentation did not yet meet the portfolio standard, and they would have to revise and re-present. Some met the minimal standard but decided to revise in order to improve the quality of their work and to obtain a higher rating. Others met the standard and were satisfied with their work, going on to work on other portfolios.

All of the students felt a deep sense of accomplishment from the experience, and, having repeated it several times before graduation, a growing sense of confidence. In follow-ups of graduates, students pointed to these research papers and presentations as a key reason they believe they have been able to succeed in college. Unlike many of their peers, who have learned passively from textbooks, they feel comfortable defining and pursuing questions, using the library and the laboratory, framing and defending their ideas orally and in writing, and managing their time to accomplish substantial tasks that require planning and perseverance.

Professional Learning and Collaboration

These schools succeed in part because of their ability to recruit and develop very strong faculties and leaders, using many of the strategies for teacher learning that are common in schools abroad but rare in the United States.

In New York City, many of the schools we studied are connected to preservice and inservice programs run by local universities that prepare teachers for progressive teaching practices, such as Bank Street College, City College, New York University, the New School, and Columbia University's Teachers College. A similar relationship exists for June Jordan with San Francisco State and with Stanford University, which supplies teachers for many small or redesigned district-run and charter schools in the Bay Area. The schools host student teachers and engage in collaborative learning through these networks. While new schools must fight the battle of potential burnout, their well-developed pipelines, collegial environments, and close relationships with students mean that most of the schools have many more applicants than they can hire, even though the districts generally have difficulty filling all of their vacancies.

The schools are able to recruit teachers who are committed to their approaches. During the 1990s, the new schools in New York City were able to negotiate changes in the collective bargaining agreement to allow them to choose their own faculty through a peer review process that allows existing staff to evaluate teaching and collaboration skills. Among the California schools, charters have the ability to select their own staff, and the district-run schools have been able to negotiate autonomy for selecting all or most of their teachers.

Collaborative Professional Learning. Many researchers have identified the collaboration associated with a professional community of teachers as a key element of successful schools.[38] Over multiple studies, Fred Newmann and colleagues found that professional community is one of three common features of schools achieving high levels of student learning.[39] (The others are a shared focus on high-quality student learning and authentic pedagogy, discussed earlier.) Their research and that of others suggest that smaller schools providing more collegial professional environments for teachers generate greater collective responsibility for school improvement and student learning.[40]

The successful schools we studied work continually to improve the quality of their instruction by making it the consistent focus of their professional learning time. Part of this commitment includes allocating considerable time for teachers to collaborate, design curriculum and instruction, and learn from one another. The schools organize extensive summer learning opportunities and retreats to look at student learning evidence and to plan and organize instruction, advisory practices, and student supports. Although faculty members participate in external professional development, most professional development is internal. Overall, the schools allocate 7 to 15 days to shared professional learning time throughout the year.

The schools encourage teachers to learn about and from their colleagues' practice, organizing substantial time during the week—usually 5 to 10 hours in addition to the teachers' individual planning time—for teachers to plan and problem-solve together around students and subject matter. With teachers operating in grade-level teams that meet regularly, the schools create structures for examining student progress, as well as for creating a more coherent curriculum and allowing teachers to learn from one another. Planning within departments also occurs regularly, and teachers develop curriculum and assessments in order to ensure that students will be prepared to meet the common schoolwide outcomes that have been established. Teachers use these collaborative opportunities to examine students' progress, determine how to adjust their instruction, and socialize new staff into the schools' approaches. Noting the power of these approaches at New Tech High, a Sacramento district official observed admiringly: "It's all about co-planning, co-teaching and analyzing, and having time out of the regular teaching day to do these analyses."

Manhattan International principal William Ling explained how collaboration within teacher teams strengthens accountability:

Everyone holds each other accountable for meeting the [school] goals. The clusters work together on the year's goals. They plan together, discuss kids together, they observe each other, and they support each other's development.

Similarly, principal Sylvia Rabiner noted that at Landmark:

Teachers share what they are doing in a formal way in team meetings. They plan together and share what they have done. There is whole school sharing and there are summer institutes where we have more time to reflect. There is more coherence than in big schools where teachers work alone.

At June Jordan, teachers participate in a professional learning retreat before school starts, and in professional learning meetings twice a month. Teachers also meet weekly, by subject matter and grade level, during common planning times to collaborate on planning curriculum and unit projects and discuss student needs. Whether in a professional development session, staff meeting, or team planning session, teachers are asked to reflect on their practice and experience in the classroom. According to one teacher:

It's easy to grab onto someone's best practices. We've developed a culture for that. . . . The practice of common planning time really lends itself to being able to serve students better and think about ways to support them.

These structural supports for teacher learning are augmented by mentoring and coaching systems for new and veteran teachers, focused inquiry about problems of practice that occurs in staff meetings, and the learning about student thinking, standards, and curriculum that occurs when teachers collectively evaluate student portfolios, projects, and exhibitions.

School-Based Inquiry. Essential to each of the schools' success in maintaining a coherent instructional focus based on its students' needs and its school vision is each school's ability to shape its own professional learning time. Most schools examine student work and other data each summer to set the focus for the coming year. Most also structure deliberate inquiries into areas of the curriculum, school organization, or instruction that appear to need attention. As a counselor at Leadership High explained:

Leadership High School has a particularly well developed model for professional learning. Everything is very intentional here. At other places I've worked, it is like, "Let's try this. Let's try that." Here, we look at the research; we look at the data and figure it out. There are reasons for everything.

The Leadership model uses a value-driven approach focused on equity to guide professional learning that is informed by data. An extensive data-based inquiry process is supplemented by regular weekly planning meetings. Department coaches (DCs) are strong, equity-minded teachers given an extra prep period to serve as the first line of support for teachers, providing coaching and one-on-one support for teachers as well as leading the inquiry process. In addition to meeting monthly with the principal, the DCs meet weekly with one another to discuss the best ways to coach, as well as how to use inquiry to build teachers' capacity for deep reflection on their practice. The DCs have 7 release days throughout the year to examine achievement data (e.g., grades, test scores, graduation assessments) and student experience data (e.g., suspension rates, attendance, measures of student satisfaction) as the basis for guiding staff-wide inquiries and professional development. According to the principal:

> Throughout all these days, particular attention is paid to surfacing patterns of achievement and failure so that we can more equitably serve all our students and narrow the predictable achievement gaps that persist in our school.

The schoolwide focus determined through the inquiry process is presented to staff during their 6-day professional development retreat at the end of the summer. Based on their work in the retreat, the staff develops a central question that they all focus on for the year. As an extension of the focus, each staff member applies the focus in their own individual work, creating an individual goal that directs personal, professional, and collaborative objectives. All staff participate, including security staff and counselors. As principal Elizabeth Rood explained, "We are trying to build a coaching culture and an action-research culture at the school and are constantly doing inquiry and constantly being reflective."

The yearly focus is carried through the 3 days a semester when staff meet all day for professional learning. In addition, these times are used to focus on individual students and continue the data-based inquiry process. For example, early in the year, the staff dedicated half a day to talk about a set of specific students, taking 45 minutes for each student and using a protocol to identify the supports that are and are not working for the student.

In their weekly professional learning meetings, attendees follow a protocol in which staff take rotating roles as facilitator, time keeper, and so on, so that all teachers get comfortable in various leadership roles. The meetings also rotate through each teacher's classroom so that every teacher can see the kind of work that is going on across the school. The principal describes this professional learning time as "intentional. . . . This is not a staff meeting [or] loosey goosey collaboration time. . . . It is important time, it is sacred time for us as a staff." Topics have included reciprocal teaching, scaffolding, student discourse, and cultural competence. All the discussions address issues of equity. For example, as staff met to discuss parent conferences, they discussed parents' potential discomfort at school because of their own or their children's previous negative experiences in school. Teachers planned how to make parent conferences constructive, given any tensions, anxiety, or concerns that parents might have.

When serious school-led professional development is in place, learning is often a vehicle for shared leadership. All the schools engage teachers in a range of leadership roles and in democratic decisionmaking. Shared governance also often involves students, parents, community members, and even industry leaders, supporting widespread commitment to the vision and mission of the school. Everyone—students, staff, and parents—works harder when that buy-in has been achieved. These schools illustrate how designs that foster intentional student, teacher, and family supports result in successes with many young people who would fall through the cracks elsewhere.

CREATING SYSTEMS OF SUCCESSFUL SCHOOLS

Designing schools that serve low-income students of color well is not impossible. Since the groundbreaking research of Ronald Edmonds more than 3 decades ago,[41] many studies have documented the practices of unusually effective schools and have uncovered similar features of those that succeed with students who are historically underserved.[42] However, to create such schools on a much wider scale, a new policy environment must be constructed that routinely encourages such schools to be developed and sustained.

Supporting Successful Innovation

Creating new schools and innovations is a great American pastime. Waves of reform producing productive new school designs occurred at the turn of the 20th century when John Dewey, Ella Flagg Young, Lucy Sprague Mitchell, and others were working in Chicago, New York, and other Northern cities, and African American educators such as Anna Julia Cooper, Lucy Laney, and Mary McLeod Bethune were creating schools in the South. A wave of new school designs swept the country in the 1930s and 1940s when the Progressive Education Association helped redesign and study 30 "experimental" high schools that were found, in the famous Eight-Year Study, to perform substantially better than traditional schools in developing high-achieving, intellectually adventurous, socially responsible young people able to succeed in college and in life.[43] Urban school reform movements occurred in the 1960s and 1970s, producing schools such as the Parkway Program in Philadelphia and Central Park East Elementary in New York, and in the 1990s when the impulse for innovation returned once again with the kinds of schools described in this chapter.

Despite more successful and more equitable outcomes than most traditional schools, few of these innovative schools were sustained over time. Any educator in the field for long has participated in what former Seattle teacher union leader Roger Erskine dubbed as "random acts of innovation"[44] that have come and gone, regardless of their success. Generally, this is because, like bank voles and wolf spiders, urban districts often eat their young. Changes in superintendents and school boards create swings in policies, including efforts to standardize instruction, go "back to the basics," and bring innovators to heel. Even when they achieve better outcomes, distinctive school models confront longstanding traditions, standard operating procedures, and expectations, including, sometimes, the expectation that students who have traditionally failed should continue to do so so that the traditionally advantaged can continue in their position of privilege. Indeed, Anna Julia Cooper's progressive M Street School in segregated Washington, DC, which offered a "thinking curriculum" to Black students and outperformed two of the three White high schools in the city, was attacked for both of these reasons in the early 20th century.[45]

Sometimes, successful schools and programs fade because special foundation or government money has dried up, and the district lacks the foresight or wherewithal to preserve what is working. Other times, the challenges of replenishing the capable, dynamic teachers and leaders who have created a successful school prove too great to sustain the model. Historian Lawrence Cremin argued that the successes of progressive education reforms did not spread widely because such practice required "infinitely skilled teachers," who were never prepared in sufficient numbers to sustain these more complex forms of teaching and schooling.[46]

New York City's unusual renaissance was facilitated by the creation of an innovation silo in the form of the Alternative Schools Superintendency—which buffered schools from many regulations and forged new solutions to old bureaucratic problems—and by a rich array of professional resources in support of reforms, including expert practitioners who created networks of learning and support, a large set of public and private universities offering expertise and intellectual resources, and philanthropists and researchers who provided additional professional and political support to these efforts. The United Federation of Teachers (UFT) ran its own Teachers Center, and many of the teachers active in this professional development were involved in the new schools initiatives. Over time, the UFT incorporated many supports for reform-oriented schools into its contracts—first through waivers and later through changes in collective bargaining agreements—and, in some cases, became part of the protection for further reforms. Even when frequent changes in leadership might have led to abandonment of the new schools initiative, these forces kept the reform momentum going.

In most places, however, the lack of investment in professional education that would allow teachers and school leaders to acquire the knowledge they need to undertake sophisticated practices has proved to be an ongoing problem. Another recurring problem is the lack of policy development that could encourage the growth of such schools rather than keeping them as exceptions, on waiver, and at the margins. As Paul Hill has argued:

> Today's public school system tolerates new ideas only on a small scale and it does so largely to reduce pressures for broader change. The current system is intended to advance individual, community, and national goals, but is, in fact, engineered for stability. That is normally a good thing. We want schools to open on time, teachers to count on having jobs from one day to the next, and parents to feel secure knowing that their children will have a place to go to school. Stability alone, however, is the wrong goal in a complex, fast-changing, modern economy. Students—disadvantaged students, in particular—need schools that are focused on providing them with the skills they will need to succeed in today's society, schools that are flexible enough to try a variety of teaching methods until they succeed in reaching these goals.[47]

In the current environment, some, including Hill, suggest that charters, contract schools, or performance schools that are essentially licensed by school boards to provide a particular model or approach may provide a way to spark innovation and protect it from the vicissitudes of district politics and changes of course. This strategy has the potential virtue of enabling continuity of educational direction and philosophy within schools—where, arguably, coherence is most important—and holding schools accountable for results, rather than for bureaucratic compliance.

Certainly, some important new school models have been launched through charters. In California, where the state has used chartering as a major lever for innovation, three of the five high schools we studied—Animo, Leadership, and New Tech—were charters. This allowed them to outline a specific approach to education and hold onto it, without being buffeted by changing district views or intruded upon by curriculum, testing, and management mandates. Although collective bargaining agreements from the industrial era often create cumbersome constraints in many districts, new approaches to bargaining have also begun to emerge, and two of these three charters employ unionized teachers.

Many other successful new small school models have been started and expanded through special arrangements for autonomy from district regulations or through charter organizations: Some, like Envision Schools, Asia Society, High Tech High, Uncommon Schools, and others, have introduced substantially new educational approaches, including performance

assessments, exhibitions of learning, curriculum focused on global understandings, advisory systems, and more. Odds are that, within many districts,
without formal protection, their adventurousness would have been quashed
by some school board's or superintendent's insistence on introducing a new
standardized curriculum or testing system, or pressuring the schools to grow
in size and revert to factory-model designs, or requiring the hiring of teachers or leaders who are not prepared for or bought into the model. (Both
district practices of centralized assignment and collective bargaining agreements that require seniority transfers can be culpable in this problem.) Even
when intentions to support innovation are good, local districts are subject
to a geological dig of laws, regulations, precedents, and standard operating
procedures that can be enormously difficult to untangle before they strangle
change efforts.

For these reasons and others, Hill suggests an entirely new role for
school districts as managers of a portfolio of relatively autonomous schools,
rather than as school operators:

> Today, boards oversee a central bureaucracy which owns and operates all the
> schools in a given district. It is time to retire this "command-and-control" sys-
> tem and replace it with a new model: portfolio management. In this new system,
> school boards would manage a diverse array of schools, some run by the school
> district and others by independent organizations, each designed to meet the
> different needs of students. Like investors with diversified portfolios of stocks
> and bonds, school boards would closely manage their community's portfolio of
> educational service offerings, divesting less productive schools and adding more
> promising ones. If existing schools do not serve students well, boards would
> experiment with promising new approaches to find ones that work.

This notion of a portfolio of schools—also advocated by the Gates
Foundation—has many potential virtues to recommend it. Certainly, choice
is better than coercion in the management of education. Students and families could find better fits with their interests and philosophies and make
a greater commitment to schools they have chosen. Choice could make
schools more accountable and attentive to student needs. Schools that create
successful designs should benefit from more autonomy to refine and maintain their good work. If a portfolio strategy works well it should "ensure a
supply of quality school options that reflects a community's needs, interests,
and assets . . . and [ensure] that every student has access to high-quality
schools that prepare them for further learning, work, and citizenship."[48] A
portfolio structure is essentially what has emerged in New York City within
the regular district structure (now divided into sets of school zones and networks) and, on a smaller scale, in Boston, which has launched a set of Pilot
Schools—alternatives that provide a variety of educational options sharing
the features described earlier in this chapter, which are succeeding at rates
far above those of many other schools serving similar students.[49]

However, neither choice nor charters alone is a panacea. And not all in-novations are useful ones. Although some public schools of choice have been successful, others have made little difference. For example, a recent eval-uation of Chicago's Renaissance 2010 initiative—which replaced a group of low-performing schools with charters and other autonomous schools of choice run by entrepreneurs and the district—found that the achievement of students in the new schools was no different from that of a matched com-parison group of students in the old schools they had left, and both groups continued to be very low-performing.[50]

Results for charters nationally have also been mixed. Reviews of the evidence have found positive impacts in some places and insignificant or negative impacts in others.[51]

A study of 16 states, covering 70% of all charter schools, found that only 17% of charters produced academic gains significantly better than tra-ditional public schools serving demographically similar students, while 37% performed worse than their traditional public school counterparts, and 46% showed no difference from district-run public schools.[52] The fact that out-comes differ across states suggests that different approaches to regulation and funding may be important. For example, in Ohio, where an unregulated market strategy created a huge range of for-profit and nonprofit providers with few public safeguards, charter school students were found to achieve at consistently lower levels than their demographically similar public school counterparts. Studies have also found lower average performance for char-ter students in the poorly regulated charter sectors in Washington, DC, and Arizona, where charters can be granted for 15 years and fewer safeguards for students are required.[53]

A recent study of Minneapolis charters found that, despite individual successes, on average they produce significantly lower achievement relative to district public schools serving similar students.[54] Indeed, the only signif-icant positive effect on achievement was for those students who were part of an interdistrict choice plan that allowed them to leave the district to attend suburban public schools. On the other hand, in Wisconsin, where laws authorize few providers (outside of Milwaukee, where different rules hold) and require more academic and financial oversight, as well as explicit attention to innovation, students were found to perform slightly better than their demographically matched peers in most areas.[55]

In the longest-standing portfolio approach, launched in Milwaukee in the late 1980s with vouchers and, later, a wide range of charters and other schools of choice, studies have found few improvements in any sector over more than 15 years. Studies of the voucher program have produced conflict-ing results, ranging from no effects on achievement for students receiving vouchers to small positive effects on achievement in one subject area.[56] And the traditional system has performed poorly overall, appearing to improve little as a result of competition, with short-lived upturns in scores generally balanced by downturns. By 2006, only 39% of Milwaukee 10th-graders in the public school system scored proficient in reading, as compared to 74% in the state as a whole, and only 29% of Milwaukee 10th-graders scored proficient in math, as compared to 70% of Wisconsin 10th-graders.[57]

The most substantial improvements in achievement occurred between 2006 and 2009, when Milwaukee superintendent Bill Andrekopoulos launched an initiative to build instructional capacity across the district, with a set of teaching standards outlining exemplary practices, a new professional evaluation system, and professional development supported by coaching for both teachers and principals.[58]

Interestingly, his journey mirrors that of Superintendent Tony Alvarado, who first initiated a choice plan in New York City District 4, which produced some extraordinary schools, including Debbie Meier's first school in East Harlem at Central Park East Elementary. However, Alvarado decided that the "let a thousand flowers bloom" approach often resulted in only a few flowers blooming, so it needed to be supplemented with a districtwide capacity-building approach to enable strong instruction in all schools, which led to his more systemic approach to reform when he moved to District 2.

Finally, the pressures under recent accountability regimes to get test scores up have led to growing concerns that some new schools—charters and otherwise—have sought to exclude those students who are the most challenging to teach, either by structuring admissions so that low-achieving students and those with special education or other needs are unlikely to be admitted, or by creating conditions under which such students are encouraged to leave. Studies of new schools created in New York City after 2000, for example, have found that these schools, unlike the earlier pioneers, enrolled more academically able students and fewer English language learners or students with disabilities than the large comprehensive schools they replaced. This enabled them to show better outcomes.[59]

Thus, it is not the governance mechanism or the degree of autonomy alone that determines whether schools will succeed. In places where new school models and redesigned schools have done well without ignoring or pushing out struggling students, attention has been paid both to sparking new educational possibilities and building schools' capacities for good instruction, and to removing unnecessary constraints and creating appropriate safeguards for students.

Sustaining Change

The goal, ultimately, is not just to support a vanguard group of unique schools but to enable all schools to adopt practices that will be more successful for all of their students. For this to happen, districts must find ways to foster innovation and responsiveness without compromising equity, access, and the public purpose of schools to prepare citizens who can live, work, and contribute to a common democratic society. This will require redesigning districts as well as schools, rethinking regulations and collective bargaining, while building capacity and allocating resources in smarter and more equitable ways.

Redesigning Districts. For successful schools to become the norm, districts must move beyond the pursuit of an array of ad hoc initiatives managed by exception to fundamental changes in district operations and policy. Throughout the 20th century, most urban districts adopted increasingly bureaucratic approaches to managing schools. They created extensive rules to manage every aspect of school life—from curriculum, instruction, and testing to hiring, purchasing, and facilities—along with complex, departmentalized structures to manage these rules and procedures. Siloed bureaucrats have had the mission of administering procedures that often block practitioners' instructional efforts, rather than managing quality by being accountable for figuring out ways to support success. To create a new paradigm, the role of the district must shift in the following ways:

- From enforcing procedures to building school capacity
- From managing compliance to managing improvement
- From rewarding staff for following orders and "doing things right" to rewarding staff for getting results by "doing the right things"
- From rationing educational opportunities to expanding successful programs
- From ignoring (and compounding) failure in schools serving the least powerful to reallocating resources to ensure their success

To a large extent, these changes represent a switch from bureaucratic accountability—that is, hierarchical systems that pass down decisions and hold employees accountable for following the rules, whether or not they are effective—to professional accountability—that is, knowledge-based systems that help build capacity in schools for doing the work well, and hold people accountable for using professional practices that enable student success.

In a new paradigm, the design of the district office should also evolve from a set of silos that rarely interact with one another to a team structure that can integrate efforts across areas such as personnel, professional development, curriculum and instruction, and evaluation, with the goal of creating greater capacity in a more integrated fashion. These supports should include

- Recruiting a pool of well-prepared teachers and leaders from which schools can choose, and building pipelines to facilitate their training and availability

- Organizing access to high-quality, sustained professional development and resources, including skilled instructional mentors and coaches that schools can call upon and that can be deployed to diagnose problems and support improvements in struggling schools
- Ensuring that high-quality instructional resources—curriculum materials, books, computers, and texts—are available
- Providing services, such as purchasing and facilities maintenance, to school consumers in effective and efficient ways—if schools choose to acquire them from the district

If they incorporate choice, districts will need to ensure that all schools are worth choosing and that all students have access to good schools. This means they must continuously evaluate how schools are doing, seeking to learn from successful schools and to support improvements in struggling schools by ensuring these schools secure strong leadership and excellent teachers, and are supported in adopting successful program strategies. Districts will need to become learning organizations themselves—developing their capacity to investigate and learn from innovations in order to leverage productive strategies, and developing their capacity to support successful change. Where good schools and programs are oversubscribed, districts must learn how to spread good models rather than rationing them, and where schools are failing, they must learn how to diagnose, address problems, and invest resources to improve them. These capacities are needed in all systems, whether or not they adopt choice strategies.

If education is to serve the public good, it is critical to guard against the emergence of a privatized system in which schools are separated by their ability to choose their students, rather than by the ability of students and families to choose their schools. For choice to work, districts must also not only provide information and transportation to parents but manage parents' and schools' choices so that schools recruit and admit students without regard to race, class, or prior academic achievement, both to preserve the possibilities for integrated, common schools and to ensure that some schools do not become enclaves of privilege while others remain dumping grounds. Managed choice arrangements in cities such as Cambridge, Massachusetts, and (in some areas of) New York City have created strategies for doing this, allowing parents to state several preferences and requiring schools to admit a diverse student body from all parts of the achievement range. However, these districts have also learned that such strategies require constant vigilance and are not by themselves enough to guarantee access to quality schools for all students. In particular, without the right support and incentives, many schools will seek to recruit the most advantaged students and deflect or push out the least advantaged ones. These incentives, as I discuss below, have to do with the level of capacity to serve students well, with resources, and with accountability measures.

Building Professional Capacity. Building professional capacity ultimately requires investments in effective preparation, hiring, mentoring, evaluation, and professional development for school leaders, as well as teachers and other staff. In addition, systems need to develop strategies for sharing good practice across schools, ranging from research that is widely disseminated to the establishment of networks of schools, teachers, and principals that develop and share practice with one another, to the creation of strategies such as school quality reviews that allow educators to examine one another's practice and get feedback that can help them grow.

Growing successful new schools or improving existing ones is not likely to be accomplished merely by a replication strategy in which external agents seek to transplant programs or designs from one school into another. Replication efforts have an inglorious history, largely because they quickly run up against differences in staff knowledge and capacity, resources, and contexts of receiving schools. Unless they are accompanied by intensive, long-term professional development support, schools can rarely attend to the nuances and implications of new strategies in ways that would permit strong implementation over the long run. When the purportedly effective techniques don't work immediately, especially for students who are challenging to teach, staff will tend to revert to old approaches and/or focus on reaching those who are easiest to teach given what teachers already know how to do and have the resources to support.

Another approach was used to achieve the surprisingly consistent and sophisticated practices we found across the Coalition Campus Schools we studied, which allowed them to be successful with normally low-achieving students. Following what might be called a birthing and parenting strategy, many of the new school "launchers" had been teachers in the older, successful schools. They were mentored by expert veteran principals and teachers while belonging to a set of networks that facilitated ongoing sharing of practice and supported problem solving.

Networking strategies have increasingly been found to be powerful for sharing practitioner knowledge. Teacher-to-teacher networks such as the National Writing Project help teachers develop effective pedagogical practices; principal networks have become critically important within many districts seeking to support stronger instructional leadership and create opportunities for shared problem solving; and, in both the United States and abroad, school networks are enabling educators to share departmental and schoolwide practices through collective professional development, observational visits, and pooling of intellectual resources.

Managing and Allocating Resources. For schools to succeed with all students, they must be adequately resourced to do so. As we have seen, disparities in funding between states, districts, and schools often leave those working with the neediest students with the fewest resources. States can begin to change this by costing out what would be required to provide an adequate education to graduate all students, having met the state standards, and then allocating resources equitably to each student on a per-pupil basis adjusted for regional cost-of-living differentials and pupil needs. The weighted student formula approach, advocated by many school finance reformers and adopted in some cities to equalize within-district funding, is intended to provide an added increment for students with disabilities, new English language learners, and low-income students, determined by estimating the costs of educating these students to the state's standards. Schools serving large concentrations of high-need students would receive additional funds to provide the services that so many of their students require.

Schools and districts also need the flexibility to spend their funds in optimal ways. Among the distinctive features of successful, redesigned schools is that they use the resources of people and time very differently from traditional systems in order to provide more intense relationships between adults and students and to ensure collaborative planning and learning time for teachers, as schools in other nations do. As described earlier, the United States spends much less of its educational budget on classroom instruction and on teachers—just over 50%, as compared to 70% to 80% in other countries.[60] This weakens instruction in the United States.

The United States spends more on several layers of bureaucracy between the state and the school, made necessary in part by the dizzying array of federal and state categorical programs schools are expected to manage because they are not trusted to make good decisions about resources. These categorical programs themselves create inefficiencies in spending—requiring administrative attention and audit trails, as well as fragmenting programs and efforts in schools in ways that undermine educational outcomes. Often, these programs and other regulations prescribe staffing patterns and other uses of resources that reduce focus and effectiveness.

In addition, the United States spends more of its personnel budget on a variety of administrative staff and instructional aides rather than on teachers directly, implementing the outdated model that added a variety of pull-out programs and peripheral services to make up for the failures of a factory-model system, rather than investing in the instructional core of expert teachers given time to work productively with students whom they know well. Thus, whereas full-time teachers engaged in instruction comprise about 70% to 80% of education employees in most Asian and European nations, they are only about half of education employees in the United States.[61] In 2003, for example, only 51% of school district employees in the United States were classroom teachers, whereas the proportion of full-time classroom teachers in Japanese schools was 89% of all educational staff. If the large number of doctors, dentists, and pharmacists based in Japanese schools is included in the calculation, the proportion is 72% of all employees (see Figure 13.1).[62] Indeed, Japanese schools had, proportionately, as

Figure 13.1 U.S. and Japanese School Staffing Patterns, 2003.

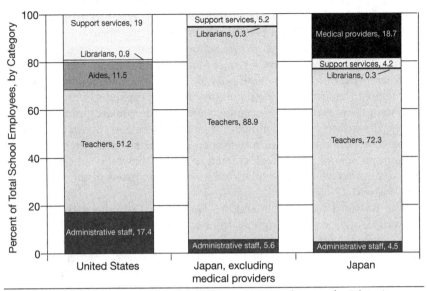

Source: Japanese Ministry of Education (2005) and National Center for Education Statistics (2005).

many doctors as there were instructional aides in U.S. schools, but only one-third the proportion of administrative staff.

Successful, redesigned schools often invest more of their resources in classroom teachers and organize teachers in teams that share students over longer periods of time, to create more sharing of knowledge, as well as to focus on accountability for student needs and success. They consolidate their resources to offer a strong, common core curriculum and key supports, resisting the temptation to diffuse their energies or spend on peripherals at the expense of the central goals of the school. The implications for staffing patterns, resource allocations, and the uses of teachers' and students' time are even more distinctive for schools that engage students in extended internships outside the school, as the Met and its network of schools do; for schools that are engaging students in a range of college courses while they are in high school; and for schools that are embracing technology-based approaches to project work as the New Tech network of schools does.

States and districts will need to encourage more thoughtful and inventive uses of resources by resisting the temptation to prescribe old factory-model requirements for staffing and uses of time and funds, and by providing supports for school leaders to learn how to design organizations that use resources in ways likely to produce the desired outcomes.

Deregulating Strategically. As I have suggested, a challenge in scaling up more effective school designs is that the century-old model of school organization that has shaped most schools is now reinforced by layers of regulations that often do not produce the most effective forms of education. Most state regulatory frameworks for schools have not yet shifted to accommodate or encourage the design choices made by new school models.

Where innovations are made possible by relief from regulations, they cannot spread unless the same regulatory relief is applied to other parts of the system. Few states have examined ways to deregulate public schools strategically in ways that would permit greater focus and success while preserving core public values. In recent years, as charters and other relatively autonomous schools have been created to permit flexibility in one part of the system, heavy-handed regulation has often increased in the remainder of the system.

The Boston Pilot Schools and the New York City alternative schools are proof that large public organizations can create organizational firewalls that allow space for successful innovation. But to do so, they must always be conscious of the impact of their policies on school-level practice, and they must, over time, allow innovators to help change the rules as well as avoid them. Regulations protecting access and providing equitable allocations of resources should provide the foundation of a redesigned system, while professional standards and investments in professional capacity that allow educators to be trusted should replace efforts to micromanage teaching and the design of schools.

Changing Contracts. Over time, many of the features of the factory model have been incorporated into collective bargaining agreements by both unions and school boards. Among the most problematic aspects for school reforms are constraints on how time and work are structured and procedures for faculty hiring and assignment that have assumed, in the assembly-line era, that teachers are interchangeable parts.

The success of schools committed to a set of educational principles depends on their ability to hire faculty who believe in those principles and have the capacity to enact them. Thus, centralized assignments of teachers can be a problem, whether in the initial hiring of teachers or due to seniority transfers that give teachers rights to transfer into schools where their skills and philosophy may not fit. Some districts have begun to change these traditions by taking on the responsibility to build a strong pool of well-prepared personnel from which schools can then recruit, and by placing teachers who want to transfer schools into this pool when openings are available, with rights to an early interview but not to placement in a specific school.

In New York, for example, the new school development process triggered important system reforms, including in the key area of selecting teachers. With the cooperation of the Board of Education, the United Federation of Teachers

(UFT) and the CCS Project negotiated a process for selecting staff in which a committee of teachers reviews resumes, interviews prospective candidates— and often observes them teaching or planning collaboratively—and selects those most qualified for the available positions. Where teachers are equally qualified, seniority is the decisive variable. UFT representatives participated in these hiring committees, and were so pleased with the outcomes that the union introduced the process into contract negotiations and recommended its adoption more broadly. The contract now includes a peer selection process for teachers in all nontraditional schools, illustrating how innovation can be used as a lever to transform system policies.

In addition, in any New York school where 55% of teachers vote to do so, the school can trigger a School-Based Option that relieves it from many contract constraints and allows new arrangements to be substituted. Many innovative schools have created their own contracts for teachers which, for example, may recognize teachers' roles as advisors and acknowledge different uses of time during the day and week in return for smaller pupil loads and greater autonomy.

Rethinking Accountability. Finally, policymakers must learn new ways to manage the tension between fostering innovation and holding schools accountable for the other purposes of public education—equity, access, development of citizenship, and progress in learning. One critical aspect of the state's role is to ascertain that students are being adequately taught to become productive citizens of society. In recent years, accountability in the United States has largely come to mean tracking test scores on increasingly limited measures, rather than ensuring access to adequate and equitable learning opportunities and the achievement of a broader set of outcomes. As we have seen, the allocation of sanctions to schools based on these high-stakes measures also creates disincentives for schools to admit and keep the neediest students.

Some states, such as Nebraska and Rhode Island, have allowed schools to develop and implement broader, more ambitious assessments of student learning that are approved by the state and examined for accountability purposes along with other documented student outcomes. In New York, 31 schools in the Performance Standards Consortium, including many of those we studied, have developed their own graduation portfolio of challenging research papers and exhibitions. This collection of required products treats both academic outcomes and civic and social responsibility—the latter demonstrated through community service and contributions to the school—and is approved for use in lieu of some of the New York State Regents examinations, with the expectation that schools also track evidence of college admission and completion.

In the long run, accountability systems that provide the right incentives for school quality and equity will need to examine student growth and school progress on a range of high-quality measures, not just their status at a moment in time on one limited measure, include evidence of students' opportunities to learn as well as their outcomes, and enforce professional standards of practice that assure parents their children will be well taught, not just well tested.

CONCLUSION

A growing number of schools have disrupted the status quo by providing opportunities for low-income students of color to become critical thinkers and leaders for the future. Unless policy systems change, however, these schools will remain anomalies, rather than harbingers of the future. Creating a system that supports the learning of all students is not impossible. It will take clarity of vision and purposeful, consistent action to create a web of supportive, mutually reinforcing elements. In particular, dismantling the institutionalized inequities that feed the racial, socioeconomic, and linguistic achievement gap will require substantive policy changes in redesigning schools, developing teachers and principals, expanding our conceptions of curriculum and assessment, rethinking funding strategies, and reconceptualizing accountability.

NOTES

1. Darling-Hammond, Ancess, & Ort (2002).
2. Darling-Hammond, Ancess, & Ort (2002); Fine, Stoudt, & Futch (2005); Friedlaender & Darling-Hammond (2007); Wasley et al. (2000).
3. Darling-Hammond, Ancess, & Ort (2002); Bosman (2007).
4. Ravitch (2009).
5. Ravitch (2002).
6. Darling-Hammond, Ancess, & Ort (2002); Fine, Stoudt, & Futch (2005); Lee, Bryk, & Smith (1993); Newmann & Wehlage (1995); Wasley et al. (2000).
7. Kearns (1988).
8. Deming (2000); Senge (1990).
9. Braddock & McPartland (1993); Gottfredson & Daiger (1979); Lee, Bryk & Smith (1993); Wehlage et al. (1989).
10. Lee & Smith (1995).
11. For reviews, see Lee, Bryk, & Smith (1993); Newmann & Wehlage (1995).
12. Newmann, Marks, & Gamoran (1995).
13. Lee, Smith, & Croninger (1995).
14. Friedlaender & Darling-Hammond (2007).
15. The state graduation rate calculation in 2007 and preceding years used a formula from the National Center for Education Statistics, which adjusts for transfers in and out of schools. In 2008, the state adopted a different graduation rate calculation proposed by the National Governors Association.

16. Friedlaender & Darling-Hammond (2007).

17. Darling-Hammond, Ancess, & Ort (2002).

18. See Ancess (1995); Bensman (1987, 1994, 1995; Darling-Hammond (1997); Darling-Hammond, Ancess, & Falk (1995).

19. The 4-year graduation rate reflects the proportion of a class of students who began as 9th-graders in a school and have, within 4 years, graduated from that school or any other in New York City or have received a GED. Data are from New York City Public Schools (1994).

20. Darling-Hammond, Ancess, & Ort (2002).

21. Fine, Stoudt, & Futch (2005).

22. See, for example, Wasley and colleagues' (2000) analysis of more than 50 Chicago new small high schools, which found much lower dropout rates, higher grade point averages, stronger reading achievement, and comparable math achievement for students in the new smaller schools as compared to peers in larger schools, controlling for student characteristics and prior achievement, and Fine's (1994) study of small school units, called charters, in Philadelphia high schools, with similar outcomes. Both identify small size, personalizing structures, teacher collaboration, project-based learning and performance assessment as critical features of the more successful schools. French (2008) documents much stronger achievement for Boston's Pilot Schools than other city schools serving comparable students, attributing the differences to personalizing structures that produce lower student-teacher loads, wraparound student support (including advisory structures), substantial time for staff collaboration (285 minutes per week plus 6 professional development days versus 29 minutes per week and 3 professional development days in other BPS schools), and authentic instruction and assessment through internships, research projects and demonstrations, exhibitions, portfolios, and performance assessments.

23. The following section draws on Darling-Hammond, Ancess, and Ort (2002) and Friedlaender and Darling-Hammond (2007) and includes quotations originally published in these sources.

24. Darling-Hammond, Ross, & Milliken (2007).

25. For a review, see Darling-Hammond, Ross, & Milliken (2007).

26. Howley and Howley (2004) found that optimal school size varies by student socioeconomic status, with schools in the smallest decile nationally maximizing the achievement of the lowest-income students. They observe that achievement equity in mathematics is maximized in high schools enrolling fewer than 300 students, and equity in reading is maximized in schools enrolling 300–600 students; inequity is greatest in schools enrolling more than 1,500 students. Another group of studies conducted by Friedkin and Necochea (1998) in California and replicated by Howley and Bickel (1999) across six other states also found the relationship between school size and student achievement to be related to the socioeconomic status of the community, with smaller schools appearing to be most beneficial in low-income communities.

27. Howley (1995), p. 2.

28. Howley (1995).

29. Verlinden, Hersen, & Thomas (2000).

30. Lee et al. (2000).

31. Lee, Bryk, & Smith (1993).

32. Powell, Ferrar, & Cohen (1985).

33. Miles & Darling-Hammond (1998).

34. Bryk, Lee, & Holland (1993); Lee, Croninger, & Smith (1997).

35. Black et al. (2003).

36. Glaser (1990), pp. 16–17.

37. Newmann, Marks, & Gamoran (1995).

38. Little (1982); McLaughlin & Talbert (2001).

39. Newmann, Marks, & Gamoran (1995).

40. Darling-Hammond, Ancess, & Ort (2002); Lee & Loeb (2000); Wasley et al. (2000); Bryk, Camburn, & Louis (1999).

41. Edmonds (1979).

42. For a review, see Levine & Lezotte (1990).

43. Eight-year study

44. Erskine (2002).

45. Robinson (1984).

46. Cremin (1961).

47. Hill (2006).

48. Gates Foundation (2005), p. 3.

49. French (2008).

50. Young et al. (2009).

51. Imberman (2007); Miron & Nelson (2001), p. 36.

52. Center for Education Reform (2009).

53. Carnoy et al. (2005).

54. Institute on Race and Poverty (2008).

55. Miron, Coryn, & Mackety (2007). For a review of charter school governance issues and outcomes, see Darling-Hammond & Montgomery (2008).

56. General Accounting Office (2001).

57. Council for Great City Schools (2008).

58. Data on Milwaukee schools achievement trends, which include district schools, instrumentality charters, noninstrumentality charters, and partnership schools, are from Milwaukee Public Schools District Report Card 2007–2008 and the Wisconsin Department of Public Instruction web page. Retrieved from http://data.dpi.state.wi.us/data

59. Advocates for Children (2002).

60. NCTAF (1996); Darling-Hammond (1997).

61. NCTAF (1996).

62. Japanese statistics are for elementary and lower secondary schools, as reported in Japanese Ministry of Education, Culture, Sports, Science, and Technology (2004); U.S. statistics are from National Center for Education Statistics (2005), Table 79.

REFERENCES

Advocates for Children. (2002). *Pushing out at-risk students: An analysis of high school discharge figures—a joint report by AFC and the Public Advocate.* Retrieved from www.advocatesforchildren.org/pubs/pushout-11-20-02.html

Ancess, J. (1995). *An inquiry high school: Learner-centered accountability at the Urban Academy.* National Center for Restructuring Education, Schools, and

Teaching, Teachers College, Columbia University.

Bensman, D. (1987). *Quality education in the inner city: The story of the Central Park East schools.* Rutgers University.

Bensman, D. (1994). *Lives of the graduates of Central Park East elementary school: Where have they gone? What did they really learn?* National Center for Restructuring Education, Schools, and Teaching, Teachers College, Columbia University.

Bensman, D. (1995). *Learning to think well: Central Park East secondary school graduates reflect on their high school and college experiences.* National Center for Restructuring Education, Schools, and Teaching, Teachers College, Columbia University.

Black, P. J., Harrison, C., Lee, C., Marshall, B., & Wiliam, D. (2003). *Assessment for learning: Putting it into practice.* Open University Press.

Bosman, J. (2007, June 30). Small schools are ahead in graduation. *New York Times.* Retrieved from http://query.nytimes.com/gst/fullpage.html?res=9C06E1D8173EF933A05755C0A9619C8B63&sec=&spon=&pagewanted=1

Braddock, J., & McPartland, J. M. (1993). Education of early adolescents. In L. Darling-Hammond (Ed.), *Review of research in education* (Vol. 19, pp. 135–170). American Educational Research Association.

Bryk, A., Camburn, E., & Louis, K. (1999). Professional community in Chicago elementary schools: Facilitating factors and organizational consequences. *Educational Administration Quarterly, 35*(5), 751–781.

Bryk, A., Lee, V., & Holland, P. (1993). *Catholic schools and the common good.* Harvard University Press.

Carnoy, M., Jacobsen, R., Mishel, L., & Rothstein, R. (2005). *The charter school dust-up: Examining the evidence on enrollment and achievement.* Economic Policy Institute.

Center for Education Reform (2009). Understanding charter achievement research: The CREDO report. Retrieved from https://edreform.com/2012/09/understanding-charter-achievement-research-the-credo-report/

Council for Great City Schools. (2008). Beating the odds: Assessment results from the 2006–2007 school year: Individual district profiles. Retrieved from www.cgcs.org/pdfs/BTO_8_Combined.pdf

Cremin, L. (1961). *The transformation of the school: Progressivism in American education, 1876–1957.* Vintage Books.

Darling-Hammond, L. (1997). *The right to learn: A blueprint for creating schools that work.* Jossey-Bass.

Darling-Hammond, L., Ancess, J., & Falk, B. (1995). *Authentic assessment in action: Studies of schools and students at work.* Teachers College Press.

Darling-Hammond, L., Ancess, J., & Ort, S. (2002). Reinventing high school: Outcomes of the coalition campus schools project. *American Educational Research Journal, 39*(3), 39–73.

Darling-Hammond, L., Barron, B., Pearson, P. D., Schoenfeld, A., Stage, E. K., Zimmerman, T. D., Cervetti, G. N., & Tilson, J. L. (2008). *Powerful learning: What we know about teaching for understanding.* Jossey-Bass.

Darling-Hammond, L., & Montgomery, K. (2008). Keeping the promise: The role of policy in reform. In L. Dingerson, B. Miner, B. Peterson, & S. Waters (Eds.),

Keeping the promise? The debate over charter schools (pp. 91–110). Rethinking Schools.

Darling-Hammond, L., Ross, P., & Milliken, M. (2007). High school size, organization, and content: What matters for student success? In F. Hess (Ed.), *Brookings papers on education policy 2006/07* (pp. 163–204). Brookings Institution.

Deming, W. E. (2000). *The new economics for industry, government, education* (2nd ed.). MIT Press.

Edmonds, R. (1979). Effective schools for the urban poor. *Educational Leadership*, *37*(1), 15–18, 20–24.

Erskine, R. (2002, February). *Statement on school reform and the Seattle contract*. Society for the Advancement of Excellence in Education. Retrieved June 9, 2009, from www.saee.ca/index.php?option=com_content&task=view&id=319&Itemid=90

Fine, M. (1994). *Charting urban school reform: Reflections on public high schools in the midst of change*. Teachers College Press.

Fine, M., Stoudt, B., & Futch, V. (2005). *The internationals network for public schools: A quantitative and qualitative cohort analysis of graduation and dropout rates*. New York: City University of New York, Graduate Center.

French, D. (2008). Boston's pilot schools: An alternative to charter schools. In L. Dingerson, B. Miner, B. Peterson, & S. Walters (Eds.), *Keeping the promise? The debate over charter schools* (pp. 67–80). Rethinking Schools.

Friedkin, N., & Necochea, J. (1998). School system size and performance: A contingency perspective. *Educational Evaluation and Policy Analysis*, *10*(3), 237–249.

Friedlaender, D., & Darling-Hammond, L. (2007). With A. Andree, H. Lewis-Charp, L. McCloskey, N. Richardson, & A. Vasudeva, *High schools for equity: Policy supports for student learning in communities of color*. School Redesign Network at Stanford University. Retrieved from www.srnleads.org/resources/publications/hsfe.html

Gates Foundation. (2005). *High performing school districts: Challenge, support, alignment, and choice*. Bill and Melinda Gates Foundation.

General Accounting Office. (2001). *School vouchers: Publicly funded programs in Cleveland and Milwaukee*. General Accounting Office.

Glaser, R. (1990). *Testing and assessment: O Tempora! O Mores!* University of Pittsburgh, Learning Research and Development Center.

Gottfredson, G. D., & Daiger, D. C. (1979). *Disruption in 600 schools*. Johns Hopkins University, Center for Social Organization of Schools.

Hill, P. (2006). *Put learning first: A portfolio approach to public schools*. Progressive Policy Institute.

Howley, C. (1995). The Matthew principle: A West Virginia replication? *Education Policy Analysis Archives*, *3*(18).

Howley, C. B., & Bickel, R. (1999). *The Matthew project: National report*. Appalachia Educational Laboratory.

Howley, C., & Howley, A. (2004). School size and the influence of socioeconomic status on student achievement: Confronting the threat of size bias in national data sets. *Education Policy Analysis Archives*, *12*(52).

Imberman, S. (2007). *Achievement and behavior in charter schools: Drawing a more complete picture* [Occasional Paper No. 142]. New York: National Center for the Study of Privatizations in Education.

Institute on Race and Poverty. (2008). *Failed promises: Assessing charter schools in the Twin Cities*. University of Minnesota, Institute on Race and Poverty.

Japanese Ministry of Education, Culture, Sports, Science, and Technology (2004). *Japan's education at a glance, 2004, School education*. Tokyo, Japan. Author.

Kearns, D. (1988). A business perspective on American schooling. *Education Week*. Retrieved from www.edweek.org/login.html?source=http://www.edweek.org/ew/articles/1988/04/20/30kearns.h07.html&destination=http://www.edweek.org/ew/articles/1988/04/20/30kearns.h07.html&levelId=2100

Lee, V., et al. (2000). Inside large and small high schools: Curriculum and social relations. *Educational Evaluation and Policy Analysis, 22*(2), 147–171.

Lee, V., Bryk, A., & Smith, J. (1993). The organization of effective secondary schools. In Linda Darling-Hammond (Ed.), *Review of research in education* (pp. 171–267). American Educational Research Association.

Lee, V., Croninger, R., & Smith, J. (1997). Course-taking, equity, and mathematics learning: Testing the constrained curriculum hypothesis in U.S. secondary schools. *Educational Evaluation and Policy Analysis, 19*(2), 99–121.

Lee, V., & Loeb, S. (2000). School size in Chicago elementary schools: Effects on teachers' attitudes and students' achievement. *American Educational Research Journal, 37*(1), 3–31.

Lee, V. E., & Smith, J. B. (1995). Effects of high school restructuring and size on early gains in achievement and engagement. *Sociology of Education, 68*(4), 241–270.

Lee, V. E., Smith, J. B., & Croninger, R. G. (1995, Fall). Another look at high school restructuring: More evidence that it improves student achievement and more insight into why. *Issues in Restructuring Schools*. Issue report no. 9, pp. 1–9. Center on the Organization and Restructuring of Schools, University of Wisconsin.

Levine, D., & Lezotte, L. (1990). *Unusually effective schools: A review and analysis of research and practice*. The National Center for Effective Schools Research & Development.

Little, J. W. (1982). Norms of collegiality and experimentation: Workplace conditions of school success. *American Educational Research Journal, 19*(3), 325–340.

McLaughlin, M. W., & Talbert, J. E. (2001). *Professional communities and the work of high school teaching*. University of Chicago Press.

Miles, K. H., & Darling-Hammond, L. (1998). Rethinking the allocation of teaching resources: Some lessons from high-performing schools. *Educational Evaluation and Policy Analysis, 20*(1), 9–29.

Miron, G., Coryn, C., & Mackety, D. M. (2007). *Evaluating the impact of charter schools on student achievement: A longitudinal look at the Great Lakes states*. The Great Lakes Center for Education Research and Practice.

Miron, G., & Nelson, C. (2001). Student achievement in charter schools: What we know and why we know so little [Occasional Paper No. 41]. Teachers College, Columbia University, National Center for the Study of Privatization in Education.

National Center for Education Statistics (NCES). (2005). *Digest of education statistics, 2005*, Table 79. Washington, DC: U.S. Department of Education. Retrieved from http://nces.ed.gov/programs/digest/d05/tables/dt05_079.asp?referrer=list

National Commission on Teaching and America's Future (NCTAF). (1996). *What matters most: Teaching for America's future*. NCTAF.

New York City Public Schools. (1994, February 22). *School profile and school performance in relation to minimum standards, 1992–1993.* New York City Public Schools.

Newmann, F. M., Marks, H. M., & Gamoran, A. (1995). Authentic pedagogy: Standards that boost performance. *American Journal of Education, 104*(4), 280–312.

Newmann, F. M., & Wehlage, G. G. (1995). *Successful school restructuring: A report to the public and educators.* Center on Organization and Restructuring of Schools.

Powell, A. G., Farrar, E., & Cohen, D. K. (1985). *The shopping mall high school.* Houghton Mifflin.

Ravitch, D. (2002, August 12). *A visit to a core knowledge school.* Retrieved from www.hoover.org/pubaffairs/dailyreport/archive/2856501.html

Ravitch, D. (2009). What about 21st-century skills? *Education Week.* Retrieved from htpp://blog.edweek.org/edweek/Bridging-Differences/2009/03/what_about_21st_century_skills.html

Robinson, H. S. (1984). The M Street School, Records of the Columbia Historical Society of Washington, D.C., Vol. LI (1984), 122. In T. Sowell, *The education of minority children.* Retrieved from www.tsowell.com/speducat.html#copy

Senge, P. M. (1990). *The fifth discipline: The art and practice of the learning organization.* Doubleday.

Verlinden, S., Hersen, M., & Thomas, J. (2000). Risk factors in school shootings. *Clinical Psychology Review, 20*(1), 3–56.

Wasley, P. A., Fine, M., Gladden, M., Holland, N. E., King, S. P., Mosak, E., & Powell, L. C. (2000). *Small schools: Great strides; a study of new small schools in Chicago.* Bank Street College of Education.

Wehlage, G., Smith, G., Rutter, R., & Lesko, N. (1989). *Reducing the risk: Schools as communities of support.* Falmer Press.

Young, V. M., Humphrey, D. C., Wang, H., Bosetti, K. R., Cassidy, L., Wechsler, M., Rivera, E., Murray, S., & Schanzenbach, D. W. (2009). *Renaissance schools fund-supported schools: Early outcomes, challenges, and opportunities.* Stanford Research International and Consortium on Chicago School Research. Retrieved from http://ccsr.uchicago.edu/publications/RSF%20FINAL%20April%2015.pdf

Afterword

Margaret Smith Crocco

I am honored to have been asked to write the afterword for this commemorative volume marking the 25th anniversary of the Multicultural Education Series edited by James A. Banks. Having greatly admired Professor Banks's work, as well as that of the other authors featured in this volume, his invitation to reflect upon the impact of this series and these chapters offers a unique and humbling opportunity. On behalf of all those who have benefitted from the research in this series, a note of gratitude is in order to Professor Banks and the more than 70 authors whose work comprises the Multicultural Education Series and contributes so much to our understanding of many vast and complex topics and to our practices as educators and scholars as well.

My engagement with ideas about multicultural education as a teacher, teacher educator, and researcher has a long history. Back in the 1980s, Professor Banks's work shaped my high school social studies teaching. I was fortunate to work at a school that sought to engage its faculty in a comprehensive effort to make subject matter more inclusive of diverse perspectives. Although it may come as a surprise, even back then many teachers were modifying their practice in line with Professor Banks's concept of multicultural education as curriculum change. At that time, most curricular standards, to the degree they existed at all, tended toward broad and flexible thematic constructions. The deleterious effects of the standards-and-accountability regime (Mehta, 2015) stimulated by passage of the No Child Left Behind Act (2002) had not yet introduced the high-stakes testing mechanisms experienced by many teachers as constraints on their roles as curriculum-instructional gatekeepers (Thornton, 1991).

In the early 1990s, I became a professor in the Program in Social Studies at Teachers College, Columbia University. Professor Banks's growing body of research and launch of the Multicultural Education Series served as a lodestar for reshaping our program to better meet the needs of our student teachers in New York City's public schools. We introduced several new courses and redesigned others along the lines of the principles and practices laid out in these books in an effort to be more attentive to diversity, equity, and social justice in teacher education.

During this process, we came to understand that the concept of multicultural education could not be reduced to curriculum change, especially of the "heroes and holidays" sort. Instead, we recognized that multicultural education demanded a fundamental accounting for and addressing of structural racism, sexism, ableism, and other inequities of K–20 education. This platform calls for nothing less than the transformation of education through content integration, knowledge construction, prejudice reduction, equity pedagogy (see Chapter 2), and thorough reconsideration of traditional policies and practices. What was being asked of educators, it is important to note, had neither been achieved nor attempted by any other institutional sector of American life. That this educational transformation project remains only partially and unevenly realized today should not come as a surprise, given the magnitude of the ambition. In many ways, education is asked to serve as the leading edge of cultural and social change through its embrace and application of multicultural precepts.

Besides the aspirational scope of this change process, efforts are often vitiated by deep-seated cultural beliefs. Among those challenges are an unwillingness to confront racism and a social order characterized as a caste system (Wilkerson, 2020), along with cultural commitments to individualism over the common good, narrow views of meritocracy, colorblindness, and willful ignorance of the uneven playing fields upon which individuals compete.

The summative chapter in this volume, by Linda Darling-Hammond, highlights the ambitious goals of multicultural education that now transcend national boundaries. Her chapter reminds us of how challenging educational change is in the United States by contrast with many other nations, given the former's highly decentralized context of schooling and its loosely coupled companion enterprise, teacher education. Darling-Hammond's chapter also calls for major changes in school organization and systems, including reconsideration of approaches to school financing. She cites as keys to reform the positive benefits of smaller schools grounded in communities, reduced pupil loads for teachers, enhanced opportunities for teacher learning and collaboration, and authentic instruction and assessment. She offers examples of places where such reforms have succeeded. She frames her case in terms of the acceleration of globalization over the last two decades (Friedman, 2007), highlighting the fact that in response many U.S. states have raised the bar for success in schooling, using metrics emphasizing higher levels of literacy, numeracy, critical thinking, and participation in postsecondary education (Schneider, 2011).

In looking at examples outside the United States, a recently published book in the Multicultural Education Series—*Race, Culture, and*

Politics in Education: A Global Journey from South Africa (2021) by Kogila Moodley—provides personal insights into how enactment of multicultural education has spread as nations come to understand that their future success will rest on their ability to draw upon all human capital, not just that of an elite group. Other books in the Series address a range of global issues including human rights, migration, language differences, and democratic citizenship education, all essential elements of a comprehensive platform of multicultural education.

In supporting calls for change sensitive to the needs of the present and future, we should not ignore the lessons of the past, especially the long history (Beard, 1946; Crocco, 1997) required for transformative efforts like those of the feminist or civil rights movements. As Cherry McGee Banks and James Banks explain in their chapters in this volume, historical antecedents for multicultural education can be identified, albeit without many of the features of today's platform. From early in the 20th century until today, movements labeled cultural pluralism, intercultural education, ethnic studies, and women's studies arose to address the needs of immigrants (Selig, 2011), rewrite the canon (Gates, 1992), transform knowledge (Minnich, 1990), and overhaul the curriculum (Au, Brown, & Calderon, 2016). As James Banks explains, the civil rights movements of the 1950s and 1960s by African Americans played a central role in revitalizing the women's rights movement and stimulating demands by other groups such as Latinx, Asian Americans, Indigenous groups, and the LGBTQ+ community. Pertinent to this context of social and political change was the overhaul of federal immigration law (1965), which expanded the opportunity of individuals from Asia and Africa to gain entry to the United States.

In the midst of social change, multicultural education answered a felt need among many practitioners and teacher educators in rethinking practice along fresh lines, consonant with the intellectual currents of scholarship in the disciplines and the growing diversity found in their classrooms. By the 1990s, publishers often marketed their textbooks as multicultural, even if their revisions were superficial, comprised mostly of names and vignettes found in sidebars accompanying a narrative that remained focused on the achievements of White men. Despite backlash at that time against "multiculturalism" (Bernstein, 1994) and shibboleths about the "culture wars" (Hunter, 1992), by the end of the decade well-known scholars such as Nathan Glazer (1998) proclaimed, "We are all multiculturalists now" in the title of a book by that name.

Few of the historical antecedents of multicultural education provided instructional guidance along the lines found in this commemorative volume or across books in the Series. Traditional responses to new immigrants, for example, emphasized schooling as an instrument of assimilation. By contrast, chapters in this book advocate "culturally responsive" forms of teaching (Tyrone Howard) grounded in and tailored to the students in classrooms (Carol Lee; Christine Sleeter and Miguel Zavala) and more sophisticated understandings of language and culture (Sonia Nieto; Guadalupe Valdés) than prior renditions.

Although the emphasis on practice as well as principle in these books is critical, it also needs to be acknowledged that enacting pedagogical differentiation, along the lines described in chapters by Özlem Sensoy and Robin DiAngelo, Gary Howard, and Paul Gorski, especially in classrooms with large numbers of students, is not easy. Just as society is demanding more of students and schools, so too is it demanding more of teachers, and it bears repeating that teachers have been asked to promote social justice for a society that refuses to support its children and families in meaningful ways. During the decade preceding the launch of the Multicultural Education Series, the prevalent political ideology advocated shrinking government and the public sector while challenging the legitimacy of teachers' unions and public education and promoting privatization via charter schools.

From the 1980s onward, such neoliberal policies resulted in enlarged class sizes, heightened emphasis on accountability, and threats of global competition that were often used to shame teachers into getting on board with certain types of "reform." Whatever good intentions and merits NCLB may have had (see Chapter 8 by James Loewen and Chapter 10 by Guadalupe Valdés in this book for different perspectives on this matter), the additional burdens on schools and teachers and the consequences of its narrow focus on implementation via standardized testing greatly outweighed the positive aspects of the legislation, on both teachers and students.

Over the last two decades of such change, some teachers have become "demoralized" (Santoro, 2018), turning to "principled resistance" (Santoro & Cain, 2018) or leaving the classroom entirely. Today's latest challenges to educators' work, for example, legislation by some states against teaching U.S. history in honest and accurate fashion (Romero, 2021) or critical race theory (O'Kane, 2021), these new strictures may prompt acceleration of teachers' departures from public schools (Smith, 2020). Despite these difficulties, many teachers remain committed to addressing structural racism (see Chapter 11 by Noguera and Syeed) in their schools. According to attitudinal studies, younger generations seem to understand that racism can be both interpersonal as well as structural and that teaching for racial justice is necessary. In polling conducted after the murder of George Floyd in Minneapolis, the Pew Research Center (Horowitz, Parker, Brown, & Cox, 2020) reported:

> Two-thirds of White adults younger than 30 say they've done a lot or some to educate themselves about race recently. This compares with roughly half or less among older age groups. The age gap is apparent among both Republicans and Democrats, with 53% of White Republicans ages 18 to 29 and 81% of their

Democratic counterparts saying they've taken at least some steps to educate themselves about race in recent months.

In addition, White adults with a bachelor's degree or higher are more likely than those with less education to say they've done a lot or some to educate themselves on these issues (62% vs. 44%).

Despite a few positive developments in Americans' reckoning with racism in recent years, major changes in institutions and society always provoke backlash. This does not mean, however, that change cannot happen. Certainly, one of the greatest threats to bringing about change is cynicism. History demonstrates that organized, strategic efforts, especially those using nonviolent civil resistance, can produce significant change (Chenoweth & Stephan, 2011).

Today, youth activism on many fronts such as criminal justice, climate change, and racial injustice holds the promise of providing the sustained pressure necessary to effect change. Attitudinal shifts, at least in part due to activist efforts, can be seen in recent social surveys about topics such as same-sex marriage (Pew Research Center, 2019) and national identity (Silver, Fagan, Connaughton, & Mordecai, 2021) that demonstrate the efficacy of coordinated campaigns focused on social justice.

School change presents different challenges, to be sure, but as Pedro Noguera and Esa Syeed assert in this book, it is important not to underestimate the role that schools can play in addressing structural racism and other forms of discrimination. Their chapter and many others in this volume underscore the need for attention to intersectionality and the multiple forms of oppression faced by many students in today's public schools. Chapters like Paul Gorski's, while acknowledging the role played by character and family in shaping youth and their life prospects, offer antidotes to an exclusive emphasis on bootstrapping as a solution for educational and social inequities. As Linda Darling-Hammond notes, if changes of the order of magnitude necessary to effect greater equity in schooling across the country are to be made, radical revision of approaches to school financing will be necessary (for recent commentary on this subject, see Kristof, 2021).

Gorski argues that only cultivation of an understanding of structural racism among teachers, administrators, policymakers, politicians, and school boards will make the changes advocated by multicultural education's platform possible. The opposition to such understanding is fueled by those who fan the flames of racial resentment for their own political purposes (Davis & Wilson, 2021) and has been seen recently in schoolboard elections (Henig, Jacobsen & Reckhow, 2019) as well as attacks against those who support public education itself (Gott & Seidman, 2018).

At this 25th anniversary of the Multicultural Education Series, paradoxically one measure of its success might be attacks against it like these examples. However, the great conceit of such an approach to gauging success would be to consider two and a half decades as a fair timeframe for assessing change of the magnitude being called for in these books. As Americans accustomed to the rapid generation of technology change every few years, we have perhaps come to assume that everything changes at this pace rather than the more typical, incremental pace of social and cultural change.

Historian Eric Foner (2019) has described the long arc of historical change related to this country's constitutional reckoning with slavery in passage of the 13th, 14th, and 15th Amendments after the Civil War and further changes brought about by the Civil Rights Act of 1965. Likewise, the over 100-year quest for women's right to vote in the United States serves as an important reminder of what has been called the "long history" of social and political change (Beard, 1946). The labor organizer Myles Horton (1997) spoke of the need for commitments that he dubbed the "long haul" project of supporting workers and communities.

In 2020, the election of Kamala Harris to the vice presidency, a first in over 250 years of American history, illustrates how long it has taken to achieve success and in this case redress, even partially, the patriarchy, sexism, and racism embedded within our society. One might also add to this list the George Floyd verdict convicting Derek Chauvin of murder, which perhaps only 2 or 3 years ago might have seemed improbable if not impossible, and the widespread calls (e.g., *New York Times* Editorial Board, 2021) for ending the qualified immunity of police officers.

In these cases, things unimaginable a decade or so ago became possible due to the efforts of organized and strategic advocates over many years, whose persistence, vision, courage, and clarity of goals kept their cause moving forward, even in the face of defeats alongside victories. Success demands faith in the future, the power of persuasion, especially moral suasion and even moral outrage (Crocco, 2018) in the face of injustice, and sustained dedication over the long haul, as the above examples illustrate so vividly.

As scholars (Sunstein, 2019) argue and research confirms, a critical force in advancing social, political, and educational change depends on shifts in norms about what is deemed acceptable behavior, as seen in the civil rights movement, the #MeToo movement, and the environmental movement. Normative change shifts perception of what is viewed as possible in terms of public policy, which capitalizes on the insights of behavioral economics and nudges individual behavior in new directions (Thaler & Sunstein, 2008). Given the decentralized system of schooling in the United States, change will need to come about one teacher and one school district at a time but can be supported vigorously by policies and practices in teacher education programs and professional organizations nationwide, which are generally less vulnerable to political interference.

The Multicultural Education Series provides a blueprint for educational transformation whose success can only be measured in terms of long history. Its ultimate achievement will depend on new coalitions of committed educators who pledge to continue the fight for social justice in the nation's schools. To accomplish the goals of multicultural education, however, it will be critical to rededicate schooling to its original mission of citizenship education in a democracy (Stitzlein, 2014) and to yoke multicultural education, as Professor Banks has done in other writing (2017), to citizenship education and human rights globally.

Reclaiming a more robust vision of democracy such as that espoused by John Dewey (1916) as a form of "associated living" is essential. The pandemic and its attendant crises in public health, the economy, and political institutions have revealed the need for renewed emphasis on communal concerns and shared responsibility in addressing the work that needs to be done. Arguing forcefully and consistently for good public schools, ones that prioritize the welfare of all students and champion active forms of citizenship in pursuit of the common good, will be critical to the creation of a society that benefits all citizens.

In conclusion, building more just schools within a stronger democracy are urgent endeavors that require attention to the pedagogical, policy, and research platform whose myriad dimensions are described throughout these chapters and in every book of the Multicultural Education Series. Sustaining progress toward these goals requires the creative leadership demonstrated by Professor Banks and his collaborators in the remarkable achievement represented by the 25th Anniversary of this Series. One can only hope that a new generation of leaders (and followers) will carry on the visionary project of transformational change outlined in these books.

REFERENCES

Au, W., Brown, A., & Calderon, D. (2016). *Reclaiming the multicultural roots of U.S. curriculum.* Teachers College Press.

Banks, J. A. (2017). Failed citizenship and transformative civic education. *Educational Researcher, 46*(7), 366–377. https://doi.org/10.3102/0013189X17726741

Beard, M. R. (1946). *Women as a force in history: A study in traditions and realities.* Macmillan.

Bernstein, R. (1994). *Dictatorship of virtue.* Vintage.

Chenoweth, E., & Stephan, M. J. (2011). *Why civil resistance works: The strategic logic of nonviolent conflict.* Columbia University Press.

Crocco, M. S. (1997). Forceful yet forgotten: Mary Ritter Beard and the writing of history. *The History Teacher, 31*(1), 9–31.

Crocco, M. S. (2018). Moral outrage and teaching about Hurricane Katrina. *Theory into Practice, 57*(4), 270–280.

Davis, D. W., & Wilson, D. C. (2021). *Racial resentment in the political mind.* University of Chicago Press.

Dewey, J. (1916). *Democracy and education*. Macmillan.

Foner, E. (2019). *The second founding: How the Civil War and Reconstruction re-made the Constitution*. W.W. Norton.

Friedman, T. (2007). *The world is flat*. Picador.

Gates, H. L. (1992). *Loose canons*. Oxford University Press.

Glazer, N. (1998). *We are all multiculturalists now*. Harvard University Press.

Gott, M., & Seidman, D. (2018). Mapping the movement to dismantle public education. *Jacobin*. https://www.jacobinmag.com/2018/06/public-education-privatization-koch-brothers-teachers. Accessed on May 19, 2021.

Henig, J., Jacobsen, R., & Reckhow, S. (2019). *Outside money in school board elections: The nationalization of education politics*. Harvard Education Press.

Horowitz, J. M., Parker, K., Brown, M., & Cox, K. (2020). *Amid national reckoning, Americans divided on whether increased focus on race will lead to major policy change*. Pew Research Center. https://www.pewresearch.org/social-trends/2020/10/06/amid-national-reckoning-americans-divided-on-whether-increased-focus-on-race-will-lead-to-major-policy-change

Horton, M. (1997). *The long haul: An autobiography*. Teachers College Press.

Hunter, J. D. (1992). *The culture wars: The struggle to define America*. Basic Books.

Kristof, N. (2021, May 23). If only there were a viral video of our Jim Crow education system. *New York Times*. https://www.nytimes.com/2021/05/21/opinion/sunday/education-racism-segregation.html?searchResultPosition=1

Mehta, J. (2015). *The allure of order: High hopes, dashed expectations, and the troubled quest to remake American schooling*. Oxford University Press.

Minnich, E. (1990). *Transforming knowledge*. Temple University Press.

Moodley, K. (2021). *Race, culture, and politics in education: A global journey from South Africa*. Teachers College Press.

New York Times Editorial Board. (2021, May 22). End the Court doctrine that enables police brutality. https://www.nytimes.com/2021/05/22/opinion/qualified-immunity-police-brutality-misconduct.html

No Child Left Behind (NCLB) Act of 2001, Pub. L. No. 107-110, § 101, Stat. 1425 (2002).

O'Kane, C. (2021, May 20). Nearly a dozen states want to ban critical race theory in schools. https://www.cbsnews.com/news/critical-race-theory-state-bans/

Pew Research Center. (2019). Changing attitudes on same sex marriage. https://www.pewforum.org/fact-sheet/changing-attitudes-on-gay-marriage/

Romero, S. (2021, May 21). Texas pushes to obscure the state's history of slavery and racism. *New York Times*. https://www.nytimes.com/2021/05/20/us/texas-history-1836-project.html?referringSource=articleShare

Santoro, D. A. (2018). *Demoralized: Why teachers leave the profession they love and how they can stay*. Harvard Education Press.

Santoro, D. A., & Cain, L. (Eds.) (2018). *Principled resistance: How teachers resolve ethical issues*. Harvard Education Press.

Schneider, J. (2011). *Excellence for all: How a new breed of reformers is transforming America's public schools*. Vanderbilt University Press.

Selig, D. (2011). *Americans all: The cultural gifts movement*. Harvard University Press.

Silver, L., Fagan, M., Connaughton, A., & Mordecai, M. (2021). *Views on national identity becoming more inclusive in U.S. and Western Europe.* https://www.pewresearch.org/global/2021/05/05/views-about-national-identity-becoming-more-inclusive-in-us-western-europe/

Smith, C. (2020, September 14). As teachers retire amid the pandemic, schools are left scrambling for substitutes. *Chicago Tribune.* https://www.chicagotribune.com/retirement-aging/sns-school-teacher-opt-out-virus-outbreak-20200914-wco5rwwkbvb6nm3omcqt5a6igq-story.html

Stitzlein, S. (2014). Habits of democracy: A Deweyan approach to citizenship education today. *Education and Culture, 30*(2), 61–86.

Sunstein, C. R. (2019). *How change happens.* The MIT Press.

Thaler, R., & Sunstein, C. R. (2008). *Nudge: Improving decisions about health, wealth, and happiness.* Yale University Press.

Thornton, S. J. (1991). Teacher as curricular-instructional gatekeeper in social studies. In J. Shaver (Ed.), *Handbook of research on social studies teaching and learning* (pp. 237–248). Macmillan.

Wilkerson, I. (2020). *Caste: The origins of our discontents.* Random House.

Credits

Chapter 1: Cherry A. McGee Banks (2005). Responding to diversity in the early 20th century. *Improving multicultural education: Lessons from the intergroup education movement* (pp. 11–30). Teachers College Press.

Chapter 3: Özlem Sensoy and Robin DiAngelo (2017). Understanding the structural nature of oppression through racism. *Is everyone really equal? An introduction to key concepts in social justice education* (2nd ed., pp. 119–140). Teachers College Press.

Chapter 4: Gary R. Howard (2016). White dominance and the weight of the West. *We can't teach what we don't know: White teachers, multiracial schools* (3rd ed., pp. 32–55). Teachers College Press.

Chapter 5: Sonia Nieto (2010). Culture and learning. *The light in their eyes: Creating multicultural learning communities* (10th anniversary ed., pp. 77–100). Teachers College Press.

Chapter 6: Tyrone C. Howard (2020). Culturally responsive pedagogy. *Why race and culture matter in schools: Closing the achievement gap in America's classrooms* (pp. 65–87). Teachers College Press.

Chapter 7: Carol D. Lee (2007). Modeling with cultural data sets. *Culture, literacy, and learning: Taking bloom in the midst of the whirlwind* (pp. 59–79). Teachers College Press.

Chapter 8: James W. Loewen (2018). Introduction: History as a weapon. *Teaching what really happened: How to avoid the tyranny of textbooks and get students excited about doing history* (2nd ed., pp. 1–22). Teachers College Press.

Chapter 9: Christine E. Sleeter and Miguel Zavala (2020). What the research says about ethnic studies. *Transformative ethnic studies in schools: Curriculum, pedagogy, and research* (pp. 44–68). Teachers College Press.

Chapter 10: Guadalupe Valdés, Sarah Capitelli, and Laura Alvarez (2011). Realistic expectations: English Language Learners and the acquisition of Academic English. *Latino children learning English: Steps in the journey* (pp. 15–42). Teachers College Press.

Chapter 11: Pedro Noguera and Esa Syeed (2020). The role of schools in reducing racial inequality. *City schools and the American dream 2: The enduring promise of public education* (pp. 33–65). Teachers College Press.

Chapter 12: Paul C. Gorski (2018). Embracing a structural view of poverty and education: Ditching deficit ideology and quitting grit. *Reaching and teaching students in poverty: Strategies for erasing the opportunity gap* (2nd ed., pp. 57–66). Teachers College Press.

Chapter 13: Linda Darling-Hammond (2010). Organizing for success: From inequality to quality. *The flat world and education: How America's commitment to equity will determine our future* (pp. 234–277). Teachers College Press.

About the Contributors

James A. Banks is Kerry and Linda Killinger Endowed Chair in Diversity Studies Emeritus at the University of Washington, Seattle. He was the founding director of the Center for Multicultural Education from 1992 to 2018, which was renamed the Banks Center for Educational Justice. Banks is a past president of the American Educational Research Association (AERA) and the National Council for the Social Studies (NCSS). He is a fellow of the American Educational Research Association (AERA) and a member of the National Academy of Education and the American Academy of Arts and Sciences. His books include *Citizenship Education and Global Migration: Implications for Theory, Research, and Teaching* (AERA, 2017) and *Diversity, Transformative Knowledge, and Civic Education: Selected Essays* (Routledge, 2020).

Cherry A. McGee Banks is a founding faculty member in the School of Educational Studies and Professor Emeritus at the University of Washington, Bothell. In 2000 she was named a Worthington Distinguished Professor, and in 2013 she was elected a fellow of the American Educational Research Association. Her research focuses on intergroup education and the role that public school educators played in linking schools to communities and helping students and parents appreciate diversity and embrace democratic ideals. Professor Banks is associate editor of the *Handbook of Research on Multicultural Education*, coeditor of *Multicultural Education: Issues and Perspectives*, and author of *Improving Multicultural Education: Lessons From the Intergroup Education Movement*.

Margaret Smith Crocco is emeritus professor of social studies and education, Teachers College, Columbia University. She has served on the faculties of the University of Iowa and Michigan State University, and has authored or edited nine books, numerous book chapters, and articles in journals such as *Theory and Research in Social Education, Journal of Social Studies Research, Journal of Curriculum Studies, Phi Delta Kappan, Democracy and Education*, and *History of Education Quarterly*. She also directed development of the award-winning curriculum guide accompanying Spike Lee's film about Hurricane Katrina, *When the Levees Broke*, as well as other documentary film-related curriculum projects.

Linda Darling-Hammond is the Charles E. Ducommun Professor of Education Emeritus at Stanford University where she founded the Stanford Center for Opportunity Policy in Education and served as the faculty sponsor of the Stanford

Teacher Education Program, which she helped to redesign. Darling-Hammond is past president of the American Educational Research Association and recipient of its awards for Distinguished Contributions to Research, Lifetime Achievement, and Research-to-Policy. She is also a member of the American Academy of Arts and Sciences and the National Academy of Education. From 1994 to 2001, she was executive director of the National Commission on Teaching and America's Future, whose 1996 report *What Matters Most: Teaching for America's Future* was named one of the most influential reports affecting U.S. education in that decade. In 2006, Darling-Hammond was named one of the nation's 10 most influential people affecting educational policy. She led the Obama education policy transition team in 2008 and the Biden education transition team in 2020.

Robin DiAngelo is an affiliate associate professor of education at the University of Washington, Seattle. She is the author of numerous publications and books. In 2011 she coined the term "White Fragility" in an academic article that has influenced the international dialogue on race. Her book, *White Fragility: Why It's So Hard for White People to Talk About Racism* debuted on the *New York Times* Bestseller List and has been translated into 10 languages. In addition to her academic work, Dr. DiAngelo has been a consultant and educator for more than 20 years on racial and social justice issues.

Paul C. Gorski is the founder of the Equity Literacy Institute and EdChange, organizations that support schools and school districts as they strengthen their educational equity commitments and efforts. He has taught education and social justice courses at several universities, including George Mason University, Hamline University, the University of Maryland, and the University of Virginia. He served 8 years on the board of the National Association for Multicultural Education (NAME) and 5 on the board of the International Association for Intercultural Education (IAIE). He has authored, coauthored, or coedited 12 books, including *Reaching and Teaching Students in Poverty*.

Gary R. Howard has over 40 years' experience working with issues of civil rights, social justice, and equity in education, including 25 years as the founder of the REACH Center for Multicultural Education. His landmark book, *We Can't Teach What We Don't Know: White Teachers/Multiracial Schools* (3rd edition, 2016) examines issues of privilege, power, and the role of White leaders and educators in a multicultural society. His current work, documented in *We Can't Lead Where We Won't Go: An Educator's Guide to Equity* (2015), centers on providing schools with the internal capacity to strengthen the cultural responsiveness of their practices and build long-term systemic change strategies for achieving greater equity and social justice in their outcomes.

Tyrone C. Howard is the Pritzker Family Endowed Chair at the University of California, Los Angeles. He was the founding director of the UCLA Black Male Institute, and currently serves as the director of the UCLA Pritzker Center for Strengthening Children and Families and the UCLA Center for the Transformation of Schools. He is a member of the National Academy of Education and a fellow of the American Educational Research Association (AERA). His books include *Why Race and Culture*

Matters in Schools (Teachers College Press, 2020), *Black Male(d): Peril and Promise in the Education of African American Males* (Teachers College Press, 2014), and *All Students Must Thrive* (Houghton Mifflin Harcourt, 2019).

Carol D. Lee is professor emeritus at the School of Education and Social Policy in the Learning Sciences Program at Northwestern University. Her research focuses on ecological supports for learning, specifically in terms of the teaching and learning of disciplinary literacies, with particular emphasis on the role of culture and identity processes. She is the president-elect of the National Academy of Education, a past president of the American Educational Research Association (AERA), and a member of the American Academy of Arts and Sciences. Professor Lee is also a fellow of AERA and the National Council on Language and Literacy and a member of the Reading Hall of Fame.

James W. Loewen was an independent sociologist and historian from 1995 to 2021. From 1968 to 1975 he taught at Tougaloo College, a historically Black institution in Tougaloo, Mississippi, followed by 20 years at the University of Vermont. His book *Lies My Teacher Told Me* is a best-seller. Other books include *Lies Across America*, which critiques about 100 historic sites, *The Confederate and Neo-Confederate Reader*, *Sundown Towns*, and a short memoir, *Up a Creek, With a Paddle*. He believed that teachers can transform lives.

Pedro Noguera is the Emery Stoops and Joyce King Stoops Dean of the Rossier School of Education and a Distinguished Professor of Education at the University of Southern California. Prior to joining USC, Noguera served as a Distinguished Professor of Education at the Graduate School of Education and Information Studies at the University of California, Los Angeles. Before joining the faculty at UCLA, he served as a tenured professor and holder of endowed chairs at New York University, Harvard University, and the University of California, Berkeley. He is the author of 15 books. His most recent books are *A Search for Common Ground: Conversations about the Toughest Questions in K–12 Education* (Teachers College Press) with Rick Hess; and *City Schools and the American Dream 2: The Enduring Promise of Public Education* (Teachers College Press) with Esa Syeed.

Sonia Nieto is professor emerita of language, literacy, and culture, College of Education, University of Massachusetts, Amherst. Her research on multicultural education and teacher education has been published in 13 books and dozens of journal articles and book chapters. A member of the National Academy of Education and a fellow of the American Educational Research Association, she has received numerous awards for her scholarly work and advocacy, including nine honorary doctorates. The first edition (1992) of her classic text, *Affirming Diversity: The Sociopolitical Context of Multicultural Education*, was selected for the Museum of Education Readers' Guide as "one of the 100 books that helped define the field of education in the 20th century."

Özlem Sensoy is professor of social justice education in the Faculty of Education, the associate director of the Centre for Education, Law, and Society, an associate member of the Department of Gender Sexuality and Women's Studies, and an affiliated faculty member with the Centre for Comparative Muslim Studies at Simon Fraser University in Canada. She teaches courses on social justice education, critical media literacy and popular culture, and multicultural and antiracism theories. Her research has been published in journals including the *Harvard Educational Review*, *Gender and Education*, and *Race Ethnicity and Education*. She is the co-author (with Robin DiAngelo) of the award-winning introductory text on social justice education, *Is Everyone Really Equal? An Introduction to Key Concepts in Social Justice Education* (Teachers College Press, 2nd ed., 2017).

Christine E. Sleeter is professor emerita in the College of Education at California State University Monterey Bay, where she was a founding faculty member. She is past president of the National Association for Multicultural Education (NAME), and past vice president of the American Educational Research Association (AERA). Her books include *Un-Standardizing Curriculum* (2nd ed., with J. Flores Carmona, Teachers College Press, 2017), *Transformative Ethnic Studies in Schools,* with M. Zavala (Teachers College Press, 2020), and *Family History in Black and White* (Brill, 2021). She is a fellow of the American Educational Research Association and a member of the National Academy of Education.

Esa Syeed is an assistant professor of sociology at California State University, Long Beach. A former teacher and youth development worker, his research and teaching are shaped by concerns for equity and justice. His current work explores sites for educational change and resistance in communities of color. An interdisciplinary scholar, he has published in a variety of journals, edited volumes, and popular venues.

Guadalupe Valdés is the Bonnie Katz Tenenbaum Professor of Education at Stanford University. She specializes in applied linguistics. Her work has focused on the English–Spanish bilingualism of Latinxs in the United States and on discovering and describing how two languages are developed, used, and maintained by individuals who become bilingual in immigrant communities. She has carried out research in elementary, middle school, high school and college leading to six books and over 90 articles. Two recent articles are ("Mis)educating the Children of Mexican-Origin People in the United States: The Challenge of Internal Language Borders" (2020) and "Analyzing the Curricularization of Language in Two-Way Immersion Education: Restating Two Cautionary Notes" (2018).

Miguel Zavala is director of urban learning and associate professor of education at California State University, Los Angeles. A former middle school teacher, over the last 2 decades he has been in the field of teacher education, and is currently co-president of the California chapter of the National Association for Multicultural Education (NAME). His recent publications include *Transformative Ethnic Studies in Schools* (with Christine E. Sleeter), *Rethinking Ethnic Studies* (co-edited with leading educators and scholars), and *Raza Struggle and the Movement for Ethnic Studies*. His research interests explore the intersections of ethnic studies, critical literacies, and participatory movements.

Index

NAMES

Note: **Bold** type indicates contributors and their respective chapters. Page numbers followed by "n" indicate material in numbered endnotes.

SUBJECTS